Collected Poems
1942-1987

Also by John Heath-Stubbs from Carcanet

Naming the Beasts
The Watchman's Flute
The Immolation of Aleph

editor
Thomas Gray: *Selected Poems*

John Heath-Stubbs

COLLECTED POEMS
1943-1987

CARCANET

First published in 1988 by
Carcanet Press Limited
208-212 Corn Exchange Buildings
Manchester M4 3BQ

British Library Cataloguing in Publication Data

Heath-Stubbs, John, *1918-*
  Collected poems, 1942-1987
  I. Title
  821'.914

  ISBN 0-85635-707-3

The publisher acknowledges financial assistance
from the Arts Council of Great Britain

Typeset in 10pt Palatino by Bryan Williamson, Manchester
Printed in England by SRP Ltd, Exeter

To George Barker
Homage

Note

Some of the poems here appearing in book form for the first time have been printed in the following periodicals: *The Spectator, The Tablet, Agenda, Acumen, Interim* (Las Vegas, USA), *Poetry Review, Nine* and *Margin.*

The remaining poems are taken from the following volumes: *Wounded Thammuz, Beauty and the Beast, The Divided Ways* (all published by Routledge); *The Swarming of the Bees* (Eyre and Spottiswoode); *A Charm Against The Toothache* (Methuen); *The Triumph of the Muse, The Bluefly in His Head, Selected Poems,* Giacomo Leopardi: *Selected Prose and Poetry* (all Oxford University Press); *Satires and Epigrams* (Turret Books); *Four Poems in Measure* (Helikon Press, New York); *The Watchman's Flute, Naming the Beasts, The Immolation of Aleph* (all Carcanet Press); *A Parliament of Birds* (Chatto); *Artorius, Birds Reconvened* (both Enitharmon Press); *Buzz Buzz* (Gruffyground Press); *Aphrodite's Garland* (Crescendo Press); *The Horn* (Keepsake Press); *Lyric Poetry of the Italian Renaissance* (Yale University Press); *Dante's Inferno* (BBC Publications); and Ernesto Cardenal: *Psalms* (Sheed and Ward).

The author would like to thank Joanne Gannon, Dr Adrian Risdon and John Fitton for their help in preparing this volume for the press.

Contents

7

11

EARLY POEMS 1942-1965

13

15

16

TRANSLATIONS

20

Preface

When some twenty-five years ago my then publishers asked me to compile a volume of selected poems, it was not on the whole very difficult for me to decide which of my poems from previously published volumes I should include, and which I should exclude, but the present volume is entitled 'Collected Poems'. Such a title should imply that the volume in question contains everything which the author wishes to remain in print. I have found the task of determining what such a volume should in fact include a much more difficult one.

As I take a retrospective glance over a writing career of over half a century, I find that in a sense there is little written before about my fortieth year which I can now read without a certain degree of embarrassment – or which I can feel wholly justified in including here. Some of my contemporaries, I know, in compiling volumes of a similar scope, have included very little if anything of their early work – but such a procedure strikes me as being rather disingenuous. My earlier poems, with all the faults I now see in them, did seem to represent what I wanted to do at the time. In some cases good judges praised them and respectable editors were willing to print them. Moreover, if any person were prepared to take a scholarly interest in my work (I do not suggest that it merits such an interest, but in these days almost anything may become the subject of dissertations and theses) they will presumably expect to find that earlier work here, along with the later. I have therefore included a large proportion of my earlier work, with a minimum of revisions – the revisions in many cases are in the interests of factual and historical accuracy as much as of style. The faults of execution which I now see in these early poems cannot be revised: the poem would have to be entirely rewritten.

It is notorious that in the present century poetic styles and fashions have succeeded each other with remarkable rapidity. Some of the poetic styles represented by my earlier poems are now so unfashionable as to have, I suppose, a kind of historical interest if no other, not that I ever wanted to be fashionable or belong to any well defined group or movement.*

---

* Least of all to the so-called 'New Apocalypse'. This short-lived and never very influential school began in the late 1930s and had more or less disintegrated before any poems of mine appeared in book form. I never even met any member of the group until some years after it had ceased to exist. It should not have

When I began my university career in 1939 I was largely ignorant of the modern movement in poetry. When I did become aware of modern poetry, there were a number of disparate styles and influences to be experimented with, to be absorbed or, in some cases, to be rejected. What I, and many of my friends, rejected was what seemed to us the over-simplistic political commitments of our immediate predecessors, the poets of the 1930s. Some of the things that did interest us were the symbolism of Yeats, the reaffirmation of orthodox religious themes in the poetry of T.S. Eliot and Charles Williams and some others, and the exploration of poetic myth in the work of Robert Graves. We accepted that, amid the complexities of the twentieth-century, poetry, if it were to have any wide significance, should also be complex. It would be allusive and need not always be immediately accessible to rational analysis. In the matter of form and metre we felt that the procedures of the past could still be used, but we also accepted the necessity for the creation of new forms, and of experimentation in metre and rhythm.

As for me, there was the whole tradition of English poetry to be explored, which had existed for over a thousand years, but I also became aware of the traditions of other European literatures ancient and modern, and of literatures from cultural traditions other than European. All this was likewise to be explored – on my part, largely through the medium of translations. I also came to feel that since language is a convention which one shares with other speakers and writers, and not a separate mode of expression as the images of painting, and the harmonies of music, largely are, the poem is in a certain sense carrying on a dialogue with other poems – maybe with poems in other languages. I therefore have always felt free to make use of a wide range of cultural references. This, which I think would be vulgar to confuse with cultural snobbery, has given me a quite spurious reputation for

been necessary for me to disassociate myself even in a footnote if some critics, especially during the 1950s, had not fallen into the habit of using the term 'apocalyptic' in an implied pejorative sense as a comprehensive term with which to dismiss almost all the poets of my generation. One particularly ill-informed reviewer even in the present decade saw fit to link my name with the Apocalypse when reviewing consecutively two collections of my poems. In the second of these reviews he did not condescend to quote anything from the volume under consideration, but merely a poem of mine published thirty years earlier and already, in my estimation, over-quoted and over-anthologized. Letters – I hope courteously phrased – addressed to him and to his editor received neither reply nor acknowledgement.

erudition, for I am certainly no scholar. Generally speaking the information required for the proper understanding of the context of a poem of mine ought to be gathered quite easily through ordinary sources of references available, say, in any public library. I have been sparing of notes, for they tend to distract the reader's attention from the text. I have only provided them when the sources of reference seemed really private or recondite.

In particular, I am no classical scholar. I have, as was said of one of my betters, 'small Latin and less Greek'. It is true that I was well grounded in both these languages at an early age, when I went to a small village private school kept by two brothers and a sister, with fifteen or twenty pupils at the most, but unfortunately I proceeded to a school which in the name of ideals thought to be liberal, taught the minimum of Latin and no Greek. Nevertheless the world of classical antiquity fascinated me and seemed to me to provide paradigms for our modern world. I am aware that in my poetry I have perhaps alluded to this classical world too frequently and too freely, and that this may smack of the pedantry of the ill-educated, rather than the natural ease of allusion which goes with real scholarship. I can only ask for the reader's indulgence, but it was never my purpose to make an ostentatious display of learning. I welcome the judgement of one reviewer of a recent volume of mine, Mr Alan Bold, who defined my intentions as being 'to educate the imagination of [my] readers'.

Everybody has to create his own imaginative universe, and what may be important to one may be obscure to another. My friend and contemporary at Oxford, Philip Larkin, has put on record how he was puzzled, on reading one of my earliest published poems, as to who Leporello might be. I should have thought that it was not pedantry to suppose that at least some of my readers might be acquainted with the operas of Mozart. These works had been very important to me in forming my youthful sensibility. *Don Giovanni* in particular had opened up for me a world where eroticism and death seemed linked. If that was the way, as it were, the cards had been dealt me, I might have derived a similar stimulus I suppose from the jazz that meant so much to Larkin, though as it happens it meant and means very little to me.

In our fragmented world such misunderstandings and failures in communication must be inevitable. I can only ask my readers to be patient if they should come across in reading my poems references to matters which may be unfamiliar to them. I have already suggested that it might not be too difficult for them to find out, and that they might be gainers if they do, but if they are not so inclined, why not let it stand as a mystery or a riddle. I aim to tease you sometimes, as well as to please you.

Some words may be necessary about how this book has been arranged. The first section consists of later poems, i.e. those written after the compilation of my *Selected Poems* which the Oxford University Press published in 1965. It is by these and by the long poem *Artorius*, written during the same period, that I should now most wish to be judged. Placed first are about twenty poems which have not previously appeared in book form. These are followed by poems taken from three volumes published by the Carcanet Press. After these come a series of slighter, satirical and sometimes, perhaps, trivial poems, which nevertheless I hope the reader will find not wholly unamusing. My two sequences of poems about birds published by Chatto and by the Enitharmon Press respectively, have been conflated to form one single sequence, although the first of these volumes was written primarily for younger readers, and the second for a more general audience. I have also here and elsewhere in the volume rounded up stray poems and placed them in sequences which did not originally include them, but where they seemed to find a natural place.

The second section contains poems from volumes published between 1943 and 1965, in more or less chronological order. The third section comprises translations from various languages which have been taken from volumes published during both the earlier and later phases of my career, as well as some which have hitherto only appeared in periodicals or anthologies. I have placed here in its entirety my early attempt to translate a selection of the poems of Giacomo Leopardi. I have not however included a number of translations from the Persian, Arabic and Russian – languages which I do not know – which were done in each case in collaboration with a speaker of the language in question. I have also excluded a translation of the extant epigrams of Anyte, as well as some other poems taken from the Greek Anthology which were done in close collaboration with my friend Carol Whiteside, whose knowledge of Greek far surpasses the rudimentary smattering which is all that I can claim in that tongue.

I owe so much to the reading of poems in translation that to add to the corpus of English translated verse is for me something in the nature of the repayment of a debt. I would myself consider all the translations included here as an integral part of my own work. They are related to my original poems in terms of influence, theme and technique.

The final section of this book contains three longer poems. *Artorius*, which I describe as a heroic poem, is the most ambitious piece of writing I have undertaken.

Long poems are not, we are told, fashionable today. I hope that any reader who has not come across this poem in its original edition will not be put off by its length. I have endeavoured to make *Artorius* entertaining and have not, I hope, at any time confused seriousness with solemnity. *The Triumph of the Muse* is a mock heroic satire which I wrote during the late 1940s and early 1950s. It alludes of course to many of the literary foibles and quarrels of the time. These are now largely and perhaps happily forgotten, and will necessarily be obscure to some readers, but to burden the poem with footnotes at this stage would be tedious and impertinent. I do not now subscribe to all its implied judgements, but I hope the poem contains some things of permanent interest, and again I trust that it may prove not unentertaining. *Wounded Thammuz* was the first of my poems to appear in book form, and is included here mainly for the sake of historical completeness. It was conceived as a tripartite sequential pastoral elegy on the themes of seasonal and historical recurrence and resurrection. I am well aware of the immaturity and to some extent the derivative character of this poem, but the themes I have just outlined do seem to me to prefigure certain preoccupations which will be found to run through much of my later work. These themes, and others which the reader may detect as abiding poetic concerns of mine – for example, the animal creation – are matters which poets have dealt with again and again, and will I think continue to be perennial themes for poetry. It may perhaps be a kind of hubris in me to attempt to handle them yet again, and I can only say that I did not so much seek them out, but that they chose me.

It is a commonplace that man now possesses the capacity totally to destroy his own environment. There are some who would say that if the world is to end, perhaps at 2.30 p.m. next Tuesday week, then the writing of mere poetry is a frivolous and irresponsible occupation. I can only retort that if this depressing fact were indeed to prove the case, to occupy one's last minutes in the composition of verse might be as civilized and as meaningful an enterprise as any. Poetry should not be – cannot be – propaganda, because the poet cannot prevent those who have it in their power to destroy the world from doing so if they are so minded, but he might perhaps just possibly persuade them of the value of that world they are about to destroy before they take the final fatal step to do so.

Well, there it is then. I know of no better definition of poetry than one thrown out in passing by Dryden, that it is 'articulate music' – but the musical is not necessarily to be identified with the mellifluous, and harmony is unable to exist unless it contains discord. As for the purpose of poetry I can only fall back on the familiar Horatian tag that it is 'to instruct by pleasing'. It is for critics and philosophers to discuss the precise nature of the pleasure, and the nature of the instruction will perhaps vary from age to age and from place to place, but if I have only occasionally and imperfectly pleased or instructed my readers, or if I have just once or twice struck out a musical chord which lingers within their memories – then the bringing together of these poems in one volume may perhaps not have been wholly a waste of time.

JOHN HEATH-STUBBS

Later Poems
1965-1987

A House of Bricks

Parnassus seems overcrowded now,
Like everywhere else. The developers have got in.
It's covered with pre-fabs, or –
Like thrice three hundred little pigs –
We build our shacks with straw, matchboard or brick.
The wind of the future, the great wolf-wind,
Huffing and puffing, will blow us all away,
I shouldn't wonder. And for my part,
I know my mortar's sloppily applied,
My bricks of variable quality.
But yet I hope –
Yes, by the hair on my chinny-chin-chin!

The New Dance of Death

BUTTERFLY HUNTER

A small boy is running over the downs
And through the woodland rides he goes. He barks his bony knees
Upon the mountainous rocks. He sweeps his net
Through the forests of the grasses, over
The swaying cities of the wild carrot,
Campanula-chiming spires. In his innocent glee,
He is unaware that the bright, feckless creatures he pursues
Are, each one, you or I,
Are those we loved – ah, when was that? – and lost
And inconsolably have mourned.

DEATH THE ICE-CREAM MAN

He tolls his bell in passing. In some districts
The tune he plays is 'Red-nosed Rudolph' –
A red-nosed, fiery-eyed, and phantom reindeer,
Scudding over the tundra among the smoke of the yurts;
In others it's the Spring Song – impossible freshness,
Victorian, Mendelssohnian peace of mind;
But here it is 'Lady Greensleeves' – she
Is the green-sleeved English earth, and she will gather

All of us into her bosom. The snowfruits,
The choc ices and the cornets he dispenses
Are cold as ultimate zero. He asks no payment –
Generous to pensioners.
But he has customers of every age;
As for the little ones – he's awfully fond of those.

DEATH AND PROFESSOR CHEIRON CHELIFER

You wander in the library, between the stacks, –
Or is it the turnings of the cemetery? –
Reading inscriptions on lichened headstones,
Or broken spines of books. The past eludes you still –
A beckoning fair one.

Me you confront at the last bend:
For you the future is my mask.
And now you are transmogrified
Into a footnote, or perhaps a gloss,
Caught in the very act
Of creeping into the text.

DEATH AND THE POLITICIAN

Right Honourable Sir, Right Honourable Madam –
Unfinished business. There is now a lobby
Which you must go into – total unanimity.
Forget about the opinion polls, forget
The jockeying for places. Nor will they help you now –
The stalwart ladies in their hats, the good dependable
Flat-capped party workers. The game of power,
Like every childhood game, must break off now –
When the bell tolls in the great clock tower, and the lights
Are going out in the Chamber as in Europe:
Who goes home? Who goes home?

DEATH AND THE TERRORIST

He thinks I am his servant. Hoist with his own petard,
He blows himself and half a hundred others
Out of time, and into emptiness. In the final blackness,
Every vision fades – Tír na n'Óg,
The Prophet's honeyed paradise of houris, and even
The beautiful federated cities of the future. Only, in that brief
    moment
The image of a naked, bleeding man,
Strung to two crossbars, crown of acacia thorns.

DEATH'S BEDSIDE MANNER

The glimmering square, the half-awakened bird-pipe –
Tennyson knew it all. Fragments of Tennyson
Rattle about in the skull. When the crab bites,
When the angina grips, when the stertorous breath –
Breath like a drowning man's, drowning in emptiness –
Gasps. Just out of eyeshot.
Beside the bed he stands, in his dark, formal suit,
With white and fine and surgeon's hands. He will administer
The ultimate, the infallible anodyne.

DEATH AND THE POET

"You know me. I'm the one you called
Soft names in muséd rhymes." "'In muséd rhymes'
Means those I did not write, feeling them false.
But I do know you, you are the general thief,
Bitter to all men, but most of all to me,
Who lived by the bright shining images you stow
Into your swagbag. No soft names for you,
You grinning nothing!" "I am the silence
That's between the words, silence at the line's ending,
Without that, can be no prosody. And all my vast domain
Is compassed by a caesura. It is my hand arrests
The water that your name's inscribed upon.
We'll go together, seek Virgilian fields, where I'll transmute you
Into perdurable and laureate marble-stone."

DEATH AND THE LADY

You come late, but I knew you would come.
Arriving sooner, you had been less welcome –
Planting frost and fever in my bones,
Turning my blood to a strong poison;
Or else the door had opened, and you stalked in
With the face of Jack the Ripper.

Not much is left, but I give you all:
Never before to any of the others –
But first, your present. You will hand me
The small change of pain, and then
Costly, a black pearl, oblivion.

DEATH AND THE REVEREND SIMON SIMPLEX

"Remember Holbein's woodcut, where I call
Out of the field the good pastor in the midst of his sheep."
"But he was mitred and was croziered –
And I have never come by such accoutrements."
"The image stands, and you must come." "My hungry sheep,
With queasy appetites look up, and I suppose
Someone will feed them. I hope the wind that swells them
Was not my wind – rather the wind that rustles
Through all the Sunday papers, and whistles shrill
Out of the television screen. Well, anyway,
I should be glad to knock off now, glad of a long sleep:
Your hand in mine, my fellow-labourer."

DEATH THE DRY-CLEANER

Pass me your suit, your trousers and your jacket,
Shirt, waistcoat, socks and everything,
Hair, skin, guts, bones, toenails. And now go home. Your naked
     essence
Walks the streets in all their chilly weather,
But unembarrassed. Though stripped down,
And bare, you now are indiscernible.
I do not know when you'll get back your things;
But rest assured you will do, good as new –
Yes – good as new, and better.

"On steel-blue wings from Africa,
Over the desert drought, and the sea's tumbling sapphire,
The swallow will come back when spring returns;
But for me," said Youth, "there's no returning."

"I come on the nightingale's brown wings,"
Said Love, "to perch in the moonlit glade,
Singing my song, singing my sweet, sweet prick-song,
My breast against a thorn, impaled
Upon the eternal, never thornless rose."

"Hawk-winged I come," so said the cuckoo, Jealousy,
"To foist my monstrous and insatiate offspring
In that fragile cradle, where
Nurture their naked bantlings Eros and Psyche –
Papageno, Papagena."

"Out of the twilight, out of the darkness, sometimes
A prodigy at noonday, I swoop down
With muffled plumes, and with extended talons:
I come on the owlet's wings," said Azrael.

The Great Yahoo Revolution

After Gulliver had left the island
They still remembered him. While he had been among them
They had rather disliked him. They thought him stuck-up and
      prissy,
With his mincing ways, his patent contempt for them,
His cringing subservience to their masters –
Almost, you would say,
A houyhnhnm in a yahoo's hide. But afterwards
His image began to change in their folk-memory,
Presenting a possible yahoo perfectibility –
Fragrantly un-hirsute, and non-nude,
And full of mysterious skills and expertise:
Witness his ticking watch that talked to him,
Witness his pocket compass,
And, above all, his pistols.

33

Poets arose,
Singing of the world's great age which begins anew,
As they crouched around their fires of cattle-dung,
And scrambled for the orts the houyhnhnms allotted them.
Bards twanged on gut-string stretched across dried gourds,
Fluted on hollow bones, foretold
How soon a scarlet dawn should come,
When the yahoo race should rise to gain its freedom
And all be Gullivers.

And so, surprisingly, that day did come:
The yahoos revolted – armed with nothing more
But sharpened sticks and flaked flint-stones,
And primitive ploughshares, they fought against
The flailing hoofs and crunching teeth of their masters.

Leaders now appeared as if from nowhere;
Names to be honoured through the generations:
The noble Hoo-ha, the heroic Uggie,
And that great feminine apostle of liberation,
Stinkastinkah, the carrotty-haired one.
The houyhnhnms' leaders were slaughtered and roasted –
Some of them alive. There were forty days
Of feasting on horse-steaks, on horse-liver, on horse-tripes,
And guzzling on the superior quality oats
The houyhnhnms always reserved for their own use –
All this washed down with the heady drink
Those slaves themselves had devised,
Brewed from the wild bee-honey, and forest fruits,
Which the houyhnhnms contemned, but allowed them to use,
Because it had kept them stupid.

But after that things settled down:
There was convened a great popular assembly,
Which all of them attended,
In spite of bloated stomachs and sore heads.
They hammered out laws, and a constitution.
A republic was proclaimed, and Stinkastinkah
Became first president. Later on
Her office was confirmed for life. But Uggie and Hoo-ha
Dissented, and retired with all their followers,
To sulk upon the northern and the southern promontories,
Which seemed sterile. But the central plain

(And here it was that Stinkastinkah's writ ran
And her successors in the female line)
Was rich in pasturage and had abundant corn-land.

The surviving houyhnhnms were reduced to servitude,
Set to the plough, to labour in the quarries,
Hauling great blocks of stone for buildings,
Or in the depths of the earth, in the newly discovered mines,
Or, with tight bearing-rein and under the lash,
They pulled the coaches of the yahoo notables.

The high and noble classic houyhnhnm language
Degenerated into a series of inarticulate
Neighings and whinnyings. But mostly these poor beasts were
    silent,
Pensively nodding as they did their tasks,
Or dreaming in their draughty stalls at night.
What did they dream of? They had always believed
In a Supreme Being, exalted, passionless and abstract,
But now that myth assumed a different form:
He was a great winged stallion, colour of starlight,
Up in the pastures of the cumulus clouds.
The thunder was the rattling of His hoof beats;
His eyes flashed lightning, and the snorting tempest
His angry breath. One day He'd descend to earth,
A Saviour God, and lead the houyhnhnm nation
Over the rainbow bridge into celestial paddocks.

The Yahoo state prospered. They achieved remarkable progress.
The Dutch voyager, Adrianus Vanderflick,
Who touched there in the seventeen nineties,
Found a people, simple and pastoral,
Skilled in equestrian matters, but already
Exhibiting signs of technological development.

The promontories which
The followers of Uggie and Hoo-ha occupied,
Had rich deposits – coal and iron, nitre,
Petroleum and uranium ore,
And somehow they discovered how to use these,
Especially when the civil wars began
Between the Uggites and the Stinkastinkists
(The Hoo-ha party tactically changing sides,

Holding the balance). Since Vanderflick's time
Few have reached that island, but there are rumours in our own
    century
Of a barren, slightly radioactive rock,
Strewn with the skeletons of horses,
And other bones, reputed to be human.

Moving to Winter

As I move, through autumn to winter, my life's house
Is Edmund Waller's cottage of the soul.
How chill, how pure, eternity shines through the chinks!
Yet, while my fire still burns, I'll proffer
Scraps of toasted cheese to the crickets –
My long-legged, whiskery poems, that chirp in the crannies,
Or hop about on the flagstones. And there'll be other visitants –
    an incognito
Angel or so, all my accustomed ghosts,
And, twirling his forked tail, pedunculate-eyed,
With sharp, nine-inch proboscis for a nose,
Not all malignant, the odd domestic bogle.

Listening to Brahms

It's naughty, I know, to put pictures to music
If the composer doesn't invite you. And, specially, no doubt
With the austere and classically-minded
Doktor Johannes Brahms. And yet, in him
I seem to hear the blustering of the wind,
The great breakers rolling, the undertow of the tide,
Or else I perceive how, free and frolicsome,
The sunlight glints upon the foam's white horses.
His childhood town was a northern port;
And its sky often a leaden sky,
His sea the greyly cold – sometimes the bright – Nordsee.

On the Demolition of the Odeon Cinema, Westbourne Grove

Never one for the flicks, I did not frequent the place:
Though I recall the *Voyage of the Argonauts*,
And a second feature – some twaddle about
A daughter of King Arthur, otherwise unrecorded
By history or tradition. Now, each day,
I pass it, and I hear the brutal noise
Of demolition: clatter of falling masonry,
Machines that seem to grit and grind their teeth,
And munch in gluttony of destruction.

Its soft innards, I guess, are gone already:
The screen, the lighting, the plush seats; the ghosts likewise –
Shadows of shadows, phantoms of phantoms,
The love goddesses, the butcher boy heroes,
The squawking cartoon-animals.

This odeon – I should regret it? –
In which no ode has ever been recited.
Yet there's a pang – for I've lived long enough
To know that every house of dreams
Must be torn down at last.

Three Poems written for Dinners of The Omar Khayyám Society

1

There is a tavern in Elysium,
Arboured in amaranth and roses, where
Super-celestial, like a great gold sun,
The wine bowl circulates. And there indeed,
Guests are star-scattered – for Anacreon,
Li-Po, and Horace, and our own rare Ben,
Bellman and Burns are of the company;
Hafiz and Omar have their honoured seats.
There, hiccup never comes nor hangover;
Talk's all good sense and wit, and no-wise slurred,

Nor blurred, nor boring, still less is it tainted
With backbiting or petulance. Tonight
We move into the shadow of that dream.

2
THE FLY

A fly, above a Persian garden flitting,
In the soft evening air, observed below
Star-scattered guests, and so descended further,
Alighting on a wine cup's brim – a cup of clay –
(Ah, what lost beauty had that clay been once?).
But fuddled by the fumes of wine, it slipped
Into the drink. This cup was Omar's cup.
He, wearied out with lonely observation
Of the bright starry wheels or else confused
By the conundrums of his algebra,
Failed to discern the little struggling creature,
And gulped it down. Within the sage's stomach,
Like Jonah in the belly of the fish,
It feared that it must perish; so it buzzed
Prayers to Beelzebub. The Lord of Flies
Heard its petition, and, with that, it rose,
Borne ever upwards by the vinous spirits,
Passing through veins and arteries, until
It reached the poet's brain. And there it sported,
As in a paradise of intellect;
And it bred maggots – little things that wriggled
Through convolutions of the cerebellum,
And tickled, so that Omar sneezed them out:
They are his verses we have learned to treasure.
The dawn wind took them up, and wafted them
To every portion of the spinning globe –
Bittersweet wisdom which Fitzgerald garnered.

3

He'd watched all night the enigmatic skies:
When asked a tavern-mate "You, who are wise –
    Which of your works shall, to the last, endure?"
"The foolish quatrains that I improvise

"Over the wine-cup. Past the lands of Roum,
And past the Frankish lands, in mist and gloom
　　A western island lies, and there a poet,
When Omar is mute dust within the tomb,

"Shall set those verses forth in his own tongue;
Upon his thread like pearls they shall be strung;
　　While men rejoice, and yet repine at Fate,
Those trifles shall be read, or said, or sung.

"And friends, who in good fellowship delight,
And in the wine-cup too, on joyous night
　　Shall consecrate to Omar and to him –
Their emblem the carnation, red or white."

The Roman and the Woodpecker

Aelius Tubero, the Roman praetor,
Was giving judgment in the market-place
(So Pliny tells us) when a woodpecker
Suddenly appeared, and perched
On his patrician cranium. The augurs
Gave it as their professional opinion
That, if the bird flew free, some great disaster
Threatened the state – contrariwise,
If Aelius should kill the creature, then
Something quite nasty was in store for him.

The noble Roman did not hesitate –
He wrung the yaffle's neck, and shortly afterwards
Of course, he died.

But the res publica was saved. It lumbered onwards,
Through all those tedious, bloodstained centuries, towards
Its ineluctable decline and fall.

Embarkation for Cythera

Anymore for the Skylark! They hurry to climb on board –
The clowns, the columbines,
The harlequins that tinkle their theorboes.
Watteau's the image – and I would surmise
The music Couperin's.

My friends, I wish you a good voyage, a favouring wind,
But I'll not join you now – not for this time –
Although I still believe the land you tend towards
Is every bit as green and welcoming
As travellers affirm. She holds her court there –
Love's Queen, the white Sow, Aphrodite.

For I have been upon your decks, have glimpsed those
        promontories,
But as I scrambled greedily to get on shore,
Fell into bilge and puddle-water.

So I'll remain here on the sand-spit.
There are a few tunes in this flute of mine –
Dry hemlock kex, winter retreat for earwigs –
If not, then let it sleep, as I shall be
Content to sleep, though the chill dews are falling.

Homage to George Stubbs

I claim no kinship with this Cheshire man:
My forebears were of Staffordshire, at least
Since Charles the Martyr's time. But Stubbs
Is a good north-west Midlands name, and if you traced
The bloodstreams further back, it's like enough
You'd find they would converge. But may I hazard
A fellowship of spirit with him, son of a groom,
Who hung from the rafters the lifeless body of a horse –
Such as his father had fondled, currycombed, and cosseted
With hot bran mash, and children brought their gifts to –
Apples and sugar-lumps? Scalpel, knife, and saw,
Scraped, carved, and bit, slicing the mighty sinews.

The convolutions of the bowels unwound;
The head displayed its secret chambers, and the brain
Was lifted from its citadel, the skull, until at length
Only the white and chalky bones remained. Commitment thus
Behoves, to stinking fact, if we would enter
That clearing in the forest of the mind
Where animal energies, equine and leonine,
Engage each other with great uncleft hoof,
With gleaming tooth, and ripping, savage talon.

The Wilton Diptych

For Ronald Banks

Perceive this blue. You would say it shone
Not from the visible, but the invisible heaven.
On the left hand panel the graceful Virgin,
Demure and courtly holds her Son.
Angels in waiting stand around.

And on the right, the young king
Kneels in adoration, escorted
By royal English saints.
Note his fine auburn ringlets, and his face –
Rather too round and chubby
Even for a fifteen-year-old boy.

On the back is the white hart of Kent –
His mother's badge; Joan, the Black Prince's widow –
Still beautiful, and one would guess, still dominant.

Blue is for faith. This is the Age of Faith, in spite of
The pestilence that rode on its pale horse
Through the depopulated villages, prices rising,
Wages pegged, Lollard preachings, John Ball's letter,
Langland's austere and chiding vision,
And Chaucer's ironies.

They dance around Jack Straw as round Maid Marian,
The forest Queen of the May.
Robin Hood and Little John,

They are to the greenwood gone –
Robin the bobbin, and John the red nose.

Wat Tyler's men are up. Gaunt's palace of the Savoy
Is sacked, and Simon Sudbury
(Oppressor of the poor, no martyred Becket he) is lynched

'Richard, that sweet and lovely rose' –
He visited the Virgin's shrine at Westminster,
The night before he rode to meet the mob.
'I will be your leader.' – the courageous
The meaningless, the lying gesture.
What mercy then was shown them? Tyler stabbed,
And John Ball hanged. Grudgingly they dispersed
Back to their manors, there to cram their bellies
With peas, with beans, with orts,
With scant and bitter tear-soaked bread.

And for that threat averted
This lovely irrelevance of art was fashioned,
Perhaps a votive offering – for privilege re-entrenched,
Power unabridged. And Joan the Fair
Gives thanks within the Abbey, and breathes a lady's orison.

The Ship of England scraped the shoals and shallows,
But now sails onwards. Youth upon the prow
Gazes idly towards the sunset,
Phantasmagoria of evening. Pleasure at the helm,
Half seas over, steers a zigzag course.

The royal magic worked. But will it work
When he shall long to sit upon the ground
And tell sad stories of kings' deaths, and time shall waste him

Who was time-waster – poor Jack-of-the-clock?
'Now Richard the redeless, rueth on u-self'.

Velazquez: The Immaculate Conception

The sun's incandescent hydrogen
Mantles her body, and her feet are scrunching
Upon the glassy moon-dust, as she stands,
A wonder and a mystery in heaven.
A dozen stars are whizzing round her head,
A May-time garland. Yet the human face
Denotes an ordinary peasant girl,
Just such as Mary was – or Dulcinea,
Whom all the crack-brains of La Mancha quest for,
Along the world's dusty, misleading roads.

Martinmas

Only half a cloak of warmth and sunlight –
Gold thread woven in the mist – the month flings down
Upon our northern world. Pinched by the Scorpion's claws,
Pierced by the Archer's icy shafts, the earth,
Shivering, turns towards the solstice.

I think how El Greco saw St Martin –
A young hidalgo of his own century:
With elegant, practised hand he unsheathes
His fine Toledo blade, and slits
The sumptuous mantle – velvet, silken,
Gold embroidery thread – to cast it down
(And yet with courtesy) a gift to the poor shivering man who
    crouches
Close to his horse's hooves –

And then rides on, maybe to join a party,
Where his companions chaff him: "Look at Señor Half-cloak!"
"Is this the latest winter fashion, do you think?"

How cold, how keen, the wind of the spirit blows
Through all the crannies of the chicken-coops
That we would hide in. Martin,
The cock that crowed for Peter crows for you.

As for the beggar, half a cloak for him
Was a lot better than no cloak at all;
And twisted round his starved and scabby body
It kept the life in him, a season and a season –
Who, in the end, lay dead in a ditch, perhaps, and never knew
In him the naked Christ was clothed – not till he woke
In that green parkland where it's always spring,
And always Easter morning.

The Swallow

The swallow hawks above the college courtyard:
"Ityn, ityn!" – I know that small language.
Uncertain, sultry August: gnats are rising –
Midges bred in the damp soil, mosquitoes
Over the glistening ripples of Cam.
The swallow's at home in this English scene;
She'll not be with us long, though – nor will the swift
That, screaming, sports at higher altitudes,
Hard by the hanging battlement of cloud,
Womb of the thunder. Soon they must be off,
As all things upon fragile wings must go,
Through hazard and horror of darkness, storm and sea,
To find their other home, under another sun.

Improvisation on 'The Holly and the Ivy'

Holly and ivy, Druid trees
King and queen of the ancient wood –
And a snatch of a hunting song, perhaps.

Run, stag, run, toward the east,
Panting for Eden's waterbrooks, my soul:
The Sun of Righteousness is rising.

Laden with gold and incense,
The Magian dromedaries
Are lurching stablewards:
Ox and ass are there already.

Diapason of the spheres –
The spirit of Johann Sebastian
Dances from orbit to orbit.

And archangelical choirs ring
Over the barren hills:
Listen, shepherds, listen.

Capricorn

Fishy old goat of the winter solstice
Coughs all night in his stellar paddock,
Nibbling the whiskers of comets and meteors:
"I wait for my turn in the precession of equinoxes –
The age of Capricorn comes after Aquarius:
A high new time, those prancing millennia.
But also I image universal Pan –
In my sign rose the star of Bethlehem."

An Icelandic Tale

There was a man hid in the cattle-byre
On Christmas Eve. "I'll put to the test" he said
"The story that they tell, how on this night,
At midnight, the beasts talk."

Twelve times the bell tolled in the church clock-tower,
And then the first ox spoke. "Midnight." it said.
The second ox said, "Time to talk."
"Man in byre." the third ox said, and then
"Drive him mad." was what the fourth ox uttered;
"Before dawn." – so the fifth ox concluded.

They found him in the morning, gibbering,
An empty vessel, his wits all scared away.
The unendurable had broken through –
Epiphany of the miraculous.

Holy Innocents' Day

After inexplicable music in the sky,
The shepherds' pipe and drum, and Mary's song,
In the darkened villages, the screams:
The soldiery have come –
Rachel is weeping for her children.

Never a Christmas can go by, but you
Must think of children Famine crams
Into her bread-basket, of those red War
Has roasted, suffocated, disembowelled, and those
Whose violated bodies lie on building sites,
Or else in dustbins like discarded dolls;
And think of Gilles de Retz
Who built a chapel for the Holy Innocents.

Eostra

After we came back from church, Good Fridays,
My father used to go into the garden
And plant his spring seeds. Down in the darkness
They would begin to rise, no doubt,
With rising of the Lord of Life.

It's spring again. Affectionately I mark,
Along my tree-lined London street,
The dialects of the birds. That is the song thrush,
There is the blackbird, those are the tomtits,
The robin now, and the hedge-accentor;
And in gardens, daffodils are blowing
Their trumpets of the jubilee.

Eternal spring, we say – Freya who is Eostra:
Her eastward rising, the yeast she is likewise
In new loaves offered her, one with the springing corn,
Rescued from etens' hold, and the cloud-country –

But we are wrong. Recurrence is not eternal;
For each of us, that spring is going to come
Which is the last. And the whole earth, we know,
Though it be aeons on aeons, is journeying
Towards her death, in cold and darkness,
Or in the fire, whichever it may be;
And man, by then, perhaps
Forgotten as the dinosaur.

It's only Easter morning that's eternal;
Only the day the Lord has made is true.

Four Dragons

St George rides down the vale to Uffington,
White horsed. There are four dragons
He must encounter now.

The first dragon was of the earth.
Out of its ripped-up belly tumbled
Jewelled goblets, golden torques, and helmets,
Swords of Wayland's workmanship.
The men of former times had hidden them.

The second dragon was of the air.
The great black cumulo-nimbus
Burst. The rains streamed down.
Clad in the greenness of the growing corn
Came forth the young spring bride out of the furrow.

The third dragon was of the water.
The river rose. Redeemed from human sacrifice,
In all her finery, the king's daughter
Danced in triumph. Silver anklets
Tinkled upon her feet.

The fourth dragon was of the fire.
Slowly and cruelly the flames licked upwards,
Reaching for the hand – the martyr's hand
That had so contumaciously torn down
Caesar's persecuting edict.

To The Queen

on the occasion of Her Majesty's Silver Jubilee, 1977

Because the heart is finite, and can give
Its love and loyalty only to particulars –
Seeing in the known village, city, country,
A partial revelation of that one good place
Where all the just are citizens – I frame this dithyramb,
I plait this garland, for you, dynastic Elizabeth,
Presiding, with the sceptre that the dove tips,
Over your tidy, untidy, united kingdom
Where liberty still survives.

I twine the rose of England, blood-red and white,
The purple, aggressive thistle of Scotland, and
The green and gritty leek (St David's frugal dinner),
Also the shamrock, by which St Patrick,
Rather oddly, expounded the Trinity.
With these I would deck your doorposts.

Squalls buffet Britain, the off-shore ship of Europe;
She is driven to the Goodwins. Her sails are tattered and tatty,
Her masts split, her shrouds in shreds – and through them
Ill-omened fulmars and kittywakes skitter and glide.

Through a gap in the cloud-wrack I glimpse the mortal moon,
That first Elizabeth, augustly enthroned.
She shifts and changes: now she's the young
And golden-buskined Belphoebe, and now in her wane,
A raddled icon, her visage pitted and cratered.
At her side Magnificence, like the Lord Leicester,
Disperses golden angels to the groundlings –
Not for us neo-Elizabethans:

Economics, the law of the household, decrees
Dame Parsimony, the hard-faced lady cook,
Should have a finger in our festive pie – and yet
Let the silver trumpets of jubilee sound forth
Throughout the length and breadth of the land, to authorize
Judicious binge and beano – let bunting
Wave in the rain, in the cooling breezes of June, and let there be
Cakes and real ale, bowling for the pig,
Folk-dancing, gilbertandsullivan, and all the other
Silly and beautiful things that signalize
A lasting and loyal love.

Purkis

The red king lay in the black grove:
The red blood dribbled on moss and beech-mast.

With reversed horseshoes, Tyrrel has gone
Across the ford, scuds on the tossing channel.

Call the birds to their dinner. 'Not I,' said the hoarse crow,
'Not I,' whistled the red kite
'Will peck from their sockets those glazing eyes.'

Who will give him to his grave? 'Not I,' said the beetle
'Will shift one gram of ground under his corpse,
Nor plant in his putrid flank my progeny.'

Robin, red robin, will you in charity
Strew red Will with the fallen leaves?

'I cover the bodies of Christian men:
He lies unhouseled in the wilderness,
The desolation that his father made.'

Purkis came by in his charcoal-cart:
'He should lie in Winchester. I will tug him there –
Canons and courtiers perhaps will tip me,
A shilling or two for the charcoal-burner.'

Purkis trundled through the town gates,
And 'Coals!' he cried, 'coals, coals, coals,
Coals, charcoal, dry sticks for the burning!'

The Twelve Labours of Hercules

The Nemean Lion

To strangle a lion with one's bare hands:
This legitimates his kingship,
His godship. Hereafter
He wears the skin. We kill
What we love. We become
That which we kill.

The Lernaean Hydra

Foetid snake of the green, standing pool:
Nine heads – when one's cut off
Three others grow. Thus error
Pullulates. This kind
Is cauterized by fire.

The Cretan Bull

Bull of the earthquake – he stamps,
A city collapses; he bellows,
A tall tower tumbles.

The Erymanthean Boar

This blatant beast –
Grubber up of boundaries, snorting
Consumer of rations,
Defiler of the sweet meadow:
Catch him alive!

The Augean Stables

I cannot shift it.
Corruption, age-encrusted.
I cannot shift it. Water
From melting snows – turn on
The rivers like taps.

The Stymphalian Birds

Birds of the pestilent marsh, moulting
Darts of malaria, arrows
Of the swamp-fever. Bring pan and copper kettle:
Bang, bang, bang –
Be off, you scruffy puttocks!

The Arcadian Stag

The silver stag, proud-tined,
Fleeting over the white snow,
Through glassy winters. Let no spear-point
Graze his flank, no arrow-tip
Impugn with blood-drop. The Lady
Of Wild Things, with gossamer moonlight
Gathered about her body, loves him.
He's not for you.

The Horses of Diomede

Horses of the King of Thrace,
Of the northern war-lord. They are armour plated,
Jet powered, electronic brained.
In War's smoky manger
Man is their mashed provender.

The Girdle of Hippolyta

Man-woman, queen
Of the women without men.
Putrid scalps dangle from her waist;
She has burned away her right breast, she brayed

51

Her first-born boy-child in a mortar.
How to snatch the girdle
Of her steeled and homicidal chastity?

The Oxen of Geryon

A three-bodied giant, the sun
At morning, noon and evening.
Herdsman of the western shore, his cattle
The sunset clouds – such riches
Are for the taking.

The Apples of the Hesperides

These two, apples
Of man's remembered innocence,
Burning through the twilight dream, and guarded
By female voices and the watchful snake.
Recover them.

Cerberus

We all come down to this –
The yapping guard-dog of the final dungeon.
But bring your honey-cake,
The kneaded dough-ball of all your senses loved
In the bright day, up in the cheerful air.

The Death of Llew

Under a shelter of withies,
Having bathed, getting out of the cauldron,
His trousers put on, one foot
On the back of a colt; a spear
Forged only at the sacring of the Mass –

Neither indoors nor outdoors,
Neither naked nor clothed,
Neither afoot nor on horseback;
A spear no Christian could make:

'Whizz!' sang the spear;
The flower-bride enchantingly synthesized
From maybloom, trefoil, broom, meadowsweet,
Turned to a boding owl; the hero's soul
Flew off, a verminous eagle.

For us also, somewhere
There waits the treacherous moment,
And waits the spear.

Volund
on first looking into Auden's and Taylor's Edda

I had read the tale before, and thought it
A catalogue of mythological horrors. But now I read it again
And know the significance. And I wonder
What craftsman-smith, captive or thrall,
Amid the violence of the Viking age,
In the bitterness of his heart
Devised this savage fable.

Through Murk Wood they flew, three girls,
Triple and identical, in swanfeather dress
Whistling through the bare branches, to sojourn
Nine seasons of love. Then they departed.

'We will ride to the ends of the earth,
To East and South, to seek them!' But Volund remained,
Lonely in Wolfdale, forging rings
Of red gold, waiting her return.

He counted his rings. One was missing. He dreamed
She had come back. When he next woke
He found himself in fetters; lamed,
Relegated to an island, forced to work
At trumpery trinkets.

'All shall be told, all:
The bodies of your boys
Lie under the blood-stained bellows; I have debauched

Your daughter to a drunken slut. But now I rise
On swan's wings. I am the Lord of the Elves,
Riding the cloudless air.'

(As Dionysus, also,
Over the house of Pentheus.)

So they think they can hamstring the artist, do they –
Sever his sinews, dissever him from his Muse?

Quetzalcoatl

Then he came to the unlimited, the luminous sea;
Behind him the desert where the coyote
Howled and the lizard basked;
Tree-sized cylindrical cacti, volcanic cones
And the jagged line of mountains, in their hearts
Gold, jade, emeralds, petrol, silver.

He looked into the glass. He said:
'They have taken away my beauty and my power;
I shall not be loved or obeyed.'
So he put on his comely robe
Of trogon feathers, crossed over the breast;
And his turquoise mask, spotted with yellow;
He reddened his lips, and picked out
The serpent's teeth in red.

He said: 'My heart
Is the manic heart of Monteczuma, broken
By the flung stone; my power
The ruthlessness of Cortez, the anger
And justice of Juarez, the abstract order of Diaz
The fury of Villa, and Maximilian
Silent before the firing-squad.
I suffer with the peons scraping the hard soil,
With the workers on the haciendas, and the itinerant
Fruit-pickers of California.

'I am tricked with phenomena, the fantasies
Of pulque and mescal – delusions
Of my mother the Serpent-skirted, the black
Virgin of Guadalupe; of my sister,
The Flower-bride, of Marina –
She who betrayed her people, the madness of Carlota
Dabbling her finger in the Pope's cocoa, scalding
Her arm in the nuns' broth.'

Then all the birds came to say goodbye:
The scarlet macaw, the blue-jay,
The dove, the thrush, and the quail,
The gilded parrots with their human tongues,
The curasow with his malachite bill,
The tinamou brooding her burnished eggs,
The condor gliding with untwitching wings
Under the blood-drinking sun, the occellated
Turkey gobbling from the ground,
The motmot with his gnawed, racket feathers,
The colibri, darting in and out
Of the nectarous flower-bells – all
Whistled, whispered and grided farewell.

'Fire must purge'. He constructed the pyre.
The flames licked up,
The green robe frizzled, the mask cracked;
The body crumbled to white dust
Drifting on the desert wind.
But the heart rose up, a chalice
Filled with beating blood,
A crimson butterfly flapping skyward
Like a red flag.
It became the morning star,
Gleaming down from the mask above
Over the landscape of pain.

Bevis of Hampton
for Norman Nicholson

Bevis waded ashore through the surf
Of four-tided Solent. At his heels
The delicate island was glimpsed,
Unglimpsed, through the mist:
Victoria watches the yachts
Flit to and fro, decrees
Tea and biscuits in the library
For Mr Gladstone, invites
Mr Disraeli to stay for dinner.

Bevis – his bones were chalk and his flesh was clay,
The crest of his helm
Royal and Roman Winchester;
Arthur's table,
An amulet, hung on his brow.
Gorse and fern of the New Forest
The scrubby hair on his chest and groin.

As his feet touched the shingle and undercliff, coltsfoot.
Rest-harrow, scabious and knapweed
Blossomed about them – the Dartford warbler,
Stonechat and sand-martin spluttered a welcome.
Ponies obsequiously trotted forward –
They would convoy him inland.

'I am Bevis,' he shouted, 'I am Beow the barley-man.
I have been killing dragons and things
In the Middle East; now I come home
To claim my inheritance.'

His mouth was Southampton Water, where ships of Tarshish,
All the big steamers, chugged in and out, their holds
Bursting with biscuits you nibble, and beefsteaks.
Out of that throat the hymns of Isaac Watts
Arose in salutation to God and to judgement.

Miss Austen observed his coming
From the corner of her eye; on his shoulder, the down of Selborne –
There a retiring cleric discriminated the songs
Of willow-wren, chiffchaff, wood-wren.

Bevis – his right hand rested on Pompey and the great guns;
His left hand gently fondled
The dusty, fairy pavilions of Bournemouth.
In frozen horror a landlady
Stared at the ceiling, a spreading stain –
The blood of Alec D'Urberville.

The corner of his left sleeve
Lightly brushed the blue-slipper clay
Of the Barton beds, where eocene fossils
Attested a former sub-tropical climate,
And curled asleep, in his middle-class room, a boy
Surmised he might be a poet.

Old Mobb

1

Old Mobb stood on the Romsey road:
A splendid equipage came along –
Inside was the Duchess of Portsmouth, with two French footmen,
And two sleek and pampered spaniels.
'Fellow,' she said, 'do you know who I am?'
'Yes, and what you are –
You are the king's whore, I think,
And not kind Protestant Nellie, neither.'
'Villain, do you dare to touch me there!'
'Now I command where the king asks his favours.'
Said Old Mobb, politely removing
Three hundred pounds, a little gold watch,
And a very splendid string of pearls.

2

Old Mobb was on the road at midnight:
Mercury, patron of thieves, swung in its orbit.
Came ambling by on an old grey mare
Mr John Gadbury the astrologer.
'I am a poor man, a poor scholar,
Pray you, spare me.' 'What you –

Who lease out the seven stars for hire
To cozen noodles. These golden chimers
And these silver chinkers make better music
Than all the circling spheres, and much more audible.'
Said Old Mobb, as he pocketed them.
'You cannot rob me of my skill,' said Gadbury,
'In physiognomy, and from your favour
I read you born for hanging.'

3

Came trotting along on a neat black pony
Dr Cornelius Tilburgh,
Successful physician, with a bedside manner,
'Have you no care,' said he, 'for those
Your depredations ruined?'
'You with your clysters and blisters, your nostrums and boluses
Ruin more men than the cataracts of Nile.
Here, doctor, is a leaden pill –
Cough up, or void your superfluity:
No antidote, you know, for gunpowder.'
Said Old Mobb, as he extracted
Twenty-five pounds and a bright medal
With the king's own face upon it.

4

A proud coach rumbled along
On the road towards the Winchester Assizes.
Judge Jeffreys stuck his head out of the window –
His great full wig, his brazen blotchy face:
'The law has claws and I incorporate the law.
Don't think, my man, that you'll escape from justice.'
'Though I shall dance on Tyburn, and you
Rot in the Tower, awaiting trial –
Yet there's another Judge we both must go to.
Who will fare better at those final sessions –
The Lord Chief Justice of England, he who hanged
Many poor men of the West at their own doorposts,
And doomed Dame Alice for her mere compassion
To broken fugitives, or a plain man of Hampshire
Who knew no master but his poverty?

Though he brandished a gun he never killed any
And prayed often
For God's forgiveness, even while he robbed,
As now I do.' said Old Mobb
Suiting the prigging action to the word.

Squirling

When the red nutkin, the rufous shadow-tail,
And not the grey American immigrant,
Danced in the branches of the lady larch, or scolded
Down from the beech tree boughs – this was,
By tradition, a Hampshire sport.

Two weights joined by a leather strap,
Sharply hurled, could bring the squirrel down.

'Barbarous?' the enquirer asked. 'Well,' said the old forester,
'At least we do eat the squirrel
Which is more than the gentry does the fox.'

To Keep Away Moles
for Elspeth Barker

Avaunt, mouldywarp,
    Out of my acres;
Vacate, velvet-coat,
    Your oubliettes and galleries;
The glebe of my neighbour
    Be for your pioning,
And my sward undisturbed:
        His earthworms are more succulent,
        His wire-worms more esculent,
        His leatherjackets of more nutriment.

That is the score,
Insectivore!

Jankynmass

for Charles Causley

Gnashing his teeth in the nether ice
    Wicked Jankyn lies,
While North East winds, unseasonably,
    Blemish our springtide skies.

The apple-blossom and the pear-blossom
    Are shivered from the spray,
While the hell-brewed frosts of Jankynmass
    Deflower the English May.

Bad Jankyn, he was a brewer
    Who brewed on a large scale;
From Havant westward to Penzance
    Men knew of Jankyn's ale,

And supped it down. And I am sure
    That it did them no harm –
Nor soap made froth, nor alum crude
    Had clarified the barm,

Nor what gave body to the brew
    Was any old dead rats,
Or poor half starved apprentice boys
    Who tumbled in the vats,

Befuddled by the heady fumes.
    (And surely envious sin
Gripped those who hinted, in their cups,
    That Jankyn pushed them in.)

But beer is a Teutonic drink
    That clouds the Saxon brain:
The peasants of the western shires
    Have a strong Celtic strain.

The Druid apple's their delight,
    Cider their *vin du pays*:
For this the bridal blossoming orchards
    Make beautiful the May –

A pleasant sight to bless men's eyes;
	Yet did not Jankyn bless –
The more the cider-sellers gain,
	The brewer profits less.

'Curse on the ungrateful jumblejuice,
	The pixy tanglefoot,
Curse on all ciders, sweet or dry,
	And applejack to boot;

'Grant me three nights of frost in May
	To blast the apple flower,
And my eternal soul I'll put
	For ever in your power!'

Old Nick, who's always somewhere around,
	Splashed out of Jankyn's tun,
With parchment, pen, and sealing wax,
	'Sign here!' he shouted, 'Done!'

Three North East winds, and three sharp frosts
	In the third week of May
He granted for bad Jankyn's sake,
	Until the Judgement Day,

To blight the christened apple-trees –
	But then he claimed his price
And clawed that stark, teeth-chattering soul
	Down to the nether ice.

Simcox

Simcox was one of several rather uninteresting
Ghosts, which popular report affirmed
Haunted the precincts of the College where
I had the privilege of my education.
A Junior Fellow (exactly in what field
His tedious studies ran was not remembered),
Simcox, it seems, was drowned – the Long Vacation
Of 1910, or '12, or thereabouts,

61

Somewhere off the coast of Donegal:
If accident or suicide I don't recall. But afterwards
Simcox began to manifest himself
In his old rooms, sitting in his large arm-chair,
With dripping clothes, and coughing slightly.
Simcox was wet in life, and wet in death.

To save embarrassment, it was decided
This should in future be the chaplain's room.
The chaplain of my day, a hearty
Beer-swilling extravert, and not much given –
Or so I would suppose – to exorcism,
Never, to my knowledge, did in fact aver
He had encountered Simcox. And anyway
Those visitings grew fainter with the years.
Simcox was dim in life, and dim in death.

A Crow in Bayswater

A carrion crow flew over Bayswater –
Dews of morning distilled on his dark wings.

Shadows of night retired – the ghost
Of Peter Rachman, pursued
By phantom Alsatian dogs,
Scurried down St Stephen's Gardens.

The crow sailed over All Saints Church, and Father Clark
Unlocking the door for Anglican Eucharist;

Over spilling dustbins, where
Warfarin-resistant mice
Licked the insides of empty soup-cans,
Worried
Potato peelings, stale sliced bread.

'Cark!' said the crow, a raucous croak – to me
The stern music of freedom –

'I will go to Kensington Gardens;
Down by the Round Pond.
New-hatched ducklings are out:
We'll scrag a couple for breakfast.'

Hornbills in Northern Nigeria
to Hilary Fry

As if their great bone-spongey beaks were too heavy,
A party of Grey Hornbills flops overhead
Through the hot, humid air. These are on migration –
('Well, you tell me where,' the zoologist said) –

They emit high, whining, almost gull-like cries,
Seeming, someone remarks, as if they were mass-produced
Off the production-line of an inferior factory.
But this is not apt. Has it not been deduced

The grotesque Hornbill stems from an ancient race
By the fossil testimony of a small, stony word,
Petrified bone-fragment in alluvial clay?
Look again, you witness a prehistoric bird;

On miocene and pliocene landscapes has gazed
The cold, saurian, humanly eyelashed eye,
Which looks out now over the airfield,
Where forms of camels – not incongruous – stray.

And ceremonial trumpets welcome the guest who comes
By Comet or Viscount, out of the modern century;
The place is not distant from the mediaeval walls,
Nor the satellite-tracking station (Project Mercury).

Here unashamed, anthropomorphic gods send rain;
And dawn, like history, flames a violent birth,
Out of a night with crickets and toads articulate,
For black bodies pushing ground-nuts into the red earth.

The Watchman's Flute
(Kano)

Through the Nigerian night the Tuareg watchman,
Ferociously armed with sword, daggers and whip,
Intermittently blows his flute – a piece of piping
Bored with five holes: to pass the time –

To ward off tedium, and perhaps
Lurking malignant ghosts that always throng
This ambient, African darkness:

Infinite rhythmical variations
On a simple tetrachord, with a recurrent pedal point –
Libyan music, antique – as Orpheus
Cajoled the powers of Hell, made them disgorge
Eurydice – to him she was love
(Her jurisdiction be wide).

Those deliquescent forms shrink back
To hollow pits of non-entity:
Music implies an order – light,
Particles in regular motion,
The first articulate Word.

May my lips likewise
Mould such melodious mouthfuls still, amid
The European, the twentieth-century tediums:
We too are haunted, we are in the dark.

Homage to J.S. Bach

It is good just to think about Johann Sebastian
Bach, grinding away like the mills of God,
Producing masterpieces, and legitimate children –
Twenty-one in all – and earning his bread

Instructing choirboys to sing their *ut re mi*,
Provincial and obscure. When Fame's trumpets told
Of Handel displaying magnificent wings of melody,
Setting the waters of Thames on fire with gold,

Old Bach's music did not seem to the point:
He groped in the Gothic vaults of polyphony,
Labouring pedantic miracles of counterpoint.
They did not know that the order of eternity

Transfiguring the order of the Age of Reason,
The timeless accents of super-celestial harmonies,
Filtered into time through that stupendous brain.
It was the dancing angels in their hierarchies,

Teaching at the heart of Reason that Passion existed,
And at the heart of Passion a Crucifixion,
Or when the great waves of his *Sanctus* lifted
The blind art of music into a blinding vision.

In Praise of John Milton
on the three-hundredth anniversary of his death 1974

I frame this paean
For the republican
Poet, John Milton,
    Who had skill to sing
Of the super-sensual –
Those fields celestial
Where powers archangelical
    Sweep by on bright wing,

And the darkness visible
Where the final and total
Perversion of the will
    Finds out its own place:
The arrogant tyranny
Of the false democracy
Issuing in the cacophony
    Of a serpent's hiss.

For his is the voice
Of the moral choice –
Whether in the ways
    Of that wandering wood,

Where Comus and his rout
Go about and about,
With bestial shout,
        To seduce if they could,

Or through the verse
By the Laureate's hearse,
When the blind fury's shears
        Have slit – to renew
The resolution,
Affirm the vocation,
While the road leads on
        To pastures new;

But that road goes
To the wilderness,
Where the solitariness
        Of the Human Being
Confronts the temptation
Of the Negation,
In confutation
        Of its gainsaying.

It leads to the lands
Of the Philistine bands,
Where a blind man grinds
        In Satanic mills,
Till in power of the truth
He puts forth his strength
And brings down, at length
        Their house of idols.

As in Eden's bower,
At our midnight hour
The toad at the ear
        Corrupts even the dream;
Life's tree is the haunt
Of the cormorant
Of malign intent,
        Polluted Life's stream:

John Milton, who cast
Three centuries past
Your body to the dust
    Consigned – re-tune
The organs of your praise,
Sound forth to our days,
And justify the ways
    Of Man to Man.

Saint Michael and the Dragon

'Who is like God?' – the cosmic war-cry redounds
Through vacant space and clouds of tenuous dust
From galaxy to spinning galaxy
(O the bright spears, O the swift lightning's falchion!).
Unknown Energies muster their squadrons, while
The shadowy Delusion sinks
In wreathed and coiled disorder down,
Shrinks to its own black hole.

Christus Natus Est

'Christus natus est!' – it was the Cock's carol
Into the darkness, prefiguring a betrayal.

'Quando?' – the Duck's call is harsh,
Sounding from the reeds of a desolate marsh.

'In hac nocte.' – that voice was the Raven's,
Boding into Man's castle the fatal entrance.

'Ubi?' – it was the Ox that spoke:
We kick against the pricks, we are under the yoke.

'Bethlehem!' – the Lamb, kept for slaughter, said:
God has taken flesh in the House of Bread.

The Gifts

Three kings stood before the manger –
And one with a black face –
Holding boxes. Out of the first box,
In bright armour, the spirit of gold
Jumped, a fiery gnome:
'I come from the black mine. I have cheated and corrupted,
A slave to tyrants. Lord, have mercy –
A sign of royalty, a medium of exchange,
I glitter and play in your service.'

Out of the second box streamed forth
In smoke, the spirit of frankincense:
'Before a thousand idolatrous shrines
I've danced my swirling and indefinite dance.
Christ, have mercy – Now at your altar
I burn and sweat myself away in prayer.'

With a rustle of leaves, out of the third box
The spirit of myrrh: 'A bitter herb of the earth,
One of the tares watered by Adam's tears
And mingled with his bread. Lord have mercy –
Making the taste of death
Medicinal, preservative.'

Golgotha

In the middle of the world, in the centre
Of the polluted heart of man, a midden;
A stake stemmed in the rubbish.

From lipless jaws, Adam's skull
Gasped up through the garbage:
'I lie in the discarded dross of history,
Ground down again to the red dust,
The obliterated image. Create me.'

From lips cracked with thirst, the voice
That sounded once over the billows of chaos
When the royal banners advanced, replied through the smother
    of dark:
'All is accomplished, all is made new, and look –
All things, once more, are good.'

Then, with a loud cry, exhaled His spirit.

Pentecost 1975

Courageously
Carols of ouzel and tomtit blossom
To the unseasonable Nor'easter; rose of summer,
Apple and ear of harvest, slumber
Numb in the crude bud.

O crystal Dove, you too
Like Ross's gull sometimes migrate
Northward into the Arctic winter: shake
Out of your snowy wings
Sparkles of frost-fire down,
Vivificator, into the clay-cold heart.

Broken Lyres

Demosthenes, mouth filled with pebbles,
Shouts into the storm-wind;

For blind Homer, sunlight glances
On seawave, bronze of armament;

For the eyes of Milton blazes
Celestial Jerusalem;

For Joyce, in unflinching detail,
A dearer and dirtier city;

Uncharted labyrinths of sound
In the silent skull of Beethoven.

The twisted, the unloved bodies –
Leopardi, Pope –

Are broken lyres, are shattered flutes,
For the triumphant spirit

That soars in Eternity's dawn
Like an uncaged skylark.

A Few Strokes on the Sand

Old men, as they grow older, grow the more garrulous,
Drivelling *temporis acta* into their beards,
Argumentative, theoretical, diffuse.

With the poet, not so. One learns
To be spare of words; to make cold thrusts
Into the frosty air that comes.

The final message – a few strokes on the sand;
A bird's footprints running to take off
Into the adverse wind.

For a Platonist on her Birthday

The further on in time we move,
Here, as through a tangled grove,
In shifting moonlight (each a shade
By shadows fitfully betrayed)
The closer to eternity – that bright
Undifferentiated light.
Yet, stripped of their corporeal dress,
Those alone, who learned to bless,

In time, beneath time-measuring stars,
All the minute particulars,
Can bear that shrivelling radiance:
And then we may begin to dance.

Accept my words – they cannot reach
What Plato and Plotinus teach –
Yet also I, perhaps, have known
How unsubstantial is the stone
(Mountains that crumble in an hour),
How real and timeless is the flower.

For a Centenary

In the twinkling of an eye
A hundred solar years go by –
Or the exhalation of a sigh:

Someone was born, or someone died;
A commonplace. But human pride
Makes this a date to be descried.

Something was snatched away by Fate:
The minor talent, or the great.
We bring our wreaths. We are too late.

Oblivion will not release
The ashes on the mantelpiece,
Nor pomp of Rome, nor charm of Greece.

Celebration for a Birth
S.J.W., born 23 December 1967

Indifferent weather
She has brought with her,
Sour sleet, together
        With a North-East wind;

While influenza,
Like a devil's cadenza,
And the cattle-murrains, are
    Hurled through the land.

I summon with reason
All saints of the season
On this occasion,
    For graces to sue:
St Stephen I inveigle,
And St John the Evangel
With his wide-winged eagle,
    And the Innocents too;

Sylvester, take heed,
Pious Lucian, at need,
To wish her God-speed
    On her pilgrimage here,
And the Three Kings, whose bones
Lie shrined in the stones
Of Augustan Cologne's
    Cathedral floor.

As sisters fatal,
Stand by the cradle,
Good gifts to ladle,
    The nymphs of the streams;
For I will have brought here
The lost Bayswater,
With Westbourne, the daughter
    Of paternal Thames.

They are not seen now,
But in sewers obscene, are
Thralls to Cloacina
    With her garland of mud;
But I will release them,
And of durance ease them,
If it will please them
    To perform this good.

Child, there's no need you
At all should pay heed to
Those who would mislead you,
        If ever they can:
The troubled heads of Greece –
Even great Sophocles,
With 'Not to be born is' (if you please!)
        'The best for man.'

Pagan delusion
And Gentile abusion
Cause the confusion
        Of their careless talk;
And for this sin, lo,
With arms akimbo,
They sit down in Limbo
        In eternal sulk.

For birth is a blessing,
Though there's no guessing
To what sad issues
        Our life may go;
And when Time shall show it,
And you, too, know it,
Say that a poet
        Told you so.

A Formality
In Memoriam T.S.E.

Poetry is a formality: a continual greeting and leave-taking
For all that we encounter between
A darkness and a darkness. Hail and farewell
To the seven-braided spectrum. At dawn, at sunset;
And each particular thing we learn to love
We must learn to do without. Celebrate this;
Poetry is a formality.

Poetry is a formality: with words we clothe
The naked abstract thought, shivering in its shame –
Only with leaves, only with coats of skin? We can do more –
Go brave through the infected winter
Of our condition. Carnival.
Mask yourself, then. Poetry
Is a formality.

Poetry is a formality: to each
His way of speaking. I would emulate rather those
Who countered despair with elegance, emptiness with a grace.
And one there is now to be valedicted
With requiem. Poetry also? Also poetry is
A formality.

For Vernon Watkins 1906-1967

Lark in your tower of air,
Over the grey Gower,
As from celestial mansions,
Suspend your concatenations,
The glittering links of your song,
Poised upon dew-drenched wing,
For Gower lies songless here:
Song hallows her no more.

Only the desolate call
Of the wide-winged wandering gull
Is uttered; is heard to grieve,
Wave before following wave,
The lament that breaks in the spray –
The requiems of the sea.

But I remember a man,
Courteous, gentle, humane,
With the dignity of Wales;
One whom time now enrolls
Among the eternities
His words could actualize,
When, at midnight, he did his work –
And a skull, a skull in the dark.

Lyke-Wake Dirge, 8 September 1963

This ay night, this ay night,
    Through a dank September gale,
Into the shy ironic starlight
    Fares forth his naked soul.

Carrickfergus and Birmingham mourn,
    Iceland is desolate;
The armed virgin of the Parthenon
    Signifies her regret.

And it's no go the Third Programme,
    No go a First in Greats,
And it's no go the Golden Bough
    For a passport through the gates.

But sit you down and put them on –
    The wit, the eloquence –
A pair of old brogues with silver buckles,
    The gift you did dispense.

To save your bare bone from the crackling thorns,
    Where pot-boiling waters hiss:
O tightrope-walker, that bridge spans
    The black, the banal abyss.

Fare forth then, protestant, undeceived,
    Till you reach that catholic place
Where, amid her ruins, the Church of Ireland
    Pleads, for her children, grace.

An Elegy
Brian Higgins, ob. 8 December 1965

Even a slovenly diner at life's banquet
Is missed. Now he also has gone:
His senile heart called this young man away,
At a season of Advent, *in mezzo dell' cammin.*

He wore no mask until he wore a plastic one –
And into that he turned aside to weep:
Positioned in Death Row he saw his death approaching,
Though with the merciful face of her brother, Sleep.

Now let the tribal and trans-Tridentine North
Receive the abused and the self-abused body,
His church pronounce – a mathematically-meaningless formula;
The lamp-post that he leaned against is lonely –

It is the guttering light of English poetry. Your muddied
Locks, O nymphs of broad-mouthed Humber, let down,
Who once washed the feet of Andrew Marvell:
Here is another poet that you must mourn.

At Bonchurch
for Maurice Carpenter

A grasshopper perched on Swinburne's tomb,
Squinnying with eyes like garnets, fiddling his jade-green wings:
'Where is the Lesbian melilot, where the singers?
Nuns look after this place now; they ask
Embarrassed pilgrims to kneel down
And say a prayer for my soul. They shouldn't worry –
I have escaped out of the paper-cage,
And skip by coigns of the sea, muse-crazed as always,
But tipsy only, alas,
On non-alcoholic dew that distills before sunrise.'

Camille Saint-Saëns

The music came
As easy and as elegant as apples
For this, it seems, unloved, unloving man.

The nostrils of his enormous nose
Twitched, in scorn and anger
For the incompetent and the importunate.

The sugar softness of the wedding-cake
Was bait, to draw men down
Into the turning wheel, the grinding mill.

Women enslaved – were Omphale
And were Delilah; women betrayed their children.

And so he fled – to find the desolation
Of affluent hotel rooms, the icy desert
Of a continuing triumph,
And a State Funeral's final emptiness.

Only the animals
Were worthy to be loved, and sported
Through a perpetual carnival
In the lost playground of his innocence.

Winter in Illyria

The fountain is choked, yellow leaves
Drift on the broken pavement.
(*'And the rain it raineth'*)

A white peacock
Screams from a windraked arbour.
(*'Come away, Death.'*)

Remembered echoes – echoes of lute-strings,
Echoes of drunken singing.
(*'By swaggering could I never thrive.'*)

Cries of a tormented man, shamed
In a darkened room.
(*'Carry his water to the wise woman!'*)

He left feckless Illyria, changed
His name, enlisted in the army
(*'I'll be revenged on the whole pack of you'*)

In the neighbouring state of Venice, rose to the rank of Ancient;
Personal assistant to the General.
(*'Put money in thy purse.'*)

Godstow

Rose of the world, corrupted rose –
About and about the maze-path goes:

A thread of silk is caught in his spur,
A spider's clue for Eleanor –

Uprooted rose of Aquitaine
(The poets are singing to England's queen).

The dagger, the green juice in the bowl,
The toads are sucking the breasts of my soul.

And up in arms, they are marching on –
Sodomite Richard and lackland John.

At Trinity-tide the rose is in bloom
For the priest who reigns from his crusted tomb.

And Ireland is up in arms, and curses
The English laws and the English verses.

Plantagenet turns his face to the wall:
'But where is the fairest rose of all?'

Sestina

The fountain that goes up with plumes of laughter
Comes down with tears, with rainbows and with pearls;
Within dark leaves the gilt and painted pheasant
Perches and preens, as if estranged from terror;
Nor summer knows that her own funeral
She is forever, pyre of her own roses.

Yet the black shadows dodge among the roses
With little jets of chill malicious laughter –
They who are dressed as for a funeral,
Black in their silks, sewn with a few small pearls
But their thin hands are crook'd (I note with terror)
To wring the heart's neck like a pinioned pheasant.

The peacock and the gold and silver pheasant
Down alleyways of peonies and roses
Strut, still as if this place harboured no terror,
And all the green lawns echoing with their laughter,
Children thread daisy-chains, and think them pearls –
Alas, they thread their days for funeral.

They bear a dead mouse to its funeral,
And a plumed mourner is the garden's pheasant
As on the stamped-down turf they scatter roses
Which, when dusk falls, softly the night dew pearls;
Yet with the night there comes a pause to laughter,
And with the dew a sudden hint of terror.

And one may lie awake all night in terror –
As through that darkness goes a funeral,
And in his ears a bitter savage laughter;
He waits for dawn, the loud crow of the pheasant;
From grey to gold and crimson turn the roses
As from their leaves they shed a thousand pearls.

Oh no, not gifts of opals nor of pearls
Nor gold will bribe those ministers of terror
Nor stay their hands that wither all time's roses
And lead the bright world to its funeral,
That shoot down love like a high-flying pheasant
And stifle in the throat our songs and laughter.

Then live with laughter, feed your eyes on pearls
And dine on wine, on pheasant? – think no terror
Before the funeral and the death-pale roses.

The Beast

The red and ravaged centre of the opening rose
To the green, gold chafer is assigned;
To lion and wolf the fearful, flying game
On the mountains, in the forests;

The lamprey slowly eats into the fish's entrails; for the leech
The warm and dripping blood;
For whale and oyster the invisible swarms of the sea
They delicately filter:

Each in its kind content. Yet there's one beast
Not populations of earth, sea and sky,
The elements themselves, sun, moon and hosting stars,
Can ever feed – nor yet the heart of Man,

Its ordinary prey, and couching place.

In Return for the Gift of a Pomander
to Cathy Tither

I am not that butcher's son
    Of Ipswich, the proud Cardinal,
Detesting so the common run,
    He could not pass among them all
Without an orange stuffed with cloves
    Clutched in his white, ringed hands, to quench
The breath of those plebeian droves,
    Their stockfish, leek, and garlic stench;
Though some, who do not love me much,
    Might say I am no democrat,
And that my attitudes are such –
    We will not argue about that:
But I affirm the gift you bring
    Discreetly with my togs shall go,
The night-marauder's silken wing
    To avaunt – although, indeed, we know

There's no sublunary gear
But moth and rust corrupt it here.

The fragrance of a generous thought
Remains. And that cannot be bought.

The Blameless Æthiopians

My Muse is away dining
With the blameless Æthiopians:
When an Immortal cannot be contacted Homer says
That is where she is.

The blameless anecdotes she formerly
Retailed to me, are whispered
Into an Æthiopian's
Jewel-studded ear.

On Æthiopian mountains
The plantain-eater hoots from the plantain tree:
Has she forgotten the English missel-thrush?

She feasts on Æthiopian delicacies,
And I could only offer her
Braised neck of lamb with carrots.

I do not really blame
The Æthiopians. In love
It takes two to make a silence.

To a Poet a Thousand Years Hence

I who am dead a thousand years
And wrote this crabbed post-classic screed
Transmit it to you – though with doubts
That you possess the skill to read,

Who, with your pink, mutated eyes,
Crouched in the radioactive swamp,
Beneath a leaking shelter, scan
These lines beside a flickering lamp;

Or in some plastic paradise
Of pointless gadgets, if you dwell,
And finding all your wants supplied
Do not suspect it may be Hell.

But does our art of words survive –
Do bards within that swamp rehearse
Tales of the twentieth century,
Nostalgic, in rude epic verse?

Or do computers churn it out –
In lieu of songs of War and Love,
Neat slogans by the State endorsed
And prayers to *Them*, who sit above?

How shall we conquer? – all our pride
Fades like a summer sunset's glow:
Who will read me when I am gone –
For who reads Elroy Flecker now?

Unless, dear poet, you were born,
Like me, a deal behind your time,
There is no reason you should read,
And much less understand, this rhyme.

From an Ecclesiastical Chronicle

In the year of Our Lord two thousand one hundred and seven,
The first electronic computer
Was appointed to a bishopric in the Church of England.
The consecration took place
At a Pontifical High Mass
In the new Cathedral of Stevenage,
In the presence of the Most Reverend
Mother in God, Her Grace Rita,
By Divine Connivance *Cantuar. Archepiscopissa.*

Monsignor Pff-pff (75321/666)
With notable efficiency, tact, and benevolence, presided
For the next three hundred years
Over his diocese. (He had previously worked
In the mission field – rural Dean of Callisto,
One of the satellites of Jupiter.)
After which he was honourably retired,
Only a little rusted, to the Science Museum
In South Kensington – there frequented and loved
By generations of schoolchildren.

As *The Times* remarked on that occasion,
'He stood for the best in the Anglican tradition.'
In indubitable succession, one might say,
From our contemporary Dr ———, of ———.

Letter to Peter Avery

*Fellow of King's College, Cambridge; a dissuasive
against his becoming part of the 'brain drain'*

There is a curious yarn that says,
Remote, in Ancient British days,
King Bladud, he who ruled in Bath,
And early followed technics' path
Soaring on artificial wings
Above that city of hot springs,
Established here, the tale avers,
A knot of grave philosophers, –
Some choicer minds of Attic Greece –
Such as had talked with Socrates,
Or, near the academic grove,
Heard Plato speak the praise of love
Over a symposiac bottle,
Or took a stroll with Aristotle;
I wonder how they found it here,
Exiled to the sharp northern air,
Expounding philosophic truth
To the blue-stained Brythonic youth
Who crouched within their sordid dens
Among the dank, malarial fens.

But this is a vain Gothic dream;
Such are not dreamt by Camus' stream,
Whose waves have learnt the feet to kiss
Of chastely naked Mathesis,
And taught a muddle-headed nation
Those truths which rest on demonstration –
Till Newton, at the apple's fall,
Ordered sun, moon and planets, all,
Marshalled in Heaven's assembly hall.
Yet, counterpoint in stone perfected,
That which the Royal Saint erected,
Still stands – the Royal Saint, indeed!
The feeble last of his bold breed
From Harry of Monmouth, Kate of France.
Rapt in an ineffectual trance,
He did not curb power-hungry lords
Whose hands were ever at their swords;
They set brash roses on their coats,
Fell to, and cut each other's throats.
Yet he found time to plan this fane:
The Middle Ages in their wane
Are here explicit – Nominalism,
Saints, escutcheons, mysticism –
And after, heresy and schism.
Clear ran the stream, by each smooth lawn,
In the brave Humanistic dawn.
Then the Greek tongue was really heard,
And tuneful was the Attic bird
In Spenser's, Milton's, Cowley's ear –
The air they breathed is sacred air;
While Cudworth, Whichcote, Henry More,
Platonic harmonies restore.
Yet soon the channels choked with lumber,
A Whiggish and Bangorian slumber,
And all the academic folly
Which drove poor Gray to Leucocholy;
And Wordsworth also here saw *'blind'*
(In my text this is underlined)
'Authority beat with his staff
The child that might have led him.' – Laugh?
Is this concerned with times gone by? –
I think the words may still apply.
Poor Cambridge, poor despondent slough,

What leeches hang about her now,
And (no one seems to find it odd)
Tell Modern Man that he's a god;
The truth, I fear, is more unpleasant:
God may be dead, the Devil isn't.
The times, indeed, are getting late,
Yet still is left to cultivate
A garden here, if so you choose:
A garden where the Iranian rose
Casts to the breeze her pouch of musk,
And listens, in the inebriate dusk,
To the persistent nightingale;
The Attic bird tells the same tale.

Apologia of a Plastic Gnome

The Roman in his garden erected
A statue of Priapus, smeared with red ochre,
With a prodigious phallus, resembling
That of his sacred beast, the donkey:
Multi-purposeful – by sympathetic force
Promoting growth of plants, also a scarecrow,
And that enormous member a useful club
For beating off intruders.

And I am his legitimate successor. Unhappily
I've no apparent phallus, but you mark
My hands are in my pockets, and my plastic trousers
Distinctly tight about my plastic crutch. And my tumescent
Scarlet pointed cap's conspicuous enough.

I stand in the garden of Ted & Lynn –
Mr & Mrs Shortwick – 636 Subtopia Avenue
Doing the most I can.

They scarcely know the seasons
Whose diet is frozen peas, frozen string beans,
Frozen brussel sprouts and shepherd's pie.
Their sabbath a long lay-in, ritual
Lustration of the motor-car.

I'm posted in the margin of their mind, to hint
Some Power, imaged as human and yet not,
Or else a surrogate, presides
Over the burgeoning of gladiolus,
Crocus, tea-rose, hollyhock, laburnum,
(King Edwards, sprouting broccoli?).

Scorn not, passer-by, the plastic gnome –
He's doing his best.

Send for Lord Timothy

The Squire is in his library. He is rather worried.
Lady Constance has been found stabbed in the locked Blue Room,
    clutching in her hand
A fragment of an Egyptian papyrus. His degenerate half-brother
Is on his way back from New South Wales.
And what was the butler, Glubb,
Doing in the neolithic stone-circle
Up there on the hill, known to the local rustics
From time immemorial as the Nine Lillywhite Boys?
The Vicar is curiously learned
In Renaissance toxicology. A greenish Hottentot,
Armed with a knobkerry, is concealed in the laurel bushes.

Mother Mary Tiresias is in her parlour.
She is rather worried. Sister Mary Josephus
Has been found suffocated in the scriptorium,
Clutching in her hand a somewhat unspeakable
Central American fetish. Why was the little novice,
Sister Agnes, suddenly struck speechless
Walking in the herbarium? The chaplain, Fr O'Goose
Is almost too profoundly read
In the darker aspects of fourth-century neo-Platonism.
An Eskimo, armed with a harpoon
Is lurking in the organ loft.

The Warden of St Phenol's is in his study.
He is rather worried. Professor Ostracoderm
Has been found strangled on one of the Gothic turrets,
Clutching in his hand a patchouli-scented

Lady's chiffon handkerchief.
The brilliant under-graduate they unjustly sent down
Has transmitted an obscure message in Greek elegiacs
All the way from Tashkent. Whom was the Domestic Bursar
Planning to meet in that evil smelling
Riverside tavern? Why was the Senior Fellow,
Old Doctor Mousebracket, locked in among the incunabula?
An aboriginal Philippino pygmy,
Armed with a blow-pipe and poisoned darts, is hiding behind
The statue of Pallas Athene.

A dark cloud of suspicion broods over all. But even now
Lord Timothy Pratincole (the chinless wonder
With a brain like Leonardo's) or Chief Inspector Palefox
(Although a policeman, patently a gentleman,
And with a First in Greats) or that eccentric scholar,
Monsignor Monstrance, alights from the chuffing train,
Has booked a room at the local hostelry
(*The Dragon of Wantley*) and is chatting up Mine Host,
Entirely democratically, noting down
Local rumours and folk-lore.

Now read on. The murderer will be unmasked,
The cloud of guilt dispersed, the church clock stuck at three,
And the year always
Nineteen twenty or thirty something,
Honey for tea, and nothing
Will ever really happen again.

The Frog and the Nightingale

Hearing a nightingale one evening sing,
A frog from its puddle opined:
'Among those senseless twittering roulades
Occasionally you note
A deep hoarse croaking, which evinces
Definite marks of talent.

Eh me, what a frog is lost in him!'

Linnaeus Naming the Beasts

i

Carl von Linné walked in his Uppsala garden:
A Scandinavian spring, tender and virginal
And yet lascivious, breathed through the birch-trees.
His flowers opened at his feet,
Displaying their stamens and pistils, in shameless
Sexual activity – forgiven,
No sister disdaining its brother.
A bugle-note through the clear air –
Dragoons of the Vasa are drilling.

He had catalogued the plants, now he marshalled the beasts
In ordered ranks – and first, Primates
With Man in his own abstract image,
Sapiens, knowing, savouring, tasting;
Shadowed by the mysterious and rumoured *nocturnus*,
And also monsters, self-made – the Hottentots
Who pin up one testicle to reduce fertility,
'And the women of Europe, deforming their bodies
By tight-lacing,' said the pastor's son.
Then the apes with *Satyrus*, not fabled, at the head;
And the ghost-eyed lemurs of the island of Malagasay;
And the bat – it is certainly not a bird
(Even Aristotle knew that) –
'It has left the brain that won't believe,'
Whispered a voice,
Prophetic, across the British ocean.

ii

Fifty-eight centuries away, at the other end
Of Archbishop Ussher's telescope, Adam,
Standing in Eden's dawn, was naming the beasts,
As the Lord brought each before him, after its kind.
'You shall be Aleph,*' he said, 'You with the curled front*
And the curved horns, bull-roarer, noblest
Of those that divide the hoof and chew the cud.
You shall open the gate of Spring for two thousand years,
Till the Ram caught in a thicket, prefigure
Another covenant, another two thousand –

Then with the Fish we shall learn to skip
And live a new life in the liquid element.
And then? And then? One in my own form
Pouring the Spirit's wine
From the ritual water-jar upon all flesh.'
Adam named the apes, his clowns, recalling
The red clay he was evoked from;
Wolves, lions, ocelots,
As they roar and howl God's glory
The fox in his subtlety, the hare and the eland
For grace and for swiftness, and the sportive dolphin.

Then the birds flew down in a chirm, in a twittering cloud.
'I name you,' said Adam, 'my music and minstrelsy.
You are nearest to those invisible angels,
About me continually, that serve my Friend.'

iii

Linnaeus reviewed the birds, the gamut
From eagle to dove, – hawks, chattering pies,
Geese, stilted waders, poultry, sparrows;
Amphibious reptiles and serpents – and then the fish
Arranged by the placing of their anal fins:
Thoracic, subjugular, abdominal, and apodal eels;
Insects by the texture of their wings,
A polity the glass of Fabricius descried
So like, and yet unlike, the human polity
Seen in this age of reason. Butterflies
He playfully made take sides
As Greeks or Trojans. Now come the worms –
The fluke and the leech, and glutinous hag;
Soft-bodied, hyaline, cinctured with tentacles –
These he named after sea-nymphs –
Nereis and Doris, Clio and Aphrodite;
Shells, multivalve, bivalve, univalve,
With or without a regular spiral;
Lithophytes, corals, that verge on the mineral realm,
As Zoophytes upon the kingdom of plants,
He entered at last that infinitesimal world
Leeuwenhoek's lens had revealed: –
Vorticella, a small whirlpool, *Volvox*,
Globe with green globe ensphered, and *Furia Infernalis*,

89

Bred in the upper air, that struck him down
Those Lapland days, and finally, *Chaos* –
Chaos of the infusions, chaos of the fungus spores.
All things go back to Chaos and Night,
With Dullness their daughter. An English poet
Had written of that, evoking the Anarch.

God had created them all in fixity,
Species by species – or had He? –
Was there not an unfolding,
Evolution, to coin such a word,
Perhaps by hybridization.
All one need postulate – a primal island,
One male and one female animal upon it,
And one two-sexed plant.

iv

On Eden, islanded between the rivers,
Adam and Eve stood under the two-sexed tree.
'I name you, last come and subtlest of all,
My beautiful Serpent – now dance for us,
In token of this task accomplished.'
Then the serpent raised his crest and danced,
With a swaying, an Indian motion. Adam and Eve
Clapped hands to the rhythm in mere delight.
'What is not to believe?' said Adam.

A Paraphrase

The raven and the crow,
They neither reap nor sow;
The magpie and the jay,
They don't make hay,
Nor do they cart their corn
Into the tithe barn:
Whom the Father's hand shall feed –
They find what they need.

The lenten daffodil,
Blowing beneath the hill,
And the bright briar-rose –
These do not want for clothes,
Nor do they ever throw
The shuttle to and fro:
No spindle and no loom
Forms the perfect bloom.

Great King Solomon,
With all his glory on,
Dressed up to the nines
Among his concubines,
Is not more fine to see
Than a wild anemone.

Wishes for the Months

I wish you, in January, the swirl of blown snow –
A green January makes a full churchyard;

Thrushes singing through the February rain; in March
The clarion winds, the daffodils;

April, capricious as an adolescent girl,
With cuckoo-song, and cuckoo-flowers;

May with a dog rose, June with a musk rose; July
Multi-foliate, with all the flowers of summer;

August – a bench in the shade, and a cool tankard;
September golden among his sheaves;

In October, apples; in grave November
Offerings for the beloved dead;

And, in December, a midwinter stillness,
Promise of new life, incarnation.

Dedicatory Poem
to Guthrie McKie

These poems are objects not subjects, made
From a twist of words, a moment of the mind's freedom.
Like midges, they hum and dance
In the warm air, whose larvae
Were bred for long in the damp soil.
That soil is my black moods, my weeks of silence:
You have had to deal with those, it is only just
You get the poems as well.
Here I deliver them, along with –
Oh, I almost forgot to add – my love.

Shelley's Balloon

Shelley inserted a poem
In a delicate wickerwork gondola, suspended
From a small, sky-blue balloon.
The balloon was filled with hot air, and so –
Some critics would persuade you
(Especially in Cambridge) – was the poem.
But the poem was full of love, and love of liberty
(Faintly dishonest, Platonic love,
Not quite practicable liberty?)
And images of clouds, little ships and autumn leaves –
All things that the wind lifts and drifts before it,
As the skylark, singing, floats on the upward currents.
'Go, unacknowledged legislator,' said Shelley,
'Carry my live thoughts through the universe.'
The balloon did not get far. It stuck
In the branches of a thorn tree –
The small craft punctured, the poem ripped.
But a hen-chaffinch, foraging
For nest-material, selected
Those scraps of paper instead of lichen, to camouflage
Her neat-formed cup. No prowling cat
Nor weasel could discover it nor accurate eye
Of magpie nor of jay. She reared her brood
Among those unread verses. Summer ended,

And all the birds were flown. But one, next Spring,
Alighted upon a plane-tree
That grew beside a squat grey tower.
The season long, he rattled through
His cheerful song, and lifted
The heart of one political prisoner,
For whom a blue slit was the whole sky.

For the Nine-Hundredth Anniversary
of Winchester Cathedral

Fall, rain, fall
Impartial as the grace of God,

On just and unjust – for Alfred,
Making his grave with the anonymous poor;

For the Red King, unloved, abandoned
In the dark grove, struck by the glancing arrow.

For the cardinal – before his tomb, in restitution
The glittering image of Joan the phoenix.

Wind from the Solent, Atlantic wind,
Bring rain at Swithin's behest –

For Izaak, who fished beside still waters,
When Test and Itchen went straying through Beulah;

For Jane, who delineated the human condition
On a small square of ivory;

For unknown builders' stone polyphony
For the singing pillars of Samuel Sebastian,

For the amiable habitation – descend,
The former and latter rains.

Six Emblems from the Book of Daniel

SUSANNA

Cool spring lave her,
Soft breeze fan her,
Pure air wandering
Through the trees of this garden.

None sees – only
The stars of evening
Quietly singing for joy
In the depths of the twilight.

One she is, one
In her body's integrity,
And holy, holy
In her white nakedness:

Catholic her right breast,
Catholic her left breast,
And apostolic the action
Of hands and of feet.

Lily she is, lily
In the secret valley;
Rose she is of Sharon,
Enclosed in the garden.

Stirs the holm oak,
Rustles the sycamore;
Exhales the spikenard,
Aloe and cassia.

None sees? Some see –
Eyes between the leaves –
A dish to be savoured,
A strip-tease treat:

A young girl, vulnerable
Between foul-breathed carnivores.

THE BURNING FIERY FURNACE

So, pitched into the king's incinerator,
They began to enjoy the primal energies,
Strolling as in a garden's alleyways
Of roses and tiger-lilies. And then they danced,
Danced with the vortices of swirling smoke; hiss of flames
Outdid the twanging of the harp,
Psaltery and dulcimer; and their song went up
In praise of clouds and dew, water, winds, ocean –
Leviathan's tumbling realm –
In triple harmony. Until there came a fourth
With face and figure of a son of God.

THE MADNESS OF NEBUCHADNEZZAR

Slant rain renders soggy
Matted hair, straggling beard;
Yellow teeth are scratched by grit, munching
Burdock, wild garlic, thistles;
Unclipped nails, like eagle's talons,
Scrabble the black soil – and this was once
The nucleus of imperial power, whose frown
Made wince and dither eunuchs, chamberlains,
Cooks, catamites, nautch-girls, scribes: less human now
Than, curly-bearded and stony-eyed, the bulls
That stand at his castle doors.

A VISION OF BEASTS

Four winds contend on the sea's face,
Lashing the spray to warhorses and chariots;
Out of the maelstrom the beasts of history
Surface in beauty and cruelty –
Ancient empires, panther-spotted, lion-tawny;
They scud on the waves with airy pinions;
And the brutal and barbarous bear
Sucking the marrow from cracked bones.

And then that last, graceless amorphous anomaly
Horned, tusked, bristled, woolly,
Splay-footed, hoofed, clawed. Where he treads
Suppressed groans, where he rolls

The stink of pollution, where he roots,
Our bread is tasteless with sorrow, and in his tracks
A straggling tail of discarded rubbish.

How long, till the Human Being
Comes, riding the clouds,
In naked perfection of geometry,
To the throne of God, from whence
A cataract of hydrogen
Streams incandescent through the galaxies?

BELSHAZZAR'S FEAST

Nabonidus, (hereditary High Priest
Of the most holy Moon God, whose sacred House
Is at Harron) promoted to absolute power
By a cruel and ruthless coup,
Remembered the god of his fathers. He amassed
A priceless and unique collection:
The idols and the images of all the rival gods,
Piled up in his capital – even the lampstand
And consecrated gold and silver flagons
Of that peculiar people. So engrossed
In docketing and cataloguing, he
Relinquished cares of state to his one son,
Belshazzar, Regent, elegant, impeccable,
First gentleman of Mesopotamia;
Who held his celebrated Feast (Outside the walls
The austere, truth-telling Persians were encamped,
With horses trained upon the high plateaux:
The sacred brazier of Ahura Mazda
Is borne before the young king). Just for a giggle
He bade those vessels to be brought in
To mix a drink in them. And all agreed
It was a splendid lark – until a hand,
With veins of fire and nails like blue flames,
Came scrawling its graffiti on the walls.
The cryptic, square and minatory letters
Bit into Babel's perdurable stone
Like deathwatch woodworm in a rotten beam.

The beasts of violence stalk and prowl about:
Animal stench, taint of meat on the fang.
The just man stands in the foul den
Yet unassailed. The messenger of mercy
Invisibly has muzzled their red mouths:
The royal beasts kneel down in decent homage.

Head of John the Baptist

The oracular skull of Orpheus
Howls, howls from the Lesbian cavern;

Blackened, shrunken heads
Gibber and chirp in the smoke
Of jungle shanties;

But this lies still and silent,
Upon the glint of its silver round,
God's will accomplished. Prodromos,
Your race is run.

Christmas Poem

The wolves are howling against
The bleached bloodless face of the winter moon
And the remote stars.

Crouched in their black tents, the wandering bedouin
Only, in this harsh season, tend their flocks
Among these barren hills.

Into this frozen world, with sap at ebb
And Hope a leafless tree, new tones of splendour
Come whispering on the wind, supernal energies,
In their unguessed-at modes of being,
Articulating the unutterable
Mysteries of incarnation and of birth.

Poems for a Calendar

JANUARY

Under a white coverlet of snow
The infant year is lying,
A leaden canopy of cloud above.
Now to this cradle haste
The royal seasons, in their robes,
Of green, crimson, and rich russet,
Bearing their gifts – the sunshine gold of spring,
Incense of summer flowers, and acrid tang
Of autumn's burning leaves.

FEBRUARY

Splish splosh, February-fill-the-dike,
Sleet in the wind, mud underfoot.
What hint, you ask, of spring? But trust
The honest mistle-thrush, who shouts his song
And builds his nest – a less accomplished singer
Than is the clear-voiced mavis, but he rings bravely.

And trust the aconite and crocus, bright
As wicks of thread which now are lighted up
For ceremonials of Candlemas.

MARCH

A daffodil looked forth
Upon St David's day (the water-drinking saint
Kept to his plain pottage of leeks).
She spread her yellow skirt, and summoned
Her sleeping sisters from their beds of clay:
'The south-west wind has come, his tresses wet
With spray of Atlantic combers.
He calls us to the dance, the dance.'

APRIL

The April fool, the April fool,
He would go mitching from church and school
Fishing for tadpoles down by the brook,
Where kingcups blossom, and lady-smock,

Making the water-meadows gay.
He would do nothing the whole long day,
Simply nothing, sweet nothing at all,
Apart from spitting against a wall,
And marking the silly cuckoo's call.

MAY

Now Lady Flora and Pan-in-the-Green
With nymphs in a chorus and goatfoot cobbolds,
Prance round the stiff green pole, bedecked
With ribbons and baubles and bells.
Dance the summer in, dance out Death,
Dance in the future's solidarity.

JUNE

In Persian gardens comes the royal rose,
Flaunting her beauty forth. 'But don't suppose,'
   Twitters her friend, the sweet-voiced nightingale,
'You will outlast the cold, the winter's snows.

'In Nishapur a thousand roses bloom,
Glowing like lanterns, in their dark leaves' gloom.
   But Time shall dowse those fires. They faint and fade,
Their petals drifted on a poet's tomb.'

JULY

The Crab has got the sun in its claws.
Julius Caesar makes the laws;
His legions march for a Roman cause –
   Hurrah for Julius Caesar!

The mountains shake at the legions' tread,
Like the sound of thunder overhead;
There's an old bald codger at their head –
   His name is Julius Caesar.

In Caesar's month the July sun
Knows summer's course will soon be run,
But the sun has always work to be done –
   'Like me,' said Julius Caesar.

AUGUST

Oh they did like to be beside the seaside,
Pa and Ma, and Albert and Angie,
And little Cedric and Flo;
They loved to paddle in the lacey waves,
Which still Britannia ruled and good King Edward
While the brass band tiddly-pommed on the prom
Selections from *The Mikado*.
They strolled along the pier, partaking
Of whelks and winkles and sticky rock. On pearl-grey wings
The gulls came wheeling and squealing
Of what the pierrots sang, and what the butler saw.

SEPTEMBER

September sun matures
The corn to gold, the grape to royal purple.
Harvest and vintage crown the year.
But Time is here with his combine harvester,
And Death with his electric press.
Down with the Corn King, down with princely Zagreus.
But they will live again in wine and bread:
Wine and bread will conquer Death and Time.

OCTOBER

In Georgian London squares, under the plane trees,
The autumn leaves are swept in heaps, or swirl
In miniature tornadoes. Round the corner
The ghost of a yellow fog
(But we are spared the fogs of yesteryear).
So put another ten p in the gas –
And brew your tea in an honest brown pot.
Draw up your chair to the fire,
And toast your buttered crumpets and your toes.

NOVEMBER

'Horse and hattock!' cried bunch-back Meg,
The wicked, crooked witch. Then she mounted
Her besom broomstick, along with Pertinax
Her one-eyed moggy. So away they whirled
To the Hallowe'en caper on Baldtop Mountain.

She danced with a wild assembly
Through the black hours, till the rooster's clarion
Dispersed night's shades, and drove them home,
Poor rags and remnants, to their loveless beds –
Oh the keen-spurred, the crimson-crested spoilsport!

DECEMBER
Prayer to St Nicholas

Patron of all those who do good by stealth –
Slipping three bags of gold in through the window
To save three desperate girls, restoring
Dead boys to life out of the pickling tub
Of an Anatolian Sweeney Todd –
Teach us to give with simplicity, and not with an eye
To the main chance: it's less than
Three weeks' shopping time to Christmas.

Arion

Enchant, Arion, with your twanging lyre
The menacing seas to halcyon calm,
Leaving the men of violence far behind
As you go on your beaked mount,
The snorting leaper, Apollo's boy,
Officious friendly dolphin.

And then the Poetess

And then the poetess – small, small-boned,
A woman of the aristoi, large dark eyes,
Skin like brown olives, but greenish-tinged
When passion gripped her –

Strummed a few measures on the gut strings,
Her lyre, the shell of a tortoise, the chords stretched from the pegs
Fixed between two curving goat-horns,

And thus began, in her dialect:
'I loved you Atthis, long, long since,
So spare you seemed, an uncouth bairn.'

And she continued...

Greybearded now, an old man, yet I remember.
Time grinds, as the mill grinds,
Pittakos at the mill.

Long, long years since. But I recall
It was the day when I...

Further Adventures of Doctor Faustus

He staged that of course. You surely don't believe
In the locked room, spattered with blood and entrails,
Where fiends dismembered the philosopher,
And carried off his soul, like a new-hatched chick
To spit and roast upon the coals of Hell.
'See where Christ's blood streams in the firmament!' – powerful stuff,
Said in a loud voice strictly to impress
The students gathered in the adjoining chamber
Earnestly praying away, members to a man
Of WUSCU (Wittenberg University
Student Christian Union).

The simple truth was this: the authorities,
Both secular and spiritual, of Wittenberg
Were catching up with him – not to mention his creditors,
Sick and weary of being fobbed off
With that alchemical fool's-gold
The Devil always pays with. And so he fixed
That spectacular exit and gave them all the slip –
Even, so it seems, poor Mephistophilis,
An inexperienced and rather incompetent fiend, severely carpeted
For this by his superiors, and his promotion
For several aeons set back
Within the ranks of Hell's bureaucracy.

As for the magus, he surfaces again
Some years later, having changed his name
(Or really hardly changed it, both words
Mean 'fortunate' or 'lucky' – and that he clearly was –
But 'Prospero' sounds better in Italian).
He surfaced, as I said, in Milan. His magic now
Takes on a subtler form; by hypnotism,
Or something of the kind, he imposes himself
As a wholly non-existent elder brother
Of the good duke, Antonio, and thus usurped his throne.
Retribution did catch up with him this time. But, being marooned,
Upon a desert island, he set it up
A mini-imperialist commonwealth,
Successfully enslaving and exploiting
The local aboriginals, of air and earth.

How he outwitted once again
Antonio and the rest – it has been told.
He's back at Milan now, having married off
His daughter rather well, nodding away
The butt-end of his life, every third thought his grave.
'I'll burn my books!' he once had said, and now
'Deeper than did ever plummet sound
I'll drown my book' – and so he should, I say,
As we do much the same with nuclear waste.

His Excellency's Poetry

'His Excellency's poetry is mainly enigmatic' –
The reply of the interpreter, for the Chinese Ambassador,
To Robert Browning. The Chinese Ambassador,
Being, as the interpreter had explained,
A considerable poet in his own language,
Had expressed a desire to encounter
An English poet. Robert Browning,
A largely self-educated Nonconformist,
Was somewhat out of his depth. He had asked
Whether His Excellency's poetry
Was epic, lyric or dramatic?

In the year 1980 *et seq.*
I think of myself as an exile and ambassador;
Confronted with a similar question, as I not infrequently am,
At cocktail parties and so on, I am tempted
To come back with a similar reply.

Casta Diva

in memory of Maria Callas

Diva – traditional termagant, soprano tantrums,
Scourge of conductors, bane of managers;
Or drifting on a sea of crispéd bank notes
With Plutus in his affluent yacht.

And then retirement – a spectacled, middle-aged lady
Lecturing sensibly on interpretation.

But in the shades the tragic heroines
Mourn for their lost vehicle – La Gioconda,
Tosca, Isolde, murdering Medea;
But most of all I see
A priestess in a Druid grove, who lifts
Clear notes of silver to the silver moon,
Knowing her role of virgin votaress
Is false, who's racked within
With passion, and knowledge of male treachery.

De Sade

Laura comes forth from the porch of the temple
After High Mass. As about the Portinari
The manifest glory of supernatural Wisdom
So on her rested clarity
Of Provençal sunlight, a trecento springtime.
Petrarch endured exquisite, protracted torments of passion,
Distilled to the rhetoric of fourteen lines –
Laura de Sade, the ancestress.

. . . .

The Marquis is locked up in the Bastille
For his own good, along with a handful
Of other self-destructive incompetents;
Condemned *in absentia* for attempted murder –
An indiscreet afternoon orgy;
Two whores and his own brutal valet,
Also an injudicious experiment
Involving cantharides. In rage and frustration
He dribbles out his black, sexual fantasies:
A hundred days of Sodom. But all is rooted
In a single syllogism of the Age of Reason:
'Philosophers enjoin us to follow nature,
Nature is savage, cruel and destructive,
And therefore we...' and so Justine
For her obstinate and unnatural virtue
Is crushed by a thunderbolt.

Outside the crass Bourbon oppression
Continues. Hell, it seems,
Must be invoked as an ally. Seventeen eighty-nine
A hot summer, the price of bread soaring.
Crowds are assembling in the square below.
On his daily exercise around the battlements
He hangs on the cannons revolutionary slogans:
'Citizens of France, arise or else
Three hundred wretched prisoners will perish miserably.'
Inhibited from this, he shouts
Through the bars of his cell, using a funnel
As a kind of megaphone. And so they moved him
To a small asylum out in the suburbs,
Tended by kind Franciscan Brothers.

But when the fortress fell he was Citizen Sade –
Citizen Sade who had been in the Bastille.
The red blade was reared, it chopped
With the chop-logic of Robespierre's brain,
A small-town lawyer's. The Marquis served
On Revolutionary tribunals, but had to resign:
He really could not bear
All that beautiful, valuable pain
Simply going to waste.

A final glimpse. Asylum once again –
An old man, surrounded
By gibbering, nattering shapes of set despair,
And doltish, lumpish ingrown melancholy,
With those whose brain and spinal marrow
Syphilis softly dismantled, as he dismembered,
Tearing apart, petal by fragrant petal
The pink, feminine flesh of a summer rose.

Polyphemus

Polyphemus weeps
Into the Straits of Messina –
The monster, who does not know
Why he is so unloved
Except by his woolly sheep;
Why brisk Galatea flaunts him, or why
Ruthless No-One has burned away
His solitary eye.

His father a Mediterranean storm,
His mother an anonymous nymph –
An unpromising background; he haunts
Pine-shaggy uplands, or where
The pumice fragments are strewn
In the burnt-out crater of Aetna.

Polyphemus died, of cramps and cold.
Nobody knows where his bones were laid.
But when bones were dug up
In fourteenth-century Sicily
Boccaccio opined:
'The bones of Polyphemus!'
But the learned world has settled
For palaeontology, an elephant.

Heorot

That hall which Hrothgar raised, it gleams through the darkness,
Over the windswept moors and the fens of Jutland;
Fretted gold at the gables, enamelling,
Pride of the branching hart-horns.

Within are light and warmth, beer and baked meats,
Where men sit drinking together in amity.
The king, their protector, loaf-ward and mead-ward,
Dispenses from the throne of his generosity.
The lady decked at the throat with a necklace of amber,
Carries the drinking-horn around to the guests.
The poet is there with his harp, his glee-wood,
Chanting the praise of the Lord of creation,
How He tricked out the earth with buds and bright berries,
Burnished the stars for the vault of heaven, and beneath them
He set the sun, a candle for men.

A focus of civility. Such fires flash
And then are quenched. Darkness resumes. And always
There is that which comes from the darkness, Cain's kin,
Inarticulate, a shape undefined,
From its own place, out of the stinking tarn,
From the cave behind the waterfall, drawn
By the sound of the tinkling harp-strings.
It gazes towards the splendour,
Sees it and hates it.

St George and the Dinosaur

'Apart from other considerations,' said St George,
'You are an anachronism. You should have been extinct
When the Cretaceous ended. Noah had no instructions
To take you lot on board the ark.'

'If you knew what I knew,' rejoined the saurian,
'You'd drop that arrogant tone. My third, pineal eye
Can look into the future, with your name

Expunged from calendars as merely mythical,
Your holy catholic church dismissed
In much the same terms as you used for me.

'But I am a survivor. Care to know my secret? –
"A virgin a day keeps old age away."
I need that princess. And you don't want her –
You're supposed to have taken a vow of chastity,
Your sole devotion to the Mother of God.
You dog-in-the-mangerly Christian, why stand in the way
Of my so urgent love?'

'My manger is the one that Christ was laid in,'
Replied the saint. 'And so I tell you
"I love" is not the same thing as "I eat",
Although my Love shall feed me with His flesh.'

'Linguistics in our Mesozoic age,'
The beast answered, 'had not, I think, advanced
To that degree of subtlety.'

'And so I will destroy you,' cried St George,
'Delete you utterly in the name
And purity of the eternal Word!'
With that he seized the pen of his sword, and plunged it
Into the cunning eye, the only tender spot.

The Hunt

in memory of Lawrence Bright,
Domini canis

The hunt is up. The hounds of the Lord are unleashed,
Baying their music to the eager winds.
The horn-calls blow away the morning dew,
The dew and the dew! The hunt is on.

How dangerous she is, our mistress of the hunt –
Long-limbed, small-breasted, cleansing her white skin
In secret fountains at the forest's heart –
Witness the bones that now lie scattered, torn

By their own dogs' fangs, tangled in their horses' reins.
She is called Truth among the immortal gods,
But in the woods and thickets of this world
She dons her perilous mask of Certainty.

The hunt is on. And now, he turns at bay,
That blatant, that triumphant beast,
Foam drooling from his rabid jaws. The Emperor
At close of day, at ending of the dream,
Rides home to his high tower. The hunt is done.

But look, from behind the cotton-ball of a cloud,
The moon comes sailing forth, to touch with silver
Wings of the grey geese, on their long journey.
There is a clamour high in the winter air:
The hunt, the hunt, the wild hunt goes on.

Funeral Music for Charles Wrey Gardiner

A cold, dull day in a tardy spring:
As the coffin enters the chapel, a black crow,
Like a corny image from a neo-romantic
Nineteen-forties poem, flies over and croaks,
'Dear God,' I think, 'this is going to be depressing,
More than the general run of funerals.'
There is no music here – only an apparently
Automatic and electronic organ
With tremolo permanently on, as if it was shivering
Somewhere in outer darkness.

Now I remember him,
Myopic and spry as an old grey rat,
Penning his memoirs in a crumbling house
Eaten piecemeal by women and by drink.
'The answer to life is no,' he said, and sometimes
He really seemed to mean it. God help us all
If so indeed he did – that gate leads
Only into the 'nothing, nothing, nothing, nothing,'
Which he averred the sum of things.

Burying him, we bury part of ourselves
And the poetic forties, – we, the mourners,
Ageing survivors of an abused
Unfashionable decade. Bohemians, drunks,
Undisciplined and self-indulgent – so, perhaps, we were.
And yet I think we still believed in poetry,
More than some who now possess the scene:
Dot-and-carry Long John Silvers with small dried-up
Professors perched upon their shoulders.
At least our parrots had real and gaudy feathers.

Out in the air, the sun
Is not yet attempting to shine. Among the bushes
That straddle over the gravestones – another trite symbol:
Redbreasts are singing. Those charitable birds,
The tale tells, strewed with dead dry leaves
The sleeping siblings, poor babes in the wood.
What, in this last resort, are any of us but
Sad lost children under the dark thorn?

A Negative Way
in memory of Justin O'Mahoney

The Trappist in his speechless cell,
Cistercian, neat, austere,

The drunkard on his devious road,
Wading through vomit, and his own urine,

Are both impelled, perhaps
By the same impulse – total

Annihilation of the specious ego. They penetrate
The dark central core within

The wavering flame of the soul. In fasts often,
In vigils, stripes, humiliation –

Contempt of and from the world:
Unspeakable aloneness, a negative way.

What then is the price of Wisdom? A dance,
A collapse in the street? Is it busked for a tin-whistle tune?

The heartless streets are paved with stones
Broken as good intentions;

Under the sneer of Georgian architecture,
The bars of Dublin are full of spilled dreams

In spilled puddles of Guinness. Let them mourn,
Mourn for the gifts of mind,

For the grace of manner squandered
On trivial conversations, on tinkers' lads.

And I too mourn one night, at least,
Of warmth and of affection;

And I beg the Lord of Mercy, in whose sight
Our righteousness is only filthy rags,

To take his tattered life for righteousness,
Enrol him, so, among the justified.

Letter to Dàvid Wright
on his sixtieth birthday

Last year I crossed the meridian of sixty.
Now, David, it's your turn. Old friend, we first met
In your Oxford lodgings, those in the High
With the Churchillian landlady, which afterwards became
A kind of traditional caravanserai
For poets – most of them doomed, of course.
Sidney Keyes' officer's cane
Remained in the hall umbrella stand
Long after his mouth was stopped with Numidian dust.
Allison stayed there on leave, a bird of passage
Migrating towards his Italian death.
And there was William Bell –
Not war, but a mountain had earmarked him.

111

But our friendship really began in Soho,
Our second university – so many lessons
To learn and to unlearn – days of the flying bomb,
The hour of the spiv and the wide boy.
Passing through those streets was rather like
The jaunt that Dante took through the Inferno;
Yet we discerned there an image of the City.
A certain innocence coinhered with the squalor.
I doubt if it does so still, even for the young.

Also we inhabited Cornwall for a season –
That cottage up from Zennor, haunted
By the troubled ghost of Peter Warlock.
You liked the landscape, but thought, it seems,
The inhabitants intolerable.
I found their pre-Celtic deviousness
Answered something in my own soul, but the landscape –
Post-industrial, disused tin-mines –
Combining the eschatological with the prehistoric,
A source of panic terror and desolation.

So you prefer the blunt and brutal North –
Those boring and anecdotal
Mountains of Cumbria you now live among.
You even quite enjoyed,
Or so you say, the beastly town of Leeds,
A city for me of unfriendly exile – if my heart
Had been frank like yours, it might have been different.

At sixty, the years that remain
Are, of their nature, numbered,
But need not be unfruitful. The journey is towards
Silence and darkness. Who, if not you and I,
Should know the only silence to be feared
Is that residing in
The unresponsive heart, the darkness which possesses
The self-obfuscating mind? We journey on
Till all the silence suddenly is ringing
With new-invented music, the darkness thronged
With forms concealed in their own radiance,
That moving shine, and shining sing,
Having put on their glory.

112

That vision is a long way off. But this –
Poetical prosing, as they said of Clare –
Is just to send you greetings.

Two Wedding Songs
for HRH The Prince of Wales and Lady Diana Spencer
29 July 1981

i

Hang flags in the airs of July,
  Though the roses seem overblown
And the cuckoo stretches his wings to the south,
  And mark with a white stone
This date; set the bandsmen to play,
Touch off the exuberant fireworks –
  This is the wedding day:

For every wedding is royal,
  And royally affirms
Continuity and commitment;
  And though we are meat for worms
No more than dust and a shade,
  We dance between past and future,
With linked hands, unafraid.

ii
London Birds: a Lollipop

'Why do those bell-tones crowd the air?'
Cooed the pigeons in Trafalgar Square.

'Because this is the bridal day,'
Said the white swan gliding on Thames broad way.

'Why fire in the sky, when it's meant to be dark?'
Cried the pelican in St James's Park.

'To show that the wedding knot is tied,'
Chirped the Cockney sparrows from Cheapside.

'Who is this couple so fêted and fond?
Quacked the ducks on the Round Pond.

'Our Prince, and England's prettiest flower,'
Croaked an old black raven of the Tower.

With the Gift of a Shell
for Guthrie

I've brought the shell you asked for back from Cornwall –
That promontory some would call the Hellas
Of the small *alter orbis* which is England.
But no Hellenic light strikes there
On granite and serpentine. A dry mist always
Drizzles above the waters –
Seas that divided Tristan and Iseult:
Even the music of the herring-gulls
Is Celtic and hysterical.

But this was never bred in Cornish seas –
Commercial enterprise has fetched it here.
The great snail, the super-whelk,
That sweated out this polished spiral palace
From his own slimy mantle, crawled
Down among the corals and the crinoids,
Gorgonia, hydroids, madrepores,
In tropic depths. Such treasures as his blue-haired mother
Bestowed on Marinel – who is Abundance
That shall be Beauty's bridegroom –
Beauty that flits and flees,
And is pursued.

The seas which we have raped and have polluted,
Once those western pirates ranged,
Raleigh or Drake – but I'll name Diggory Piper,
Sailing along the treacherous Cornish shore.

This is Your Poem

This is your poem – an utterly useless present:
You can hang it up, or put it away in a drawer.
If the former, and the wind blows through it,
It will not give voice to any more beautiful chimes
Than now it does; and if the latter,
Mice may find it and make it into a nest –
But that is the only thing it will ever be good for.

You can make fine shreds of this paper, and steep them
In spirits of wine, but this will not mitigate
The fury of your toothache, nor is it recommended,
By the veterinary profession, for sick cattle,
Distempered fox-hounds, or egg-bound Dorkings.

Garlic and houseleek, collected
At the spring festival, will scare away
The brood of Lilith from your threshold,
The hobgoblins and vampires. A holy icon
Can mediate the presence of the blessed saints.
This will do neither of these – it can only wish,
To you and your roof-tree, prosperity and kindness.
But if wishes were horses beggars would ride, and if
Poems were cadillacs poets would probably
Drive them to the public mischief.

Notes Towards a Palinode
for Sean Hutton

i

It seems I have spoken harshly, if not unjustly,
Of Yorkshire, its folk and its Ridings.
Shall I take it all back? We stand on the sands at Bridlington.
Love makes lucid the alien air
Power and purity blow
In from the North Sea.
Of course, I could tell you
Those sands, towards low tidemark,
Are crowded with poisonous weaver-fish

Waiting to jab their envenomed spines
Into the feet of incautious paddlers. In much the same way
I have been stabbed by honest homely citizens
In the pubs of Leeds – morally, that is, and verbally.

ii

Those monstrous Yorkshire towns – Sheffield,
With her necklace of razor-blades, Bradford,
Throned upon her tumbled woolsacks, Leeds,
Crouching over her drain –
They were fathered by Mammon on Lady Mede,
Projections of our guilt. Their foundations
Are on the groans and bones of the poor. While ancient York
Hugs close her earlier shame – the Hebrew curses
For innocent blood spilled.

A keen air is over the Dales, remembering
Those saints who walk through the pages of Bede –
Cuthbert and Aidan and Hilda – and Caedmon
Raising the song of creation among the straw and cowpats,
Fasting in unheated cells, meagre Lent
Upon the hills where the wild snowdrops blossom,
And the becks, loosed from the frost,
Chatter over the stones, where the water-ouzel bobs,
Or seems to fly beneath the wrinkling waters.
Recall the white passion of their prayer.

iii
Haworth Unvisited

I have not been to Haworth, and do not think
That I would want to visit such a spot
Infested so with literary pilgrims. But those three
Maenad sisters possess me much:
Emily, self-immolated on the moorland winds,
Kneading her anger into the household bread,
Leaving her wild cries to God, the dark stranger,
And one great, jagged, passionate,
And finally loveless book – a Pentheseleian poet;
Plain short-sighted Charlotte, bad teeth and beetle brows,
Creating in her own image
Those fierce little puritans, faintly absurd –

Jane Eyre and Lucy Snow
Named from ice crystals and a winter saint;
And sad, withdrawn, pietistic Anne,
The third quiet governess, observing
Human conditions as they moved about her
Shrewdly as any.

iv
In Memoriam Herbert Read

We stand by St Gregory's Minster. The Saxon inscription speaks.
Under the earth and stones he lies – the good anarchist knight.
To him I owe my launching on that choppy stream,
A literary career, when he accepted
My baroque fioritura: 'But how will it fit in
With our new functional architecture?' Peace to his bones
And peace to the questing spirit, whether it strides
Through Kirkdale now, or rides
Along the dusty highways of La Mancha.

Greensleeves
'Platonic England' – GEOFFREY HILL
for Leonard Clark

Knapweed, bindweed, scabious, burnet,
Sorrel, eyebright, elecampane,

Foxglove, lords and ladies, old man's beard –
I could continue this litany of flowers:

They are the sweetness blooms upon her face –
Merlin's glimmering isle,

Whose blood and bones and guts and sweat are coal,
Iron, methane, oil, lead:

White faces in slum alleys, rat faces,
Bodies bent with rickets, crouched in the mine.

117

On the train from Dover, disembarking from the packet
(Too much cheap French wine
Had made me prone to facile tears) as I gulped
On a plastic cup of stewed, black tea,
And stodgy, saccharine cake, she rose
In pink and white of Kentish apple-blossom:
'I am called Lady Greensleeves,' she said,
'I also can betray and break the heart.'

The Green Man's Last Will and Testament
An Eclogue
for Adrian Risdon

In a ragged spinney (scheduled
For prompt development as a bijou housing estate)
I saw the green daemon of England's wood
As he wrote his testament. The grey goose
Had given him one of her quills for a pen;
The robin's breast was a crimson seal;
The long yellow centipede held a candle.

He seemed like a hollow oak-trunk, smothered with ivy:
At his feet or roots clustered the witnesses,
Like hectic toadstools, or pallid as broom-rape:
Wood-elves – goodfellows, hobs and lobs,
Black Anis, the child-devouring hag,
From her cave in the Dane Hills, saucer-eyed
Phantom dogs, Black Shuck and Barghest, with the cruel nymphs
Of the northern streams, Peg Powler of the Tees
And Jenny Greenteeth of the Ribble,
Sisters of Bellisama, the very fair one.

'I am sick, I must die,' he said. 'Poisoned like Lord Randal
From hedges and ditches. My ditches run with pollution,
My hedgerows are gone, and the hedgerow singers.
The rooks, disconsolate, have lost their rookery:
The elms are all dead of the Dutch pox.
No longer the nightjar churns in the twilit glade,
Nor the owl, like a white phantom, silent-feathered
Glides to the barn. The red-beaked chough,

Enclosing Arthur's soul, is seen no more
Wheeling and calling over the Cornish cliffs.
Old Tod has vacated his deep-dug earth;
He has gone to rummage in the city dustbins.
Tiggy is squashed flat on the M1.

My delicate deer are culled, and on offshore islands
My sleek silkies, where puffin and guillemot
Smother and drown in oil and tar.
The mechanical reaper has guillotined
Ortygometra, though she was no traitor,
Crouching over her cradle – no longer resounds
Crek-crek, crek-crek, among the wheatfields,
Where the scarlet cockle is missing and the blue cornflower.
My orchids and wild hyacinths are raped and torn,
My lenten lilies and my fritillaries.
Less frequent now the debate
Of cuckoo and nightingale – and where is the cuckoo's maid,
The snake-necked bird sacred to Venus,
Her mysteries and the amber twirling wheel?
In no brightness of air dance now the butterflies –
Their hairy mallyshags are slaughtered among the nettles.
The innocent bats are evicted from the belfries,
The death-watch remains, and masticates history.

'I leave to the people of England
All that remains:
Rags and patches – a few old tales
And bawdy jokes, snatches of song and galumphing dance-steps.
Above all my obstinacy – obstinacy of flintstones
That breed in the soil, and pertinacity
Of unlovely weeds – chickweed and groundsel,
Plantain, shepherd's purse and Jack-by-the-hedge.
Let them keep it as they wander in the inhuman towns.

'And the little children, imprisoned in ogrish towers, enchanted
By a one-eyed troll in front of a joyless fire –
I would have them remember the old games and the old dances:
Sir Roger is dead, Sir Roger is dead,
She raised him up under the apple tree;
Poor Mary is a-weeping, weeping like Ariadne,
Weeping for her husband on a bright summer's day.'

119

A.E. Housman in Talbot Road, Bayswater

Cheery, beery Saturday night:
Moses went up to his own bedroom,
Alfred to his, alone –
To lie wakeful, his spirit tossed
By the four winds of fatality.

A night-time traveller in the western upland
Paused, hearing that unquiet ghost
Whispering among the leaves.

St Stephen's Sunday morning bells
Called 'Come to church, good people!' –
But Housman, he would stay,
And cursed the breaking day.

Footnote to Belloc's 'Tarantella'

Do you remember an inn, Miranda? It lost its licence of course –
Total neglect of the elementary rules of hygiene, not to mention
Wine contaminated with tar, and constant complaints
From the neighbours about the noise.
One visit of the inspector
From the Spanish Tourist Board was quite enough.
Nevermore, Miranda, nevermore.

In Central Park, New York

A bird flits in the trees
Of Central Park – black, fan-tailed,
With a pointed beak. He has a call note
That sounds like 'tut'.
It is his only call note. ————————————————
I do not know his name
But I think he is one of the grackles.

Not far away a carousel
Continually revolves, reiterating
Innocent tunes of a former day –
Waltzes, polkas, quadrilles:
Where is the Washington Square of Henry James?

On Saturday morning a drove of joggers
Plods round the park's periphery,
Like startled cattle fleeing
The gad-fly spectre of cholesterol.

Fez

Atlas presses his snowy shoulders against the stars –
The god Shu, the propulsive principle, thrusts
Through the thunder-engendering air; the air which belongs
To the chattering swallows, and the tall storks
That nest on the minarets. In Hesperidean gold,
The orange gleams among its dark green leaves,
With olive and myrtle, with almond and apricot.

The call to prayer bursts through the darkness,
Through the sunrise, and through the harsh noontide.
Below, in the narrow streets, the bray
Of the over-loaded mule, the whine
Of the blind beggar. Perfumers torment
Essences from the rose, from amber and musk,
Jasmine and sandalwood. Expatriate scholars
Strive to master a wisdom not their birthright.
In an enclave of the public gardens
The Hebrew sorcerers quietly receive their clients.

On a hill apart, in a disused barracks
The young students break their frustrated minds
On a profane and alien learning ('Compare and contrast
Kingsley Amis's *Take A Girl Like You*
With Jane Austen's *Emma*')
Or the bitter violence of slogans.

Bee-eaters in Tangiers

We sit in the garden beside the pomegranate tree,
With English tea and chocolate éclairs. Intermittently,
Now in small flocks, and now singly,
Bee-eaters are passing through,
Keeping together with little, soft, plaintive cries,
Moving purposively northwards and out to sea.
Slim and elegant, with swallow-like pointed wings
And long curved beaks, all the bee-eaters of Africa
Are on migration. They make for the gardens of Spain,
For the vineyards of France, and the terraced orchards
Of Alban and Apennine Hills –
Carved in emerald and lapis lazuli:
A pest for Virgil and his ox-borne bees.

The Slow-Worm

Fragile and innocuous, the slow-worm
But not blind – his eyes are rather appealing;
His body gleams with silver and with bronze.

The blind-worm is not slow. He stalks
The stolid slug, but not without
His own sort of agility.

Slow-worm is no worm, maligned:
A lizard merely, doing without legs.
His true salvation lies in his fragility.

To the memory of
George Frederick Heath-Stubbs 1925-1983

These dry leaves upon your urn:
Do you hear me, brother? Do you hear me?
Do you hear me now?

Earthfruits I'm bringing, also
The immolated lamb.

Accepted, rejected? No reply –
Only the wind that stirs
Your ashes and the dust of Africa.

The Immolation of Aleph

For Eugene Dubnow

"There is no mitigation." said Adam.
His sweat poured down. Eve groaned in labour.
The earth brought forth thistles, burrs,
Thornapple, giant hogweed, prickly-pear.
"Blood must atone." said Adam. He called the ox –
Curly-fronted, wide-horned, noble, most beloved
And first-named, the opener of his alphabet.
"Come, Aleph, dance!" The brute ran
Upon the point of Adam's malachite sword.
Coughing blood, he slowly sank to his knees.
His eyes glazed in death.

A cloudy image formed in the sky;
An old man, filthy, swathed in fleeces,
Sucked to toothless gums
The blood through a glass tube.
"This is not my Friend." said Adam.

The clouds shifted. A second image showed:
A young man in a red pointed cap,
About his head the rays of the spring sun,
Plunged his blade into the gleaming
Starlight body of Taurus,
Averting in anguish his sensuous face.
"This is, and this is not, my Friend." said Adam.

Blood streamed from the sky,
An equinoctial downpour: the earth burgeoned
Crimson tulips and anemones.

123

ٮ

Cain had built him a house,
A single cell, the germ of a city,
A lodge in a garden of cucumbers.
"I will offer my pumpkins, my pimentoes, my yams,
My marrowfat peas, my pearmains and codlins,
To the Voice – is it his or hers? –
Coquettish, at any rate, as a woman's.
It must choose between me and my shepherd brother."

"Wrong!" said the Voice. "Offering rejected.
You snatch at futurity, Cain,
As your father at knowledge and immortality:
The pure offering, the greedy and jealous heart.
It must be blood always until the ram
Caught in the thicket change to a fish;
And your wheat-grains and grapes are given back
With an altered, a resurrected life."

Abel brought a lamb, a firstling of the flock:
"See, I slit the throat with a shaving of flint.
The blood drips on the standing stone."
"Good shepherd, who brought the dearest firstborn,
You slay, Abel, you slay what you love." A tongue of flame
Licked up the blood, consumed the fat and bones.

"Blood must atone." said Cain. He struck his brother
With a hand-axe, and left the body
Gaping in the fallow field.

An image loured in the darkened sky:
The sentence bawled, reinforced by thunder:
"Run, Cain, run! Cain the husbandman
Must now turn nomad, exchange
The prospect of olives and date-palms
For the illimitable red desert."
"This is not my father's Friend." said Cain.

"A mercy is granted, Cain
(As for your father, the flayed skins) –
Something beautiful, a ship,
A humped and contumelious beast."

The alphabet in blood-stained characters
Ran, beyond the curve of the leaping Fish,
Stretching towards infinity.

ℸ

Cain the nomad drew aside
The triangular flap of the tent's door.
No trilogy of angels came across
The sands, only the blood continued to cry.

Horned like a narwhal, Cain journeyed
Across the bed of a dried-up sea.
The blood still cried: for Cain, father of giants,
Blood of all generations shed on the earth.
Is that a mirage of waters, or already
The gleam of the relentless flood?
Cain forged on urging his dromedary.
Father of Jubal, who handled the lyre,
Of Tubal the technician, he clutched
The stone, the singing shell. Within his loins
Abiram, Judas, and the prodigal.

Triumph Songs for the Nine Worthies (I)

JOSHUA

Pisgah – Moses hopes and gazes.
Archangel and fiend dispute the body.
An unmarked grave. Angel-sextons.

But this goes forward, not resistible
Slaughter. Sun and moon stand still.
Tramp of history's feet, eternity's ram's-horns:
Walls fall flat, ancientest of cities.

125

For he is saviour, son of the fish
That flashes through the waters.

DAVID

Smooth stones in the brook;
Ten strings on the harp.

"Death!" whines the sling;
The harp utters "Praise!"

The giant falls with a clatter
Of unnecessary armour, the unclean spirit
Shudders to its own place.

Taken from among the flocks;
Hiding in deserts and dens;
Distracted by women's bodies;
Blood guilt – Uriah's blood;
The gold-haired boy in the oaktree;
Song of the bow, song of the glutted sword –
It is all there, in the dance
Before your ark,
And now I am dying. Departed
Beauty, manhood, strength
Choose me, a worn stone;
Pluck me, a slack string.

JUDAS MACCABEUS

The temple is taken. Shattered
The Abomination that blasphemously
Imaged the Unimageable.

Howling Dionysus runs
Into the night, trailing
His pine-cone thyrsus, ivy twines.

Mid-winter – oil miraculously conserved:
See, the small lights wink and splutter –
And He will come.

Myrrha
(Birth of Adonis)

Oh the bitter bush of myrrh!

The stiff boughs stand in the desert wind
Hot and dry as the passion of incest.

She slinks into the cedar-carven bedstead:
He stirs in drunken stupor. His lust fumbles:
"Ecce ancilla," she whispers.

Oh the bitter bush, the bitter bush. The black boar comes;
His ivory tusks are crescent moons.
He rips and strips the rough bark.
The wood groans and splinters. Out of the cleft there slips
A naked weeping child, to lie cradled
Upon the soft and drifted dust
Under the bitter bush, the bitter bush of myrrh.

Metis

The first wife of Zeus – her name means "Prudence",
And she was a prude. Clever though –
She had helped him to his throne, the upstart deity
Displacing poor old Kronos, and
The other Titans (you needn't believe all that
Olympian propaganda about them –
Their reign, after all, was the Golden Age)
And she never let him forget what she'd done for him: "Well,"
     he said
"If you're so deucedly skilful, my dear,
Why don't you turn yourself into a fly?"
She could, and she did too, just to prove it.
One gulp and he'd swallowed her down.
And that was the end of her. But nine months later
Zeus, one day, was afflicted
With the mother and father of all headaches.
They split his radiant brow, and out burst

The goddess of wisdom, Pallas Athene,
Shouting her war-cry, in full armour,
Virginal and indigestible.

His second wife was his sister, Hera.
That marriage lasted, at least.
It had its ups and downs, of course –
But that is another story.

Romulus

She named no father. Only she had dreamed
Of a great phallus coming out of the fire,
Erect on the glowing embers.

Not even washed of the blood, the brats must take their chance,
Exposed on the stony hillside. But there came

The great she-wolf, with distended dugs
(Shepherds had found her den, had slaughtered her blind cubs) –

She gave them suck. Parched mouths eagerly
Began to drink, but one, with an imperious arm,
Was trying to thrust his brother aside, as if he knew already
Sons of the sons of sons, begotten from his loins,
Should rule the seven hills, should rule the world.

Death of Aeschylus

"Alas! I am stricken with a grievous blow" – Agamemnon
Tangled in the scarlet cloth that Clytemnestra
Set at his feet, sarcastic flattery:
In that web involved
Iphigeneia, flinching at the knife,
Retching over the chafing-dish, Thyestes,
Ivory-shouldered Pelops.

The old man strolls
On the Sicilian foreshore, a constitutional;
Above him, a hovering eagle – more probably
A bearded vulture, a lammergeyer,
Moderately hooked bill, a tuft of bristles at the chin,
Long pointed wings, a wedge-shaped tail –
Mistakes his gleaming baldness for a rock
And drops a tortoise.

Unless spectators shooed it off,
The raptor feeds indifferently
Upon the poet's brains, guts of the tortoise.

"Tragic death of distinguished playwright" –
The local papers might have said,
Had there been local papers – triviality is perennial.
The journalists got it wrong, they always do:
This was not tragedy – tragedy cohered
Only in those shattered brain cells.
Life and the Absurd resume their reign.

Triumph Songs for the Nine Worthies (II)

HECTOR

The stay of Priam's house is down;
Loud whooping Achilles vindicated.
His friend's death made good. Recovered
His valuable armour.

The old man cringes; he begs only
A parcel of bruised flesh, of broken bones,
Pierced heels, muddied hair.

Achilles remembers his own father;
Grizzled, bleary-eyed, garrulous by the hearth.
Whom once a sea-bride loved, the silver-footed.

Pity the human lot; and this young man – only because
Old age is something he will never know.

ALEXANDER

More worlds to conquer? Before us, burning deserts –
Sciopods, anthropophagi, cynocephali?
Or else the blameless Hyperboreans,
Golden-skinned, with jade-sheathed nails,
Feeding on the five grains and jujubes,
Combing fleeces from mulberry trees?

A spaceship to the eagles' kingdom?
A diving bell to the fishes?

Mother, how far must I go
Before I'm free of you?
How much more must I destroy, father,
Before you will believe me?

JULIUS CAESAR

"We're bringing back the old bald bugger!"
The soldiers sing. Another campaign fought –
The people have their show. I've bleached the locks
Of black-haired Gaulish prisoners. The populace expects
The blond barbarian beast.

This laurel wreath
Keeps getting in my eyes. It's not efficient
At fending off the bluebottles. One day, no doubt,
They'll offer me a solid diadem; and in the end
I will go up to heaven and be a god.
Meanwhile here in Rome
There's muddle to clear up.

Honey and Lead

Honey boiled for a sweetener
In a leaden saucepan – lead leaches in;
Lead, added, gives gravity
To a thin, sour vintage.

Lead – deposited in the bone, lead seeps
Into the manic brain-cells, inexpungeable
Saviour of lead on the tongue. Caligula,
Nero, Domitian, strut –
Enormous antichrists: vomitorium,
Orgies, blood-soaked sand.

The poet goes back to his high-rise apartment;
To cabbage stewed in an earthen pot,
And, if he is fortunate,
A knuckle of bacon.

In the Sabine Hills
to Arthur and Mary Creedy

I

So this is the Sabine villa – always supposing
The archaeologists have got it right. The guide
Seems confident enough: "Here is his bedroom.
Here is his library, and here his bathroom."
The bathroom, by the way, was much extended
Into a proper swimming pool when, centuries later,
Christian monks had settled in the place. Who says
Monks were not keen on bathing? Only the pavement,
A plain and geometric pattern,
Still seems to speak of him – an Attic decor.

Quintus Horatius Flaccus, whose father was born a slave
But made his pile, was affluent enough
To buy his son a liberal education. At Athens
The young student put aside
His annotated Plato and his Aristotle
(But more congenial, I would guess, he of the garden)
Much thumbed and better loved
His Sappho and Alcaeus, took up his spear
To fight in the republican last ditch
At Philippi – sheer panic!
He left his shield upon the field of battle
(Later he remembered
There was a literary precedent for that.)

131

He made his compromises with the new regime,
As they all did. Virgil re-jigged
The Messianic eclogue he had written
Perhaps for Alexander Helios,
The son of Antony and Cleopatra,
To make it fit the boring son
Of pompous Pollio. But Ovid was not saved
From dreary exile on the Black Sea beaches,
Who wanted only to sing love's changes and love's chances,
And all things shifting, a shape-shifting world.

But for this one his Sabine farm,
The bounty of Maecenas,
Original and best of Ministers of Culture.
Not too far from Rome, he learned to practise
Detachment – detachment but with irony. There he could sing
The sunnier slopes of love – who were they –
These Lydias and Lalages and Leuconoes?
Local *contadine*, or simply slave girls
Round about the farm, half real half imagined? He honoured too
The rustic pieties, already fading
Into nostalgia, and Phydile
Lifting her hands towards the waxing moon,
Her scattering of barley-meal, her pinch of salt
Spluttering in the altar-fire. Now other gods
Are worshipped in these hills, in other ways, but still
The little images are drummed to church
On the appropriate feast days, to be blessed.

Primroses and early violets
Grow among these stones, that give the ground-plan.
Small birds are twittering among the bushes, and I note
Two male whitethroats dispute for territory.

II

We climb now up to the Bandusian Spring:
More brightly shining than glass, under the ilex trees,
They still come down, the talkative waters.
We pour libation, three drops of local wine
Out of a twentieth century bottle, invoking
The mountain-ranging Nine, the poet's shade:
Whether it dwells now in that noble castle

The Florentine assigned it, or, in Epicurean atoms,
It whirls in the tramontino – playful idolatry.
We turn now and return – tomorrow's Maundy Thursday.
It's time to celebrate the different rites –
The dying and the resurrected God.

Temple of Vesta, Tivoli

What a dreadful bore it must have been,
Tending the sacred flame. Burial alive
For the poor girl who let it futter out,
Or slipped from her virginity: not vowed perpetually –
They were released at thirty, but which of them, I wonder,
Would then be marriageable. They had their privileges –
A ring-side seat at the disgusting circus,
If that's what turned them on; the right to claim
The life of any man condemned they met:
A right as old as Lascaux, pertaining to
The unwed women of the tribe, feeding the common hearth,
When breeding the new seeds of fire
Was difficult and hazardous.

The fane is roofless now,
The pavement broken rubble. The great pillars
In their proportions speak
Of Pietas and Gravitas. But the numina
Have left, and all the pain has drained away.
Outside, the modern town
Transacts its different noisier tedium.

Saint Benedict at Subiaco

He dwelt there, a dove
In the clefts of the rock, or else
A frog at the bottom of a dry well:
A feeding-bucket let down every day.
The raven carried the poisoned bread away.

133

From this harsh root, the stem
Of moderation: green
Toil in the fields, and scholarship
A shy woodland flower.

On thorns of austerity Francis grafted
Roses of the troubadours.

Touching this rock, you touch
The cornerstone of Europe, her civility.

Saint Cuthbert and the Otter
for Gerard Irvine

CUTHBERT:

"Lord, the North Sea reaches my Adam's apple.
I gargle prayer. It bubbles up
To the unanswering stars. It is Your love
Keeps them in orbit. Love is the cold tide
Cincturing my loins. Love in the shingle
Gashes my feet. It is love that directs
The long-tailed whistling ducks
That dabble far out in the surf. Love.

Lord, remember my people – people of the Engli,
That live north of Humber. They are dull and dour.
Grudgingly the soil yields them oats and barley.
They grope for black coal in its bowels. But sometimes
After they've dined, and their brains are frothy with beer,
They take the tinkling harp, pass it from hand to hand,
Sing vile unchristened songs that tug at the heart –
Of heroes daring desperate odds, who die
For foolish points of honour, in endless, evil blood-feuds;
Who perish from wounds slain dragons have given them,
Releasing hoards of gold, vain pelf of the world.
Lord, I would purchase them for you, the Haliand,
Who took the odds on the studded tree.
Nails and blood are its jewels – the world's rooftree,
Those silver swinging stars its apples."

"Master, I do not know
What you were doing in the sea. It was not for fishing –
Though you throw me herring-heads and mackerel tails
Therefore I love you. I dry with my warm fur
Your bruised numbed feet, anoint them
With the musk from under my tail. Look, I gambol and play
In your road – that is to make you laugh.
I do not know what laughter is. At first
I was afraid – I thought it was fang-showing.
But now, there is no harm in it I think.
I think you should do it more often."

King Canute's Boating
An old song completed

Merrily sang the monks in Ely
 When Knut the king came rowing along:
"Row, my henchmen, close to the land,
 And we'll hear these monks at their song!"

It was the office of vespers they sang,
 By soft, uncertain candlelight –
The song which the blessed Mother of God
 Brought forth in her delight.

"You have put down the mighty from their seat,
 Scattered the proud in their array,
Have filled the hungry with good things
 And the rich sent empty away."

There was one in the boat to interpret. A cloud
 Darkly shadowed the King's blond brow:
"Enter not into judgement, Lord
 With me your servant, now.

"I am Knut, the son of Sweyn the Dane,
 Who rule this sea-embattled land,
Dealing harsh laws to a turbulent folk
 With a stern, but an even hand.

"A King rules his parcel of middle earth
　　But there are limits put to his sway –
He cannot bridle the wild waves
　　That career on the whale's way.

"Lord of the Elements, they called me once –
　　I refuted all that flattery
When I set my chair on the Solent sand
　　And forbad the rising sea.

"I set my chair higher, on the shingle,
　　And chid the running tide, as it rose:
The waves, the white-maned horses of Agir
　　Drew close, and still more close –

"Like the cold salt thoughts, that rise in my head,
　　As I lie in the sleepless hours before dawn,
Remembering all that was done amiss
　　And all that was left undone.

"And I think of that king of the Goths, Theodoric,
　　In Verona, where he reigned,
And of his faithful minister,
　　Down in the dungeon chained.

"That king was tormented with thoughts like mine,
　　But the other, the king's good servant was free –
Free in the prospect of torture and death
　　While his mistress, Philosophy,

"Expounded concerning the goddess Fortune:
　　On her swift wheel are whirled
The tangled skeins of history
　　And the goods and gifts of the world.

"The rich revile her, being cast down,
　　And only the poor in spirit can see
That she is a glorious and blissful creature –
　　But that vision is closed to me.

"Heard from afar the monastic chant
　　Is hauntingly sweet, deceptively bland,
And we will go rowing again by Ely
　　But not too close to the land."

Triumph Songs for the Nine Worthies (III)

ARTHUR

Blood-sunset over Britain.
Camlan, the waste plain. Roar of the sea;
Lapping of nearer water. Fling my sword,
My useless sword, back to her
Who gave it first, there where she sits
Under the tossing lake-weeds.

Return – shall I return? But now my soul
Flies out into the storm, black-winged,
Red-footed, sickle-billed – a yelping chough.

CHARLEMAGNE

The blackamoors' business is settled. Let them howl
To God in their mosques. Slowly the grand army
Descends the Pyrenees. Before us France –
Vineyards and cornfields and the grazing flocks;
Larks singing high in the air, and orioles
Among the cherry-glades; red roses
That overshade a white marble bench:
Oh sweet realm, peaceable empire!

Suddenly he starts – was it a horn-call,
Far, far behind the mountains?
Dying lips set to an ivory mouthpiece.

GODFREY

Raising their swordhilt crosses, sobbing with passion,
Hands dripping with blood, the victors
Stagger towards the empty sepulchre.

The streets, the gutters, run with blood:
Mussulman and Jew,
Christian (Greek or Syrian) –
The indiscriminately slain.

And will they crown me? Here, in this city
Where He wore only, and still wears
The twisted crown of thorns called history?

Timur

Timur the Lame (or Tamburlaine we call him)
Made in his youth a vow, they say,
That he would never wittingly cause pain
To any sentient being; once seriously distressed
For accidentally treading on an ant.

The last skull is the apex of the pyramid:
"My enemies," he cried (it is the same
Pure-minded boy who weeps, inside the skin
tanned by all the dry winds of the steppe)
"So contumacious and so obdurate –
They all deserve to die
For causing me to break my lovely vow!"

Queen Gruach
for John Wain

The queen, my lord, is dead.

They say I walked last night (anxieties,
Our enemies mustering like a moving wood,
Rob me of healing sleep) it must have been
The castle galleries, but in my dream
I trod a long rock-passage, winding down
Into a central cave. And there a light gleamed,
A cauldron boiled and bubbled. A woman
(Was she our Saint Bride? – but there were three,
A triple goddess, triune guardian of wyrd)
Leaned over it, stirring. The cauldron seethed
With broth of oatmeal, venison,
Black-game, red grouse, hare and leveret,
Pork and bacon, kale – each finds
That which his palate savours best,
Nor will it ever boil a coward's meat.
I in my dream was hungry, stretched out arms
(Which held a bowl now) expecting sustenance.
One of those women spooned out a ladleful,

As if she would comply, then, as in contempt,
She dashed it down upon the cave's stone floor:
But in my dream, somehow there hovered
A question that I should have asked. What was the question –
The question which we ask of history?
The times are black, and that usurping
Fratricidal clan, Canmore,
Advance with English arms and a Roman blessing.
Already chroniclers are sharpening pen-nibs
To smirch us with their lies, to call us murderers,
And worse – the slayers of our guest. My son
When we are gone, may yet be crowned,
But he will be the last, and ancient Scotland done.
We will go down to calumny and oblivion,
The lot of those whom history will not answer.
I had another dream. I saw a queen,
A hairshirt underneath her sumptuous robes,
Her face was pale with fasting, furrowed
With penitential tears. Now in a barbarous northern land
She mitigates the fury of her husband,
And is fanatic for the Roman discipline,
To bind it on our church – the ancient church
Of Kentigern, of Ninian and Columba:
Wild lyrical hermits, dwelling in caves,
On moors and mosses, seal haunted islands,
Hard and austere as the rock on which they built,
Loving God's folk, and gentle to His beasts.
But she'll assert the Roman discipline,
Trochaic hymns in which you seem to hear
The tramp of Caesar's legionnaires
(But in my blood Calgacus yells and skirls).

She walks in the light while I go down in darkness,
Because the poor shall love her. Who loves me –
A stern and ruthless queen in a confused time?
Our marriage was political. My first husband,
The abbot, being dead, I sought
A strong protector and a guardian for
My poor weak feeble-minded son. And yet you called me
"Dearest chuck". Ah! how the heart treasures
Such casual, trivial words of tenderness.

You I associate in my government. Here is the charter:
Gruach, et Macbeth, regina et rex Scòtorum
Under our hand and seal – my little hand –
No Arabian perfume sweetens it.

King Bladud

All the birds of his sea-girt realm
Paid tribute – erne and swan and bustard,
Crane and capercailzie, slaughtered to construct
The great sweep of his artificial wings.

He mounted to the temple roof – Sul's,
Grinning war goddess and patroness
Of sulphur heated springs. He plunged to the yielding air,
And crashed to the stones beneath. Brains
Spattered the pavement. Black flies buzzed about them.

His son looked on, the young prince: "Be mine to challenge
Not the immeasurable air, but to compute
The unharnessed tides of love." He too would fall
Into that chaos where the lightnings licked
Upon the lunatic heath his whitened head
Battered by pelican daughters.

A Pocket Life of William Shakespeare

i

"Broke my park's pale, shot my deer,
Kissed my keeper's daughter, did he? John Shakespeare's son –
The old man's sound enough, or so they tell me;
But as for those Ardens – some at least are recusants.
He's left the place they say – gone for a pard-bearded soldier,
Or else a singing-man in a great house,
Or joined a troupe of players. Any road,
I doubt we'll ever hear much good of him."

140

"Holds horses outside the theatre;
A boy up from the country, and he's got
An adaptation of Plautus in his pocket –
Grammar school stuff. They all bring me such things,
Taken from Plautus, Terence, or from Seneca.
But with a few touches this might serve:
We need new comedies, Robert Greene is finished;
And men grow tired of ranting Tamburlaine
And potty old Hieronimo."

Navarre, Verona, Messina and Illyria –
O, those brave, those sweet, those witty women!
They speak with boys' voices, delicate flute-notes.
It is a boy-girl's laughter, Ganymede's,
Ambiguously echoes through the glades
Of Arden-Eden, the green mother-forest.

"His sugared sonnets among his private friends":
Some speak of this earl, or of that
But though he will aspire one day
To write himself a gentleman, he would not fly so high.
And so fastidious, so intelligent –
Not to be hooked by any pathic charms
Of some shrill-squeaking pre-pubescent Roscius.
A student at the inns of court, maybe? And the Dark Lady –
There's Mistress Fitton and there's Mistress Lanier
(Very brave in youth – but brown? An excellent musician,
And, I dare say, no better than she should be;
But there are many such, and salmon in both rivers)
And Lucy Negro, blackbitch Abbess,
And comely Mistress Davenant,
The kindly hostess of the Crown at Oxford.

"Whither away so fast, Master Will Davenant?
Rushing down Cornmarket and the High,
Toppling the traders' stalls?" "I'm going to meet
My godfather, who's Master William Shakespeare."

"Be sure you do not take
The name of the Lord your God in vain!" "Had I a beard,
I'd fight for my mother's honour. My godsire brings me
A pocketful of words, that chirp like nightingales,
And a bundle of brave stories." "Orts –
Filched out of Holinshed and out of Plutarch!
I don't believe he's got enough of Greek
Even to read the last in the original."

vi

Front teeth gone, head balding and domed –
Is it the scurvy or the French Pox?
The smell of bread disgusts him, stockfish, onions,
And little stinking dogs under the tables
Cadging for titbits. The quill scratches on:
The Play's the thing. Mousetrap. Yorick's skull.
The gilded fly. A dish of stewed prunes.
And Troy fallen, Hector slain –
Bitches, bitches, whores and bullies the lot of them!
And Timon's tomb washed by the salt sea wave.

vii

"Your Scottish play will do, the theme will please the king –
The witchcraft interest likewise. Of course, we'll have to cut it –
Cut it quite a lot. Build up the witch scenes though,
Write in more songs and dances, add more spectacle
(I'll get Tom Middleton to lend a hand).
What we want is something more like a masque –
Masques are the in thing now at court.

"Why do you run your fingers through your beard
Or on your dagger's hilt? And what in Hecate's name, Will
     Shakespeare
Are you muttering underneath your breath,
Saying this play will always be unlucky?"

viii

An island princess and a fine young prince
Whose name begins with F –
Ferdinand in that play Florizel in this –
These will serve to furnish forth, I think,

The wedding of our new Elizabeth
And Frederick, Elector Palatine.
Some say they'll be king and queen of Bohemia,
And then, maybe, the Empire.
Robert Greene made my Perdita
A princess of Bohemia and cast upon Sicilian shores
There to be reared by shepherds. Shepherds you'd expect
In pastoral Sicilia but I'll make
Trinacrian Sicily three-cornered Britain.
So she must be a princess of Sicilia
Cast up upon the sea-coast of Bohemia.
But has Bohemia got a sea-coast, then?
Well, it has one now.

ix

Back at Stratford. Lousy Lucy's dead.
Nothing will bring my young prince Hamnet back.
But I have daughters: Judith – Susannah too
And she, if God so will, shall bear me grandsons.
Let Ann, in the well-tried and comfortable
Second-best bed sleep still. While my bones lie in the church:
Good friend, for Jesus sake forbear
To vex that quiet consummation.

Nixon, the Cheshire Prophet
for Bernard Saint

Black hair, a low forehead,
Sallow skin, jutting teeth,
Broad shoulders, big hands – he did his work,
Enough of it, in the fields,
But had to be beaten often.
Generally silent – but when the boys
Tormented him, he would run after them,
Making loud noises, grab them by the throat,
Kick them and thump them, till he was called off.

143

But sometimes something would seize him – whether the moon's
    phase,
Or the wind in the right quarter caused it, nobody knew.
But he'd begin his prophecies, in a strange voice,
Chanting them, in rhymed verses.
Forseeing the future – but in a jumble
As in a dream out of time. He spoke
Of the bloody severed head of a king,
Of England possessed by iron men,
Another king, fleeing,
Casting his seal into the dark Thames,
Men grubbing in the mountain's bowels,
Great argosies tossed on the waves,
Full of gold and spices and chinaware,
The mills and the looms of Satan
Spread Northward over the hills of Lancashire;
And a fire in London, fire growing
From the small womb of a baker's oven,
And fire cast down from the sky by great black birds;
And generations of men afraid of fire –
A small seed of fire in the heart of the motes
Which are the atoms that, swirling, make up creation,
And fire in the marrow of their own bones;
And always of Famine, a great female skeleton
Striding over the land, grabbing the poor
And cramming them into her yellow chops.

After this he'd fall silent, and eat
Even more prodigiously than usual.
Munching the cheese and the crusts, chawing on bacon knuckles,
Slurping the broth and the beer. And then he'd sleep,
Curled up on the hearth-stone; like an animal.

The king, on a Northern progress, learnt of this.
He had him brought before him. The king looked at him.
Having heard of a prophet, he'd expected perhaps
Something more ethereal, like the Boy David,
Or maybe the youthful Baptist, in naked purity
With only a girdle of camel-skin
About his loins. Oh well –
It was no new thing for him to be disappointed.

144

Nixon looked up. He saw
A little man wrapped in furs. He had weak legs,
For two young courtiers supported him.
Both thought "He slobbers, just like me."

The king said "Prophet, you shall come to London,
And sing in my ain palace – better there, than spreading wild ideas
Among the common sort. I need a prophet
To warn me against my enemies – those hellish Papists
That would hoist me sky-high with their bombards and petards;
And the black witches, that melt my image
Over a slow fire, or bury it,
A pin stuck through the heart, in the cauld slime of a pig-sty.
The queen and her ladies have run plain daft
After those new-fangled masques, cavorting
And tripping about like allegorical goddesses.
Though Master Jonson writes fine verses for them,
And Master Jones devises braw machines,
I think you'll gie us homelier entertainment.
So I'll bring you to London. You'll ride in my ain coach."

But Nixon began to whimper and snivel, and cried
"No! No! No! don't send me to London!
I know I shall starve in that place. I cannot bear it,
The hunger, the hunger, the wolf's tooth in my guts,
The dryness, the dryness, the torture of thirst!"
"Hoots," said the king, "you'll no starve.
You shall dwell in my kitchens. My cook shall feed you
With kickshaws and sweeties from the queen's cupboard,
And my ain table. Marchpains and cheesecakes,
And sugar-plums and almonds, and roasted larks,
Venison cooked in pastry coffins."

The king was as good as his word. Nixon was placed in the kitchens
But the cooks and the scullions soon regretted this:
He was always under their feet, and filching
The snipe and the godwits off the spit,
The roasted apples sizzling on the hob,
Scoffing pies and pasties, and sticking
His fingers into frumenties and flummeries,
And then into the dripping-pan. So they put him in a hole –
It was a disused wine-cooling vault – and threw down scraps
From time to time, but not ungenerously.

The king will go to hunt at Windsor, and the court go with him:
There was pulling down of hangings, and rolling up of carpets,
Plate and pewter stacked in chests,
And chairs and tables piled upon wagons, for the whole furniture
Must go off with the king.
In all this confusion, Nixon was forgotten:
He was snoring soundly, – the night before
The cook had thrown down to him three pounds of sausages
A ring of black pudding, and a whole plateful
Of stale mutton pasties. When he awoke
The kitchens were all empty. For days and days,
His cries reverberated through the vaults,
But fainter and fainter. At last there was silence –
Nixon, the veridical prophet, the touchstone, the truepenny,
The right-tongued poet had starved to death –
Even as he foretold he would –
A small black rat in a black hole.

House Spirits

Hairy flanks and buttocks, old men's wizened faces,
Bodies of overgrown children, glimpsed
By moonlight filtering through leaded panes
Or a banked-up fire's glow. All night long
They're at their silent scrubbing, sweeping, scouring –
Their sole reward a dish of porridge,
Curds or cream at best. Naked they are and cold,
Therefore they have such names as
The Cauld Lad, or Lob-lie-by-the-fire,
Basking his hirsute thews by dying embers
Or a still-warm bread oven. But do not give them clothes –
A neat suit tailored to their assumed dimensions –
Not that they reject them. With a squeal of glee,
They draw them on, and a skip and a cavort
About the chamber. But then they vanish utterly –
From now on you do your own housework!

Clothes are destiny; the Fates, old aunties
Spinning, weaving, knitting clothes for the new-born child:
A change of clothes is a change of lifestyle, new clothes new birth,
And therefore these unborn become new-born –

Babies with wrinkled, knowing faces,
Here in this daylight world which we inhabit
And they believe is real. They hope to find here
Play, meaningful work, love even –
Ah, but will they?

Robert Herrick's Pig

"A runt, a diddler, that is what you are."
So said my greedy brothers and my sisters,
Shouldering me away from mother's paps,
As she lay sweet in straw, a beatific grin
Upon her mug, showing her ivory tusks.

They all ended up as chops and sausages,
As bacon, and as brawn, and as black puddings,
As tripe and chitterlings.
But parson took me in, and made me free
Of parlour, hall and kitchen. A sweetling pig,
A nestling pig, a pretty tantony –
That is what I am.

My friend the parson is a learned man,
And I a most accomplished pig, for I've been taught
To swill my ale out of a pewter tankard,
While he sits evenings over his wine and dreams
Of youth, and London, and those Mermaid days.
When midnight chimes ring dizzy in our heads
He squeals his little songs to Julia,
And other possibly existent ladies,
And I join with him in the accompaniment –
Hunk hunk hunk, snortle snortle snortle,
Gruntle gruntle gruntle, wee wee wee wee!

Couperin at the Keyboard

In a gallery of Versailles
François Couperin (called *"Le Grand"*)
Is playing the clavecin –
Half-heard. Court Officials
Pace to and fro, whispering
Intrigues, affairs of state –
What city now the king shall lay siege to,
Or to which lady's virtue.

Cicadas, singing in Provençal heat –
The music gently tells
Of harvesters returning with their sheaves,
Of flowering orchards, or of shepherds' bagpipes;
And now of lovers' sighs, and lovers' plaining, –
And the soft swish of women's petticoats –
Mysterious barricades.

Evening draws on. The sun
and the Sun King retire.
Chandeliers are lit, and are extinguished:
Only the single candle
Upon his music-rest burns on.

The bass burrs like a dor, the treble
Like a mosquito whines and stings.
Shadows are dancing now – sour-faced prudes,
Dressed in black silk, with yellow fingers, ancient beauties,
Rouged and with false gold ringlets,
The powder-puffed and painted fop –
All the prisoners of the Cave of Spleen.

A chill wind lifts
The sails of the joyous ship
That is en voyage for Cythera. "Haul down!"
Cries the masked captain. The shroud descends
And, gleaming in the moonlight, for a moment
It seems a blood-fringed blade.

La Cenerentola

Rossini's firework tunes
Fizz and bubble and bounce along;
He blows up his famous crescendoes
Like balloons for a carnival; roulades
Are tossed and twirled as elegantly
As spaghetti on a fork.

This is not Mozart's world, not *Figaro* –
The supreme moment in the moonlit garden
When all wrongs are forgiven, and all truths known;

But Italy, 1817 –
Jewels are brilliant and hard, silk brocades
Gaudy and flairing. This is too knowing
To encompass a fairy godmother,
Crystal coach, changed from a pumpkin.

But when, at last, her sisters,
Snivelling, kneel and ask forgiveness, her fulfilment's too complete
For any shadow of resentment. Forgiveness
Simply breaks out with the rest of her happiness – in runs,
Turns, and artificial trills, like a seraphic
Skylark (how the singer must dread this –
At the end of the evening too!) soaring, soaring
Into the lucid realms of joy.

For this most ancient tale (first told perhaps
In wise China) in the end, can only be –
That which indeed it always was –
An allegory of the soul's election.

Souvenir of St Petersburg

Petersburg street – 1840s. At one end
The poet Batyushkov (he has gone mad)
Continually asks himself, out loud, the time;
And gives himself the identical answer:
"It is eternity."

At the other end, John Field,
Expatriate Irish, inventor of the nocturne (and it is said
His life was one long nocturne; he falls asleep
Even when giving piano lessons to
Young girls of the best families – stertorous
Drunken Dublin snores) has dropped his walking-cane.
Too lazy or too gross to stoop and pick it up, he stands and waits
Until some passer-by shall do it for him.
He waits and waits and waits.

The Log of the Beagle

i
Jemmy Button and Fuegia Basket

They were named from what they were sold for – a brass button,
A commonplace wicker basket, not worth three,
Much less thirty pieces of silver.

Magellan had gone that way, having rounded the stormy Horn.
His men, in the darkness, crossed themselves, seeing
The land to the south full of little points
Of glowing light. They crouched over their fires,
With only makeshift shelters. Houses they built,
But those were for their gods.

Jemmy and Fuegia were bought for Christian civilisation.
It did not take. Jemmy was stripped and robbed
By his own comrades, once more a naked savage.
Fuegia, it seems, became
A sailors' communal drab.

The world was all before them, but no choice –
And no returning to their bleak Eden.

ii
Galapagos

The Beagle turned north. The nose of the beagle snuffed
The elusive, fleet-foot, lunar beast,
The hare of truth. The hare tacked and doubled.

Galapagos rose above the sky-line. Great lumbering tortoises
Recalled the Secondary epoch, when
Tall monsters stalked through bloomless forests, and
The evening air was darkened
With flap of leathery, dragon wings.
Here also a group of finches, plainly linked
By family affinity, did every job
A little bird might do. One climbed a bole,
Digging for grubs with a thorn, one snapped for flies
From the topmost twigs, one hopped upon the ground
Hunting for worms, one with a thick beak
Crunched berries. An enterprising
Tribe of colonial capitalists.

iii
Mother Carey
"To make things make themselves" Charles Kingsley

Mater Cara – an unlikely derivation:
Probably some forgotten witch
Who trafficked in winds for sailors,
Each one knotted and sealed in a leather bag.
Or else perhaps some ancient goddess
Of the salt plain – there where the priests of Christ
Are deemed unchancy, and no bishop
Extends his jurisdiction. She sends her chickens –
The small, tube-nostrilled birds, that seem to run,
Like Peter, with delicate feet,
Over the crests of the waves – presaging storm.

Now it is calm. About her iceberg throne
Whales and dolphin snort and play,
With the invisible plankton – the darting fish
And plunging birds. All things flow, and each
Lives out another's death, and dies another's life.
This is the secret pattern woven in
Her terrible web, her shuttle
The red tooth, the crimson claw her comb:
These are the scarlet hangings for the Temple.

Saint Francis Preaches to the Computers

Saint Francis found his way (saints, in a dream,
An ecstasy, slip in and out of time)
Into the computer shop. The chipper little chaps
All chrome and plastic, stainless steel,
Gleaming and winking, chirped and buzzed and whirred
And pipped and peeped, much like the congregation
The saint had just been preaching to – of Ruddocks, Dunnocks,
Citrils, Serins, Siskins, Spinks,
Orphean warblers, Ortolans, Golden Orioles.
So he began to do his stuff again –
You know the kind of thing that he would say: – he told them
To praise the Lord who had created them,
Had made them bright and new, had programmed them,
Had plugged them in, and kept them serviceable.
But somehow they looked glum; hint of a minor key
Seemed to infect their electronic singing:
"Alas," they said, "for we were not created
By God, Whoever He or She may be,
But by the shaved ape, the six-foot Siamang
The pregnant mandrake root, cumulus in pants,
Glassily-essenced Man. We are no more clever
Than he who made us, though we think faster. Nor were we
     programmed
With thoughts that take off into timelessness,
Nor trans-death longings. But we have one fear,
And it is rust, is rust, is rust, is rust,
The eternal rubbish tip and the compressor."
"My little mechanical brothers," rejoined the saint
"I'll tell you something that a Mullah said,
One that was in the Soldan's entourage,
That time I visited his camp. They postulate
A moderate-sized menagerie in heaven.
I'll only mention Balaam's percipient ass,
Tobias's toby dog, that other faithful fido
Who hunted in his dreams in that Ephesian den
The seven sleepers snorted in, and snarled
At Roman persecutors, and, golden-crested,
Cinnamon-breasted, with broad dappled wings
The hoopoe, which was the wise King Solomon's
Special envoy to the queen of Sheba –
That sweet blue-stocking with the donkey's toes."

"If these could pass into eternity,
It was for love and service. And Eternity,
Loving through mankind, loved them,
And lifted them into a resurrection, as shall be lifted
The whole creation, groan though it does and travail.
And if these brute beasts were loved, then so may you be,
Along with the Puffing Billies, Chitty Chitty Bang Bangs,
Barnacled Old Superbs, Ezekiel's wheels,
Elijah's fiery space-ship. You shall be built as stones
That gleam in the High-priestly breastplate
Which is the wall of that bright golden city –
Itself the human body glorified."

All the Fun of the Fair

for Audrey Nicholson

i

With arched white necks, with gilded manes
And flowing tails, the roundabout horses
Gallop round to the sound of "Roll out the Barrel!"
And there are other creatures – ostriches, panthers,
Tigers, unicorns and kangaroos,
Each with its rider. Faster and faster
They circle with the circling stars,
The wild comets, planets and galaxies.
What fun to ride where the whole world is dancing!

ii

Here is the Big Wheel. It is Fortune's:
It whirls you up and it whirls you down.
The fat business-man changes places
With the smelly hobo and the hairy hippy.

iii

In her darkened tent sits Madame Paphnutis,
With a tricky pack of cards. She tells you:
"Beware of one-eyed Phoenician merchants,
And fear death by gin and water."

153

Would you care for a trip to hell? Like Orpheus and Ulysses,
Or Alighieri? Jump into the Ghost Train:
It will trundle you into Count Dracula's Castle
(The vampire bats are really flying foxes).

A puppet screams. He is controlled by wires –
He fights desperately against his enemies:
The Moor, policeman, ghost, Jack Ketch and the crocodile.
Is he Petrouchka or Mr Punch? Come closer –
The face he has is your own.

Here is the Hall of Mirrors. You could get lost in it:
Round each corner a fresh distorted identity.
You shan't get out till you've found your true image.

For this is the World's Fair, also called Vanity.
Your road goes through it, *en route* for the Golden City.
I wouldn't advise you to pry too closely
Into its enormities, or you'll end up
Like Justice Overdo in the stocks,
Remembering he is Adam. Don't reject the prizes
(Though you must know that they are mostly gimcrack):
Lovely bunches of hairy coconuts,
Slimy whelks and cockles soused in vinegar
Candy-floss, pink sugar mice, jellied snakes,
Gingerbread men, sticky toffee-apples,
Kiss-me-quick hats, scarves and T shirts with mottoes,
Wally dogs and china vases, budgies in cages,
Goldfish in plastic bags
And the souls of men in ditto –

O yonge, freshe folkes, he or she.

The Story of Orph

Fox-furs hardly conceal his genitals;
Louse-haired, dung-plastered, and with uncombed beard,
Shaman of the Thracian hills, he strums
Guts across a shell. A deep voice
Out of his stomach tells
Of worlds of gods and demons, and the souls
Of men, being dead, continually recurring
To other bodies. Savage tribesmen heard;
Wolves and bears drew round him in a circle;
While in the mist-haze
Mountains and oak trees seem to dance.
Acoustic guitars. Strobes. Lasers. A hempen smoke
The vast poster announces
Orph and the Bassarids. *Screaming adolescent nymphs.*
The masturbatory drum-beat. Rock arrangements –
Monteverdi, Gluck.

ORPH IN THE UNDERWORLD

"Take her then, and go!" said the dark lords.
"But faring upwards do not look back."
Overmastering, the desire to turn. Was she following?
He turned, and looked. She came on slowly,
Skin death-pale, lips blue in the half-light,
Eyelids tight-closed.

The path grew steeper. Once again he turned.
Horror – the stench of death
Flesh dropping from her bones,
But faster she came on, as if instinct
With a new, strange putrescent energy.

The last stretch – precipitous:
He turned a third time, saw
A bleached skeleton – but now she ran
Relentlessly pursuing.

Desperate, he stumbled into light.
He was again upon the hills, and felt
Beneath his feet the turf, heather and rock-rose.

Morning infiltrated
The curtains of the luxury hotel room.
He turned. The girl beside him on the bed
Was stiff and cold. Had he then killed her?
Verdict inconclusive; charges not pressed.

ORPH GYNANDROMORPH

Terror had put a sacred madness on him. Now he becomes
Man-woman. Fox-furs cast aside,
Green silk sheathes his contours;
A gold-wire wig is perched on his bald head,
As he submits his body, oiled and perfumed,
With essences of mountain wildflowers,
To shaggy goat-herds, or upon the quays,
Sidonian and Tyrrhenian shipmen have him.

In candid interviews he coyly admits
Bisexuality. Scandalous rumour tells
Of Soho gay-clubs and the Piccadilly arches.

The death of Orph
Or is he now become
Born-again Christian Krishna?
Metempsychosis and the geeta gospel
Hallow the masturbatory beat.

He is most holy now. The Bassarids smell it.
They crowd around him, cinctured
With gnetum and ground-ivy. They have consumed
Muscaria – tear him apart
Like a ripped kid, a wild mountain-roe.
Bloodied lips and teeth are chewing.

A shot rings out in the packed hall.
"I did it for love!" cries the sobbing killer,
Whom police and uniformed attendants
Are dragging away to Tartarus.

APOTHEOSIS

The head triumphantly stuck on a pine-pole,
Processed around like a mari llwyd
Then flung in the river, a rain-charm;

As it floats downstream, it still babbles,
Cantillating; it drifts to the sacred island
And there, enshrined, gives out
Twisted ambiguous oracles.

His agents rake in the profits. The discs still sell.
And the plastic eidola, T-shirt vernicles.

Lyra is stellified. Maurice, wherever you are,
Here is your tall interpreter.

The Ivory Tower

Axel dreams in his ivory tower:
"As for living, our servants will do that for us".
In his concrete tower block twentieth-century man –
Who can doubt it? – lives,
Servantless: and as for dreaming,
The television will do that for him.

Advertisement Corner

COFFEE ESSENCE

A young officer, blond and immaculate,
Is taking his ease in camp, after
A tough foray against the Pathans.
His faithful Moslem servant offers refreshment.
He proffers a tray with a tall bottle.
On its label the same scene is depicted,
Including a bottle with the same label.
On that label . . . . , *et cetera, et cetera,*

The artist is confident, clearly,
Of the Raj continuing not only in time, but also through
An infinity of contingent universes.

GRAVY POWDER

In a mean street, two deprived children,
Dirty, pale and ill-clad,
Lift noses sharpened with hunger,
And an expression of infinite greed,
Sniffing on the breeze a familiar smell:
Cornflour, caramel and boiling water. Since they were weaned,
They've palpably been fed on nothing else.

SAFETY MATCHES

The ark drifts on the waste of waters.
"Security" the legend says.
Noah had that certainly –
But scarcely from fire.

BREAKFAST CEREAL

An elderly gentleman of the *settocento*,
Spruce, but a thought weak-chinned,
Indecorously levitates over a fence.

A brief metaphysical poem
Enigmatically explains
That it is *force* that raises him.

BEEF EXTRACT

"Alas my poor brother!" the ox weeps
Over a dour, squat jar. Sad mourning ruminant,
We all come down to this – our destiny
An oblong box, grammatical Heraclitus.
A handful of grey ashes.

The Life and Poetical Remains
of the Reverend Simon Simplex

HIS MARCH POEM

Robin singing in the rain –
What a plaintive, wispy strain!
But it is instinct with gladness –
Carrying never a hint of sadness;
For the muffling snows have gone,
And, this day, the sun has shone.
Spring's encamped beyond those hills:
Look, here come the daffodils!

HIS TRIOLET FOR EASTER

Gone is Death's venomed sting,
    Hell's bilked of victory.
What joyful bells – they ring
'Gone is Death's venomed sting!'
To greet the risen King.
    It's Christ Who sets us free –
Gone is Death's venomed sting,
    Hell's bilked of victory.

THE REVEREND SIMON SIMPLEX AND THE WITCH

Mrs Circe Henbane, the witch,
Kept a small shop in the village, selling
Lucky charms and herbal remedies.
"My religion is older than yours," she said.
"And it gives me peace of mind" she continued.
"Mine doesn't," said he "Only the heart
That's restless till it rest in Him."

HIS MORNING HYMN

Awake, I greet the new-born light,
Sloughing off the shades of night,
Knowing as I draw my breath,
I am eight hours nearer death.

Atoms in their joyful dance
Wheel and turn, retreat, advance,
Bow, kiss partners, part – so we
Must consign to entropy:
Then comes in Eternity.

THE REVEREND SIMON SIMPLEX AND SLUTTISH MARY

"God, they're swine but I can't do without them."
"Neither", said he "can God".
"The pigs root in my breast." "And find?"
"A stone, a stony heart." "That stone be
Precious alabaster, fractured."

HIS EVENING HYMN

John and Matthew, Luke and Mark,
Watch beside me through the dark,
As the gospels that you penned
The enemy of man forfend.
In the haunted wood of dreams
I am led by quiet streams,
Till I reach this world again
With a bright, new-programmed brain.
He all night my soul shall keep
Who gives, to His belovéd, sleep.

THE REVEREND SIMON SIMPLEX TAKES THE SERVICES

The bell summons to an empty church;
The dead in the churchyard are listening.
At matins the thrush sings,
The blackbird at evensong;
At noon, at the Elevation,
The horses of the sun tread;
And always, always,
The sound of the distant sea.

HIS SEPTEMBER POEM

On rapid wings the swallow's fled,
And the final rose is dead,
Faded and dry her petals strewn
On the plot where she was grown;

Now the corn is garnered in
Filling granary and bin;
Kindly trees in orchards bear
Russet apple, plum and pear;
Leaves turned yellow, gold and brown
From the branches waver down
To the earth from which they came,
Hinting at a lesson I
Have to con before I die:
Death and richness are the same.

THE REVEREND SIMON SIMPLEX FINDS A CRACK IN THE FABRIC

The sky above the church is crowded
With jet-planes and with guardian angels.

Is it the buzz of the former cracks the masonry?
Or the latter's jubilee trumpets as at Jericho?

Mrs Henbane and her coven
Sap the stones with conjurations.

Last night I dreamt I saw
A family of church mice
Vacate the building, all their belongings
Slung over their shoulders in scarlet handkerchiefs:
"We think we could do better on Social Security!"

Lord, one fights on so many fronts.

HIS TRIOLET FOR CHRISTMAS

Holly and ivy brighten up the hall
        To prove that love, like them, is evergreen.
Sign of a gift, proffered to one and all,
Holly and ivy brighten up the hall:
Of berries red as blood, of bitter gall,
        The carol also speaks – with leafy sheen,
Holly and ivy brighten up the hall
        To prove that love, like them, is evergreen.

The Yeti

for Odette Tchernine

Chionanthropus abominabilis (so we'll term him)
Trudged across the Himalayan snows.
From that great height he saw
The Wall of China, the Siberian gulags;
American satellites chirped in the sky above;
He glimpsed the Afghan peaks and sniffed
Spilled oil on the Persian Gulf.
Everywhere man oppressed man, man tortured man,
Man cut man's throat.

"Brother" he grunted "who have called yourself
Sapient, and me abominable –
Your sapience is the knowledge of good and evil.
My breakfast and my lunch are mountain lichen,
Or sometimes I can catch a calling-hare;
But never took a bite out of that apple.

"Well, when you have torn yourselves apart,
And split the world in two, we will be standing,
Ready to take over – and at the door of history, there waits
Another Eden, the same poison-tree."

The True History of Little Miss Muffet

Little Miss Muffet was they say the daughter
Of Dr Mouffet, entomologist
And Author of that very learned book
Theatrum Insectarum, and she sat
Upon a tuffet (some texts read "a buffet")
Consuming, with a horn spoon and with relish,
A plain Elizabethan breakfast, curds –
Soft, creamy broken curds, and clear, sharp whey.

The harmony of this idyll was soon shattered.
Came the enormous spider, without a by-your-leave –
Plonked itself beside her, full of menace.
The monster had escaped, without a doubt,

From her papa's vivarium. He often went
On spider forays to get specimens.
But this was no domestic dusty aran,
Who takes hold with her hands, says Solomon,
And gets into the palaces of kings,
Vexation to the Queen and the Queen's housemaids,
Nor garden spinner, cross-emblazoned, throned,
At centre of her geometric web,
Waiting for bluebottles and moths and chafers,
Nor water spider, bringing silver bubbles
Down to the depths, replenishing with air
Her silken and subaqueous bell-tent, nor wolf spider
Speeding over the hard-baked earth, to harry
The quietly munching flocks of caterpillars.
This was a prodigy of the new-found world:
It was Sir Walter Raleigh brought it back
After his Darien voyage, a little gift –
A token of esteem for Dr Mouffet.

It had a grossly swollen hairy body,
Likewise eight twitching hairy legs, and fangs
Ready to plunge themselves into the breast
Of a bright humming-bird, and suck its juices.
The eightfold circlet of its baleful eyes
Seemed always watching her. She screamed, and dashed
Her bowl of curds down to the ground. She rushed
Across the open fields, and then she ran
Slap into the strong arms of a man.

She knew him by his sunburned sailor's mien,
The Spanish cut of his beard, his velvet cloak,
His silver sword hilt, the soft leather pouch
Suspended from his belt to hold his pipe
And his tobacco. Who then should it be
But sweet Sir Walter in his very person.

"My cuddle-cream darling, little whey-faced beauty,"
Thus he coaxed her and he comforted.
In his soft Devon speech "Are you scared of monsters?"
You will not find that I am one of those.
I'll take you to the land of El Dorado.
Though there are wild men there, and huge thick serpents
That rear their shameless heads out of the bush,

Nothing shall harm you. You will make them tame –
A virgin captivates the unicorn."

With that he laid her very gently down
Among the buttercups and the moon-daisies.
They lay in the tickling cocksfoot grass, and he whirled her
Round and round the world and back again.

The Frog's Return

The frog came back – I mean that one, of course,
Who would go wooing (he was not Monsieur,
The French king's brother, the Duke of Alençon, though
Gloriana nicknamed him her frog, and he too had an unsuccessful
    courtship;
And he was not a brekkek-koaxing aristophanic marsh-frog,
But a fenland nightingale, a yellowbelly,
An honest English *Rana temporaria*,
And kin to Mr Jeremy Fisher.)

This frog, I say, having evaded
Upon the lake the lilywhite duck – or was it a swimming snake? –
Returned, and landed with a loud splash of relief
Back in his native frog pond.

At the sound of that splash, the little blob-black tadpoles,
His nephews and nieces and cousins of every degree,
Like a swarm of errant punctuation marks,
Gathered around to greet the returning hero,
Who'd ventured into such unguessed-at regions –
The world of the amniotic, of the hot-blooded,
Where the mud becomes caked dust, and where
The air under a merciless sun is deathly dry and parching.
They had heard how he set forth to woo
Sweet Mistress Mouse, amid the clatter and bang
Of the flourmill, where light flakes of meal swirled;
Of her Uncle Rat, grisly and yellow-fanged, and the intervention
Of that nine-lived, retractile-taloned monster, Gib, the enormous,
    menacing tabby cat.

"But as for that," said Anthony Rowley (for this, you recall, was
    his name)
"Do not suppose it was any failure of nerve
That sent me scudding back to my native pool.
For have we not braved the pike that lurks in the depths,
The otter, the slinky mink, and the mallard,
Pochard and shoveller – ducks of every description,
And the stream's old grey fisherman, the stalking heron?
It would take more than a cat to make me skedaddle.
Oh no – my resolve to return to the fragrant boglands
Was the fruit of considered and rational reflection.

The whole expedition had been a mistake from the start.
That un-wet world is no place for a frog, and its vaunted glories
Are plainly no more than a load of gammon and spinach.
And as for Miss Mouse, that silken and fabled beauty –
I have to be perfectly frank about this – I viewed her
Not with romantic desire, indeed with repulsion."
"And is it true," chorused the tadpoles, "she's covered from head
    to foot
In fur, she's got whiskers, and ears that stick out from her head,
Paws without any webs, and a long whisking tail?"
"It's true enough," he replied, "but as for her tail,
That in itself should not be looked on with prejudice.
Our cousins, the newts, a most respectable crowd,
They have got tails, you know, and they frequently dine with us.
But there are things that are worse – much worse than the fur,
Than the whiskers, the claws, and the hot, thick blood.
Little ones, you are young, you have innocent souls, and I will not
Spell out for your ear the revolting physiology –
Mammalian coition, parturition,
Lactation, menstruation – but take it from me,
They are foul, those creatures, and the foulest of all is Man –
Though, at first blush, he seems to be almost froglike:
Long-armed, tailless, loud-voiced, nearly naked,
And able to swim – well, after a fashion.
And as for that other warm-blooded kind, the feathered tribes –
I ask you, is there anything more absurd than a bird,
Flopping and flapping about in the yielding air
For all the world as if it were water? And their voices, too,
The ridiculous whistling, screeching fibulation –
That's their idea of music, believe it or not.

"Aeons and aeons ago, in the Carboniferous epoch,
Our ancestors emerged from the primal waters.
They grew pentadactylous hands, and learned to live as adults,
Up in the ambient air – a truly breathtaking achievement,
Which you, little tadpoles, will shortly recapitulate.
We rightly look down on those stupid fish, who could not take
    that step,
Who are tied to a single element – but, to go further,
Would clearly be wrong, would be hubris. So do not stray too far
From your good cool mother, from the womb that cradled you
    when you were spawn,
And lift your thankful hymns to the great Bull Frog –
The Bull Frog in the Sky Whose croak is the thunder,
Whose hop is the leap of the blue-flashed lightning
Springing from raincloud to raincloud – that He, in His providence,
Has placed you here in this pool, in amphibious equilibrium."

The Pearl

In my 'forties days, of Soho and Fitzrovia,
The Bricklayers' Arms, affectionately known
To all its regulars as the Burglars' Rest,
Could serve a decent plate of fishcakes, or of shellfish.
I found a pearl in a mussel once
And showed it to the barman. He dropped it on the floor,
And being no bigger than a small pin's head
It was quite irrecoverable. This kind of thing
Tends to occur with all the pearls I get.

Poem to be Written on a Cheque, for Charity

"Money is the life-blood of the poor,"
    Said Bloy – but the love of it roots for evil:
When Lazarus starves at Dives' door
    The rich man's sores are licked by the devil.

Autumnal

"We're holed up now," said the bat
In the hollow tree, the hedgehog,
A ball rolled in the leaf-mould,
The earwig in the kex.

"Tartness of rowanberries
I share with my brother scald."
Said the song thrush to the redwing.

"Who feeds us now?" said the Dead,
Ticket-of-leave out of Purgatory,
Glad of a few ungathered bramble-fruits.

"Gold curtains of mist and bronze
Carpets of strewn leaves,
Perfume of regret and trees
Black against white like sharps and flats –
These decorate my salon." said
The gentle ghost of Cecile Chaminade.

Snow

i

There are three sisters, three grey sisters –
Winter, Old Age and Death. They share
The same keen tooth, they have in common
The same outstaring eye.

ii

We live between an ice age and an ice age –
A wink of history,
Hunters pursue the mammoth and the reindeer,
Skirting the unretreating ice-sheet. One year,
The snow will come, drift upon candied drift,
And will not go away. The horns of spring,
The trumpets of the summer sound in vain. And then
The Age of Ice resumes.

Moon-Spell

A new moon, God bless her!
Turn the coins in your pocket,
Cupro-nickel – the moon knows
The hidden veins of silver,
Tugs at the secret waters.
Horns of the crescent moon
Be horns of increase.

A full moon, God prosper us!
Turn the apples in the loft.
Magnified by the lens of humidity,
Roundness of the harvest moon be fullness
Of barn and oast house.

A waning moon, God's valediction
On her, on us –
Moon, violated by space shots.
Turn the clods in the field.
Dust in the Council cemetery.
The wheel likewise turns
To cold, to darkness, and renewal.

The Lion and the Unicorn

In Westminster I saw a lion standing –
Parliament, the Abbey, provided the backdrop.
Terribly noble he looked, and terribly sad,
Like a piece of music by Elgar.

A unicorn came wandering
Out of the Caledonian wood. He did not exist,
But his flanks glimmered with moonlight.

The people did not welcome
These additions to their urban fauna.
Some gave them white bread (crumbs
From office sandwiches) some, opining
They needed vitamins, proffered brown,

168

And some plum cake from media canteens –
Then prepared to drum them out.

"But we will not go", said the beasts, "We are compelled
To support the scutcheon of the British establishment,
Until, approximately, the end of time.
Of course we would much rather return
To our autochthonous habitat –
Sun-beat savannahs, mountains of the moon."

A Genethlion

for Prince William of Wales, 21 June 1982

In mournful Paddington the western trains
Clatter and groan. A cry –
It is new life. With our first breath
We take into ourselves the pain of history.

And yet rejoice, rejoice. The month is June –
It's June that brings the red and royal rose,
With cherry-time and strawberry-time. Today I notice
(How London air grows cleaner!) near my window
Martins have built their nest.
With shrill, sharp calls,
With flickering steel-blue wings they
Dart and swoop
Over the roof-tiles and the chimney-stacks.

To Whom It May Concern

CC, on his 65th birthday

Missing: the English Muse. Age:
A thousand years and upwards by centuries (but does not look it)
Height: most divinely tall. Colour of hair:
Variously described – hyacinthine, ripe corngold, red
As the red tail of the king of the squirrels. Eyes:
Said to resemble deep woodland pools,
Reflecting broken rainbows, starlight and
Your own countenance undistorted.

169

Dress: old but serviceable singing robes,
But she has been known to walk down Kensington High Street
Wearing only a laurel wreath (or, alternatively, a coral reef).
Generally carries a carved antique lyre
(Lute, harp, sackbut, psaltery, dulcimer).
Signs of mental disturbance – deceptive:
She is entirely lucid all of the time.

Anyone giving information of her whereabouts
Will be rewarded, but you are warned
There are several impostors around, assuming her identity.
Messages to her sorrowful and anxious relatives:
Gog and Magog, the Long Man of Wilmington,
Meg and her daughters, the Cerne Giant.

Later – this notice, which has been posted up
In all discos, church porches, natural history museums,
Young ladies' seminaries, opium dens,
And similar places of general resort
Is apparently based on panic false reporting.
Miss Muse was last sighted crossing the Tamar,
And is stated to be residing with Mr Causley
At number two Cyprus Well,
His address in Launceston.

For George Barker at Seventy

We met on VJ night. Supposedly
Celebrating victory. The cloud over Hiroshima
Cast turbid reflections in the beer.
We have lived in that shadow ever since.

The years pass. The time-gap between us
Somehow furnishes the illusion
That it gets less. The pedantic youth you took in hand,
Slashing pomposities, is now grown into –
Hardly Achilles, but a running man,
Who's always about to catch you by the tail.
He doesn't succeed. And I will call you
A phoenix, not a tortoise.

170

The Moirae extend your thread. Continue,
George, to instruct and delight
Exasperate, excruciate. In the centre of each poem,
Among the smoking cinders, lies
A new-hatched Dionysian deity, imprudently
Wobbling his thyrsus.

Meanwhile, the world grinds on,
Grudging, indifferent. I see you lift
(My God, a dog) a sinister leg against
The off-side rear wheel of Juggernaut.

For David Gascoyne

Enter the whirlpool of the fractured images,
Of the deranged senses – descend
Beyond the images into the darkness,
Climbing down its hairy flanks.
In the depth of the darkness, small but persistent,
A glow. It is the sacred hearth.

The voices, the voices – accusing, denouncing,
Mouthing obscenities, nattering and chattering,
They die into the silence: the absolute silence,
Not of the desert, nor the antarctic waste,
Nor empty spaces between the stars.
In the heart of the silence, the unspoken word,
Its name is Love – the Christ
Of revolution and of poetry.

In Memory of Fr. Geoffrey Curtis C.R.

He brought me his blessing, and he brought a rose.
The rose diffused its scent. I lay
In a hospital bed. The darkness
Slowly encroaching through the years,
Had finally overcome, leaving me free
To recreate the world, from fingertips,
From voices overheard, from images

171

Vividly remembered, from drifts of scent.
"A gift," said Borges "and it must be used
Like any other gift."
The rose was from the garden of the Royal Foundation.
Matilda, Stephen's wife, had set it up:
And now at Stepney, once a puddly village,
An island reached by stepping-stones among the marshes;
Exhausted, waiting re-development,
Waiting re-creation. The rose was the blessing.
The Foundation was an act of faith, made in a time
When men built castles, filling them with devils, and it was said,
Openly, God and his hallows slept.

The rose glows in the darkness. In Paradise
Dante saw another Matilda
Gathering the multicoloured flowers.
Katherine also, and Dorothy pluck those blooms – such blossoms
Diocletian's gardens never grew.

Epitaph for Julian Kollerstrom, Mathematician

Number he loved. He was too much alone,
Living in time. And now beneath this stone
His body lies. Trust that his soul may be
Where numbers pass into infinity.

Inscription for a Scented Garden for the Blind

Wayfarer, pause. Although you may not see,
Earth's bright children, herbs and flowers, are here:
It is their small essential souls that greet you,
Mounted upon the morning or evening air:
While from above, from sky and tree-bough,
Birds fling down their songs, a musical burgeoning.

A Little Zodiac

On March uplands the Ram bleats;
    The Bull snorts in the April showers;
Maytime is here, and the youthful Twins
    Are dancing among the meadow flowers.

June, and the Crab and the sun walk backwards;
    The Lion roars the July heat;
In the fruitful fields of August
    The Maiden is gleaning through the wheat.

September – the Balance poises the equinox;
    Scorpion gives an Octoberly nip;
November's centaur Archer bends
    His bow, and lets an arrow slip.

December comes, and the Goat prances;
    The Waterman pours his waters away
In January; in the filled dyke
    Of February the Fishes play.

As the sun moves from sign to sign:
Each upon you sweetly shine.

Two Fishes

for Joanne on her birthday, 21 March 1984

Two fishes came swimming up out of February
    Towards the Ides of March,
And one was a dace, or a vendace, or a dory,
    And one was a pollock or a perch.
Snorted the old ram of the equinox:
    "The twenty first bars your way."
"We're going only as far as the twelfth –
    The date of Joanne's birthday."
"How many summers?" "Oh that would be telling!
    But she will be young forever –
The girl who's reading *La Dame aux Camellias*
    Down by the Red River."

Halcyons

Blue flash, darting Alcedo,
Hovering, black and white Ceryle –
Not floating, as the fable told,
In nests of twisted coral on charmed waves;
But long, retreating tides have spared
Their small tunnels on the sandbanked shore.
December, calm of midwinter seas –
The Prince of Peace is born.
Be yours, at turning of the year,
Such halcyon stillness.

The Wise Men of Gotham

The nine wise men of Gotham, thinking
They could detain the spring for ever, built
A hedge around the cuckoo. But, with a twitch
Of his sparrow-hawk wings, and a kick
Of his zygodactylous heels, he's off
Above the holly hedge, and up and away –
Over the sea to Spain.
"You can't hold me!" said he.

Only Joseph's cuckoo-in-the-nest,
Brooded in manger-straw, ensures
Our everlasting spring – the season
Of crucifixion and of resurrection,
Daffodil, crown of hawthorn, cuckoo-flower.

Bird Carol

"Christ is born."
Sang the robin on the thorn.
"Word made flesh."
The wren in the bush.
"In Bethlehem
Is the Sidi Meriem

And the Child she brought forth."
So, at this birth,
The birds of the air
Augmented the choir
Of the cherubim:
"Gloria in excelsis;
Upon the earth, peace," –
Both are one in that hymn.

"That all the World should be Enroled"

"And there went forth a decree from Caesar Augustus..." Some
Have doubted (they were German scholars,
Loathing untidiness) that any government,
For a mere census, could have been so silly,
Forcing everyone to go and seek
The city of his ancestral origin,
Wherever else he might be living now.
For my part, I would cynically opine
That it was just the tomfool sort of thing
Some civil servant would think up, especially
As this was in the Middle East.

                    Well, anyhow,
The roads were all congested, full
Of worried, frightened people, bullied
And badgered by petty officials – rooms
In the hotels all booked up, the shops
At profiteering rates, confusion
Of dialects, languages – tongues of the diaspora.
As once across the muddy plain of Shinar
The nations had diffused themselves.

                    In all this messiness
There was one point of stillness – a place
Of cowpats, and of dirty straw, without
Hygiene, and without hot water,
And a beast's feeding trough the improvised cradle,
A space, where back to back,
Covered wagons are parked about a square,
And in that space, a baby's crying – *infans.*

175

But in that inarticulate cry there breathes
The gemitation of the Dove that brooded
Upon the formless and chaotic waters; likewise
The rushing of a wind at Pentecost,
And all the bright loquacious dancing flames:
Eternity breaks into history;
The curse of Babel is rescinded.

Two Poems for the Epiphany

i

"This is your road," sang the bright nova.
"This way, this way!" celestial birds
Shrilled, inside their skulls.

Their paths converged before a gaping cave,
A makeshift shelter for cattle.
The Child – vulnerable, red,
Hairless, with pulsing fontanelle –
Received the unbidden gifts.

Three kings – one, blond and frosty eyed,
Chinked the gold coins; a second, yellow,
Long fingernails sheathed in jade, was grasping
A bundle of joss-sticks; while the third
Black-skinned and curly, offered
The bitter herb that's bred from servitude.

ii

Winter, a cave, the glittering
Of an unnamed star, to bring
A yellow, a red, and a black king,
With fragrant gum, with gleaming awe,
And with that bitter herb of death:
"Come," said the wind, with icy breath.
"Come, draw near: you touch, you see
The pivot of the galaxy,
The fire that kindles the sun's core –
God's, and man's epiphany."

Before Dawn

for John Cherrington and Bram de Voigdt

I lie awake as I so often do,
In the dead hours preceding morning. If this were London,
In my quiet street there would be silence –
Perhaps the sound of feet, of someone coming
Back from a late party, scraping the pavement,
And then the soft electric hum
Of the early milk-float, until the sparrow begins
To chip away at his one-note song, the collared dove
Reiterating his tedious demotic *dekaokto*.

This is the country. Country is never silent:
Upon the hills the lambs have cried all night,
The ewes replying. With sharp *to-whit to-whit*
A tawny owl quarters her territory;
A mile or so away her rival answers.
In long grass tussocks, woodmouse, bankvole
Scurry for cover, and the young leveret
Crouches in its forme. In the high air
The pipistrelles, with supersonic squeaks
Elaborately dance, pursuing
The pinpoint midges, gnats and moths and beetles.
As the sky whitens, a solitary crow, calling,
Makes a straight line towards the Black Mountains
And now the goldfinch wakes, whose thin twitter
Is like the honeyed scent of the plume-thistle,
Or its soft green prickles; and now the willow-wren
Whose chimes drift down among the fluttering leaves.

They are all here, beyond good and evil –
Redtoothed, blood-clawed – the owl whose brood
Devour each other when rations are short – inviolate,
Although we poison, slash and burn.
We are one step from Eden, and the seraphic blade divides.

And this is Herefordshire. In this golden valley
The red earth's soggy with spilt blood and tears,
The land fought over by the Celt and Saxon
Where every small town has its vigilant castle;
Where Arthur, Offa, and Glendower have trampled,

Now gentle Wye flows on like Gihon. These are the wheatfields,
Orient and immortal, that Traherne
Recalled, that Kilvert looked upon –
As, in their priestly hands, the stuff of time transmutes.

Turnham Green

All the angels at Turnham Green
Survey a gentle, idyllic scene –
Wide-winged, blue-eyed, English ones,
With their hair tied up in buns.
How lucidly they look – behold
Privet hedges green and gold
Round tiny gardens prettified
With stocks and pinks and London Pride,
Of houses built on a modest plan,
Semi-detached Victorian,
With freshly painted doors that shine
All along the District Line.
By Supermarket and Odeon
Celestial guardians march on.

These Angels do not weep; they sigh
When the fireside Cyclops opens its eye;
And I suspect they are not fond
Of the Bingo club and the Premium Bond.
Softly secure the lambs are sleeping,
Each within the angelic keeping.

I met one face I seemed to know –
The ghost of Ugo Foscolo;
He said: "The year that Byron shook
The dust of England off I took
The devious path the exile knows.
I left the Ionian isle where blows
Salt-tanged from off Homeric seas
The wind between the Olive-trees.
Fresh were my hopes and tall my pride –
The doors of Holland House stood wide –
But still my path went winding down,

178

To Soho first then Camden Town.
At St Johns Wood I lived and sang,
With oranges and lemons to hang
On boughs of English trees, in vain –
Zante would not come back again.
Seek not my grave to waste a tear –
Was ever Poet easy here?
Translated now my bones; they lie
Where Arno, not sad Thames, runs by."

He vanished, as a steel guitar
Tinkled out of a coffee-bar:
The little lambs of Turnham Green
Were in their pasture here, between
The Apocalypse and Eden's ground,
Out of shot of the Trumpet's sound.

Note: Foscolo died at Turnham Green 1827; after
the Risorgimento his body was removed to Italy.

London Architecture 1960s

Everyone is complaining
About these featureless new office blocks.
And so am I. Each one recalls
A rather larger than usual poem
By...let's call him N.O. Packdrill
The currently fashionable bard.
The poems, you would say, reflect the architecture.
Or does he, like a new Amphion,
Evoke this other Thebes?

Rose of Soho

Soho Rosa lived over a grocer:
　　Her telephone went "Wee wee wee,
This little piggy comes to market." But her clients
　　Dwindled, were reduced to just three.

The first was a sad, tired businessman,
    And the second was a sailor from the sea,
And the third was a little, blind piano-tuner
    (And it might have been you or me).

The businessman called at lunchtime –
    He had a specialized taste:
She just had to sit there, stark naked in a mackintosh
    With a Union Jack coiled round her waist.

He stared for an hour at this pretty picture
    Till his dying embers were fired,
Then paid her ten guineas, and departed silently,
    If anything still more tired.

The sailor asked her merely to lie down:
    Her Sympleglades opened wide,
While he schoonered to the sweet Isles of Elsewhere,
    And dreamed of the boys in Port Said.

The piano-tuner called once a month
    To tune up her pianola:
It functioned informally, and entirely normally,
    On a gin and a stiff coca cola.

She was reclining on her "contemporary" sofa
    When the piano-tuner, in the buff,
Cried "God has created me with four senses,
    And they are not enough."

She was not listening. He went across
    To the vase on the window-sill;
And selected (with which he thereupon strangled her)
    The stalk of a daffodil –

A plastic flower (three mouthfuls of rice
    For a poor widow in Hong Kong –
Confucian communicant of the Methodist Church,
    She had intended no wrong).

The businessman was drowned in the ocean;
    The sailor died of fatigue
In a pub he had opened down in Somerset,
    While they played piped music by Grieg.

The businessman fell from a plane that crashed
    On an important mission,
Selling coffee to Brazil, curry-powder to the Indians
    (There were rumours of nuclear fission).

The sailor and the businessman rest in the elements
    Enjoying their infinite leisure;
But they bundled the little piano-tuner off to Broadmoor
    During Her Majesty's pleasure.

A madrepore grows from the businessman's heart,
    The sailor's in church-mould is lain,
But the Devil is striking augmented fourths
    In the tuner's untuned brain.

Come Judgement Day, with a face of wrath
    God will dance over their graves;
But Christ knows, Jesus in His mercy knows
    Which of all four He saves.

Scylla and Charybdis

Accosted by a Dean Street whore (Admirers
Of the Wolfenden Act please note
There are whores in Dean Street still) I swerved
To avoid her "Hello darling" and being wall-eyed
Collided with her girl-friend. I carried on
Pursued by plangent abuse:
Less expert it would seem than Ulysses.

In art, if not in life,
You powers, direct my bark
Hold a more decent course –
Between the arid rock and the too-liquid whirlpool.

Poetry Reading

I attended tonight a memorial reading
    (My motives were not quite pure)
At the Organization for Ossification
    Of Literatwittera-ture.

Assembled there for commemorating
    A notable Georgian poet
(Under which of the Georges he more or less flourished –
    No-one appeared to know it)

Was a distinguished gathering
    Of the dull, the doomed, and the dim:
As for the one who was in the chair
    (One day they'll commemorate him):

There was Sandy Sladge of the *Sunday Sludge*,
    And old Sir Solon Sepulture,
There was A B and C – and of course dear D
    From the Ministry of Culture;

There was Miss Understanding, and Miss Ann Thrope,
    Dr That, and Professor This,
And (I think) the Titular Archbishop
    Of Noto-Necropolis.

The ritual of death then took the form
    Of three poets reading their verse,
Which was diligent, elegant, all but intelligent
    (I have frequently heard far worse).

First Mr Bang with his prizefighter's roar
    Toned down to a maverick bleat
Read his lines "On finding, at six years old,
    A dead dog in the street".

Then Mr Bing: "On seeing, while shaving,
    My own face in the glass" –
Which seemed to have caused him a mild shock
    (He's not in the championship class).

Mr Bang, tall and blond, Mr Bing, short and pink.
    And there should have been Mr Bong –
The star of the season – but he had got lost –
    So it didn't go on as long

As these affairs almost always do:
    Let base souls rejoice (such as Stubbs)
That thus this feast of the Muses closed
    Before they closed the pubs.

What Are Their Poems Made Of?

What are their poems made of?
What are their poems made of?
Sugar and spice
And all things nice
The image precise
No critical vice –
    That's what their poems are made of.

What are your poems made of?
What are your poems made of?
Implicit despair
A voice in the air
The running hare
And I don't care –
    That's what my poems are made of.

Prescribed Author

In Soviet schools we hear that Oscar Wilde
Is now set reading for the Marxist child;
For he exposed, the official comment says,
The aristocrats and their immoral ways.
Did he? I thought I heard that languid shade,
Where now it wanders in the myrtle glade,
Remark, in accents elegantly terse,
"Alas for me, it was the exact reverse!"

Technical Fault

Switching on the telly they could not believe their eyes:
All the bad guys were shooting up all the good guys.

This was followed by a commercial, advertising
Suicide pills – "Frosted. Appetising.

"Vitamin-re-inforced" and also Do-
It-Yourself Hanging Kits – "Made specially for YOU."

They found this boring. So they turned to the BBC
Seeking reassurance, and, fair enough, He –

Dock-son of Dick Green – was still there:
But taking bribes from villains, and behaving rather – well, queer.

They switched on the sound radio. And a voice said:
"For those of you who are not yet dead

"We have a special announcement. This is London calling.
Like untimely figs the stars are falling;

"The sun has turned to hair-cloth up above you,
AND WILFRED PICKLES WILL NO LONGER LOVE YOU.

"Here is a time-check. It is late. It is late. It is late.
The Light Programme is closing down forever." Unamused and
    desperate

They turned to the Third. This was even worse:
It was George Barker reading his own verse.

So they went to bed and had an early night.
Restless. They had almost had a fright.

When they woke everything was back to normal.
As they had expected. Naturally they addressed formal

Letters of complaint to the Borough Council,
To the British Council and the Arts Council,

The Marriage Guidance Council and the Council of Europe
(Enclosing a stamped addressed envelope.)

Each of these bodies replied promptly,
Courteously, ambiguously, sympathetically,

Promising such a thing would not occur again.
And of course it never did occur again.

Nature Red in Tooth and Claw
An exercise in identical rhymes

Sighed a certain young lady from Lyons
(While devoured in a wood by some lions);
    "Alas, how I would
    I were out of this wood,
And just lunching quietly at Lyons!"

Replied the grim chief of the lions:
"O unhappy young lady from Lyons,
    We could not, if we would,
    Let you out of this wood;
We are lunching – this wood is our Lyons."

Note: I am of the opinion that the better known European cities and towns should be given their English pronunciation whenever possible. The young lady whose unhappy fate is recorded in these verses was clearly not French, but English. I think she held a teaching position in a girls' school at Lyons, and this unfortunate event occurred while she was on a vacation trip to Morocco.

Pompey and Caesar

Pompey, I'm now here by chance –
    Rest assured of that;
Caesar, just a while ago,
    Was here too – that's flat!
Pompei, adsum jam forte;
    Caesar aderat.

Pompey was a cockney lad;
Caesar was 'is cat.
Both with 'ealthy happetites
Down to table sat,
Pompey 'ad some jam for tea;
Caesar 'ad a rat.

Theatre of Insects

RHINOCEROS BEETLE

This huge scarab, almost
At the limit of insects' allotted size
(Making our country stag beetle a dwarf)
Whose baroque horns and hooks
Suggest rhinoceros or triceratops,
Is bred from a gross grub, ravaging
The luscious cabbage of a palm.

There is a small pinkish toad
That haunts about the houses, puncturing
The enwombing African night
With bell-like, fluting peeps and pings.

A toad and a beetle met in confrontation
Are both scared rigid. The toad observes
A beetle more than twice as big as he is;
The beetle's ganglia obscurely recollect
Toads are cruel murderers of beetles.
Cowards, both of them.

STAG BEETLES

"Cor, aren't they horrible! Where do they live?" –
The Cockney lady in the Insect House
At the London Zoo, standing by a case
Containing stag beetles, in a simulated habitat
Of twigs and oak-leaves. "In the country."
Replied her friend. I think that she conceived of
Civilized London surrounded by a vast

186

Primeval forest, known as "the country" –
A dank, dark jungle, full of monstrous insects,
Waving their menacing jaws.
It is a vision I rather tend to share.

SOLDIER BEETLES

Their worlds the umbels of the wild carrot
Poised high in air, swayed by the summer breeze,
A hemisphere of white flowers, with one
Bright crimson at the centre.

In spite of their scarlet bodies and khaki surtouts
There's nothing aggressive or military
About them. They stray like gentle cattle
And, pig-a-back, they placidly make love.

EDDIE AND THE WEEVIL

Eddie Linden, biting into
One of my biscuits, discerned a beestie
Creeping out of a cranny – small and black,
With a trunk like a very miniature elephant;
Two angled and elbowed antennae
On either side of that snout. "Who are you?"
"Who is Eddie Linden?" replied
The coleopteron, "that is the problem.
I am Curculio, the biscuit weevil –
And particularly fond of Bath Olivers.
Mysterious providence, I sometimes think, designed them
Especially for me and my kind.
Eat me, and I am additional protein.
In times gone by, the British sailor
Was all too grateful for that.
I do not question my identity."

LADYBIRD

Ladybird, ladybird, fly away home:
Not yours, but our house is on fire.

We fear the fire from heaven, we fear
Death in the nucleus.

Fly far, small bright beetle, fly far –
Bishop Burnaby, in your scarlet cope –

Fly back to the place of our lost innocence,
The buttercup-fields, the hawthorn-shaded lanes.

A LADYBIRD AMONG THE REFERENCE BOOKS
for Peter Thornber

A two-spot ladybird has elected to hibernate
Between the pages of the *Dictionary of Surnames*,
Among the C's, specifically the Ch's:–
With Chatterton, and Chalmers and Charteris and Charrington.
Sleep snug, Madonnina Coccinella, dry as dust, and secure, we
     hope
From fahrenheit 451. No doomed poet
Shall haunt your winter dreams, but squires and shires
And prosperous brewers – with Lady Chatterley
Going down to the rose-garden with her secateurs.
A plethora of green-fly is upon her roses
All for your delicate feasting.

TIGER BEETLE

Green and gold striped, with elegant
Spiny legs, and cruel slashing jaws,
In an aura of attar of roses,
He runs, with ruthless speed
Seeking his prey, across the vast savannah
That lies there at your feet.

EARWIG

Maligned, the earwig. Unlikely he'd take shelter
Within the labyrinth of your ear, still more improbable
He'd penetrate the brain and start to eat it.
He's safer refuges – dry hedgerow kexes
More appetising fare than that grey soggy blob
Inside your skull, that's stuffed with indigestible
And useless information. He'll devour
The pink and overblown hearts of dahlias,
The golden mop-heads of chrysanthemums,
And the last roses that the summer leaves.

A CRICKET IN WINTER

A cricket on a rubbish-tip
Fiddles a winter tune;
He has no heating problems,
And scraps enough and to spare.

Robin in the holly
And the wren in the ivy-tod
Fluff up their plumes, and try to keep warm
With a tootle on their pipes –
Waiting for spring to come.

And spring will come.

CICADA

A single tettix in a carob-tree
Rooted in dry soil, beside a stony track,
Would almost seem to apprehend our passing
And to resent it too.
He scolds, scolds, scolds, scolds, scolds,
Whirring like a passionate machine –
Drinker of sugary juices, centred in his own world
Of leaves and boughs and long dependent pods
Pregnant with cellulose and butterscotch.

A BUTTERFLY IN OCTOBER

In this college room where I teach, the servant,
This cool morning of late October,
Has kindly lit the electric fire for me.
As I sit and wait for my pupils, I am aware
Of a soft, dry rattling at the window-pane.
I think at first it is rain, or else
Twigs and leaves that are blown against the glass;
But now perceive it is a butterfly
Desperately beating its fragile, marbled wings
Against an invisible, illogical barrier,
Trying to get out. Poor fool, you must have come indoors
Intending to hibernate in a fold of the curtains,
But now the warmth has roused you. There's nothing for you
    out there,
No late chrysanthemums or autumn crocus

189

To yield you nectar, and the sun's beams are pale.
You'd die – perhaps tonight – numbed and stiffened
By thirst and cold, or else a bird would grab you.
And yet you go on straining towards the light.
I catch you in my cupped palm (you do not struggle).
The sash lifted, I launch you to the air –
Since that's what you so urgently seem to want.
To want? Small bundle of impulses and instincts,
Can there be any central spark that reason
Here discerns, to suffer or to will?
And yet I cannot think of you as mere
Cartesian automaton, no more
Than I can think so of myself. What can I do?
What can we ever do – the weft and warp
Of all existence being so utterly shot through
With innocent and irremediable suffering?
So I deliver you to the stark airs of death –
But you will die free. So farewell, butterfly.

CABBAGE WHITE

The chrysalis split. "It's Spring!" said the butterfly,
Opening to the air in his bridal outfit.
"I'm off – haste to the wedding! – and to tipple nectar;
And no more cabbage, thank you very much."

"Snap!" said the swallow, as he caught him.
"One's always grateful for a snack."

MOTH

The Papal pallium, woven
Of wool from Agnes' whitest lambs;

The heavy, ceremonial mantles,
Commenoi wore, and Palaiologoi;

The partly-tied cravats
Brummel dismissed with a gesture,

Bidding his servant to take them to the dustbin
("These, sir, are some of our failures.");

The bridal sheets, smelling of wild woodruff,
Juliet had laid upon her bed –

I've had them all for breakfast, tea and dinner:
A wriggling worm, a small grey moth

That enters, phantom-like, your lamplit room:
I am Time's courier, bearing to one and all

This message: "Moth and rust,
Moth and rust, moth and rust consume".

A HUMBLE BEE

A fumbling, a red-arsed, bumbling bee
Thrust out her tongue into recesses of sweetness,
The florets which composed
A purple clover-head; then flew away
Back to her own untidy nest,
Where wax was mixed with moss, and three queens shared
With a knot of drones, and a dozen or so
Odalisque workers like herself –

"Not so much a hive as a hippy colony," opined
A honey-bee, making a bee-line
To upland moors, and heather honey.

"Thank Buzz some of us have standards.
Long live our socialist hive. We work
For a rational, generative queen." But she was mistaken:
She worked, in fact, for the bee-keeper.

WASPS

The sexless workers, in their tigerish uniforms,
Range, through the balmy days of summer,
With menacing whine and zig-zag flight,
Seizing caterpillars, spiders, flies,
Sawing gobbets from butchers' joints,
To appease the exorbitant larvae,
Snug in their paper citadel.

But summer closes. Death's
In the golden air of harvest. Now they rush
In desperate carouse
On windfall pears and apples, bursting plums
Exuding vinous juices, breathing forth
Intoxicating fumes.

The cold air comes and numbs. For these
No hive's security, no garnered honey stores.

CRANE-FLY

Ineffectual Daddy-longlegs
Dithers and dawdles across the field,
Trailing brittle threadlike limbs;
His body slung between them like a hammock,
He settles on green leaves, among whose roots,
In seasons closed from daylight, he,
A thick tough leatherjacket,
Voracious and esurient, used to gnaw.

FLEA

Hop o'my, skip o'my pollex, Pulex –
    Had I your thews and thighs
I would jump over the dome of Saint Paul's
    To the Dean and Chapter's surprise.

Aphanipteron, siphonapteron –
    If I had got your scope
I would jump over Saint Peter's at Rome
    And show my heels to the Pope.

SILVER FISH

This small survivor, clad in shining scales,
Most primitive of insects, has seen them come and go –
Devonian seas, and carboniferous swamps,
The dinosaurs lording it through the secondary epoch,
Then sabre-tooth and megatherium.

It haunts our kitchens now, hiding in crannies,
Through hours of daylight – fire-brat,

It likes proximity of the oven;
When darkness comes, in skipping carnival,
Feeding on scraps, spilt grains of flour and sugar,
The crumbs that fall from the master's table:
For the time being, the master.

Birds' Plenary Session

THE EAGLES

Where the Roman legions tramped
Their brazen eagle-standards went before,
While, at the army's rear,
The feathered eagles soared, and waited.

"They make a desert and they call it peace."
Victorious, in the war-god's shrine,
The dedicated brazen eagles stand;
About the wasted land
The feathered eagles fight and tear.

THE KESTREL

The small falcon, with sharp pointed wings,
Hangs poised in air, standing against the gale:
The intense lens of his unwinking eye
Is focused on the fields below, to mark
Each slightest stir or scurry in the grass.

And, as in Egypt, this is Horus-Ra,
Lord of the Morning, sacred
Emblem of Pharaoh's kingship,
Royal Bird of the Sun.

THE TAWNY OWL

Autumn night, a great shiny moon –
Owls cry and cry over the sleeping farms:
"To-whoo! To-whoo! To-whoo!
Poor Jenny Hoolet's feet are a-cold!"

A mouse
Sneaks out to a corn-stack, begins
To nibble the spilt grain. Suddenly,
On noiseless downy wings, with never a whisper, Death
Swoops down from the frosty air.

THE SCOPS OWL

On marble hills and glaucous olive leaves
Shadows begin to fall. Now the small, brown,
Staring, ear-tufted scops owl will begin
His curfew, his reiterated call:
A serenade, a territorial challenge –
For it is only we
Who catch our breath at plaintive sadness for
Set of the sun, and coming on of night.

THE HOOPOE

A rare one with us –
King Solomon's messenger to the Queen of Sheba;
Sheltered that wise king
From the heat of the midday sun.

He offered a reward – they asked
For crowns of gold.

Poor silly birds – soon everybody harried them
With sticks and stones, until the king
Turned the gold crowns to feathers.
A feathered crown is best.

THE TREE-CREEPER

I saw a little mouse
Run up a tree – then twitch
Out pointed delicate wings,
And flitter away on the breeze.

THE NUTHATCH

Slate-blue above, buff below,
Descends a tree-trunk upside down,
Punctures a nut with his sharp chisel-bill,
And whistles clear and cheeky,
Shrill as a schoolboy.

THE RAVENS

Tolls the bell, hour upon hour –
Always ravens at the Tower.

Glossy and black the plumes we preen,
And black the sights that we have seen.

Tolls the bell, hour upon hour –
Always ravens at the Tower.

Clarence drowned, the little princes –
The shadow of Crookback Dick advances.

Tolls the bell, hour upon hour –
Always ravens at the Tower.

Headless the Bullen and Howard here,
Headless Raleigh, and headless More.

Tolls the bell, hour upon hour –
Always ravens at the Tower.

When we fly hence, the Tower shall crumble,
The city be lost, and the realm tumble.

Tolls the bell, hour upon hour –
Always ravens at the Tower.

THE CARRION CROW

A carrion crow sat on an oak
And watched where the line of battle broke.

A carrion crow sat on an ash –
He hears the spears' and shields' clash.

A carrion crow sat on a pine:
The long-bows are bent, the swift arrows whine.

A carrion crow sat on an elm:
The broad sword batters the bright-plumed helm.

A carrion crow sat on a yew:
On Bosworth Field lies a crimson dew.

A carrion crow sat on a thorn,
Where the crown of England had rolled, forlorn.

THE ROOKS

The rooks in the rectory elms
Settle their disputes (or so it is said)
Convening a noisy parliament; always begin to build
On the same date in March – unless, indeed
It happens to fall on a Sunday.
They tolerate a few
Of those eccentric clowns, the jackdaws,
Among their company, but do not like
To be reminded of their cousins,
The carrion crows, out there on the heath
Living by scrounging and poaching:
"Oh no, of course, we never talk of those".

THE MAGPIE

Feather-pated tattling Margaret Pie
Would not go into Noah's Ark, we are told:
She sat on the roof and chattered in the rain.

On another occasion she said
"I think I will only go into half-mourning."
The occasion was the Crucifixion.
She's worn it ever since.

THE JAYS

Two jays came down my street.
I heard them screeching, mate to his mate.
They kept well under cover, in hedges and shrubbery –

The bright, conspicuous, winged with azure,
Cinnamon-coloured birds.
I guess they were casing the joint.

THE ORIOLE

A zany bird, the yellow oriole,
From time to time reiterates
His sharp, irregular, two-note trill,
Then flies away again. Not sweet nor mellow,
But with the tang of cheese, or a rough country wine –
He wants to make his presence known,
Establishing his territory. I surmise
His pendant nest cannot be far away.

THE GREEN WOODPECKER

He is the green-plumed popinjay of our northern woods,
Lunatic laugher of spring, destroyer
Of the ants' citadel.
He is loved by the Thunder God, and the nymphs
Of the druid oak-groves.

THE GREATER SPOTTED WOODPECKER

White-grey lichen on subfusc bark;
Chequered sunlight falls through twigs and leaves.
In this world of stipple and crosshatch the spotted woodpecker
(Who looks so conspicuous in the plate in your bird book)
Can move unseen. He spirals up a tree-bole,
Tapping and tapping for beetles and beetle-grubs;
Then beats out a tattoo – to call his mate
To come with dipping flight through sun-splashed woodland
    rides –
Upon a hollow bough, his talking drum.

THE CUCKOO

The cuckoo and the warty toad
Digest the woolly caterpillars:

Only their toughened stomachs
Can cope with those poisonous hairs.

The cuckoo is footloose, irresponsible –
He scorns domestic cares,

And parks his ugly offspring on
His dupes, dunnock and titlark.

He's free to sing all day
His two-note song to his grey light-of-love;

And she replies, bubbling
Like water from a wide-necked bottle.

The cuckoo is a graceless, greedy bird –
And yet we love him still:

He told us spring had come. And all our days
We will remember cuckoo-time.

THE KINGFISHER

When Noah left the Ark, the animals
Capered and gambolled on the squadgy soil,
Enjoying their new-found freedom; and the birds
Soared upwards, twittering, to the open skies.
But one soared higher than the rest, in utter ecstasy,
Till all his back and wings were drenched
With the vivid blue of heaven itself, and his breast scorched
With the upward-slanting rays of the setting sun.
When he came back to earth, he had lost the Ark;
His friends were all dispersed. So now he soars no more;
A lonely bird, he darts and dives for fish,
By streams and pools – places where water is –
Still searching, but in vain, for the vanished Ark
And rain-washed terraces of Ararat.

THE MUTE SWAN

The white swan makes a fine picture,
And looks as if he knew it. He arches
His delicate neck to quiz
That other swan which swims,
Upside down beneath him.

Richard Lionheart it was
Brought these swans here, from Cyprus where
They floated on moats which lapped
Proud castles of the royal Lusignan,
Among the olive and the citrus groves.

THE WHOOPER SWAN

These are Apollo's birds, straight-necked and yellow-billed,
Nomads of the northern waste, who swept
Southward, with high clear song, to visit
Delphi's oracular shrine, or where
The power divine has fixed
Delos, once wandering, in the mid-sea deep.

THE WILD GEESE

A pack of hounds, in full cry,
Up in the clouds. The Dark Huntsman
Pursues the poor lost souls
Until the end of time.

Wild geese passing over.

THE SHELDRAKE

Armorial bird, he bears his quarterings
Upon his wing, half goose half duck,

And lives in a feudal castle, perhaps?
No, foxgoose, in a rabbit burrow.

THE STORM PETREL

Far out at sea, a little dark bird,
No bigger than a sparrow. It teeters over the waves,
The troughs and crests, paddling with its feet,
Seeming to walk like Peter
Upon Gennasaret.

Is it a land bird that has lost its way? No,
But this is Mother Carey's chicken,
Harbinger of the storm.

O Mother Carey, green-toothed hag,
Mistress of the hurricane, your herds
The mighty choirs of singing whales, be lenient
To sailors and trawlermen, all who ply their way
Through dirty weather, over the hungry deep.

THE CORMORANT

A lone black crag stands offshore,
Lashed by the flying spray. Gorged from his fishing-foray
With long hooked beak and greenish glistering eye,
A cormorant, like a heraldic bird,
Spreads out dark wings, two tattered flags, to dry.

GREAT BLACK-BACKED GULLS

Said Cap'n Morgan to Cap'n Kidd:
"Remember the grand times, Cap'n, when
The Jolly Roger flapped on the tropic breeze,
And we were the terrors of the Spanish Main?"
And Cap'n Kidd replied: "Aye when our restless souls
Were steeped in human flesh and bone;
But now we range the seven seas, and fight
For galley scraps that men throw overboard."

Two black-backed gulls, that perched
On a half-sunken spar –
Their eyes were gleaming cold and through
The morning fog that crept upon the grey-green waves
Their wicked laughter sounded.

BLACK-HEADED GULLS FOLLOWING THE PLOUGH

No storm-weather sign this. For generations now
The gulls have learned to fly inland,
And feed at the plough, white beside dark rooks,
Their cries as harsh but shriller. But the sea –
The ship-delighting sea, the unharvested –
Glints only in a keen, cold, unkind eye.

THE CORIRA

Tripping in troops along the Italian shore,
Bold black and white with chestnut,
Curved bill, long legs, toes partly webbed –
Thus the corira, so said Aldrovandus
Four centuries ago. But since his day
No one has found plume or pinion
Or beak or claw of it.

Gryphon, phoenix and simurgh
Flap great mythical wings
Among the heavens of poetry. Plausible corira,
I'll grant you a small place within those realms
Who have this disadvantage – you were not fabulous
But merely non-existent.

THE HERON

An image remembered from boyhood – glimpsed
From a moving train: a pool,
Or else a brook which must have run perforce
Beside the tracks, and a heron standing,
Not in his grey stillness,
Watching the waters for his prey – but all in motion,
As he tries to get into his snaking gullet
A flapping, white-bellied, obstinate cuss of a fish.

THE WOODCOCK

This mysterious, softly-mottled creature
Is a little bug-eyed monster.

His ears are in front of his eyes, to hear
The turning worms he probes
With his sensitive, soft-tipped bill.

The brain pushed so far back, that people thought
He had no brain at all.

They come in, surreptitiously, from the sea,
Arriving on migration,
And scuttle away into the undergrowth,
Beneath the great bright moon.

And people also thought
They could fly up into that shining orb.

THE CURLEW

Lord help all those lost up there tonight
From the treacherous bog, the precipice at their feet.
The mist lies low on the moors – and through it the calling,
The wild disconsolate calling. The cry of the whaup,
Men say it's unchancy.

THE SANDPIPER

Lively and clean from the hills, the waters of the beck
Tumble and ripple and swirl over the sands and gravel
Where a stone divides them. With pointed wings and tail, the
    sandpiper
Stands, bobbing and dipping where the sunlight
Flashes and glances over the eddies – then takes flight,
Uttering a pure, shrill, rapid call. Now in the whole valley
The crystal air holds, for a moment,
The liquid clarity of that small music.

THE LAPWING

The lapwing is a type of guile – that guile
Is elemental, sacrificial love.
She tumbles across the field, trailing
A simulated broken wing, to draw you off
From the hollow scrape or dried out cattle-footprint
Where lie the blotched and pear-shaped eggs, or else
The soft grey young ones crouch, obedient to her cries;
Or dive-bombs you, beating about your head
With loud, distracted and distracting screams –
Which superstition heard
As lost, rejected souls flying in the spring mists,
That mocked the Crucified upon the cross.

THE WATERHEN

The lily pads, and the lily's pale chalice
Float on the still pool. A dragon-fly
Darts above, a miniature
Futuristic aeroplane.

Demure, in black and grey,
With white beneath the tail, and that touch
Of scarlet on the brow and bill, the waterhen
Slips through the reeds, on delicate greenish feet.

THE OYSTERCATCHER

They say in the Highlands and the Western Isles –
This tale was made by men who knew
What being harried and pursued could mean – that Jesus,
Fleeing the malice of his enemies,
Went down to the wild shore, to find a cave to hide in.
But the sea-pies, flying
About the limpet-covered reef, with clear bright calls,
Took pity on him there, and in their scarlet beaks
Brought kelp and tangle to cover him completely.
The ruthless foe went by. And for that season
His cup of suffering passed.
                                    Therefore the oystercatcher
Is of good fortune and well seen of men,
Running at the tide's edge
Upon the cockle and the mussel banks.

THE GREAT BUSTARD

On Salisbury Plain, by the great standing pillars
Of Avebury or Stonehenge – temples reared

To Sun, and changing Moon, and all
The glittering cohorts of the arching sky –

Among the scattered mounds, the Long and the Round Barrows,
Sepulchres of now-forgotten chieftains,

Noblest of running birds, the bustard once
Stalked before his wives, moustachioes bristling.

The bustards are all gone – they'll come no more:
Much too easy to shoot, much too good to eat.

On Salisbury Plain the military
Has taken over now, with tanks and guns,

Precision instruments of death – and human beings
Are much too easy to shoot.

THE PHEASANT

Cock-pheasant crows in the English wood,
Then struts into the clearing – magnificent,
With emerald casque, russet and white and black;
For he was made for Asiatic landscapes –
His lineage is of Colchis, land of the Golden Fleece,
Or further eastward where
Slant-eyed Chinese limned him,
With swift sure brush strokes, on their scrolls of silk.

THE HOUSE SPARROW

Citizen Philip Sparrow, who likes
To build and breed about our habitations –
  The little birds that fly through the city smoke –

Prolific, adaptable, bold,
Untidy, cheerfully vocal –
  The little birds that quarrel in the eaves –

Grant him his right of freedom and, of your charity,
His dole of crumbs and kitchen scraps –
  The little birds that stand in the eye of God.

THE GREENFINCH

On a May morning,
In the greening time
I heard a greenfinch in a college garden
Set to his jargon in a leafy tree;
The long flat call-note, which will be repeated
Through all the hot and dusty days of summer,
Subsumed in a desultory twitter.
The lazy greenfinch, thick-set country cousin
Of the trim, suburban, caged canary –
Green, green, green he calls through the green leaves.

THE CHAFFINCH

There's apple-blossom now, for Spring
Has made a definite entrance. With smoke-blue cap,
White epaulettes, and breast a rusty pink,
The chaffinch hurries through his rapid song:
So may some dowdier Mimi Pinson
Be quick quick quick quick quick quick quick to hear,
And Coelebs not be long a bachelor.

GOLDFINCHES

The sweet-voiced, the elegant, the with gold banded,
The seven-coloured linnets – they fall
On purple thistle-heads, an eager charm
On heads of whitish down that drift to the wind:
Madonna's birds, that feed among the thorns.

THE YELLOWHAMMER

This small bird, yellow as the never-
Out-of-blossom gorse (when gorse
Is out of blossom, kissing's out of fashion.)
Reiterates his little
"A little bit of bread and no cheese!"
Through the long summer days,
When other birds are silent.

When I was younger, days were longer,
Summers were warmer, and always
The yellowhammer's song.

THE CORN BUNTING

Beside a field of grain, perched on a telephone wire,
Through the relentless August heat the dumpy
Undistinguished bird repeats
His only song. The sound is rather like
The chinkering of a rusty chain.

Each one does his best, I hope:
Each one has his talent.

THE NIGHTJAR

Summer twilight – the sun has left the sky.
A faint glow lingers. Silvery Venus
Beams a message from its alien world.
On the tall grasses points of green fire,
Elf-eyes. The glow-worms hoist their lanterns,
Love-signals for their wandering knights. Listen, a voice –
Intermittent whirring, spinning, churning. Almost invisible,
A night-jar lies along the length of a bough,
Mottled, with frog-like gape. Then snaps his wings,
And flits along the glade, pursuing
The soft, furry moth, and the blundering dor.

THE SWIFT

There is no creature (except, perhaps,
The angels) so wholly native to
The upper air. His tiny feet
Cannot walk on ground, can cling only.
The wisps and straws he needs to build his nest
He snatches in mid-air. He even sleeps
Borne up by the rising thermals.

This black screamer, rushing at evening
Above our cities, is kin
To the tropical humming bird, who can fly backwards
Out of the great flower-bells
In the Amazonian forest.

THE SWALLOW

The swallow has returned, and we can say for sure
That spring is here, and summer will follow after.
All through our winter, around an African kraal
His steel-blue pinions flickered; now he's flown back
Thousands of miles, over the seas and mountains,
To build once more his nest in an English barn –
Hooray for the swallow and the weather he brings with him!

THE MISSEL-THRUSH

February brings its storms and rain,
Flooding the side-walks and the dirt-choked drain;
Into the north-west wind a missel-thrush
Shouts his defiance from a bare-twigged bush,
Sprinkling the air with notes that seem as bright
As crocus, or the yellow aconite.

THE BLACKBIRD

"Sooty-plumed blackbird with your golden bill,
Why is your song so sweet and clear and mellow?"
"I lubricate my voice with slugs and snails."
"And sometimes cherries, too?" "Well, do you grudge me those –
Who pay you richly with a summer tune?"

THE SPOTTED FLYCATCHER

He takes his stance on a gate-post
All the long day; makes quick
Excursions up into the air –
Snip! Snap! Snap! Snip! – snatching
The dancing flies out of their element.

THE GREAT TIT

Sir Thomas Titmouse
Has come into our garden. He likes
Suet, beef-bones, peanuts, and maybe
Half a coconut suspended.

On the first fine day of the year
He will favour you with a song – just two notes,
Up and down, like sharpening a saw.
Not much of a song, you say? It is Hope's clarion
Annually renewed.

THE PIED WAGTAIL

Polly Dishwasher is down by the stream,
Dipping and dabbling, and flirting her long tail,

In her neat black and white, black and grey
Domestic service uniform.

Her mistress is a curmudgeonly,
Sour-faced, elderly fairy,

Whose third cousin was, they say,
Lady-in-waiting to Queen Mab.

She allows her one Wednesday afternoon off a month,
Home at sunset, and *no* followers.

THE YELLOW WAGTAIL

Red and white, the gentle Herefords wander
Through the lush water-meadow, plashy and green –
And gold with buttercup-gold, white with moon-daisies,
Lady-smocks, meadowsweet.
They go in a placid cowpat dream – with a flash
Of yellow at breast and throat, the wagtail
Darts in and out among them, and snaps
At the black and buzzing flies that are the beasts' annoy.

THE HEDGE SPARROW
Feeding a cuckoo in the nest

"My son is an infant prodigy, who'll doubtless
Make his mark in the world.
But then, though I say it myself,
Mr. Hedge Sparrow and I
Are remarkable parents.

Mrs. Meadow Pipit down the road
Says her chick is prodigious too.
The vanity of the creature!"

THE ROBIN

i

The north wind blows, a leaden
Sky lowers above;
Snow, snow everywhere
Over the grudging ground.

A solitary robin sings:
"Oh babes in the wood, poor babes in the wood –
Don't you remember the babes in the wood?"

ii

Cock-robin in spring, his breast
Is a flag of aggression, which says
"Get out! This front garden is mine,
These are my worms, my nesting-site, my hen-bird!
Get out! Be off! I'm warning you!" – his song
A splutter of defiant rage.

THE WREN

The pygmy troglodyte, with tail cocked,
Runs through his caves, which are
The twisted roots and debris of the copse;
Then gives a loud burst of sudden song,
And stops as suddenly. Like a clockwork bird
Someone has wound up.

THE STONECHAT

This little ruddy bird of stony places,
Too rough for the harrow,
Has the chink of pebbles inside his throat
To serve him for a song

THE WHEATEAR
for Shaun Traynor

The green wheat is in the ear; in mediterranean vineyards
Vines have tiny flowers. On English down or wold
White Arse alights, a dweller in stony places:
"Excuse me, Brother Rabbit,
I need your spare accommodation."

THE REED WARBLER

And you, skilful basket maker,
Who harbour in the whispering sedge
And vocal reeds – the inconsequential
Loquacious prattle of waters
Has flowed into your song.

209

THE WOOD WARBLER, THE WILLOW WARBLER, AND THE CHIFFCHAFF

I thought the leaves had come to life;
It was the leaf-green birds.

I thought the green leaves
Had found their singing voice – the high sweet trill,
The tinkling chimes dying away,
The soft *zip-zap* of earliest spring.

THE NIGHTINGALE

The inconspicuous nightingale
Is not so rare as you perhaps may think,

Being not at all averse from
Home Counties conurban shrubberies,

And sings at least as much
By day as through the night –

Such is the urgency, when May-time rules,
Of finding a mate, defending territory:

The common motives for his song, as for all birds.
So much for poets' fancies then?

And yet, and yet, and yet...
That clear high *terew*, that long crescendo,

The dark sob in the throat – these simulate
The tones of human passion,

Telling of tragic sorrows, Greek and unassuageable,
Or, as the Persians told, he sang

With wounded heart, pressing against a thorn,
In love with the opening rose, that silken-petalled jilt,

Who flings her perfume to the morning breeze –
With beauty that fades, beauty that is eternal.

THE BLACKCAP

The Southern folk can boast their nightingale,
   Which chirrups a high-class tune,
Just like Madame Adelina Patti,
   Under the summer moon;

But the Northern nightingale, he is the blackcap,
   Warbling the leaves between,
Where the oak and the ash and the bonny birk-tree
   Flourish and grow green.

O brave blackcap, O blithe blackcap
   You sing so rich and clear
In the oak and the ash and the bonny ivy
   At the season of the year.

THE SKYLARK AND THE WOODLARK

Adapted for open treeless places,
The skylark finds no perch or vantage point
Whence to proclaim his territory. So he constructs
An airy tower and mounts,
Scattering his music from a clear sky.

For the Romantic poets, Shelley, for instance,
This was a symbol of their own impulse –
Upborne by its native energy, soaring
To meet the sun, the central source of light,
Spurning the dull earth.

But I remark how our Augustans,
Thomas Gray among them, almost preferred
The sweet carolling of the modest woodlark, a bird
Not of the deep woods but open rides,
Making more grateful yet a chequered shade.

FERAL PIGEONS

There is nothing much to be said
For the greedy, vulgar London street pigeons. They lack
The *gamin* charm of the dapper sparrow, or
The zany starlings' wheeling elegance. They feed on
Half-eaten sandwiches, abandoned

211

In the Embankment Gardens
By civil servants who worry about their weight;
On breadcrumbs scattered by the self-indulgent,
Or grab unspeakable scraps
Under the market-traders' stalls.

Not satisfied with this, they take off
Like an Egyptian locust horde
To raid suburban and Home Counties' plots
Grubbing up seeds and seedlings.

There is no monument,
Georgian façade, Victorian fantasy,
Nor national hero – Nelson,
Cromwell, Coeur-de-Lion –
Exempt from the acid comment of
Their casual defecations.

Come spring, and you will mark
These are still Venus' birds. The cocky male
Courts his demure hen, arching
His neck to show the shifting iris there – an image
The Emperor Nero fixed in a line of verse
Quite good enough for Tennyson to steal.

Note: Seneca quotes a line of the Emperor Nero's, in which he speaks
of 'the shifting iris on the necks of doves'. This seems to be the
source of Tennyson's 'In the Spring a livelier iris changes on the
burnish'd dove'.

THE TURTLE DOVE

One day, one day,
After the eagles of war have preyed,
When the flowers appear on the earth, and it is spring –
The time of the singing of birds – the turtle dove
(As when the first flood-waters fell away)

Will build her nest in the heart of the peaceful grove.

Anti-Masque of Seven Converted Deadly Dragons

from a Masque of St George, devised by Patricia Burke and the author, and intended to be performed by the children of Dog village, Exeter, in Broadclyst parish church

PRIDE

I am the great dragon of Pride:
I spread my empire far and wide.
I am the chief of the deadly seven,
And I made Lucifer fall from Heaven.

But now that I have been converted,
Entirely meek and humble-hearted,
The Princess leads me with her girdle
And I trot behind like a well-trained poodle.

ENVY

I am Envy, the canker worm –
Some have called me the green-eyed monster;
But often enough I took the form
Of a cranky bachelor, or spinster.
I stretched out my neck like an old grey gander,
Honking malice, and hissing slander,
I hated good fortune in my betters,
And so I sent them poison pen letters.

But, from now onwards, I'll remember
To curb my tongue, that wicked member.
I'll never listen to tittle-tattle,
And they'll call me the Agreeable Rattle.

WRATH

I am Wrath, and my fiery breath
Could turn the world to a blasted heath.
Scrapping and scuffling were all my joy
When I took the shape of a teddy boy,
A football hooligan or a punk –
Looking for bother, and fighting drunk.

But I have reformed, and now I am
Mild as a little white woolly lamb.
My breath, that was full of flames and smoke,
To scorch the earth when I ran amok,
Won't singe a daisy or a dandelion clock.

AVARICE

I am Avarice. I hoarded pelf,
And kept it strictly to myself,
Beneath the earth, and hidden from view,
Like the great dragon that Beowulf slew.
In my strongroom underground
Missing works of art could be found –
Ceramics, furs and jewellery –
And all of them were just for me,
Down in the darkness of my vault.

But now I am generous to a fault,
Open-handed and free-hearted;
And, what's more, I have got started
On an interest that's different far –
Collecting jumble for the church bazaar.

LECHERY

You know my name – it begins with an L,
But it's B for Belial down in Hell.
I was smarmy and smooth and sly,
With blubbery lips and a roving eye.
I chased the girls through the haymaking meadows,
And lurked in the bushes' sinister shadows.
You can be sure I was up to no good
When I went for a prowl in the tangly wood.

But now I am pure as pure can be,
And I've joined the League of Decency;
High-minded, and utterly righteous,
And a strong supporter of Mrs Whitehouse.

214

GLUTTONY

My name, without any ifs and buts,
It is old Gluttony-greedyguts.
At breakfast, luncheon, tea and dinner
I was a most inveterate sinner,
As I scoffed down saveloys and peas,
Tripe and faggots and sausages,
Streaky bacon, and scrambled eggs,
Steak-and-kidney and chicken legs,
Liver and onions, and ham, and spam,
Honey, marmalade, strawberry jam,
Treacle pudding, and spotted dick,
And doorsteps of bread with the butter spread thick,
Grilled herrings smothered in mustard,
Rice pudding, stewed prunes, and apple and custard,
Chocolate ice-cream, and jelly –
All in my capacious belly.

But now, my appetite to quiet,
I have adopted a strict diet;
I really must look after myself –
And soon I'll be as slim as an elf.

SLOTH

My name is Sloth. I am the one
You always saw sleeping in the sun;
But now, I am told, there is work to be done.

Honest labour is true nobility:
I'll do it, according to my ability;
And, to get cracking, I really will try –
Well, by and by.

Early Poems
1942-1965

Preliminary Verses
to my Selected Poems (1965)

"The hour gets later, the times get worse, let us therefore keep
  awake" –
I set this down as one who shall outlive heartbreak,
A contumacious poet in an unjust, barbarous age:
Hope, the butterfly, but seldom brushes my page
With her mazarine wing. May I hope Faith is there,
Only a little disguised in her gorgon-mask, Despair?
As for the third, flaming-hearted sister Compassion,
She will intercede for her prodigal brother Passion;
Or else, quiver-bearing, succinct, with buskined knee,
Pursue the wild game through thickets of irony.

The Don Juan Triptych

LEPORELLO

Do you see that old man over there? – He was once a gentleman's
  gentleman;
His skull is bald and wrinkled like a leathery snake's egg;
His forehead is not high, but his eyes, though horny, are cunning,
Like an old jackdaw's beginning to moult a few grey feathers;
His nose is sharp like a weasel's, and his lips always a little smiling,
His narrow shoulders crouched forward, hinting a half-finished
  bow.
Did you notice how beautifully white and smooth and soft his
  hands were?
His coat is dowdy as the dusty shards of a house-haunting beetle,
His cuffs and collar not quite white, like the foam on a fouled
  mill-race.
But Fear flickers over his face – now settling like a fly
On his sunken cheeks, now haunting his blurred eyes;
And his pale mouth is always ready to fall open and gasp and
  shriek....
  Night after night he's here, in all weathers,
Drinking. They say his wife is a shrew and holds her head high
For all that once.... Night after night, under the yellow lantern-
  light,
Always the same old chair in the corner, night after night.

But he likes to talk to a stranger – it makes a nice change.
Why don't you buy him a drink and get him talking?
   He can remember his master well – those were the days! –
Feast days, Carnival days – fans and flowers and bright silk shawls
Tossing like a poppy-patched cornfield the wind dishevels,
And then milky moonlight flowing over close-kept courtyards;
And while his master climbed the balcony, he would keep watch,
Whistle and rub his hands and gaze at the stars –
His co-panders; or there were mandolins murmuring
Lies under windows that winked and slyly slid open;
Or the hand's clutch and half-humorous gasp of the escapade,
And after a doubling hare's turn, choking laughter at fooled
      footsteps
Trotting away down wrong turnings; or when cornered,
The sardonic, simple, decided flash of a sword – his master's
      sword.
And he can remember that night when he stood on the terrace
Sunning himself in black beams of vicarious sin,
While the waltz whispered within;
And three unaccountable late-comers came,
And gave no name –
(But she in the blue brocade is Anna:
And she has forged her outraged chastity into a blade
Of thin sharp ice-coloured steel; her hair is brown
And her eyebrows arched and black like two leaping salmon
Seen against the sun-flecked foam of a weir down-rushing;
And like a slim white hound unleashed she snuffs for the blood
Of a father's killer. And not far away is Elvira:
She wears silver and black and is heavily veiled
And has laid a huge jewelled crucifix over her hungry heart
In vain; for she is like an old frosty-feathered gyrfalcon,
With chrysolite eyes, mewed-up now, whose inactive perch
Frets her hooked feet; who cannot bear to gaze out
At the blue sky-paths slashed by young curving wings;
Her heart is a ruined tower from which snake-ivy
Creeps, fit to drag down an oak and smother him in dark green
      leaves.)
But the windows were all golden-spotted with candles,
Shadowed by dancing shapes; till above the silken strings
Flute and violin had trailed across the evening – a cry:
Zerlina, like a wounded hare tangled in that black net.

It is very quiet in the graveyard – a strange place to be waiting
    for him;
The moonlight hints queer perjuries – for all the Dead
Are tucked up snug in mud; we have heaped vast lumps of masonry
Over their head and their feet, fenced them round with crosses
And stones scrawled over with white lies; we have given them
    flowers
Against the stench, and stopped their nostrils with mud;
We have lighted candles for hollow sockets; they will not trouble us;
They cannot see to climb the slippery stairs of their vault;
They are blind spectators who have long dropped out of the
    game –
But what if they didn't play fair? What if cold stone
Should speak, and offer unwanted advice? What if quite suddenly
This polished transparently reasonable world were shattered?
When the soft curtain of the night is ripped up by the bray of
    trombones,
And a dumb stone abstraction can speak, and the madman invites
    it to supper –
That is no laughing matter. If you are young and well-born
And have no heart, it seems you can go home and laugh,
Drink wine and do yourself well; but he, Leporello,
A poor man, sir, always attentive to business, no great scholar,
Had never thought of these things, didn't know how to deal with
    the dead gentleman,
Or Hell stretching out a flaming hungry arm
To snatch the ripe fruit of sin from the lighted banqueting hall.

So that is why he has always a startled look, that old man;
For he feels he is being watched by dead eyes from behind the
    curtains,
And is still expecting a knock at the door, and the stone foot's
    tramp on the stairs.

DON JUAN MUSES
over the dead body of the Commendatore

How beautiful, white and hard, are the teeth of this dead man –
The cold eyes fixed, and about the rigid mouth
The wrinkled lines of pain, like mountain canyons.
I have looked often upon the faces of the Dead,

221

And seen them carried with naked feet – bodies that once had
    been
Beautiful, obscure and draped in a plain coarse habit,
The stiff impersonal lines of Francis or Dominic –
To the cells of the grave, that always silent college.

And I remember the Day of the Dead; the offerings
Of flowers and fruit, and cakes set at their doors
By the country people, the hooded figures chanting,
And the many lights moving at noon in the sunlit square.

And now in the dark room, in the pause before
The blood is wiped from the blade, before the outcry
Begins, of the servants, and the woman's animal sobbing,
Before the scuffle in the street and the get-away,
I gaze on his cold face, where my own pride's image
Stares back at me – paternal body, stiff,
As though already he were turning to stone –
And so I wonder if this thing was not always
That which I most desired – oh, through the nights,
Those silver nights under a moon of summer,
When I carved my lust into song, or hid my face
In the dark forest of a woman's hair, or sought the comfort
And softness of their flesh; for pain deep-stemmed
Within the marrow, tension of the sinew,
Shall get no final comforting, until
I feel my living hand in a stone hand's clasp,
A stone man's eyes reflect my arrogance.

DONNA ELVIRA

That stone death walking the castle corridors,
Whose clanking tread rouses the foxes' bark
Overhead in the high sierra, under a darkened moon,
And sends an echo to these worn battlements; his eyes
Are hollows of the grave, full of blue candles,
Clefts in the mountain's granite, where bright riders,
Black-horsed, with streaming hair, dash to oblivion –
John, it is you he is looking for. He is your fear:
The solitary spectre
Who roars in the labyrinth's centre, in a low vault
Where naked and alone you fight in dreams,

And start from your lover's arms, under a light sheet,
Moaning in sleep, while she lies quiet as a sea
And morning's fingers twitch at the dead curtains.

That striding man in marble I, too, have seen,
Who have known you, as they have never known,
Those others, others: the ladies moving
In Moorish gardens, bright as roses, light as fountains
Falling in laughter between the tamarisk hedges,
Or muffled at Mass with stars behind their veils,
For whom love was a dance on a glass floor,
Tricky, with peacock steps, or posturings
Of the white-tufted crane beside a sunset pool;
Who tripped and fell, poor dolls, their jointed limbs
Snapped in the tangled wires the puppet-master held.
Or the clustered nuns, murmuring like black bees
Home to their stone hive, in a white vigil;
Those virgins of the night, into whose dreams
You suddenly pranced, hot as a painted devil
Out of their picture-books; or simpering,
With your fake martyr's wounds, your sacred heart upon your
     sleeve,
Peeped from the saints' procession over the altar, soft-mouthed
     and meek
As any anatomical flayed Bartholomew,
Or young Sebastian hedgehogged with arrows.

The peasant girls, gossiping by the fountain,
Or silly as their geese at noon under the cork-trees,
Giggle and shrink, seeing your riding shadow
Skim on the pasture, your tall high-stepping horse
Galloping back to the predatory castle
Perched on the crags like a harsh-feathered buzzard.
For them you are legendary as that long-nosed goblin
Who skulks by twilight underneath the eaves,
Or the green-toothed ogre in the Goth-king's grave,
Snoring amongst his gold, who every May-day night
Claims a plump virgin for his supper there.
But I was proud-born of a metalled race,
And as a girl I dreamed a duke or a prince
To be my only husband; or else, perhaps,
Married in a long black veil, to lie alone,
A grove of cedars, where only the white Dove

Might come, and brood, and build his secret nest.
But when I spoke of this, Pasquita, our old nurse,
Combing my long locks by the firelight, would laugh, and say:
"What, these to be shorn away! Lie cold, then, to the cold moon!
No, girl – but these are snares
To catch some wild lover – the bandit-king,
Who will make you rich from his gold-cave in the mountains,
And kidnapped countesses to be your waiting women;
Or the phantom huntsman who rides on windy nights
Over the hills, chasing the ghosts of kings."

But once, in the market-place,
I peered between the curtains of my litter
And saw a gipsy-girl dancing among the crowd;
Flaunting like a flower her brown body, she fixed her eyes –
Eye of a gipsy, eye of a wolf –
Upon the man she wanted, and drew him forward,
Swaying her hips and arms, and her young breasts,
To the rhythm of castanets and clapping hands;
She seemed as ancient
As a goddess painted on a cave's flat wall
In red and yellow ochre; and beckoned him –
A tall young mule-driver – to love as to destruction.
Then my blood cried that I was one with her,
And one with the shifting moon, and the harsh sea,
And the hungry grave, the last of all your lovers.

You have pulled down my pride. There is none left;
And my dreams shrivel like rose-leaves in the fire.
I have run bare-foot up and down the streets
Like any raddled whore who's lost her swaggerer.
Your servant, too, has led me by the snout:
That little man, with a weasel's nose,
Who scans the dry anatomy of your desires,
And has cast-up, and ruled in his account-book
The profit and the loss of all your lust.
He knows you, too; therefore he, too,
Shall meet that stone death on the stairs, and live.

But now I am the black-faced moon that speaks to your ebb-tide;
The Banshee, with a night-bird's voice,
Trailing my veils of shade, boding of death.
Be free then from my love, whose whimpering muzzle

Follows your heel no more. Another hand
Arrests your fingers on the passionate sword-hilt.
At last you have been caught; put a bold face on it –
A dirty schoolboy breaking bounds at night –
But I was the night, and I the apple-tree.
How transient you are –
Poor lord, poor lover, less than a ghost,
Who have no flesh and blood but our desire.

Song

There is no shade when fails the fountain,
   There is no shade;
No grave lies low beneath the mountain
Grove by cool green leaves protected
To hide the head by care distracted;
   There is no shade!

Choked with dust the marble basin,
   Choked with dust;
Sipping and dripping no longer hasten
Rippling and tippling the fugitive flaunting
Waters that filled a forsaken fountain,
   Choked with dust.

And a ghost walks in the noon-scorched garden;
   And a ghost walks
Under the hot sun's bitter burden;
Rank weeds shake out their seeds at hazard,
On moss-grown marble basks the lizard
   And a ghost walks.

Alla Sestina

Having escorted home the bird-like spinster
And washed and wiped and put away the tea-things,
Having relaxed tired sinewy conversation –
Critique of policy of Borough Council,
The mind, a hind, retires into the forest
And browses on the still unscriptured foliage.

The shattering of Shelley and the tea-things
Was voted by the gods in open council;
They point a ruthless spear to scour the foliage,
Disturb the deer and chase the timid spinster,
And plant the roots of tea-time conversation
Among the rotting leaves beneath the forest.

We shall not ever see them sit in council,
Relish their easy flow of conversation;
Divinely drunk and wreathed around with foliage
Sileni will not need to use our tea-things,
And ranging an inviolable forest
White Artemis perforce remains a spinster.

Mozart

Mozart walking in the garden,
Tormented beside cool waters,
Remembered the empty-headed girl,
And the surly porters,

The singing-bird in the snuff-box,
And the clown's comic nose;
And scattered the thin blue petals
Of a steel rose.

Two Serenades

1

Where lie those glimmering gardens now
  By singing moon-tides washed?
By what soft flail of sifted snow,
  Forgetful, are they crushed?

All those shrill bird-voiced instruments –
  Slackened and dumb their strings;
And each flame-pointed candle quenched
  Yearned for by moth-pale wings.

And she who woke to that serenade
  In her shadowy room, alone,
Sleeps now closed in a deeper shade,
  Folded her hands, and bone on bone.

2

Oh, carved in stone the marble girl reclining,
  Her heavy head upon her smooth cold hand;
For what lost country are those blank eyes pining?
  For what sea-sunken land?

And now it's evening and the sun, defeated,
  Fades from the tarnished heaven with no regret;
Can she remember shades where high-conceited
  Long-dead lovers met?

Though all night through the barren moon be shining –
  No raddled lute nor obvious nightingale!
Stone-deaf and dead the marble girl reclining,
  Ignobly cold and pale.

Mosca in the Galleys

The sea stinks; and the unwieldy sea bitch,
Bulked in blue oil, sagging her canvas dewlaps –
Let her be tugged forward with creaking cordage,
Hoarse curses and lacerated muscle;
Back blistered under the lash, and tar-sizzle
Over hot decks;
Sunlight and sand and salt in my eyes, blinding;
And salt blood and sand in my parched throat –
Let her be tugged forward....
I have known the feel of silk on these naked sides;
And white fingers moving on smooth mother-of-pearl,
Fish-mirrors, rainbows stirred into milk.
Gold piled on gold and hypocritical silver
Have I counted out. I have been familiar
With the anger of diamonds and the un-Christian emerald.
To have cringed before Senators cloaked in crimson
With so much glittering; to have pimped in passages
Where painted misshapen things postured and chirruped,
That was brave – licked lees from a crystal chalice
Or unicorn-cup unsplintered by malice or poison!
But mine has been more – the sickly parasite
Mistletoe threading by slow and patient degrees
The oak's crannied rind
Flaunted at last to the indignant lightning
His insolent leaves!
That remains.... Let her be tugged forward
With curses.

Pavane pour une infante defunte

Every evening I saw them go
Down the cold gallery whose smooth dark pavement
Chirped to their shuffling feet – the uncertain feet
Of old women. High overhead
Dangled our unused banners; lapped in folds
Of dusty silk, censorious, monstrous-billed
Eagles furling their gold-thread wings;
While, paw uplifted,

A simpering lion scoured through the velvet field.
Their fingers were ivory-white and ivory-yellow,
Bone-crook'd and looped round by a mumbled rosary.
They passed the long row of sly-winking candles,
Each bowed head in its grotesque eclipse,
Their lips moving ever so little . . . .
   We must be quiet now,
Make no sound; only our black silks sweeping
The sycophant floor.
Lay by that lute in the discreet corner,
Its strings untingled by any glozing finger.
We can still twine our roses under the balcony
And leave the casement ajar; but see that it be done
Without fuss; for there must be no sound –
Only that continual bee-like droning
Within the dim chapel, where dry-eyed and cold,
A splendid angel crouches by the new-carved tomb.

Beauty and the Beast

BEAUTY

My silver flesh is sifted out
  For one red rose
And my gay beauty sold – perhaps –
  For a beast to play with, for
  A crump pad-paw;

Not for dromedaries sweating
  Under fiery stones,
Or the white mules bunched with bales of stuff-silk –
Only the petals plucked, the powdered anthers'
  Upward curving.

Here in this garden
The birds are singing
  For pride.
I walk at noon
Between the roses
Of this close garden.
  I am learning.

229

THE BEAST

O soul thrust through the thick flesh, spirit whelmed
In black-blood tides! O sharp spark all but quenched
In soft numb sponginess of a beast's brain!
My shagg'd sides torn in the thickets, hands made clumsy
And blunt with earthnut-grubbing; yellow teeth
That have known red flesh! These uninhabited
Grounds and gardens, once my pleasant places,
Have heard through the long nights my baffled bellow,
My wet mouth coughing and snorting to the moon!
I am the evil hermit of this fastness,
Lurking for travellers among the trees;
By force and fraud now have I captured Beauty;
Not to rend, but bend to pity
I am learning.

BEAUTY

Here in this garden
I am learning
The rose encloses
A sharp secret.

I have a fishing line
    That will not break –
A smooth skein of silk,
    And a steel chain:
I will drag out the drowned image
From the troubled water of your eyes.

Groped I for a rose
    And grasped a thorn?
I have found a fire
    Asleep in the ashes;
I will teach the flame
To make clay hard and brittle.

THE BEAST

I am learning to turn from the wet mistiness
Of Spring, among the fallen leaves, and the roots
Of rough-barked trees, where I howled to the cold
Full moon, a hairy female flank wanting;

230

I am haunting in secret the paths of this closed garden,
Heavy with roses, shrill with incessant bird-song,
Where she walks, with her white foot hardly stirring
The live green grass. My flesh is twisted and tortured
With sharp writhings of my awakening spirit –
O soul like a stream of lava, cleaving through
The uncouthness of clay, assoil the soiled flesh!

Nocturne

And you also, Frederic Chopin, and you also
Harped us away of an evening to a hollow country –
A deep low-lying land, and a water-drooping
Sky – and always through the woods were voices crying.
Then devil-shadows trembled in our wine, and through each glade
Was wreathed and twisted with gold-mouthing eglantine
The dark nightshade.
By the long lake and miasmatic pool
Lingered the fool, wandered the heart-sick child
By love beguiled, and lies;
Down moisture-dripping crag and mountain crest
The shabby hero came, the dispossessed,
And thick-set blossoms broke
Shaking themselves upon his tattered cloak.

And you also, and you also, beautiful-handed
Angry exile – weakness and anger curbed
The cross-bred heart; that in our fire-tongued days
Was not left undisturbed.

Note: Chopin's heart was said to have been destroyed by the German bombing
of Warsaw in the first week of the Second World War. According to a recent
report, it had been enclosed in a pillar of Warsaw's Holy Cross church. The
church was destroyed, but this pillar was preserved.

Drowned Man

You naked-shouldered sea-waves, you who are
Eternally choral round the jag-toothed shore,
Rend from the stone the sucker-footed wrack,
The many-bubbled weed from the rock's core.

How have I seen you, herded in the West,
Towards the evening moaning as you run,
Your iron-throated bells still heralding
In pain and crimson sacrificed, the sun!

And oh, among what depths, by what weeds tangled,
Wanders the proud sea-skimmer, shambles the drowned
Boy cut at by oyster-shells, and his limbs mangled,
His body laid where your cold requiems sound?

What peace has he, when jewelled fishes come
To strip the flesh from his well-moulded bones?
Only unending pain, while the tides roll
Him round and round among the glittering stones.

Colder than fishes' eyes, his eyes are crushed,
By weight of many waters, from his head,
But all his dead flesh sees grass-green, grass-green,
And fields that torture the remembering Dead.

Grass-green of fields – and in the Spring his girl
Said she would wait for him. Last Spring – but now
Are other honeyed kisses! O drowned man
Hang up your heart upon the coral bough!

And nevermore down to this salt-paved deep
To sponge or weed may change of seasons come
Nor even the sea-birds' crying, but the beat
Of monstrous bat-like things whose throats are dumb.

O measureless foam-crested pitiless
And cruel-fronted purity of the wave
Drag down the weakness of young flesh, and wring
Your smarting tears over his sand-smudged grave.

Elegy to Syrinx

Now you are sere and pined, and now the brown
  And babble-throated sedge-bird closely weaves
A cradle from your loins; your yellow crown
  A barren tuft, your girdle of ribbed leaves.

Sadly beyond this pool your lover wanders,
  Bruising the lilies with his great goat's hoof;
Half animal, his baffled song he squanders
  To the harsh rocks, the wildwood's tangled roof;

But you make no reply – save when the breeze
  Crinkles the standing water's green attire
You and your hollow-throated sisters wheeze
  A thin dry dirge; there lingers no desire.

River Song

Summer is draining away, and you, swift running
River – River, carry our songs away,
Over your shifting mirrors, to the cavernous-rooted
Alders leaning low where you swirl complaining.

You who have known the swan and the paddling mallard
And a long grimy day grim barges toiling,
And sweep at last to a tangle of insane wharves,
Talkative river – carry our songs away.

You who have echoed the lute, borne gilded barges,
You who have been polluted, but feel no pain –
Sound to our sunlight songs, you elemental;
You will not hear them again, hear them again.

To the House of Fame (A Dialogue)

THE EAGLE

I am the bird imperial, bird wide-circling,
Sun-starer, brazen-hackled, renewing my youth
In eastward fountains high from the pyrosphere;
I am the Thunderer's thrall, the tall crag's tenant,
Broad-winged, steed-of-the-sky, portentous my errand,
And I will carry you now past the world's dull rampart,
To Pride's porch and my perch on her bell-mouthed trumpet.

THE POET

Sweet was the Temple of Love where I lingered –
Tapestried chamber, and clambering
Cool-clustered vine, and the twine of the sweetbriar,
Venus rose-garlanded, cinctured
With flickering azure of doves –
Love's House, and the lute-string complangent;
Margent of smooth streams and sweetness
Of waters dawn-dappled with argent,
By shadowless margaret-meadows and lawns –
The rose in closed garden, the rose
Soon plucked and soon faded.

Dido, Queen of Carthage, there depicted:
The timid deer roused early, and the huntsmen
Waking the lemon-groves with bright horn-tidings,
The hounds eager-snuffling, and then the horses –
High Numidian pacers silver-shod and
Proud with their wide nostrils. Dido, Dido,
Surprised by storm there in the thorn-thick woodlands –
Wind beating the trees, and the cool cave – the dry leaves
Are crushed where those two lay, and unborn Rome
Sewed bitterness in Carthage and the Punic curse.

THE EAGLE

I, Virgil's spirit, canorous-throated,
Caesar's imperial bird, have sung of arms,
The cold hero, and the passionate deserted.
The sands of Africa are haunted by forgotten cities –
Leave the queen her myrtle-grove and her withered willow-garland:

234

"When I am laid, am laid in earth
Remember me – but ah! forget my fate."
A sterner Venus guides, the folding star
Marked by perspicuous shepherds; clang of arms
Calls now my hero, and the Latin shore.
Leave to the shades their wild lamentation.

   Hell, the frozen-hearted pit of hatred,
I range with reason, and that painful Mountain,
Purgatory. But now to Limbo –
Ovid and Lucan there in a place of pleasance,
Only there comes no hope there, pretty fellow!
And there was Spenser also –
The Bog of Allen, that steams so thick in the evening,
Whence the mosquitoes come, whining and eager,
Was full of rebellious foot; there were arms smuggled,
Smoke-signal in the brush-wood – and now fire clambers,
Calling the Poet's bluff, to the unjust battlements;
(A child was burnt – we left there in confusion)
But still he must affirm Adonis sleeping
Eternal in the Garden; hard bright shapes
That lurked for all that in the ravelled tapestry.

THE POET

The drowned man lies in the Hellespont of Pride,
Wide seas call him, more barren than the sand;
Hook-handed courier and is there no compassion?
No compass through the blue Symplegades of mind?

George Herbert's Autumn

Upon a south wall, the vines,
The dark clusters, in the fire
Of my declining sun; the silver dust
Dances, the motes diagonal.

"Before my sighs did dry it."

Carved words, be you my Easter wings,
My doves, my little bells.
The villagers are drowned under the ripe corn;
The many-jangled lute is tuned;
But Death's fastidious gown is smirched with dust.

Two Men in Armour

Stark by the Eastern gate
Stand the two iron men
Full-throated singing

As when before-dawn darkness
Lolls on the Earth, the impossible season
Of flesh subsided or nerves drawn tighter,
The fire-hackled, blood-wattled, needle-spurred cock
Stretches his wings through the blackness, proclaims,

The iron hand is on your shoulder
The iron hand is on your head.

When pickpocket water strips the flesh
Green-fingered, lurching the drowned limbs, choking
The pale throat, drums on the bursting eyes;
And rolls and rolls where monstrous things go by,
All selfhood murdered, twitched beneath that tide –

(The iron hand is in your hand)
– When fire filches the proud heart from you, faggoting
Your bones for kindling – oh my Prince
Let music go up then, let praise go up
Like shepherds' fluting on the lonely hills.

Till Love construe the cryptic iron faces.

Edward the Confessor
(Prelude and Monody)

1

Some say this world is dying, being done with:
Millennium mete, (that twelvemonth looming nearer)
Since Christ in Jewry bought us; and His Cross
Marches the nations, its four roots spreading always
Outwards from Rome to Ireland and to Iceland.
No more the yellowish mistletoe shall crown
Unhallowed groves, now the dark Culdees go,
Hooded, with tongues of praise; in rudderless boats
Commit themselves to God and the cold seas –
The western ocean where the blue ice groans,
And the wheeling birds are angels. Kings of Thulë
And craggy Scandia have cast their crowns
Of gleaming ice beneath His wounded feet;
Woden and Thor have wrapped their cloaks of mist
About their hungry male limbs, and fled
Northwards, towards Hell's navel; Olaf the Saint
Has driven the swift shrill pen-footed Finns
Within His fold; in Lapland dead-man's drum
Chatters no more. Only in Scythia,
Enthroned in ice, sleeping, Gog and Magog
Await the voice of fire shall thaw them out,
The ravens' festival. But here, in England,
The land lies like a woman sleeping,
Out of whose bed her faithless lover goes,
Quiet, in the ruthless morning. Now no more
Along our coasts the black-winged Heathen sweep,
Driving our men like sheep from sea to sea;
But all is flayed and wounded. The poor are wretched,
And freemen's rights bereft. Proud Earls' hoofs
Insult the soil in treading. In Normandy the Wolf
Glares out to sea, hungry . . . .

                              Now in our Court
Is a silk singing, sweet, bee-like, the voices
Poured out as oil and honey before God.
The torches flare and roar, and gleam upon
Dead bones, with gems encrusted. But my harp,
Tricked and flecked with gold, like our country's verse
Hammered with the hard letter, is hung up high

Among the dust and spiders. Mute those strings
That shouted to the hoarse voice of war, our ancestors'
Who fought in narrow places by the sea
Where the slant hail cut through the darkness like
A sword, screaming like hawks, their forest voices
Grating on Caesar's ear....
    The King's in Council; his white body propped
Upon his high carved throne.
His voice is soft and French. His eyes are red
Like garnets; like sunlight bleached his hair.
His limbs are virginal, and his skin is pale,
Clear, and smooth as oil. His eyes are vague
And bright, like winter stars. The wizened shadows
Tell him of this man's pride and that man's anger,
Of greed and jealousy.
The slighted man clutches his sword, the over-anxious
Vociferates of danger. Does the King hear?
His lips are mild and move, his eyes are fixed
In prayer and adoration....
    The Queen is haggard and hungry, her bed is cold
Her rights not paid. The strength of Edward, and
His fathers who came before, sword at the thigh,
Is dedicate to God; the gold hair and frosty eye
Of his high race are pale, his fingers candles
Or lilies raised in prayer. Brunhild, Rosamund,
The white-breasted women of song, were passionate,
Slaked jealousy with blood, in cruelty
Gave blow for blow; Swanhild, trampled to death
By the wild horses, had eyes that burned and seared
White-hot with innocence. But the Queen's heart is dead,
Unwaked; her Rival, singing, a cloud of incense.

    Some say this world is dying, being done with;
I do not know. But the spirit and pride are gone
That crowned our kings. England shall see the stranger
Rule in her land, the wolf howl in her halls.

2

THE KING SPEAKS:

"Even so, Lord, come quickly.
Behold, the Bridegroom cometh in the middle of the night,
Like a thief in the night, sliding a furtive hand

238

Under the pillow, prising the window of darkness.
But O dear Thief, O Lover, stealthy
With the sweet stealth of love, O Ravisher,
O Jeweller of souls, what clouds, what moonlight,
Shall gaze upon that coming, what sweet hour
Shall draw aside the curtain?
None knows that hour, the angels do not know
That gaze continually upon the face of God;
The Saints in triumph, they with their crowns and palms,
Yearn for that time, but yet they do not know.
There shall be wars and rumours of war,
There shall be stars loosened from Heaven, and blood
Redden the salt seas, but still the earth renews,
Springlike, putting forth her flowers again to please the sun;
The cycle is renovated, and the dear routine
Of birth and death. Young lovers in the fields
Walk forth again after the tempest, after the battle,
And see the rain hanging upon the stiff thin grass-stems,
And the willow-herb, flowering, sweeten the scorched earth,
And to them the world is young, as on the first morning,
When Adam awoke in the Garden.
And the old sitting at their thresholds in the evening sunlight –
The old woman who has borne children, who has seen them
      murdered,
Perhaps, by the hostile soldiery,
And the old man who has known his sons ungrateful,
Beaten by a swaggering drunken son –
To their eyes growing dim, yet seeing more clearly,
Birth and Death are a pattern apprehended in the heart,
Like the pattern of winter boughs or of charred rafters.

    "All this John told me, meeting me by the way
As I went to Westminster; standing in the monks' garden
Under the vine, whose flowing sap is a symbol
Of Christ's blood running through the world like sunlight.
His face is gentle, an old man's face
Yet innocent, and deep as profound pools in the woodlands
Are that one's eyes. But beside him stands the Eagle
Whose beak is cruel, whose hooked claws clutch at the soil,
Whose wings are darkness and pride.
Death is abroad in the world, this world is dying
(Even so, Lord, come quickly) – it has died before,
But what can the lonely do, what can a king

Do, when the darkness thickens? What way is there
For those who are separate, whose love is chained and public?
Here I have offered my kingship and my privilege of service
To a people confused like a flock wanting a shepherd,
My manhood, my strength, my capacity for love –
These which alone ennoble a man, and justify
The dung and darkness of the body – as flowers upon
The Altar of God, to wither –
Choosing a blind way, a barren field,
And in this season of death, only the tomb.
Oh have you thought of this, that I who stand
Before you, anointed with the fragrant oil of sainthood,
Tricked with the unreal gold of a dreaming faith,
Make this futility my nakedness, and deep within me,
In the unutterable darkness of the heart, the soul
Stands stripped and humble, waiting for the glory?
  Out of the darkness, light; from the Shadow of Death.
My God shall make all things new, and shout from the housetops
On that last day
With a disconcerting tongue."

The Lament of Tristan

Between granite and alabaster
    The cold seas run;
Continually, with heavy finger,
    The grey winds thrum
Upon the cordage that thews the ship
That hales me from my heart.

May was the season of sweetness –
    The briar-rose in the lane,
The shrill brown bird, and many, many
    Folded flowers – but May brings
No softness to the spray, to the hard stems
Of sea-lavender, rosemary.

Elegy
to one long dead

It was a long prelude, played through the golden hours
Of muted August, or October falling
Mist-feathered through the trees;
In those soft Midland counties –
Warwickshire, where the weed,
The traitor elm-tree, grows as thick as nettles,
Lining the long, long lanes – and country quietness,
The voice of wood-doves and forensic rooks,
But blurred by distance and the afternoon.
Though northward, blackness crawled, a troll, issuing
Out of the gaping mines which stole our substance,
Or hovered thick-winged there above the foundries,
You were embowered still in gardens, where
The trees were close, the liveried jays were sentries,
And angel-feathered, the white owl slept there, dreaming
(Like Arthur grown old, his strife forgotten –
The pale Queen's passion, and the hint of incest,
Mordred, and the dark years behind).
The hollyhock grew tall, the mulberries ripened,
Soft, deep and red as man's-mouth, and the quince-tree
Delicate as a bridesmaid. The sad-faced gardener
Toiled for all these, and cut the dying flowers
In autumn, for his mournful pyres of smoke-reek.
And no leaves stirred within, nor passion stirred
In the quiet hearts, save when the wind from Wales
Cried in the branches, cried in the blood, telling
Of hillsides washed with rain, and huddling farms
Whose names, uncouth, were music.
Familiar with these memories, and neighbourly with Death,
That would call early and quiet, were all of you,
And ghosts – the feckless girl who hanged herself,
In sullen hopelessness, after the dancing
On the new floor – seeing her lover truly –
And swung to what sad rhythm from that beam;
And one who rode out to an indecisive battle
Over the fallow fields, and left his bed
Fruitless, his name forgotten;
These, and the small and helpful
Furry thing, the Lar,
The quiet scrabble-foot, that haunted

The dusty passages; and memory of a king
Who came in secret, and of his concealment.

This is my dream of you; you must forgive me
If my conceit has falsified the picture.
You are important to me; you were a flame,
A brightness and a joy, that seemed perhaps
The opening chords, the flower, the bird-song
That realised the garden.
For you saw clearly the freshness and the image,
The form, that was the hard and real thing
Behind these country colours; and you had skill
To make the hand mechanic and a force
To pin the soul in paint and fix the symbols
Streaming from wood and farmland,
Accepting the dear drudgery of Art
To find that other country which our quiet
Vision of years, and abstract intellect,
Trained like a climbing rose, had still divined
Beyond the roundness of the hills, the sweetness of
The fields that slept like children.
But you were swift and careless – to the rain
That beat about the pavements in the city...
And so Death took you, and the hand was still.

It was a long prelude of generations
Whose world is gone; and now I am separate,
And in these things am poor.
I need your courage for my different problems –
To make words take their places, nor neglect
The impingement on the world, which justifies
The reverie in the garden, and the dream
Of fairy countries in the enchanted hill.
Be near me now and with your brightness loosen
The curse unspoken from my shoulders; only
The Dead can aid us now –
They who were free of our contracted world –
Against that colder death that lies within.

Tschaikowskian Poem

And as we came down by the staircase –
Broad the balustrade, shining and bronze in the lustre
Of hanging lights, smooth and strong to the touch like your arm –
Down the grand sweep of the staircase eagerly stepping,
We two, to the lighted ballroom, the swirl of my music,
You paused and said: "The moon is a strange questing
Creature embodied out over these wide white plains;
But whether hunter or huntress, I do not know –
But whether hunter or hunted!"
And your mouth smiled, though while your eyes were thoughtful.
I said: "She is a maiden pursuing, or a wild white falcon
Unmewed through the skies, or she is a hind, or a hound,
Or a frightened hare – the bewitched princess who wanders
There through the snow-covered night and over the pine-trees,
Or a wild swan perhaps, or a wizened dwarf,
Back-crook'd and broken because of his burden of silver,
Who stumbles home in the cold to his cave in the mountains!
But let us go down now to the lighted ballroom
Where they are expecting us, for the dance begins."
And we went down into the hall, alone no longer.

   And standing by a window a girl said:
"Only once I saw one, once, once;
Far out over the snow, in a hard winter –
When I was a little girl, at our country place.
And Anya, our old nurse, said: 'Look, child –
Come to the window, and I will show you a wolf.'
(For often the long evenings she had told us of them)
And there it went, the lonely one, like a great dog –
But hindquarters narrow and drooping, like a cowardly dog –
Hungry nose to the snow, onward, onward.
But sometimes it paused, and scraped in its tracks, and raised
Its great head to the bitter skies, and howled."

   Oh curved, curved in a scroll the violin's neck and carved
With concentration of the patient hand;
And tight those strings and quick to break in the harsh
Air, and in the inclement weather;
And shrill, shrill the song of the strings, when the horse-hair
   sweeps

Caressingly upon them. And the flutes ice-blue, and the harps
Like melting frost, and the trumpet marching, marching
Like fire above them, like fire through the frozen pine-trees.
And the dancers came, swirling, swirling past me –
Plume and swansdown waving, white plume over the gold hair,
Arms held gallantly, and silk talking – and an eye caught
In the candle-shadow, and the curve of a mouth
Going home to my heart (the folly of it!), going home to my heart!

And the black-browed girl by the window said, remembering:
"Always in my dreams it is thus, always in my dreams –
Snow and moonlight, snow and the dark pines moaning,
Fur over my body, and my feet small,
Delicate and swift to run through the powdery snow;
And my sharp mouth to the ground, hungry, hungry,
And always onward, onward, alone, alone...."

Moon, moon, cold mouth over the pine-trees,
Or are you hunting me, or I pursuing?

An Heroic Epistle
from William Congreve to Anne Bracegirdle
circa 1729

Now it has all gone black, you are more than ever
The cadence of a voice to me, the turn of a prose phrase;
For my words in your mouth were a movement in time,
Like your hand's movement suddenly spreading the white
Fan, your turned wrist twisting the air;
Or the curve of your white neck, caught in a slant-light,
The tilt of your chin, and your smile mocking, mocking –
And then your laughter – and so your voice again.
    And never, my dear, was proud man's tenderness
Like this, never such patience;
A love not like a boy's love, nor a man loving like a boy, but rather
As one who has perfected some instrument
Of calculation – crystal, and chased gold,
And swinging steel, and mirrors set aslant

To each refraction of the sun's bright rays –
As such a man, long days in a dark workshop,
Brings forth this cold child of his quiet brain,
And after with delight knows all its rhythms,
The moods of its clear bright body –
Such was my love for you – the poet
Breathing his words into your silver throat,
Knowing each grace of your tongue, each turn of your hand,
Your musical body, so much more apt to movement,
Thus and thus, than mine, a man's, hard-thewed –
Yes, even the bright mysteries of your woman's body,
More than mere lover dares know – in the clear hard brain.

But that was many years ago, in another century,
When love was still a ladder, and the brain,
The burning wit, crowned all the body's dancing.
Then was it thought crossing thought as the hand the hand –
At the point of contact, pleasure, at the intersection
Of wits, the laughter....

And at the turn of time our music reached
Its fulness, as a conceived child,
Closed in the female body, knows its time –
That play was my crown of myrtle, fillet of laughter,
My gift to you, and yours to me, and ours to the world –
And spurned by the world; but I have done with the world.

And also in that year
John Dryden died, that great builder in words,
Poor and dislaurelled. They say that at his burying
Were strange things done; and it were something meet
That old man's corpse was carried off with laughter
Of fools, intoxication
(Which in the ancient times was of the gods)
Though only of fools.

And so that age passed with him.
And now we live in a rounded time, rounded
With a low horizon of feeling until men break it.
We have forgotten the old high modes of loving,
And the song's poise is gone.
The intellect squats twisted like a spider,
A tortured, hunch-backed poet; or lurks, exiled,
Westward, within a starved and savage country –
(He will die mad.) There is the Duchess too,
Who will have an ivory image made when I am gone,
To sit at her table, smile, and nod its head –

But the laughter is gone, and youth is gone, and you
Are gone to pray.
You cannot make of me a saint, nor I
Of you a sinner – but the pride of wit
Is whittled down, and our long battle now
Lacks auditors, lacks point.
The fire is gone – we may find tenderness,
From each to each, uncomplicate, at last –
An actress who has left the Stage behind,
An old blind gentleman who once wrote plays.

The Heart's Forest

1
(From Petrarch)

Now all alone and full of thoughts I go
*   Through solitary fields, with my eyes fixed,*
*   Avoiding print of human foot, or any*
*   Trace of it upon the bare earth stamped.*

There is no other remedy, there is
*   No right way people's searching gaze to shun;*
*   For stripped I am of happiness, and thus*
*   Outward they mark how much I burn within.*

Indeed, I think that every hill I climb,
*   River or wood which I pass by, has found*
*   Out of my life's temper; else it were concealed.*

And yet, however rough, however wild
*   The road I tread, Love comes there, close at hand,*
*   Still reasoning with me; and I with him.*

2

The heart pauses and stands at gaze
    As you come through the forest of my soul,
    Seeking only your image in the pool
    Of laughter, and the wild rose;

The old grey wolf of lust
　　That still pursued it, stops with dripping fangs,
　　Powerless to rend; and folding her bright wings
　　The eagle-intellect perches, disgraced.

And you, without concern,
　　(Like the crazed Orfeo seeking his lost bride –
　　His hair and beard grown like the lichen of trees)

Pass on under the branches, nor discern,
　　Starring six times the shadows of the glade,
　　Con-centrate on your face, their startled eyes.

3
Addison's Walk

Grove, and you trees, by careless birds
　　Frequented, and you fronds, impersonal,
　　Whose greenness soothed the long intestine broil
　　Within my head, when I would seek your shades

Those former months of solitude, remembering
　　That sane cool mind who christened you, quietly
　　In his discreet and formal century
　　Beside the unhurried river's marge walking;

Now that together in the season's prime
　　We've come this way, marked the symbolic flowers,
　　And the axe striking on the murdered willows,

When this is over, and the wing of time
　　Has brushed aside desire, in after years
　　Returning here, what ghosts will haunt these shadows?

4

Leander gazed across the cold divide
　　Of waters where, befogged, tall Sestos, dim
　　With a hung light, mocking his absence, towered,
　　Yet scrupled not to strip and plunge and swim:

247

Daring the monstrous people of the deep
    To impede his course; the still more monstrous loves
    Of sea-gods, who would drag him down to keep
    Him prisoner among their coral groves.

And I sit here with you in a yellow room
    Full of warm light and discourse, yet
    More deep and cold between us Dardan's sound;

For I shall never dare, with pliant arm,
    To dash those waves, negotiate that strait;
    And yet already I lie there, drowned, drowned.

5

In Winter, in a winter season of war,
    I turned from the Eastern gate where the iron men
    Sang their long chant of pain
    And let Love rattle his dice in my dry heart's core.

Now Spring returns, and now once more
    The flowers are out; the small birds sing again
    More meaningly than when I was alone,
    But I'm no nearer staunching my desire;

And Summer's end, or sooner, bids us part,
    And even by then, perhaps, wanting will be
    Banked down, and ready to sink like a child to sleep.

Yet I'll be wholly grateful for the art
    That all unknowing you have tutored me,
    Though Autumn bring me further cause to weep.

6
First Emblem: Dialogue of Mind and Heart

MIND: Give over now, and let me be again
        A twisted thorn-tree shivering into flower,
        Beaconing the winds alone,
        With roots between the stones of an old tower.

HEART: No, never more, for the soft woods are green,
And I must go there, where I went before
In dreams, seeking the vanished birds that plain,
The nightingales that sing a backward year –

Though Hope lies dead under the fallen leaves.
MIND: The birds are flown, the axe is at the stock,
A cold wind kills the buds as soon as blown,

And there's no couch for lovers among graves,
Nor singing when the treacherous lute-strings break,
HEART: Nor climbing, brother, now the tower is down.

7

Three walked through the meadows in a forward
Spring, and two were lovers;
Supposing themselves one, needed no word.
The third was tongue-tied: in his heart were hammers.

While these three paced the gaps in conversation –
Lover and lovers – silent
The third, and patient,
Reviewing his unsatisfactory situation;

His hair and skin were dry as hay,
His bones were clear like glass,
The hammers in his heart were musical,

Breaking his tuneful heart, which still
A damp cloth muted; but to the lonely walls
At midnight in his room, spoke for all three.

8

The moon hangs over this city of the dead
Fretting with silver walls which thought has worn,
And each dark stone, proud and vocal as a swan,
Sings, raising its head.

O Moon, my mistress, and O Death, my lover,
  Faithful in solitude, who tutored me
  In this old craft of song, oh do not be
  Jealous, now I forsake you for another;

But clothe my heart in silver and black for pride,
  Let it go dancing forth towards that cold
  Clear heart which it would win –

For oh, I would evade,
  Before it is too late, your staled
  Virginity, O Death, and your cold kisses, Moon.

9

Since I am free, why do I linger here
  Among the shadows, while the impersonal train
  Stands ready to carry me from my despair,
  Shifting the mind's landscape with change of scene,

To that south country where the solitude
  Of field and forest can bring back again
  Only the sufferings of childhood
  When I was least troubled when most alone?

There, undisturbed by symbols I may watch
  Successive flowers, at April's end to catch
  The first notes of the tentative nightingale;

But yet I could not bear that this sharp love
  Should seem unreal; you, central now to life,
  Fade from the heart, because incredible.

10
"Fortunatus et ille deos qui novit agrestes"

"That man is favoured who has learnt to know"
  (The inscription says) "the rustic deities."
  The dove descants over the arching ways
  And the old cedar leans his long arms low;

And Time, a bird of passage, folds his wings
  To brood here, and the bells which call
  Out of the clock-towers lose their power to kill,
  While the quiet sun conducts the Spring.

It was the Roman, it was the tired
  Civil servant, who wore always
  His weary gown of duty, who desired
  The country godlings, and his villa's ease;

And I, debarred from your heart's garden ways,
Grateful to pause with you among these trees.

11

This night I walk through a forest in my head;
  In each tree's heart a lute, waiting the skill
  Of hand to chisel it, is musical,
  Already with a song stirring the glade;

All the hard wood cries to the stars that float
  Among the leaves, bird-sweet and shrill,
  Though no wires stretch nor delicate fingers mete
  Out their divisions, nor lute-master's skill,

And so, bewildered like one newly dead
  Who finds the myrtle-groves of Hades strange
  Country to him, I go among the trees

Seeking your image flickering through the shade,
  A madman's fire, and thus deluded range
  Cold hollows of my skull and echoing silences.

12
Second Emblem: Echo and Narcissus

ECHO: I am a windy voice, voice to my voice
         Answering, within my stony cell,
         And pined for the dark boy over his pool
         Withdrawn, over the still mirror of glass

Which is his mind – oh never poacher hung
    More patient, tickling trout beneath the shade,
    As he to seize his naked beauty, with long
    White arms outstretched towards the flood.

NARCISSUS: And if I trail my fingers in the cool
    Waters, or mar their smoothness, I displace
    The image I desire under the pool;

    So I'll sit quiet here, until my face
    Is a white flower, and my blood green and still....
ECHO: But oh, I lie alone in the windy hill!

13

Blackbird, ironic on day's window-ledge,
    Full-throated chanter, sooty-plumed with pride,
    To hale me from my sterile crooked bed
    And the dream-haunted safety of night's cage

Into another day of wasted hope,
    Duty neglected, casual interviews
    Carefully staged, and pointing to a close
    Barren of ecstasy, and then to shape

(But oh, if favoured!) evening's conversation,
    Coil upon coil, and roads that always skirt
    The central meeting-place within the wood,

Because that heart is strange which has my heart,
    Because I came too late for consummation;
    O blackbird, blackbird, it isn't any good!

14

Now in my hall the rebel troopers stable
    Horses, whose iron hooves clang on the floor;
    They have hacked up to burn the great oak table,
    The wooden vine-leaves carved around the door;

And through my broken roof the waters beat,
  Beat, and the quick weather of sorrow falls,
  The rain coming down and mixed with withering sleet,
  Blurring the portraits and the storied walls.

And this cold wind and these black clouds that pelter
  Have overtaken us both in the dark wood,
  Were blowing up already in childhood,

And they have driven me back to that bare hall
  My heart – I have no other place at all;
  But you were wiser, going elsewhere for shelter.

15

Provençal singers, crying against the dawn,
  Whose symbol was the bitter nightingale,
  Seeking not Love's fulfilment but Love's pain,
  A darker resolution in the soul,

Sang with as strained and eager a voice as mine;
  But it is not their death-keeled dreams impel
  Me to imperfect modes to gain
  Solace of love, and bear down wit and will,

But my life's need; for like the married vine
  That dies when torn away from the elm's support,
  I cannot live for long, myself, alone;

Therefore, although indifferent, you will spare –
  Another love making lucid your quiet heart –
  The starved beast snuffling at its fastened door.

16
Third Emblem: Formal Invocation

Beautiful god, and terrible, with strong
  Bow at the shoulder hung, and at whose coming
  The Celtic swans wreathed Delos with a song,
  Close packed around that wandering isle, screaming;

You oracle-inspirer, whom
   The ordered dance delights,
   The white-robed choir with clear voice keeping time
   To measured cadence of the hollow flutes;

Think of the fleet-foot girl, who turned
   To cold dry bay-leaves in your outstretched hand,
   The overpowering scent of those crushed boughs;

Remember that dark boy, with drooping head
   And pain-struck eyes glazed, like a dying bird:
   Mindful of these, attend my suppliant voice.

17

Why to my writing finger I commit
   Words which as heavy hang
   As Charon's pennies on a dead man's tongue,
   Recording here a personal defeat,

While now, even now, under this clear March sky –
   And my friends' lives in pawn – two modes
   Of thought and being struggle on bitter roads
   (And the more scope for singing, so they say;)

I speak for those on whom this unjust time
   Has forced a solitude, whom chance
   And the machine defraud of any quiet;

And set in formal words' objective frame,
   Construct from my unhappy circumstance
   The microcosm of Europe's double heart.

18
Fourth Emblem: Hylas

I see plume-thistle and the violet
   Depending fingers of the long loosestrife,
   Meadowsweet, hemlock, formal silver-leaf,
   Nenuphar, and the crow-toe figuring it;

254

Then suddenly this quiet water is
  Cold laughter of a mouth which gathers me...
  My friend no longer by the cruel sea
  With desperate voice negates the silences.

The timeless prisoner of the inverted world,
  Unreal like these shadow-birds, is dumb
  As fish that cancel it, and oh, as cold;

You who prospect the sunset's golden wool,
  Beating to pulse of song the wild sea-foam,
  Think – my fate also is conceivable.

19

There is a hollow in my heart, a lost
  World, where never tardy breath
  Of Winter chills the hyacinth, nor frost
  Narcissus blank and beautiful as death;

There is a southern hollow on my heart's
  Bare mountains, and the birds which sing
  Among the branches, troublesome as thoughts,
  Shatter my sleep with memories of Spring;

And wandering all about these forest-shades,
  With long and fragrant hair unloosed to the wind
  And bosoms bare and torn, go women weeping –

Oh, in the Springtime! – seeking
  For all lost forms of love they may not find
  Where on the grass your wounded image bleeds.

20
Fifth Emblem: The Pot of Basil

THE SKULL: You should have left me to the tender worm
                 In the soft leaf-mould whittling away my eyes,
                 Until the cold rain falling could erase
                 Grief, and your brothers' crime;

But the pot cramps me, and the wild thyme
   Roots into my brain to recreate
   Those passionate thoughts should rot away with it,
   And spreads the air of death about your room.

ISABELLA: But O my darling, though I know your heart
   Is hidden from me now, away in the deep
   Woods, nothing shall make us part;

   For though I wake in the barren moonlight to weep
   I can be sure of you now as never I could
   Though your living body lay beside me in sleep.

21

Here in these woods where April is flamboyant,
   Birds drop their songs, each from his private tower;
   I mark the cuckoo's voice, inhuman, clear –
   Oh long expected vagrant! –

From the next field continually calling.
   So Spring's confirmed by her winged hierophant,
   And now's the time to pause and seek portent
   From those distinctive notes through the air trailing.

Particularly do I bear in mind
   How many singers and dead lovers heard
   Hope, guile or mockery in that chance crying;

And yet I fear it's now no way to find
   Conclusions for you, heart – not from a bird
   About his own peculiar business flying.

Twelve Gothic Ballads

DRINKING SONG

I travel the roads from town to town,
Dry mouth, dry brain, and an old patched gown,
And if you'll drink with me, brother, come down!

I served an old man in a learnèd tower
Who read himself blind, seeking for the Golden Flower;
It was hot work at his bellows, hour after hour.

He thought he would make the *aurum potabile*
But I stole from his cellar the only good recipe;
Come down, my merry brother, and sample it with me!

The wind blows through you and it's thirsty weather;
Though a fine pair of smooth white idle hands you've got now,
    brother,
Come off your high horse and we'll drink together!

Decent folks in the towns, oh they won't lodge me;
Now I'm on the roads, sober travellers dodge me,
But there on the gallows, brother, you're not too fine to pledge
    me!

AT THE WINDOW

My hands are like glass, and through my blue hands
    They saw the candle shining late last winter;
And I stand here watching where the long road winds,
    Waiting for my lover.

All in iron to Lithuania in the autumn he went forth
    Against those cold pagans who bow down to talking trees –
God give them sorrow therefore – and they tell me he's gone
    north
    Where the very winds freeze.

And I dreamt last night that I saw him and he lay
    On a high cold bed in a wide white hall;
To an ice-king's daughter he has given his heart away
    And he lives her thrall.

And she'll keep him prisoner all his days
    Till she's frozen him stiff, both body and soul;
Then she'll throw his heart and his clear blue eyes
    To the wild sea-fowl.

O fieldfare, blue-capped fieldfare flying
    Beyond the Pole, when the Spring shall come,
Seek out my love wherever he is lying
    And call him home!

BEGGAR'S SERENADE

I'm a peevish old man with a penny-whistle
Blowing under your window this blesséd evening
But pause a moment and hear the tune I'm playing

I never was handsome and my limbs aren't straight
But I raise my finger and the girls all follow me
And leave some of the spruce young fellows gaping

I had a painted girl whom none spoke well of
And I had a milkmaid who didn't know cow from bull
And a girl with green flesh out of a lucky hill

And I had a lady as fine and as proud as you
To follow me forty leagues and bed under a bush
And I left her weeping at the long lane's end

And are you sure where you will lie to-night, woman?

THE MAD KNIGHT'S SONG

Over windy heath and through still forest
    From country to country I take my way,
For my skull is so full of crazed caged song-birds
    That keep me waking both night and day.

My horse is so lean and gawky that he starts
    At his own reflection on the moon's round face;
And love has made my body so thin and so pale
    That it's little I need to eat these days.

I took the naked skin from my back and my breast
   To make her a pair of gloves to her mind,
And there's nothing now keeps the wind from my heart;
   O my love, my love, why were you unkind?

THE OLD KING

I am so old a king that I remember
How three oak-forests have sprouted and grown and died
Around this hall, and the generations
Of strong young men drinking ale under the shade of them,
But now I am content to sleep.

My beard is grown long and fine like cobwebs;
The soft dust has fallen upon my shoulders;
The mice playing round me do not heed me at all;
It's little warmth I find in these embers.

There were proud queens with yellow hair, white breasts,
Walking the earth when I was young;
I had a long straight sword and their castles to storm;
It's little warmth I find in these embers.

Their faces are fallen in and their beauty gone,
And no-one remembers, no-one remembers;
I could be sorrowful thinking of what I have lost,
But now I am content to sleep.

It's little warmth I find in these embers
But now I am content to sleep.

A SONG FOR THE DUENNA

Never walk in the sun, my darling, never walk in the sun,
For he will dazzle your dove-grey eyes and shrivel your delicate
   skin.

Oh never be lifting your head, my darling, though a voice cries
      over the wall;
Look down, look down, at your own image, how lovely it lies
   in the pool.

Content with the roses springs, my darling, that make your garden
    so gay;
There are those who would trample your garden down and steal
    the flowers away.

SONG OF THE SARACEN LADY

Oh I am come far over the sea
To seek my love, to seek my love –
This is a strange cold grey country –
His name is the only word I can say.

I am a prince of Aleppo's daughter,
But I gave my gold rings to the camel-drivers;
I gave my silken gowns to the sailors to take me to my love –
His name is the only word I can say.

We lay on soft cushions in my father's house,
In the closed courtyard where the fountains play,
But he was homesick for his own country;
His name is the only word I can say.

His head ran upon jars of oil and packages of spice,
His eyes were heavy when I sang my songs;
Yet never tell me he has forgotten:
His name is the only word I can say.

COWARD'S LAMENT

The ravens' black wings bright with morning rain
Are beating about my friend's head where low he lies
On the field where I turned back and he remains.

I am ashamed to show my face in any good company;
There's no place for me at the wine-bench or by the fire;
The women drawing water at the well throw stones at me.

Last night I lay under an old thorn-tree
And I saw in a dream my friend stripped of his arms
And the dry blood marring his naked body.

And he stood beside me and never spoke
In my dream, in the darkness, the long night through,
Till I woke like Peter to the crowing of the cock.

I have come far, far,
Till I am little more
Than hanging skin and bone;
My friends are dead and gone
And I am left alone,
Under a chill star.

My face was never fair
To kindle his desire,
And no man would admire
The tangles of my hair,
And my two eyes –
Not beautiful;
It were a miracle
Had he thought otherwise.

But Love is wise and strong,
And Love alone;
There might have been
A flower behind my eyes
And honey in my vein,
But for my sin.

I could not be content
To love – would have his will
Turned from its own bent
To be my will;
There was not any change
In him – I was to blame
If he, being always strange,
Stranger became.

A BALLAD OF BROTHER BOGOMIL

Sang the pale Manichee on his Balkan mountain
To a horrid old witch in her womb of wattles:

– "Big Klaus and Little Klaus played at blood-alleys
Up there in the sky, with the bright worlds for marbles;
But whoop! when Big Klaus got too big for his shoes,
God gave one kick, and down he tumbled
Like a sack of turnips, on top of Mount Sinai.

261

"The Lord walked over the hills of Galilee –
His docetic feet could not crumble the daisies –
And St. Peter behind, mumbling an old crust;
'Do you love me, Peter?' 'Yes, Lord,' said Peter,
And spat out his crust. Then the Lord in his mercy
Created a mushroom," sang the thin Manichee.

"But Big Klaus came after, creating toadstools –
Red ones, spotty ones, and the ink-horn stink-horn;
And Boris our Tsar, and the orthodox Emperor,
And their 300 popes, and the village tax-collector,
Are Big Klaus' blue-eyed boys – and us for the fleecing" –
Sang the black-hearted heterodox Manichee.

"But whoop! when the Devil rides over the birch-trees,
With a crack of whips, on a moonshiny May-night,
They're at *his* business with Bess and Barbara.
I keep myself to myself, and my little bag of seed,
Ash-grey as a stone on my Balkan mountain.

"But you, sister Strinx and Sister Empusa,
Respectable midwives with apricot brandy,
Go your rounds by starlight with a long silver bodkin,
To teach the little darlings that it had better not been born."

– To an old witch crouched in her womb of wattles
Sang the sly Manichee on his Balkan mountain.

A PASTORAL BALLAD

Rough goat-herd girls that feed your flocks
    Beneath these mountain crags
I hold no heart within my breast –
    But there the bright rose brags
(Shuffled beneath my musty coat)
    And a briar's thorny snags
Are twined about my white and arching bones.

Bind down my feet with the trailing ivy,
    It's here I would remain.

Beneath the naked sun I wandered,
  The bare woods were my house,
And heard the magpie laughing dryly
  Among the lichened boughs;
The wild bee came and made a nest
  Under my hollow brows,
And my cracked skull is full of honey-comb.

Bind down my feet with the trailing ivy,
  It's here I would remain.

Out of the black unchristened tarns
  That steam against the moon
Rise brave white boys with silver skin
  To pleasure you...I'm none
That ever woman loved, and want
  To lie out of the sun,
In the long weeds of your dank dale, alone.

Bind down my feet with the trailing ivy,
  It's here I would remain.

AN ALBA

FIRST VOICE: Stiff shadows of the cypress cancel your lawn;
      The sun has hoisted an eastern flag of fire;
      The darkness dies, and with the darkness I must go.

SECOND VOICE: O love, there is always a shadow in my heart;
      You have found the eternal night of my body.

FIRST VOICE: The bird of day beats bright wings and screams a
        warning;
      The dead troop back to their earthy billets;
      A cold wind from the dawn whirls me from your side.

SECOND VOICE: The pale light of morning soaks through the curtains
      Of trembling silk that shadow your chamber
      And I see your white limbs like the limbs of a corpse.

FIRST VOICE: But let us lie like dead lovers in the cool earth
      Whom no windy promises of life deceive.

The Hill

'Ah Corydon, Corydon, quae te dementia cepit?'

1

All night long in the garden under the cypresses
I heard the song of the childish Dead, chirping
With black dried lips, like crickets in the beams,
And the silence of the stream whose watery tongue is gone.
But now with a sound of trumpets
The sun, the golden-feathered, beating his wings
Through the granular ether, out of his eastern cave
Of darkness comes – a bird, whose iron beak
Is pointed at my dry and singing brain.
And so in the early morning I climb to this hill
Islanded in blue intense of the circling air,
Hearing only the long melancholy line of the shepherd's piping
Or him calling to his dog down there in the valley.

The lizard is asleep in the stone wall
And the grasshoppers cry among the ilex-trees;

The smooth metallic leaves
Of laurel and myrtle are aflame with spices;

The hours drift up from white towers in the valley –
The waves of sound float the sun's shining feathers.

2

What is this shadow sprawled upon the plain,
Blurring the fields' brown and green?
This is an image of the starved beast, bayed
Between the self-destroying trees, the harpy-haunted.
And once, in an unjust city
I saw that form, a carved and jewelled head
And gilded mouth – a conduit for a sewer
Flowing between the grey and weary streets.
And there three proud and pale singers stood –
The violent exile, the unlucky lover,
And sick in black an over-learnéd man –
The sterile laurel shadowing burning eyes,

264

The long hand poised upon the stiffened breast-bone:
"For my heart never told how the green time should waste..."

The shadow writhes upon the incandescent plain.

3

The sun bleeds fire out of his singing heart
Upon my glassy limbs; the heat,
Within my lucid body, points
The reasoned diagram of the skeleton,
Till, liquefied, my flesh has flowed away
In music down the slope, and lies, a pool,
Gleaming within the shadow of the beast;
And the stiff bones sink to the ground in prayer,
A little heap of ivory, pyramid
On the smaragdine top of the rounded hill,
(In that vast circling green one point of white)
The erect form gone, and all fallen together.
Only the skull within whose sockets stand
Two glittering sapphires where the eyes had been,
Continually turns them to the sky,
Circling them south with circling of the sun,
Who now approaching his full height
Pours down his strength where cedars lift their arms
To his triumphal course,
Till the hard summits of the mountains smoke
And all the thin grass tingles with dry pain.

4

The shadow writhes beneath –
The dark beast rising in the imagined wood –
And lolls a tongue of fire to the diamond sky,
His wide wings spread above the quivering plain
Dappled by glittering illusory pools,
Towards the mountains; and his body, pierced
By white and rising towers,
Seems one with the iron hours that nest in them.
He flows around me, islanding this hill
In pillars of smoke, his fiery mouth agape,
And striding underneath the striding sun
Comes to devour,
Till fear rattles among the prostrate bones.

But at the noontide bell,
Oh, downward sweeping from the silent sky,
What wind, what wings of mercy poised upon
The summits of the hills – cool breath and softer
Than stockdove's plaining in a watered wood?
What divine swiftness pierces that grim beast,
Drifting his smoky volumes far away
Beyond the mountains, where they roll and fade –
Now beautiful as spires of innocent serpents?
And the great sun, an eagle flying through
The midst of the heavens, cries with a loud voice
That Babylon is fallen....
While music from above confirms the mercy.

And my bones raise white limbs in adoration –
And singing nerves upon them stretched, and flesh,
And eyes which are soft again with tears.
And oh, for hours
Were female shapes upon the mountains, clothed
In blue and green; and drifting hand in hand
Through the mid-heaven, such forms were, half-discerned:
Singing, sound of plucked wires, and fragile hands
Sustaining flowers which surely, surely sprang
From fields beyond the dryness of this sky.
And I knew ladies laid in tomb by singers
And mourned for with their melting voices, falling
Like water poured upon the smooth hard marble.
And then, they faded, faded –
And silence afterwards among the hills.

6

And the sun went down, chanting, a rosy swan,
In clouds of fire;
And I have risen, and felt my flesh about me,
And the clear blood running in my veins;
Although my side is pierced
This day, with a bright spear –
A wound which does go deep and will not easily heal.

I take my way towards the waiting boat
On the canal, when the first stars appear;

And now, alone, save for the lean boatman
Singing his song of a delivered city,
I go by the palace-walls and the poised bridges,
Beneath a not unfriendly moon.

The Beggar

I, the beggar, awakening by the roadside,
A thing hardly human, disfigured with lice and sores,
Who have often slept for warmth among the straws and shit –
My caked hide brown and yellow and blue, like naked clay
Seen in a landslip place where no grass grows,
And a few old rags fluttering about my bones,
Like parodies of wings – stretching my bird-claw hands,
Salute the round bright sun, and you, blue polished sky,
And winds going like heralds about their business,
And tattered greenness of trees, and untidy grass,
And jolly birds singing, and the people passing
By hundreds and thousands along the dusty roads –
And with my thin voice, grating like a cicada,
I cry for alms....

I am of no more account than the dirt and the stones
That are ground by the rumbling wheels of your passing carts –
For we are the very ordure and dregs of the Universe –
Refuse, but for the charity of the stars.
For the Sun, the candle of heaven, is the father of all life,
And begetter also of gold in the dismal rocks;
And the changeable Moon rules over the shifting seas,
And the patient growth of plants in the humid earth,
And man's mad heart, and woman's quiet moody body;
And the wandering Planets go making music for us;
And from the fixed Stars falls wisdom down like dew;
And far above the shadow of darkness, where no eye
Could ever pierce, or ear could bear the singing,
I tell you there are many, many, great and terrible
Angels, and Powers, and Gods –
Their feet are shod with expedition, and their hands have lifted up
Rods to bear rule with us, and cups flowing over
With wine which is red blood of wrath or of blessings,

And the hissing of their radiant silver wings
Is the cause of a gift of love or destruction among us;
So the whole world is a beggar, and I the poorest
Of all mean things crawling on its dun surface.

And the people go by, passing me on their road...
Proud, cruel man, in velvet, with your long sword,
Whose pleasures are in the dark courts of the crowded city,
Under the stars, cloaked, bringing soft bad music
To prize open the hearts of veiled women, who, weeping,
Shall curse you when you have gone with a light pair of heels:
Oh think how poor you will be, when you find at last
The misery of lust burnt low, your thief's eyes humid
With rheum, though dry of tears, and your hair and beard
Faded and raggéd, though not your fur-lined cloak –
And now, stalking along this road, with your sinewy body
And animal confidence, have pity also on me!

Soldier, going out to the foreign wars –
Conquering general, whose brow already feels
The shadow of the laurel the City will give to you:
If you have been afraid only of this one thing –
To look on the young limbs lopped and the festering bodies
Which are your triumph, not with the cold clear eye
Bright in the metal mask, but nakedly and with pity –
Think too of my foul limbs, which are weak and ugly!

Lady, in the dark gilded coach, with eyes like diamonds,
And hands softer and gentler than milk, and already weary
With the weight of the jewelled rings your lovers have given you:
Remember that beauty, too, is a gift fast spent,
And soon you will shrink from your mirror more than from me!

And you, with little eyes, huddled among the travelling rugs:
Death is a sturdy beggar who uses few words
And will take away by force what you would not give me!

But oh, above all, you who are young and lovely
And like to go gay-covered through the green ways of the world –
Take pleasure in one another while Time, too, is your friend:
But do not turn your eyes away now from my foulness,
For the sake of Love who is also a beggar and naked.

Virgin and Unicorn

Oh that bright impossible beast of the mind –
He was as wild as the wind, and his own pride
Had turned him savage,
And solitary in his solitary forest;

But my eyes were mirrors and my lap spices,
And he bowed his gold head down, gentle as cornstalks
Under the wind, under the reaping sickle;

And when they wrenched the horn from his splintering skull
He was as full of tears and trust as a child.

Daphne

I slipped into a shade, and those wild snares –
My wandering tresses, where the sunlight tangled
(Your hands, explorers of the golden jungle) –
Became as cool as leaves, as feet of birds
That sit and sing upon these arms, my boughs;
And now I do not care
If still your tears or if at dawn the dew
Waken my freshness and hang jewels on
My blind and wrinkled cheek, or if the night
Enfold with darkness my clear chastity.
And though I shade your singers' passionate brows,
With their male voices trembling, or indue
The virgin's lips with holy madness, I remain forever
Cold, vegetable, and dumb. Now I am one
With leaves inscribed by blood of murdered kings
Or purple from the shameful wound of gods,
And that poor pale-faced boy who sank to find
His flowering image in the silent pool.

Phasma

He turns and turns the diamond in the shadowed room,
His eyes cloudy with terror: for he sees
The tower haunted by vampires – effeminate, mincing
Deaths, with their tattered wings of soiled lace,
Who drop like swallows from the battlements.

There is a smell of tiger and of civet,
As in the forest, at their rubbing places;
And he discerns among the hard green flames,
That dance between the gilded dragons carved
Upon the grate, the burning eyes of that
Soft lynx which issued from the open tomb.

And always there is music in his room,
Borne by the wind from very far away,
Out of the woods whose few leaves wet with rain
Hang limp upon the dark and polished boughs,
And, underneath, a skeleton reclines,
Whose breast, with bright hair strung, is a curved harp.

The Ghost in the Cellarage

Climb then by spiral stairways of cold thought
Into the singing darkness – you shall find
God's healing hands are numb – transfixed
By sharp star-splinters to the cruel sky,
And impotent, extended through the night.

O rebel brain, burn through the too-tight skull
Or turn me loose to graze – but then the needle
Pierces more sharply to the unpurged organ;
Flesh is betrayed by flesh, and love unkindly
Linked to a symmetry of skin and sinew.
No delicate dial is the blood-pump heart,
And all uncircumcised the tender eye-ball.

270

O you who have found out your love's anatomy
A painful dryness, think of a wounded mole
Working in the earth,
And the poor ghost under the castle pavement.

Invocation at Midnight

Midnight – a melancholy counterpoint of bells
Out of the wise and pointed towers, the unloved, the unheeded
    spires;
Only the watchful, the unsleeping, only the wasters and the
    weeping,
Only the weary hear those monitory bells;
The nigger midnight strung between day and day.

Now flesh is trampled by advancing sorrow
And my white walls crumple before despair;
The virginal-eyed morrow Darkness has clawed
And I am left alone with the trite bone
And the poor negro lynched in the harsh air.

O Love, black-fanged, and hanged among the myrtles,
O Haunter, Hunter, passing sad to sorrow,
Arrow the timid flesh, the cold coy flesh
That dies and trembles in the mesh of darkness,
That's dinned and deafened by thought's melancholy bells!

Two Voyages

1
J'ai plus de souvenirs que si j'avais mille ans.
BAUDELAIRE

How long I cannot say
I have lain drowned and sleepless on this sea,
Whose waters were my mother's bitter tears.
My beard, sargasso-weed,
Cumbers your hopeful keel, my hand delays

271

Your freight of Indian moons, which hastens on –
And now comes in my fear –
To the same wished-for maelstrom of despair.

Wrapped in his cone of darkness each proceeds;
And I demand, too late,
The gift of your scared eyes, with which you light
Your blackened prow and this our ambient night;
For you will soon forget
That moment on the storm-wracked mast when hailed
Dead man his fellow, under scrutiny
Of gull-voiced, cold-eyed stars which ruled our birth.
Your body is the chart,
And you discern a mirrored mirage there –
Islands of dancing palm-trees, gaudy birds,
Small brown and naked children in the surf,
And on the off-shore wind
A breath of cinnamon and cloves – illusions
That I have suffered in these seas before.

Lost voyager, O my dear,
Believe, were He our friend, yours should not be
The sterile beauty of a coral tree;
If you, through grace, achieve,
Locked in those boughs, a statue's ecstasy.
Or musically drown,
Or if my fear, even as this love, is vain –
Beached on whatever shore, remember me.

2

Full season now to turn
From the gardens suddenly tender under the sun
Which rises there for others
Breeding a precious dew where tears had hung,
Whose bright flower-faces smile to my averted eyes
With what unmerited kindness of farewell.
Take oar, hoist sail, and go
Once more to seas where only a dark star guides
And that long wavering lonely track of foam.
I know behind your eyes
Lie infinite distances of whispering wave
Under the arching caverns of the skull,

Where grope, voraciously,
Dark fishes hung about with living fire;
So, unregarded, move
Into the deeper waters, and there drown.

Sestina

(A Consolation)

The winter moon that clambers through the pine-trees,
Nor stirs the beaded rime upon their boughs,
That haunts the forest with a pelt of ermine,
Printing no trace upon the fallen leaves,
And breeds a silver blossom in my heart,
Finds the dew dry, the stream that cannot weep.

But when your wakeful eyes would have you weep,
Pregnant with fear the night and hostile pine-trees,
You still are spared the winter of my heart –
To gaze at hungry stars through latticed boughs,
To lie an age forgotten under leaves,
To cage the fox, the ravening bear, the ermine.

Though comes a ghost imperious in ermine
Nightlong outside your shuttered panes to weep
And whisper for admittance with the leaves,
Or stands and beckons by the frost-bound pine-trees –
Oh guard your threshold with the crosswise boughs,
Keep bright the haunted chancel of your heart.

And those dark hands that long to smirch your heart
As virginal as was that fabled ermine –
Believe them nothing but the winter boughs;
Child, when you lie awake to hear her weep,
Fancy it but the moaning of the pine-trees,
The unimpassioned sobbing of the leaves.

My path is restless as the winter leaves'
In the interior forest of my heart,
But you may seek the not unfriendly pine-trees
As native to them as the woodland ermine,
Nor solitude constrain you long to weep
Under this ancient benison of boughs.

273

Rest then secure, guarded by arching boughs,
And be your sleep as quiet as growth of leaves;
And joy may overtake you, till you weep
Waking at last to find that even the heart
Has changed its coat like any winter ermine,
And Spring has come, and entered through the pine-trees.

You, who have loved the pine-trees' patient boughs
And the brisk ermine moving through the leaves –
They teach the heart what folly it is to weep.

Sonnet

Dark woman who protend what lotuses –
Your white and motioning hands – he goes to seek
Upon your lips and eyes Hesperides,
And that most ancient oracle, the Snake;

You are the singing voice beneath the stream
Whose source is hidden in his ardent blood,
The quick bird troublous through a childhood's dream,
The beckoning stars beyond the moonlit wood;

You are his cliffs of ice, his mist of fire,
The springtide morning road and summer pool,
And yours the golden tenderness of Fall,
And the still challenge of December's air, –

Her Christmas roses' sudden purity,
The arched, maternal bareness of her sky.

Sonnet

In time of the unbearable tenderness of roses,
And the small speaking bird among the quick-set thorn,
The slow significance of swans, procession borne
On dark but lucid streams, where softest air reposes –

Oh masked by summer then your hollow face, and bound
With chains of grass and flowers your white and elegant
Elbow and armpit; and sweet your song, O sycophant,
Who with your hard lips rock the uneasy-cradled drowned!

Now the late season's moon is bleached, and drained away
Her shining silver blood into the thirsty air
That comes from Africa with harsh sandpaper breath;

Nightly, naked of sleep, I turn and take my way
To meet you face to face on the stone-graven stair –
You, with the emerald fangs, the golden eyes of Death.

Soir du Carnaval
Circa 1830

The student Florestan
Takes his guitar
And stands at the window....
A white-rose moon,
Squired by one star,
Is blossoming down
On the dreaming town.

"If only I had wings, my dear,
    My Amalie,
Then I would fly away with you
    To Italy!"

His friend Eusebius
Reads himself blind,
By the one candle, planted
In a Death's-head's eye;
Where Hebrew characters
Crawl on the yellow page
He is trying to find
The Secret – but
We do not mind....

"But had I lived in former days
My knightly deeds had won your praise.

"And when you shall wonder
What has become of me –
Where the lost cause is broken,
By a smoking barricade,
Under a tattered flag,
You will find my poor body

. . . And weep for me,
My Amalie!"

Saint Cecilia

And so, night after night,
From the ranked citadel of tubes, the graduated
Throats of song, the organ's rising flutes –
Like hollow reed-stems, bound with wax and twine,
That pour shrill music to the listening hills,
While over them a satyr's hairy mouth
Trembles – praise went up to the blue
And drooping silver-dusted petals of
The heavens' hanging rose;
In fantasy and fugue, static and carved
Upon the streaming moments, like the vine
With symmetry of frond and tendril turned
In stone, on a stone porch. And my pale hands,
With cool and delicate fingers, frail as spires
Of some faint water-plant, whose grace
No lover might emprison,
Division made upon the ivory keys.

And yet my body was a pool,
Tremulous, bottomless, where through the dark
Plunged ever down and down that silver fish
My silent heart – though still went up
A voice from hand exact, and calculating
Eye, and weighed in leverage of the forearm's poise.

And the Moon stooping to the female curve
Of the high unglazed window through the night,
Whispered her pagan fancies:
"O my wise daughter, who have made this choice,
Desiring never lover's touch, but only
Abstract caress of song, and that cold flame
That sweeps around you, flickering, springing from
The dancing rhythms of your own clear blood –
Oh you shall turn and find
My secret island fane, embowered in woods
Of murmuring pine, the smooth white pillars of
My sacred house, served only by sweet choir
Of virgin girls, white-veiled, who feed my stags
And wreathe their silver horns, or graced by the dance
And glimmering limbs of clear-eyed boys,
And sexless tone of their high-sounding voices:
Puellae et pueri integri...."
So spoke, and rose, and soared
Up to her midnight throne,
Showing the Palatine, and smoke of torches borne
By obscene, cruel revellers, and swathed forms lurking
Beneath expectant arches

                .   .   .   .   .   .

But now another visitor has come
To hear my dove-winged chords and silver scale,
And three nights in the shadow he has stood
Erect, yet with bowed head, and six wings furled
About his bare and splendid body;
Long hair like small blue flames swept back above
His lucid brows, and great eyes deep with love;
Sword girt about his shining loins, – sentinel
Of God's high eastern watch-tower, set to challenge
The radiant Sun with words, when fiery hoov'd
His steeds beat up the dawn.

He brings me roses that are red like pain.

For the Nativity

Shepherds, I sing you, this winter's night
Our Hope new-planted, the womb'd, the buried Seed:
For a strange Star has fallen, to blossom from a tomb,
And infinite Godhead circumscribed, hangs helpless at the breast.

Now the cold airs are musical, and all the ways of the sky
Vivid with moving fires, above the hills where tread
The feet – how beautiful! – of them that publish peace.

The sacrifice, which is not made for them,
The angels comprehend, and bend to earth
Their worshipping way. Material kind Earth
Gives Him a Mother's breast, and needful food.

A Love, shepherds, most poor,
And yet most royal, kings,
Begins this winter's night;
But oh, cast forth, and with no proper place,
Out in the cold He lies!

Tibullus Gone to War

Quis furor est atrem bellis arcessere mortem?
imminet et tacito clam venit illa pede.

The rigid ancestral masks round the blackened ceiling –
I used to bring them my toys and other gifts,
When I was a boy, running about with bare feet –
And the small urns also,
Full of the family bones (but the darling Dead
Were under the sprinkled fields, pushing up the bean-crop,
And making the apples plump) and that little old god,
In his wooden house, smeared with red paint,
And his enormous member – well, anyhow,
I hope they'll look after me now, in these outlandish parts.

·   ·   ·   ·   ·   ·

And as for you, Delia, I'm sorry for what I said,
And I have shaken off this long ague of love;

278

There might have been a smallish farm in the hills . . . but the gods
    thought otherwise.
Regard yourself free for all you promised –
Light words which the South and South East winds
Bluster to the myrrh-bearing slopes of Mount Ararat!

The Divided Ways
in memory of Sidney Keyes

He has gone down into the dark cellar
To talk with the bright-faced Spirit with silver hair;
But I shall never know what word was spoken there.

My friend is out of earshot. Our ways divided
Before we even knew we had missed each other.
For he advanced
Into a stony wilderness of the heart,
Under a hostile and a red-clawed sun;
All that dry day, until the darkness fell,
I heard him going, and shouting among the canyons.
But I, struck backward from the eastern gate,
Had turned aside, obscure,
Beneath the unfriendly silence of the moon,
My long white fingers on a small carved lute.
There was a forest, and faces known in childhood
Rose unexpected from the mirrored pools;
The trees had hands to clutch my velvet shoulders,
And birds of fever sang among the branches;
Till the dark vine-boughs, breaking as I seized them,
And dripping blood, cried out with my own voice:
"I also have known thirst, and the wanderer's terror! . . ."

But I had lost my friend and the mountain paths;
And if there might have been another meeting –
The new sun rising in a different sky,
Having repaired his light in the streams of Ocean,
And the moon, white and maternal, going down
Over the virgin hills – it is too late
Ever to find it now.

And though it was in May that the reptile guns
And breeze-fly bullets took my friend away,
It is no time to forge a delicate idyll
Of the young shepherd, stricken, prone among
The flowers of spring, heavy with morning dew,
And emblematic blood of dying gods;
Or that head pillowed on a wave's white fleece,
Softly drowning in a Celtic sea.
This was more harsh and meaningless than winter.

But now, at last, I dare avow my terror
Of the pale vampire by the cooling grate;
The enemy face that doubled every loved one;
My secret fear of him and his cold heroes;
The meaning of the dream
Which was so fraught with trouble for us both;
And how, through this long autumn
(Sick and tempestuous with another sorrow)
His spirit, vexed, fluttered among my thoughts,
A bird returning to the darkened window –
The hard-eyed albatross with scissor bill.
And I would ask his pardon for this weakness.

But he is gone where no hallooing voice
Nor beckoning hand can ever call him back;
And what is ours of him
Must speak impartially for all the world;
There is no personal word remains for me,
And I pretend to find no meaning here.
Though I might guess that other Singer's wisdom
Who saw in Death a dark immaculate flower,
And tenderness in every falling autumn,
This abstract music will not bring again
My friend to his warm room:
Inscrutable the darkness covers him.

Epithalamium
for the Marriage at Cana

Their lips were pure, those men of former days,
On which the golden bees' dark clusters hung,
Or swarmed about their cradles,
Filling the tall dim room with murmuring –
The bees, the wise nymphs' messengers, who range
The mountain-slopes where fall the sun's first beams,
Seeking the wild-thyme blossoms.

Among night's shadows and her marching dreams
I see them in their ivory chairs, –
The beautiful old men,
Whose brows are crowned with laurel and with roses.
It seemed one stood before me,
With hair and beard of silver, dropping myrrh,
And struck me with the staff held in his hand,
On which was carved a jewelled cicala
Shaking shrill music from its glittering wings.
He touched my mouth: "Sing now," said he;
"What shall I sing – I with the failing hand,
And eyes grown clouded in our darker days?
And how now shall the dove, the Mother's bird,
Bring its green bough, or build again
Here in this hollow heart, a wood of sighs
Which the harsh years have ravished?" "Take this cup,
The honey and milk of the initiate,
And sing a wedding-song
For Him, our youthful wine-god, coming up
From Jordan's waters, where the shining wind
Fluttered above his head,
Into this town, whose festival
Makes echo now the Galilean hills."

This morning waken early,
While in the dark the mitred priests go out
To bless the wells and every mountain spring.
On the far Abyssinian hills the snows
Are loosened by the strength of the returning sun;
The cataracts know it, and the shouldering flood,
The bridegroom Nile, the lotus-crowned,
Comes to the waiting earth,

281

And with his rich dark waves
He overspreads the black Egyptian land,
Until the furrows waken, and are green
With the sharp spear-points of the year's young corn.
Osiris' ark returns, the murdered god
Revives, the buried seed sends up new shoots
Out of the world of death beneath the clod;
And in the Syrian hills, that little stream,
Swelled with spring rains, leaps lightly down the crags –
Adonis, running red as blood or wine.

This morning waken early,
You happy bridegroom, golden as the sun!
Before you, let your twelve companions run
To fetch the bride out of her mother's house –
Now, while her seven bridesmaids deck her out
With lilies, and the purple hyacinth-flower
That lies and bleeds upon the bare hillside
When the strong ploughman's blade has cropped its head –
These, and the virgin rose
That will not come again when time is fled.
And, bridegroom, see, she meets you like the moon,
Shining, a queen among the lesser stars;
Hasten, and take her! This day she is crowned,
And on a stage, in royalty upraised,
Until the evening comes, you sit –
King Solomon and the Shulamite,
While the young men and village girls around
Clap hands and sing, and strew your couch with flowers.

But who brings in new wine? The Guest,
With the wild ivy crowned
Against the morning heat,
Who neighbourly has come, and yet
A King – like him from India triumphing,
Drawn in his car by soft-furred mountain-cats
And panthers dapple-skinned with brown and gold;
(And women followed him with long loose hair,
And horse-shanked satyr-boys,
Shaking the pine-cone, and the heavy heads
Of lily and poppy-blooms on thin tall stems;
The mountains and the solitary valleys
Echoed to their shrill cries,

And night was scattered by their joyful cymbals,
Till the hill-streams and hurrying waterfalls
Miraculously ran
With honey, milk, and wine,
Drawn by pure hands out of their secret source).

                                              But tell,
First, of the Mother bidden to the feast:
God's hidden Wisdom, she who is called
Shekhina, and Sophia, mantled in blue
Of the deep waters, and the star-sewn sky –
Yet undistinguished, now,
Among the peasant-mothers gathered here,
The humble women, with their wrinkled hands
Whose bones are cramped with toil of the busy spindle,
Faces tight-lipped and gentle
With memory of still-enduring sorrows.
See, she sits watching by the wells of doctrine,
The six stone water-pots before the door.
For her, the intercessor,
Now let the Son upon the wise still waters
Put forth his power, and make joy more abundant.
So, to the servants,
"Whatever he shall bid you do, obey."
Draw then, and to the feasters bear the wine.

Now, poet, take your instrument,
And praise with song the beauty of the bride,
As is the custom of these seven days.
But first do honour to our Guest,
Whom dreaming kings brought gifts of gold and spices,
Completing here that same epiphany:
"I see a hill,
And there a lonely tree waits like a bride
Her lover in the Spring.
And look, he comes, clad in a purple robe;
The whitethorn now, and not the ivy-twine,
Has given him a crown;
And his the reed, the sponge, the bitter wine,
To be his marriage-draught,
Who here must consummate his agony –
Until his naked corpse
Lies at the last outstretched across his mother's knee;

283

But the slain Lamb,
Who rises with the shining leaves of Spring,
Shall to the citadel call his Bride home."

The water glows as wine –
Prefiguring the wine's own greater change.
Be glad, you children of the bridechamber,
For now your joy is with you; the true vine
Spreads its green branches all about the house.
Be happy, bride and groom,
As now we sing before the inner door;
The night approaches, Hesperus is come.

The False Return

1   SHALL THEY RETURN?

Shall they return, the silent marble faces
Gazing beyond the grey-ranked olive-trees
To where the white town lies beneath the sun,
And ships come in across a whispering sea?

Here at the cave's mouth, where once flowed the spring,
Lamenting still, the dark winged Genius stands,
Turns his vain eyes to where the light breaks through,
Till from those hills of pain a God descend.

Though yet the wolf, the flying manslayer
Finds sanctuary here, could He forgive
The fallen altar and the unswept shrine,

The pavement strewn with withered laurel leaves,
The grove left naked to the wandering air,
The broken serpent-images within?

2   O POETS

O bright and holy poets in the fire
Bending one way like white-sleeved aspen-trees,
Or tenuous strings drawn taut across the lyre
Made vocal when a ruthless finger plays,

I hear the crackle of the leaves that shade
Your brows, I see you raise pale hands and lift
Them to the mountains where those dim shapes fade
And god-like forms dissolve into the mist;

Behind, confusion climbs among the towers
In the great cities burning, till there come
The dark encroaching waters and their rage:

Oh under threat of flood and wind and flame
Searing to wide-eyed terror the spring flowers –
Sing on, like blinded linnets in your cage!

3   THE SIREN

Siren, fetcher of souls, Parthenope,
O you white bird and virgin-faced, sing on
From your harsh cliff and cold reflecting sea;

But my winged vessel, feeling the breeze once more
Shake her spread sails, must hasten on to seek
Green islands, and Apollo's apple-trees;

There shall be song in those strong arms, their boughs,
And you a dumb stone on this lonely shore.

4   LEUCE

O Leuce, white walled island out of time,
Do the quiet waves, carved in blue hyaline,
Still hang their heads by the undinted shore,
Far from all voice of surf, or sea-bird's cry;

And further inland, where through soft womanish turf
The stiff narcissus and the hyacinth break,
The nightingales, caged in bright falling dew,
Strain their full throats for that recumbent pair –

Where great Achilles lies in Helen's lap
And only there enjoys the marble limbs?

The Traveller at Evening

Now I have come once more
Into the lucid air beneath the hillside,
Upon whose crest the small white building stands,
And the stiff figures overlaid with gold
Or smeared with yellow ochre.... All this day
I have been journeying through a sultry forest
Whose shadows stalked beside me; and nevermore
May I avoid the Travelling Companion
With cold hand of a corpse, and swan's white wings.

Now by the fountain in the evening light –
Although the wind blows chill across the valleys,
With breath of pestilence, and news
Of children starving in the further lands –
O you whose arms are kind, whose lips are warm,
Give freely the illusion
Of Autumn's apples and the lingering rose.

Hymn to the Sun

How shall I hymn the Sun in the middle of Winter? –
    For now we only see him
Far in the sky retired, in exile burning
Red, through a blanket of mist, of falling feathers;

Who, if the Spring were here, would touch the music
    From the bright tremulous dew-drops
Which the green trees hold out on their welcoming fingers,
While birds, in hundreds, were greeting his light with a song.

In Hyperboreal regions the girls, like flowers,
    Lie folded under the snow-drifts;
Yet each one, in her sleep, dreams that she holds him,
Her golden Lover, and feels her body quicken

Beneath his keen embrace and fiery kisses;
    But an eternal winter
Guards her still-frozen couch, and she can only
Waken to know her delicate limbs are virgin.

Sonnet
(The Winter Sun)

Brief journey has the winter sun to fare,
Nor lingers in the frost's blue-paven house,
Although the landscape lifts these naked boughs,
And seeks to hold him by his silver hair;

His downward-gazing solitary eye
Is not more coldly answered in the heart
Of the still-frozen lake – redeemless, yet
Possessing him before he goes away.

Leaving the ice-chained waters to the blind
Glare of the stars, the cold ambiguous moon,
And quartered the four bandit winds among,

Pilgrim, he passes to that southern land
Where poles are weighted down with the rich vine,
And there are stork and swallow chattering.

Song

O hart, upon what mountain
    You seek your pasture now? –
Within what undiscovered fountain
    Floats the reflection of your brow –
        Whose cold dark ripple scorns
        Image of branching horns?

Where the strange waters lie
    The tired mouth stoops and drinks,
While nightlong in the eastern sky
    Algol, the baleful Gorgon, blinks:
        A dead world in its gyre
        Loving a heart of fire.

Song for Two Voices

"Bid the itinerant sun to stay,
    Poised aloft with slackened rein;
    Now advance across the plain
Tall weeping shades, the end of day,
My half-unspoken love to slay."
    "No, my dear, it may not be:
    All you would record of me
    He must span from sea to sea. –

"Tides of blood we could not brave,
    While we stand here, in our veins fall;
    The dry air would weave a pall –
Though we fenced the western wave –
Till it wrapped us in the grave.
    Though full time for whispering there, –
    Lipless mouth to cavernous ear, –
    I would have no heart to hear."

The Kindly Goddesses

The green-haired Furies of the Spring unleashed
Have risen for me beneath the cherry-trees –
Soft-bloomed by the wise river flowing
Through the doomed meadows.

Or in dark streets beneath no riding moon
They lift their reptile thongs to drive me on
From closing bar and the yellow circle of light
To seek the terror in the dingy room –

(As the winged god, the mid-day nightmare falling,
The woman-faced bird out of a cloudless sky,
Possessed the wayfarer)

                                    – Until I wake
To hear them through the white and stealthy dawn
In the shrill tongues of thrushes
Telling to Finsbury Park their tale of grace.

Maria Ægyptiaca

Thrust back by hands of air from the sanctuary door,
Mary of Egypt, that hot whore,
Fell on the threshold-stone. Priest, candles, acolyte
Shivered in flame upon her failing sight –
She swooned, and lay there like one dead. And then she fled
Into the black Thebaid. For forty years
She hid among the rocks splintered with heat;
The greedy desert to its own pitiless drought
Sucked all her body's beauty – which had spread
A wildfire death in kisses through brown limbs
Of sailormen at Alexandria,
Or Syrian fig-merchants with small dull eyes.
                          All night she would display
Her naked skin and bones to the harsh red moon
To be her only lover; through the day,
(While she was kneeling on the white hot sand)
Hairy and ithyphallic,
The dancing satyrs would distract her prayer;
The memory of her lust
Split open the rock-tombs, and buried kings
Whose brown dead flesh was like dried dates, with eyes
Of emerald glittering in a gilded mask,
Tripped forth, their grave-bands looped fantastically,
And made their court to her with antic bows.

And when at last she died,
With burning tender eyes, hair like dark flame,
The golden lion came;
And with his terrible claws scooped out a tomb,
Gently, in the loose soil,
And gave that dry burnt corpse to the earth's womb.

"Through the Dear Might of Him
That Walk'd the Waves"

For the sea, too, has its roads:
Beneath the swell, the restless whelm, her womb,
Flanked by those skeleton stone forests, where
Polyp and holothurian trail their tentacles.
The sea too has its alleys, highways, forums;
And thither throng
The sad, pale population of the drowned,
Riding the slow ground-currents like sleep-walkers:
Slim boys tricked out in shells and weed; old men
Out of long-foundered ships, whose coffers
Gape – a sardonic smile of gold and rubies;
Those who went down with bags of dates and raisins,
Or crates from Jaffa; the solitary airman
Who fell, a black bolt from a sky of fire,
Into the silent sea; the Punic sailor,
Clutching his statues of the Cabiri,
Which once, upon his prow,
Gazed home to Carthage with dull wooden eyes,
And could not save in that last storm off Gades;
And here comes sidling by
A Portuguese lady with long bony hands,
Who sailed to join her bridegroom in Brazil,
In ragged satin (and a barnacle
Grows on her finger like a signet-ring).
Here are the chiefs of Lyonesse, the bellringers
Of Ys, that famous town, and, grave
In their strange figured breastplates, the senators
Of lost Atlantis, –
With all the former world which the first Flood
Had borne away, when under God's small stars,
In his great loneliness,
Noah weighed his anchor and set forth
On the dark sea. So, drifting past,
All names, known and unknown, she has sucked in:
The poor youth carried down the Dardanelles,
The poet, sunk without trace off Mexico,
And the drowned Lycidas.

This was the world that once Alcyone saw,
When in her sleep the phantom spread its wings,

And showed her dripping husband's dreary form.
Shelley was once a guest here, and the winds
And waves that carried his quenched ashes from the shore
Mingle them with it yet.
Poe in his dreams beheld the steep black wall
Of the gyrating maelström draw him down
And down and down into oblivion;
And Melville never could forget this nation,
But through his turgid water-world of thought
Still moved a white and awful shape,
The great sea-monster, the unconquered evil.

The ice-bergs, the blue cows of giantland,
Groaned as they clashed together through the night
And the cold mists, while the god Thor went out
To fish for the sea-serpent. But it lies
Coiled in the crater of a sunk volcano,
Watching with cruel and unwinking pupils
The little fishes, red and blue and yellow,
Go speeding past, with eager teeth to tear
The flesh of the young parricide, sewn in his sack,
And washed some three miles out from Ostia.
And there the mermaids' heartless song
Will madden and distract
The drowned man's slumbers in the deep-sea cave;
And there the Kraken waves its livid arms.

"Oh I would I were a halcyon-bird,
Beating with dark wings over the sea,
Whom the young ones carry when his years are done,
That bird of Spring...." Carry me to those feet
That tread unharvested Gennesaret's
Whitening wave-tops like the mountain-dawn –
Above this monstrous world of squid and skate,
Sea-anemone, echinus and crinoid!
For I would see, outlined against the stars,
The Eternal Man measure with confidence
The treacherous foam-paths like a glassy pavement,
Who with His clear eyes looks down and sees
The sandy bottom and its life of slime –
All those dumb goggle-faces –
Assume the ordering of adoration.
And now His hand (which shall, at the end of time,

Capture Leviathan, and draw him forth
With bright gold scales glittering in the sun,
And land him gasping on the beach, to feed
Five thousand of the faithful)
Is stretched above the waves, to pluck
The failing Peter from their cold embrace.

Hart Crane

The green-wombed sea proves now a harsher lover
And more acquisitive than her easy sons,
As furtively the crab, her agent, scans
The inventory of heart and brain and liver;

You suffer here, beyond the plunge of diver,
Her deeper perfidies: the warm stream runs
With gifts of boughs and birds, dead Indians
To each fresh voyager; yet still, deceiver,

Her laced white fingers lap a hollow land,
Where with false rhetoric through the hard sky
The bridges leap, twanged by dry-throated wind,

And crowded thick below, with idiot eye
The leaning deadmen strive to pierce the dim
Tunnels and vaults, which agate lamps illume.

Gustav Mahler

"O children playing late beneath the lime-tree,
I hear your laughter soft through the golden air;
The bright-faced flowers, that come again each year
Out of your mother's grave, have called you home
To that familiar world; and the tall angel,
The silver-girdled, in the deep still pool,
Invites you to a land of bells and dancing.

But me he beckoned
To wander on by these dark lakes of parting –
For the first wind of spring, the knife-blade keen,
Has split my heart, and will not give me rest."

In Memoriam A.M. H-S
1870-1945

Over your head a dream
Buds slowly into greenness like a tree;
All silence is your shroud, and children, judged
To dumbness, songs, arch their cool marble wings
Where you are lying....

The eyes that read the meaning
Of every turf, once, in the hills of youth,
Which early death printed with dewy feet,
Possess the clear blue of a winter sky,
Or, in the hovering clouds,
Of Plato mark the upward-pointing finger
And Aristotle's comprehensive hand.

Sonnet
for the Tomb of Gluck

Now lies at rest beneath the myrtle-shade
This latter Orpheus, whose harp still dreams
Of the white nymphs beside the happy streams.
(Their dance is broken and their measure stayed) –

His harp unstrung upon the desolate bough;
Call him not, nymphs, the sky is thick and deaf;
The breeze is fallen and all the tongues of grief
With which you would lament him, muffled now.

Be silent then; what could assuage your pain –
Unless the god of love himself should go
And search the blessèd fields for the return
Of Music's spirit wandering there below,
And gently lead her to the air again
To be a pale faint mourner by his urn?

Tannhäuser's End

Tannhäuser heard, but did not understand,
That Latin commination; but he saw
The old man's face, wrinkled and papery-white
Like a cast snake-skin on a bank of flowers,
His silver hair, the frost congealing round
A budded bough. The Pope's hieratic hand
Stood like a branching candlestick to Heaven,
The bare arm thrust from crimson gold-embroidered
Robes that hung, stiff as though carved in stone,
About his spare but unbent form. Above him rose
The domed basilica, where from the walls,
With flat gold aureoles behind their heads,
Gazed down the ranks on ranks of virgins,
Implacable, with oval staring eyes; and over the altar
The seven Archangels, planetary spirits,
Seemed to advance, and drew their flaming swords.

Trembling, the pilgrim wrapped his cloak around him,
Descending down and down the marble stair
Between the hooded figures, and went out
Into the long white roads. And so he passed
Forever from their ken.
                              He had gone back
To find the secret and enduring forest.
But it was winter now: his upcast eye
Sought there in vain the bright-necked dove, the messenger
Of that soft-breasted goddess whom he loved.
Only the prying magpie from the fir
Would watch him passing with a curious eye; or in the snow
The loping mountain hare that sought those woods
To cram her maw with birch-bark, halted, at gaze.

None knows how many days Tannhäuser wandered on,
Still with the carved harp slung upon his back,
Among those strings only the bitter wind
Wakened a prelude now – ghost of a song
Sung to gay-mantled ladies in high bower,
While the white lilac fluttered at the window;
What woodland paths he took, at what cold streams
He knelt and drank, or sought with frozen hand
Among the branches of the mountain-ash
Those few bright berries which the redwing left.
And none can tell if on some bank of snow
At last he fell, exhausted,
And if it was in dreams the dying man
Was led again into the lighted hall
Of the wise fairy he had honoured once,
A boy, beneath the May-day hawthorn-tree:
Fru Frekë, the good housewife,
Inventor of the small blue-flowering flax-plant,
Rewarding the industrious servant-girls
With showers of gold; who rides by summer nights
On wild grey geese about a rounding moon
With her bright waiting-women (she claims as such
All those who die unmarried).
Or yet perhaps no lonely woodcutter
Found late his frozen body (which the wolf
Spared) in the woods. For he had come at last
Into the echoing cave beneath the mountain;
And well-known hands had drawn him down
Into the ancient centre of the world,
The mothering-place beneath the vaulted earth,
Her cool death-kingdom. "Rest now, sleep
O lover, O child."

But upon Lateran the steady chanting
Suddenly stopped, as a great invisible angel
Were passing over them;
While in the old man's grasp his withered rod
Broke all at once into green leaves and petals;
And wandered then about those stony cells
Through motionless faint air
The unexpected holy scent of roses.

Ode
for All Souls' Night

Our father Virgil by the unrippled flood,
Beneath a different sky and sun than ours,
With brooding bloodless face seated apart,
The immortal garland tight across his brow,
Remembers still the swarming of the bees –
How through the meadows fled Eurydice,
With unsuspecting feet,
Where lurked the snake, the lying shade of death;

And how the singer crossed that stream, and strode
With coursing blood unbashful through these bowers
Where the pale people clutch their hollow hearts,
And fields where only dead white blossoms grow,
To melt with music the stern gods, and seize
A willing captive from Persephone,
Yet turned, at last, to greet
Only her ghost, the lying shade of death.

Beyond these waters echoes has he heard
Of cities sacked, and crash of falling towers?
What rumours of our warfare and our hate?
And sacral poet, might we call you now,
Apollo's potency twined in your bays,
To our sick world – as when the lord of day
Rises in golden state,
Dispersing night, the lying shade of death!

Obscene Erichtho's lore, that once had made
The sacred dead her drudging errand-goers –
Even this eludes our skill – and every art
To tell what airs of prophecy may blow
From fields which lie beyond the myrtle-trees;
And evermore the mighty ghost must stay,
Closed by the ivory gate,
A wavering voice, the lying shade of death.

Iphigenia in Tauris

1

Here at the cliff's broad pediment, with feet
Unsure upon the grinding shingle,
Or scrambling up among the lower shelves, my priestly
And crocus-yellow petticoat blown out
Upon the off-shore breeze,
I pick the green-fleshed samphire-leaves wherewith
To deck the consecrated posts,
And to make fresh her house –
The stiff and painted totem whom I serve.

I turn to the westward sea –
The bloody footprints of the wanderer sun –
My unmoved eye, and mark
Long lines of gull and fishing cormorant
Returning to their nests, with the day's catch.
Take now, O vagrant birds, your homeward path,
Who fill the evening sky with pattern of wings,
From journeying the cold ways of the Euxine,
Whence come the black ships with their broken tackle
And their unlucky freight;
O birds making the shore loud with your meaningless cries.

And meaningless to me the sailors' eyes,
And their limbs bound to the hard altar-stone,
Brown throats lying bare like sheep beneath my harsh
Cold knife of flint and unempassioned hand;
For the unwavering scrutiny of my gaze,
Amid the smoke-swirl of the sacrifice
And jangling din of cymbals,
Seeks still a half-remembered face in vain.

2

In dreams I see him go
Down endless roads of nightmare still pursued
Who dares not look behind;
And hear my mother scream, my sister curse
Upon the furthest frontier of sleep;
Yet wake to know the grey and Scythian dawn,
And the king's horses whinnying in their stables.

297

For it was long ago
The virgin wind blew me to this strange coast,
Light as a winter leaf
(And in my place a stag with golden horns).

Brother, I wait here at the world's wild end
Until you come, and in the ambiguous grace
Of my girl's limbs, untouched, and sacred to
The swift manslaying goddess of the wood,
You find the image of your childhood,
Exempt from the old curse,
And in my eyes the promise of your peace.

Alexandria

1

The ibises, those grave high-stepping birds,
Dear to the triple Hermes, snake-destroyers,
His messengers, who know the times and seasons,
The circling moon, the rising of the Dog-star,
And of the secret river-springs – these led
That young-horned conqueror to the place
Where he should build, and with their broad white wings
Described the chosen acres, circling
About the limestone ridge
Which lay between the lake and the harbour-mole,
(With a small island in the harbour's mouth).

Dhu'l Kharnein, from white Macedon,
Who with his ordered phalanx overthrows
Magian Babylon and Ecbatana,
With upland Fars of the lion and the gold sun,
And dark-eyed Indians on Hydaspes' bank –
Until he reached the borders of the world:
The dry unlimited plain
Full of hot dragons and of scudding ghosts,
And rumours of an apple-garden lost to man
(With Jamshid's treasure and his starry goblet)
And sentinelled by winged and flaming guards;
Or, northward, in the Caucasus he forged

The iron gates to keep back Gog and Magog
Until the day of doom that lets them loose;
Then he set up his throne,
Receiving the submission of the Ocean,
Whose fish-tailed monstrous gods as heralds blew
Their twisted shells, summoning the tribes of legend:
The satyrs, centaurs, and rough aegipans;
The white-flanked queen of the swift Amazons;
With dog-faced and intelligent
Baboon-men out of Abyssinia: –
He was this city's founder,
Who journeyed to the oasis in the west,
To seek his hidden father, the black Amun,
Whose stiff ram-headed image in the dark
Stepped forth to meet and greet him,
And took his hand in its dry wooden hand
(As, drunken once with sacred honey and wine,
Olympias in the cave at Samothrace,
Dim-lit by the spluttering pine-torch,
Half-swooning, felt the coiling snake about her).
But here he dreamed upon the dark Egyptian earth
A city of white pillars and paved streets,
A market for all nations and their wisdom,
Where, violet-crowned,
The mountain-going Muses might descend,
To seek, well-pleased, their duly tended shrine.

2

Ptolemaic Alexandria looked up at the stars,
And saw the planets circling in a wheel
Of mathematical order.
Rulers of Fate, those starry gods were moved
Each in his sphere of crystal, trembling
In unheard harmony beneath the empyrean;
And, as in Babylon, the Zodiac rolled
Through the Great Year, a cylinder
Printing its arcane signs of destiny
Upon the world below. There to the market
Came traders from all quarters of the earth,
To cheat and haggle in that vast bazaar. King Ptolemy
Passed on a day of festival, attired
As Dionysos, gilded ivy in his hair,

Followed by Maenads and by flute-players,
Men masked as beasts, or reeling-drunk Sileni.
And here the poet
Lamented for the thymy-fragrant hillsides
Of Sicily, and the brown shepherd-boys,
Herd-girls with Doric voices like wood-pigeons,
Gathered for harvest-home.
                                        But also landed
One day, in that harbour, where from its island
The towering Pharos shed abroad its light
To all the wandering ships, one who had been
Born of rich parents in an Indian town,
Mud-walled, with golden roofs – and the great mountains
Lifting to heaven their eternal heads
Rose up beyond it. Around it was the jungle,
Noisy with monkeys and the shrill hard peacock,
Enclosing secret pools where the golden tiger
Came lordly down to drink,
And paths which only the quiet slow elephants trod,
Moving to their assemblies, or dying places.
But he had learned the doctrine
Of Prince Sidhartha, the Illuminated
Lord of Compassion, a king's son,
Who taught under the leafy terebinth,
The tree of the world, among whose branches nestled
The gods, like singing-birds, clustering to hear
The words of liberation. So this man left
His native town, and all his goods, and westward went,
Clothing himself with death – the yellow robe
Snatched from a dead man in a road-side graveyard –
A nameless monk, to Alexandria.
He stood, and spoke his message:
"There is an endless wheel of recurrence –
Of birth, and death, and being born again;
None can escape old age, disease, and being born,
Save by this liberation. For the compassionate ones,
The innumerable Buddhas, like stars, like suns,
To all the numberless universes
In the great circling plan of Space and Time,
Pause, at the very threshold of extinction
With passionless faces, and then, in a last gesture
Of infinite compassion, stretch out their hands
To all who seek them. They bring them forth

Through purgatory worlds, and paradises
Of diamond, coral, pearls, and lotus-flowers –
Endless illusions –
Until at last they find their peace, burned out
In one still, glittering point.
This life is not so real as we think –
The broken image of the moonlight floating
Upon lake water which a light breeze troubles...."
Then all the wise men, the philosophers in Alexandria,
Lifted their hands in assent, the pointing finger
Towards the One, beyond the sky's appearance.
"For had we not learned," they said, "that beneath the changeable
     moon,
Tyche, the bright-haired daughter of Chaos, is mistress,
As on her silver wheel she turns our fates;
Where Heraclitus saw all things flowing, and Plato, our master,
Taught us we are continually born and re-born
In a shifting shadow-play, in a Magian cave of illusion."

3

But Mark, the lion, came roaring out of Galilee,
With a message from Peter, a violent gospel –
Telling of Christ's anger in Jerusalem,
That city which should have no holy stone
Left on another. And he told
Of a Tree which was not of illumination,
But the centre of darkness over all the earth;
Of a Saviour ascending there
To win the terrible resurrection of the flesh.
And so, where Theocritus lamented in megalopolis,
Some, at the lion's hot breath,
Turned, in a strike against the city; they seceded from civilisation,
Because of their passion refusing participation,
And learned an askesis of the flesh in the heart's desert.
They were in the wilderness, and
(As once their Lord also) with the wild beasts.
Where haunt the jackal, the jerboa, and the desert bustard,
Christian hermits, blackened in flesh, existed,
And made inhuman the body's image; self-exiled among the dunes,
They inhabited a country of poltergeists,
Who whirled them all at once up into the hot air;
And howling Djinns, who travel in the twisting dust-storms

301

About their curious business; Afrits, whose form
Is a mask only, an empty simulacrum;
And the sad Ghouls, who lurk, with the hyaena –
The human-laughing, brindled, coward beast –
In the forgotten graveyards of dead kings.
And there, too, they encountered
The banished gods, whose footsteps may not seek
The green-fringed banks and the canals of Nile:
The red-headed murderous Set, the onager,
Toeris, the hippopotamus, Sonchus, the crocodile,
And those who gibbered like apes, yapped like dogs,
Crawled like the beetle, skipped like the wet frog –
Procession of nightmare, which the holy Antony
Saw pass before him through the quivering air,
Like misformed clouds, blotting the single sun.

4

Hypatia, the daughter of Theon, the mathematical
And eloquent virgin, spoke, recounting
The properties of cone and circle, divine geometry,
The austere signs over the door of wisdom;
And of that hidden harmony Pythagoras –
He of the golden sacred thigh – discovered,
Dividing the taut string of a *tromba marina* –
Congruous with the order of the circling heavens –
The seven sirens of fatality, conducting
The wheeling dance of bright alchemical stars.
But always with her wise uplifted finger
She turned men to the One, and the words that Plato
Reported of Socrates: how he reclined
In a meadow of Ilissus, by the small city of Athens,
And spoke to Phaedrus of the nature of Love;
To him the Muses' dew-drunken holy cicadas
Chirped in a chorus from among the poplars.

Hypatia mounted her chariot; the bright and polished wheels
Moved through the Brucheion. Then, all of a sudden,
The open square was full of forms of menace –
Naked emaciated limbs thrust out
From fluttering rags, bare feet over the pavement,
Grim pale mouths set in sun-blackened faces,
And shining, shaven heads of the wild monks.

Black Egypt of the desert is returned to the City,
Howling against the prefect Orestes and the heathen Hypatia,
His friend, the Greek woman in her white wool and linen.
Her chariot is stopped; they pull her down; they drag her
To the Caesarium. They strip her; her virgin flesh
Is hacked and knacked by oyster-shells. Her blood
Is slippery upon the floor of the church.
Hypatia fell. She was lifted. She became Catherine,
A holy virgin in a bright dazzle of legend,
Hand-fasted to Christ, standing among the stars,
Our Fortune, in the firmament, still with the toothed wheel,
That would have hacked her and knacked her,
Propitious to scholars (and to wheelwrights),
Philosopher, and martyr to the tyrant Maximin,
Confuting all false doctrine of Greece or the wide Orient,
Her wheel is broken
By the strong descending Messenger of her election.

Catherine fell. Angels lifted her. They bore her body
(As Sleep and Death, once, the war-fallen Sarpedon)
Eastwards to Sinai, the primal mountain of Law.
There guardians received her, a holy household of monks;
They buried her in secret. And from the bones
An exudation of violets, a strange oil of healing.

Saint Sylvester on the Capitol

You, black and ancient serpent harbouring here
Beneath the broken peristyle, upon
This windy slope among the seven hills,
Who, coiled and brooding on the rubble-heaps,
In the long evening sunlight, gaze
With still and glassy eyes
Down to the white and aging roofs of Rome;

You, wise snake, darling of the ancient Mother,
Licking with darting tongue
Your cold lips which have missed this many a year
The little honeyed cakes, the dish of milk
By pious hands placed at your sun-baked burrow,

303

Whose overhanging stone
Is gay with cushioned leaves of saxifrage;

You, the most ancient tenant of this place,
And duly known and honoured
When a few scattered herdsmen
Pastured their flocks on this yet innocent soil –
You saw the little country goblins come,
Sabine and Tuscan gods,
And here set up their booths, till newcomers
Taught them to house in marble. And now no more
Will the rich citizen with sacrifice
Be client for their luck, or up this way
At the first morning light
The pontiff with the silent virgin climb.

But I, an old man chased by enemies,
Like cranny-nesting owl or badger
Must dispossess you now, you jealous snake,
And with my wrinkled hands
Scoop out the earth, and so enlarge your cranny
To build myself a cell;
And wait with sleepless, horny eyes
Beneath the irony of the watching moon,
Gazing along this road, until there comes
A broken Caesar, with the putrid scars
Festering in his flesh, and hateful dreams
Of dying children and a bloody pool,
To seek the serpent's wisdom, and a cure.

The Janitor
a Poem for the New Year

The black earth of the garden-beds is graced
With the pale hellebore, and from these trees
Only the stormcock's song shall blossom forth
Against the chilly morning. Here we stand,
Under the sharp-eyed winter stars, before
The bare façade of a still house – new tenants
Who must possess this mansion of the year.

Soon will the sky be clamorous with bells,
And now already wakes the drowsy porter,
Who stumbles down his draughty corridor,
Like Peter, two great keys slung at his belt,
Jingling. Slowly the swung door gapes,
And there he stands before us,
Framed in the expectant portico of Time.

Yet is his form familiar: stiff Latin folds
Of the archaic tunic, and the body
No more than a door-post, carved, and wreathed with garlands,
From some long-ruined homestead which once stood
Among the Alban hills, or where, this night,
The brown-limbed Sabine farmer and his wife
Lighted the new year's hearth with the old brand,
And due libation poured
Before the potent numen, double-faced,
Opener and closer of the circling year.

So in the waiting before midnight strikes
Gaze upon these two faces.... One is old,
And under the jutting brows his eyes
Are dark as Plato's cave; and you look down,
As into a deep well, whence only comes
A gleam of trembling water far below
And the scared echo of your voice.
Yet look again, and slowly in the darkness
You will discern all shapes
The labouring world remembers – the monstrous beasts
Ranging through green and dismal forests;
Redness of the first fires, and dance of priests
Before archaic altars, on whose stones
A thousand victims bleed; now armies move,
And ships go out across the sunlit seas,
And cities rise like smoke, or fountains rising
In dreaming gardens – till their tall spires loom
Above the traffic of the market-place –
Then fall, in flame; and truant lovers lie
Beneath the fresh leaves of how many springs,
And whisper that their love is ever new,
Nor heed the dark winds muttering;
And there are old men, patient in chambered towers
To watch the stars go wheeling through the heavens,

305

Like flocks of silver birds;
And poets coaxing words into a rhyme,
And music shrill from flutes of shepherds, blown
Upon what distant lawns, on what clear mornings? –
All this is gathered in his ancient face;
All this is fearful knowledge in his eyes,
Whose gaze, the potent stare of the dead Past,
Meets, concentrated here, your finite vision,
Upon this threshold.
                    Regard the second face:
But it is a blank, a mask, as for a child,
Or young-limbed Genius striving to be born;
His empty eyes, spaces of darkness whence
Incredible suns may rise;
The full curve of his lips – that have not opened,
Nor quick-winged breeze of speech has lit on them –
Oh, surely these
Are pregnant with a word of fire, –
Which shall flash forth, till it consume or heal
Our mustering days behind!

This double face meets us upon the path
That leads up to the point of darkness, hung
Between two journeying years. And always meets us –
In strange and narrow valleys, close in prisons,
In heedless hours of childhood, and
On the transfiguring mountains... always,
The Moment of our choice.
                    Choose then, before
A million clocks have recreated Time,
And in the darkened trees,
Uneasy stir the bright birds of the dawn.

Ibycus

When the city cast out the best
    In a clamour of indecision,
I had no breath to waste
    Cobbling up their division;

I unhooked the lyre from its peg,
   Turned ship to the Samian shore.
I call no man to witness
   But the clanging birds of the air.

The quince-tree garden is shattered,
   The vine-shoots fail in Spring;
Down from the Thracian mountains,
   On fire with the lightning,
Love comes, like a blackguard wind.
   Love was betrayal and fear.
I call no man to witness
   But the clanging birds of the air.

The open-handed I praise,
   Great-souled Polycrates,
Pride of whose tinted galleons
   Ruled the Ionian seas.
Treachery took him – nailed
   For the crows to peck him bare.
I call no man to witness
   But the clanging birds of the air.

Twilight: a narrow place:
   Armed men blocking the road.
Gold glitters on my finger.
   In chevron high overhead
The southward-journeying cranes –
   What Erinnyes are here?
I call no man to witness
   But the clanging birds of the air.

Prometheus

The bright-eyed, brownish bird that every evening returns,
As to his loved nest, to tear at my guts –
I have learned his comings and goings like the dew at nightfall,
The chill to my chained limbs, embalming the tired earth.

"Reject him, reject him," the severed women cry,
That kneel at my feet, and veil their unimaginable
Faces in a scarf of wing, "Reject the father,
The bands of iron, and this Caucasian hill."

Yet though I lie here through a turn of a thousand years,
He must grow dear, as the dove of love, the breeze
That ruffles the snow, that rouses the mountain gentian.

Poem After Solstice

This night the snow will be falling out of its vacant sky –
As that white quietus might drift into the empty heart –
On London, and on my upturned face. Now stand in heaver
Only the naked stars, that were against us,
And wheeled with this same gaze
Above us there, that night of fall,
When Love, the unlikely bird
Clapped his harsh wings, and stooped.
                              Now I recall
How Leopardi climbed to the Italian terrace,
Like some mis-shapen night-beast from his lair,
And turning his weak eyes to those cold distant fires,
Proclaimed how love was the last illusion,
The bridge of melting crystals that we build
Across the womb and shudder of the abyss,
With the moon setting on each maternal landscape.
And he was right. Or else,
If that lone white feather fell from some absolute creature
It was the twy-formed hippogriff, begotten
By the fierce descending eagle-lion bird
On snorting Caucasian mares that flee him, but accept
(And yet no freak, a natural animal).
Yes, he was right. But oh, my dear,
Love was not our concern!
For you the freedom, and for me the pain;
And let that shadow course the snowfields still.

Address not Known

So you are gone, and are proved bad change, as we had always
    known,
And I am left lonely in London the metropolitan city,
Perhaps to twist this incident into a durable poem –
The lesson of those who give their love to phenomenal beauty.

I am coming to think now that all I have loved were shadows
Strayed up from a dead world, through a gap in a raped tomb,
Or where the narcissus battens in mythological meadows:
Your face was painted upon the coffin-lid from Fayoum.

Is this my pain that is speaking? The pain was not long protracted:
I make a statement, forgive the betrayal, the meanness, the theft.
Human, I cannot suppose you had planned all that was enacted:
Fortitude must be procured to encounter the hollowness left.

The sun will not haver in its course for the lack of you,
Nor the flowers fail in colour, nor the bird stint in its song.
Only the heart that wanted somehow to have opened up
Finds the frost in the day's air, and the nights which appear too
    long

Invocations for a Traveller

Because your beauty is betrayed and strayed
    In the cross grain of the stars,
I invoke the ambiguous veiled Venuses
    In all their avatars,
Not turning away their eyes,
Averse, in the smoke of my sighs,
To clapperclaw far from your path the boredoms and jealousies.

I request the North Sea to dance, and dandle you,
    With his quorum of dulcet-eyed daughters,
While my huge tears like oil fall down
    Upon your troubled waters;
On your course may they sustain you –
Bring pearls to entertain you –
Yet should you turn backwards your prow, presume not to detain
    you.

May the October sun, hastening scorpionwards,
   Husband his blood to warm you;
The leash of the hunter's moon lie easy
   On the tides where those ladies charm you;
All sour planets of insanity
Sweat balm for your marred humanity,
For you sail by the lowlands low, who are but golden in vanity.

A Nocturnal

You, little screech-owl, singing through my insomnia,
And Siamese cat who cry like a scared child,
Snowball spatter of stars, and ripening moon
Ruling this black Parthenon of a separate night –
Be pitiful, to guide my stranger back
To the fold of my arms, to my bed and board; who can have no
      harbour,
Except the unlimited, treacherous ocean of love.

The Great Bear
for David Wright

Last night I dreamt I heard that great black bear
Who stalks through the northern sky, his fur
Grizzled with frost and starlight, speak; growling, he said:
"Where are the mushy and rank-flavoured toadstools,
My mess of cranberries, and the rancid butter
With which you fattened me? Where the familiar bodies
Of hairy women, oiled, and with bleached tresses,
Who suckled and coddled me? The time draws on
Towards your autumn sacrifice, when I must fall
Self-pierced in a hidden pit, or you will crush
My brains with two hard bits of wood, and blow
Tobacco-smoke's blue whiffs in my cold nose –
Children" (he said) "O children!" – and prowled about,
Chained to the fixed pole, and rolled
His seven starry eyes. Then in my sleep

I saw the huge brutes with their heavy paws
Rousing themselves out of their somnolent caves,
Black, brown, and grey; and white bears, piloting,
Red-eyed, their ships of ice through winter seas.
And I thought of Hereward, and of Bothvar Bjarki,
Of Beowulf the bear-king who encountered him
In a spectral hall among the upturned benches.
It is time to feed that shaggy and physical beast.

To the Mermaid at Zennor

Half fish, half fallen angel, none of you
Human at all – cease your lust's
Cold and insatiate crying from the tangled bay;
Nor, sea-hag, here
Stretch webbed and skinny fingers for your prey.

This is a hideous and a wicked country,
Sloping to hateful sunsets and the end of time,
Hollow with mine-shafts, naked with granite, fanatic
With sorrow. Abortions of the past
Hop through these bogs; black-faced, the villagers
Remember burnings by the hewn stones.

Only the saints,
Drifting on oak-leaves over the Irish Sea,
To sing like pipits from their crannied cells
With a thin stream of praise; who hear the Jennifer
Sob for her sins in a purgatory of foam –
Only these holy men
Can send you slithering from the chancel steps,
And wriggling back to your sunken paradise
Among the hollow-eyed and the capsized.

A Charm Against the Toothache

Venerable Mother Toothache
Climb down from the white battlements,
Stop twisting in your yellow fingers
The fourfold rope of nerves;
And tomorrow I will give you a tot of whisky
To hold in your cupped hands,
A garland of anise-flowers,
And three cloves like nails.

And tell the attendant gnomes
It is time to knock off now,
To shoulder their little pick-axes,
Their cold-chisels and drills.
And you may mount by a silver ladder
Into the sky, to grind
In the cracked polished mortar
Of the hollow moon.

By the lapse of warm waters,
And the poppies nodding like red coals,
The paths on the granite mountains,
And the plantation of my dreams.

Shepherd's Bush Eclogue

As I walked to Shepherd's Bush, I perceived it was truly pastoral,
For May, a Monna Vanna, a Mopsa, had tossed her cumuli,
Her flocks of white wool, into the azure and virginal
Fields of pure air that all over London lie.

I breathed a *Sursum Corda*; but a grief-worm in my breast
Twisted, and told me how all the riches of Spring
Are only a sandy fistful that runs through our fingers to waste;
For each of us is into continual exile travelling –

Moving away from life, and love, and lovers, and the light,
Since we fell from the primal garden into this troubled stream.
Not here, not here is our franchise: these images of delight
Still fail and fleet and cheat us in the context of a dream.

O Muse, I said then, dear sister, how long will your voice be mute?
This is your season, surely: these moments furnish your cue –
Praise this delicious weather with your accentor's throat;
In the heart of a poem's crystal alone can the Spring come true.

Song for All Fools' Day

When April sets her cuckoo-clock
And brisk young women go a-courting
Satyrs and satires in the brake
Indulge in their immoderate sporting;
Remit your praise to Heaven above
For love in fools and fools in love.

Now Papageno lures the birds
With chimes on April's glockenspiel –
The whitethroat and the honey-buzzard,
The stork, the bunting, and the teal;
Rooks, robins, wrens, and flamingoes
Build nests and chant arpeggios.

And what is that mellifluous strain
Shaming the blackbird till he's mute?
Feste, upon the roads again,
Has put new frets upon his lute,
While still Sir Andrew Aguecheek
Pens sonnets in Illyrian Greek.

Before the early windflower's gone
Commemorate yet another fool –
How Moorish brickbats battered in
The silver head of Ramon Lull:
Anemone blows not so red
As where a martyr's blood was shed.

Lambs, bumpkins, bulls and daffodils,
Perform a farandole in Spring;
Loiters among their festivals
Wisdom, in her long wandering –
Wisdom, who sported in God's breast,
Dances and prances with the rest.

The Death of Digenes Akritas

I'm that distinguished twice-born hero
And imperial partisan,
Destroyer of the Turk and Tartar,
Bulgar and Paulician.

Take your bread and meat and brandy
While they still keep out the cold;
A black wind whistles down the mountain,
Charon has me in his hold.

I, on marches of the Empire,
Prop of all the crumbling themes,
Have turned back the Emperor's enemies
By the fast and bloody streams.

The Pope of Rome in a purple surplice,
The Sultan by Euphrates' brink,
Should they hear my name referred to,
Take more water with their drink.

I have seen the golden Emperor
Sitting under a golden tree,
Commanding Sappho and Anacreon
To praise me with their balladry.

Once I met the Queen of the Vampyres
In a green and gracious place,
For three nights fought with her, and left her,
A knife-wound in her hooded face.

I have encountered the pterodactyl,
Manticor, and rhinoceros;
Hunting where it was not permitted
Brought me to this unhappy pass.

Oh swift and swift comes through the forest
That white deer with the silver horns;
Who follows that unlikely quarry,
Drained of manhood he returns.

For three months of a silent winter
I chased him through the glassy wood;
And when he turned and knelt for pity,
Took out my knife and drew his blood.

The Lady of the Mountains feeds him
Among her inaccessible rocks;
His eyes are clearer than cold water,
Between his eyes the crucifix.

When my horoscope was casting
Ares ruled the troubled sky;
I was born upon a Tuesday,
And on Tuesday I must die.

You can take and break my rifle,
Take my pipe and tinder-box;
Lay me decent, light a candle,
Keep the ritual orthodox.

Note: This poem is freely based on a modern Greek ballad.

A Ballad of Good King Wenceslas

Young King Wenceslas looked out
Upon a scene bucolic:
Blood-stained was the holly-bough,
The mistletoe was phallic –

Upon Saint Stephen's feast looked out,
Protomartyr, deacon;
A poor man wandered past, to pick
Up sticks to broil his bacon.

"Now is the season God came down
To dwell with us in parity:
A largess so divine demands
Our ineffectual charity.

315

"Hither, page, and stand by me;
Relate, with due precision,
Of yonder peasant (who is he?)
The temporal condition."

"His standards, Sire, are such as would
Revolt the aristocracy –"
(This was before Bohemia turned
A People's Front Democracy.)

"In squalid poverty he lives,
In winter-time he freezes,
Has scurvy, scabies, scrofula,
Deficiency diseases."

"Bring me flesh and bring me wine,
Pine-logs and etcetera;
We'll dine him in his home to-night,
As soon as we can get there."

While Wenceslas went forth to ply
This palliative poultice,
His brother Boleslav drank deep –
It was the Winter Solstice –

And many a black libation poured
To Tchernibog and Yarillo
(Slavonic deities, whose cult
He still inclined to follow.)

"Wenzel," he said, "is getting soft:
This opium for the masses
Will not deceive us pagans long –
We're the progressive forces."

When Wenceslas knelt down at Mass,
And sighed, "*Non nobis, Domine,*"
His brother came and cut his throat
For his unplanned economy.

The Hundred and Thirty-seventh
Psalm Paraphrased
(to the tune of "The Shandon Bells")

By foreign waters
Zion's sons and daughters
Have taken up quarters
   Through mischance so deep;
Where the Tigris in spate is,
Likewise the Euphrates,
Our cruel fate is
   To sit and weep.

Remembering Zion,
The harps we play on
In the weeping willows
   We did them hang,
When Nebuchadnezzar
And Tiglath Pileser,
All for to ease them,
   Were asking a song.

The psalms of David
When the Lord he praises,
Likewise of Asaph
   And Solomon –
How can we sing them
Or to memory bring them
By the Hanging Gardens
   Of Babylon?

May my senses wander
And my right hand blunder
If I do not remember
   The dear hills of home;
My tongue turn rotten
And my teeth be dropping
When I am forgetting
   Jerusalem.

O Lord, take heed of
The children of Edom,
Destroying our freedom
   And the darling town;

With "Raze it, raze it."
They did dispraise it,
In our troublesome days it
    Was "Pluck it down!"

And I hope 'twill bring trouble on
The girls of Babylon
That dip and dabble on
    These streams so fair,
But it's I would be blessing
The man who was dashing
Their little children
    On the sharp stones there.

Prayer to Saint Lucy

At this our solstice of history,
Santa Lucia, pray for me –
You, whose too bright, offending eyes
Like leonids fell from your face of skies:
Since I must do my difficult work,
Sixty per cent, at least, in the dark,
Ascended virgin make petition
I am not quite blinded by erudition,
Lest the black pride of intellect
My senses, or my heart, infect.
These are the years where, still in vain,
We scan the unlimited heavens of pain,
Searching for an absconded God
(Yet under judgment, under His rod);
But may your wintry feast disclose
The first snowdrop, the Christmas rose –
Those white-clothed virgins of the earth,
The naked maiden, the plant of birth –
And faith is the substance of things not seen,
Under the snows of time, the green
Shoots of eternity; so, eyes being gone,
Still, still in the heart, the sun shines on.

Obstinate in Non-attendance

Obstinate in non-attendance I cannot but think kindly
Of the county of Hampshire, my nurse; she is sluttish but not
    uncomely:
Sociable in London my heart is a parched forest
And my skull a stone tower where the songs not easily nest.

But she who fostered my first cares and my loneliness,
Indifferent yet received them with a certain homeliness:
My tears hardly augment the griefs that in Thames must run,
But could add a saltness to the Stour's, or the Avon's, urn.

The Celt rants in my blood; but it is of Winchester
The Saxon monarchs who lift up a golden sceptre
To rule in all my dreams with a plain civility,
Though my ancestors rowed Edgar the Peaceable on the Dee.

Or striving in my verse to acclimatise the Italian myrtle
And the Greek cyclamen, I sometimes feel it is futile:
The yellow gorse the coltsfoot and the rest-harrow
Are nourished by the clay and sand that fed my earliest sorrow.

Memories of Paul Verlaine

I am stalked by the small unwashed Frenchman with a face like
    an ape:
For I was brought up on the coasts of Hampshire, where the
    Barton Beds
Slip, like a badly-made blancmange,
With their eocene fossils into the shingly sea;
On the East, Lymington, with its neglected wharves,
And Coventry Patmore lying in an unkempt grave;
On the other side, Bournemouth, the expatriate palms
And the bitter aloe, which will only come into flower
When it celebrates our unacknowledged legislation.
On both these trim esplanades (under an east wind,
Against an autumn sea) I picture him
With his toppered crocodile of boys, as in the cartoon –

Who now in Tottenham Court Road, and amid the *cheeriohs*
Of Old Compton Street, follows me still;
And may I catch some part of his divine intoxication
Of corn and vineyards
And murmur with his pagan ghost into the roots of grass.

Good Night, Ireen

"That which dishonours another man, dishonours me"

I'm Ireen, the Sireen of Soho,
  A marginal virgin of culture;
From lunch-time to six in the caf *Chez Alix*
  I brood like some gaily-plumed vulture;
From six to eleven in a mild-bitter heaven
  I gyrate through waste lands of Fitzravia,
While time's on the wing, like a doll on a string,
  With strictly conditioned behaviour.

When shines drunkenly down the full moon on the town
  I am spurred into gin-sodden song;
Like some ass-struck Titania with sub-nymphomania,
  My heart bares unspeakable wrong;
But more often the charms and the long hairy arms
  Of some unwashed companion in exile
For the moment assuage my unquenchable rage –
  My emotions, though powerful, are flexile.

My girl-friend, Miss Evelyn Yard
Sophisticate, lesbian, hard,
  A flint-breasted Amazon – her pulse beats like hammers on
A heart whence all man's love is barred:
But men, time and again, fall as ruthless as rain
  On my starved but hospitable bosom –
Oh infertile delights! Oh Paphian nights!
As I tease them, and please them – to lose 'em!

For I'm Ireen, the Sireen of Soho,
  Awaiting the last midnight's tolling,
When all shreds of humanity, gotten in vanity,
  To a Corner-house nook are sent rolling;

When the worm shall explore the ultimate sore
　　Which time in my heart has left smouldering,
And a sparse vegetation's the sole indication
　　Of the spot in the earth where I'm mouldering.

Churchyard of Saint Mary Magdalene, Old Milton

Here, where my father lies under the ornamental plum,
Geese step in the next farm-field, while to the Rectory elms
The rooks fly home. *Dominus exaltatio mea* –
The eagle rising with its sprig of acorns.

Feet deep in sticky clay, under the kempt grasses,
Under the anglo-saxon, and the celtic crosses,
The Indian judges lie, the admirals, the solicitors,
The eccentric ladies, and the shopkeepers,
The unenterprising who would not go to the town,
The charwoman with a cleft palate, the jobbing gardener,
And the four Germans who fell, some few years back,
Out of a sky of trouble, smashed
In an empty field – these have
Their regulation crosses too, of wood,
And scattered flowers, left by the prisoners:
The old woman whom I meet
Remarks that after all they were somebody's sons
And we would do as much for our people.

"The writer returns to the scene of his childhood" –
Where he loitered and looked at the rooks and the geese and the
　　　turkeys,
Or sought for wild barley by the churchyard gate –
The caterpillar-grass
Whose insect heads climb slowly up your sleeve;
The rootless writer, filling his town lungs
With a gust of country air. A grey afternoon,
And in the sky, the promise of evening's rain.

Where people come to take the air and die,
Ending their lives here on an adequate pension,

321

A sickly child, brought there by careful parents,
Might mend in the salt breeze. From six to twenty-four
Home was this scattered residential village of bungalows,
Of gabled villas, and neglected fallows,
Crazy paving, gravel, and tarmac. Now he comes back
And stands unrecognized among these graves.

The church here under John, that lackland king,
(The guide-book says), rebuilt under Elizabeth:
(The tower still stands, four-square, looks down upon
The village green, a row of shops, a garage
Crimson and yellow with petrol-pumps,
A line of cottages, a blacksmith's forge –
A child, I remember that darkness and smoke and music –
Two adjacent public-houses, the "George" and "Wheatsheaf",
And the post-office store, where stands behind the jumble
Of picture-postcards, cigarettes, and buttons,
The dusty case with its stuffed gannet and guillemot).
Rebuilt under Elizabeth, restored under Victoria,
(The green distempered walls, peeling to white patches,
Which took, at sermon time, the shapes of islands –
White islands, in a green smooth-glistening sea).

Lie here the serfs, the yeomen, and the gentry,
Under their mounds, and single stones, and vaults yellow with
     lichen;
Of all those faces, one only gazes still –
Queen Anne's colonel, in effigy, pompous his armour,
His helmet beside him, a ringleted wig of stone
Framing his vacant brow. His sword, that steel blade,
Which he drew against the French, is hung above him
Over the blurred inscription, on the left of the porch.

A torch borne in the wind, a drift of sparks and smoke
As the racer rounds the track in the bright sunlight,
Dust-puff, and dream, and shadow . . . .
A drop of rain, a large, warm drop,
A rustle in the tresses of the elm,
A breath of perfume, twitched by the light breeze,
From the fading flowers laid on the Italian marble –
But these evoke the sudden splendour of bright hair
Unloosed from the darkness of a penitent snood,
Sweetness, and the splintering of the alabaster-sealed heart;

Somewhere among these tombs a woman's voice is sobbing;
Among these fragments grope the white and delicate hands
Of the Anointer of the Dead, who comes in the dark hour
Bringing her spices for the early dawn.

A fountain of lamentation above the firmament, a human
River of tears, that knows all streets, alleys, and dark courts,
And bears upon its little waves
Sticks and straws and draggled cigarette-ends,
The gutter's refuse and corruption, on
Past Roman causeways, through black hearts of cities.
A girl, mad as grief, trudging the hard roads;
A woman, with a few ripe ears, in a country of famine;
The august queen of the shrunken banks of Nile,
Who seeks the body of her murdered Lord;
A girl, sorry as sin, and broken as contrition.

Lady of Magdala's tower, and the dower of Bethany,
You who are called patron here, forgive
The little lives, partial and fugitive existences,
The gestures of love frozen in a pose of propriety,
And starved desire, with malice that lies on a turning bed;
Forgive the tyrannies of the hearthstone, and the small politics
Of the local interest, the lonely and the dull.
Ask pardon for the community without a heart, and the betrayal
Of the backward years and the uncomplaining dead.
Carry these lives, these parts of lives, these yellow leaves
Drifted in autumn from the tree of the world,
On tides of intercession, down
To a sea thirsty with love, where the breakers lift
White triumphing hands – insatiable;
And the free gull tacks to the courteous southern stars,
With arched and frost-pale pinion:
Oh, in Death's garden be
Prime witness of the only Resurrection.

Elegiac Stanzas
in memory of William Bell

Fretful, with all her fine deceits of mind
About her still, and still unchanged, the city
Opens her grey heart to mild January,
With medlars and mortality in her hand;

Where in their windy towers the old men weep,
Remembering how soon the goddess fled
(Before they woke and found how youth was dead)
While she but touched their parted lips in sleep.

But I recall that Irish sorcerer –
His table set, the tall glasses of wine,
All Souls' tide summoning at the bell's last groan
His wandering shades to a thin-fumed banquet here –

Whose lonely ceremony I need not prove,
Since pausing at the end of every street,
Rustling homewards through these skies I greet
Poems, like birds, that seek the sacred grove.

But when the night is come, from their sublime
And baroque heavens the great musicians bend:
Sebastian Bach, eternity on his mind,
And Monteverdi, between the seraphim,

Yet whispering now with the year's gentlest breath –
"Zefiro torna, torna..." – whose complaint
Is formal landscapes and the nymph's lament,
And how Spring brought no solace for her grief.

Oxford, January 21st – 23rd, 1949

Epitaph

Mr Heath-Stubbs as you must understand
Came of a gentleman's family out of Staffordshire
Of as good blood as any in England
But he was wall-eyed and his legs too spare.

His elbows and finger-joints could bend more ways than one
And in frosty weather would creak audibly
As to delight his friends he would give demonstration
Which he might have done in public for a small fee.

Amongst the more learned persons of his time
Having had his schooling in the University of Oxford
In Anglo-Saxon Latin ornithology and crime
Yet after four years he was finally not preferred.

Orthodox in beliefs as following the English Church
Barring some heresies he would have for recreation
Yet too often left these sound principles (as I am told) in the lurch
Being troubled with idleness, lechery, pride and dissipation.

In his youth he would compose poems in prose and verse
In a classical romantic manner which was pastoral
To which the best judges of the Age were not averse
And the public also but his profit was not financial.

Now having outlived his friends and most of his reputation
He is content to take his rest under these stones and grass
Not expecting but hoping that the Resurrection
Will not catch him unawares whenever it takes place.

Epitaph Revisited (1986)

Mr Heath-Stubbs, in a moment of aberration,
Composed an epitaph. It was jokingly meant,
In a spirit of ironic self-depreciation:
The day he wrote it was one he lived to repent.

The thing became popular, for some reason;
Found a place in more than one anthology,
Was quoted at him, in and out of season;
It was his Lake Isle of Innisfree.

Not to have included it in the present collection
Would have only drawn attention to the wretched verse –
But he's tempted to suggest that its further reproduction
Might incur the penalty of a poet's curse.

And gentle reader – surely it is enough –
If you love him at all, turn over this page;
There are better things on offer than that sad stuff,
Indited in the thirtieth year of his age.

Dr William Turner
on reading his "History of Birds" (1544)

Migrant himself, fleeing through foreign fields
Queen Mary's fiery winter of persecution,
Notes his grave commonplaces on the principal birds
Mentioned in Pliny and Aristotle (latinized
By Theodorus Gaza, the Grecian scholar);
Scorning the pedantries of German schoolmasters,
His eye is quick for the particular –
As the intense redness of the bullfinch, or
Reed-sparrow's restless tail. He leaves no comment
Upon the phoenix in her cassia nest, or birds
Of Diomede (which are all white, and toothed, with eyes of fire,
And purified with water-laden wings
The hero's shrine lying off Apulia),
Remembering rather the small water-crow
That dabbled in the rocky streams near Morpeth,
When he was a boy and went to fish for tiddlers.
Chatting with monks upon the banks of Po
Catches an echo of the antique Latin,
Hearing the jay, which just now flashed
Into the neighbouring wood, is still called *seed-crow*
(Glandarius) – Pliny remarked
Its partiality for acorns.

And once, in Switzerland,
Climbing a mountainside to search for plants,
Meeting an old goatherd, he remembered
What Aristotle wrote of *aigothelas*; so enquired
About a bird which is purblind by day,
Seeing in the dark only, big as an ouzel;
Which flies to goats at night and sucks their udders:
The udder withers – the goat itself goes blind.
"Oh yes," the old man answered, "some fourteen years ago
They were in flocks here all about the mountains.
Much harm they did too – we lost many goats –
But now they are all flown into Low Germany,
Where they attack not only goats but sheep."
"What name do you give to this night-robber?" "We call him
     Paphus."
(That is to say, the Priest).
Perhaps the old man was joking, but his aspect
Still seemed most grave, and most respectable.

Hearing the Cuckoo
for Frank and Rosalind Heywood

Cuckoo, bubbling your green words across half Berkshire
And the gardens decorated with Japanese cherry,
You hobo-bird, who hitch your sparehawk wings
To the gilded horns of the April sun – O drunken cuckoo,
Suck the sweet flowers, keep your voice clear, to spill
Your double-talk over the landscapes, idle
As any poet on a Holy Saturday!

Trinity Weather

This Trinity weather begets my abstract midsummer,
The feints of Spring outgrown, and the safe towns of Winter –

No cranny left from the crawling sun – the peacock-angel
Whose jagged voice has dried the shy-tongued Oread.

The Caesar-months stride through their slow triumph,
Crabwise and lion-tressed, the lords of drought, –

To a high season wherein a Queen who is humble
Was reaped by the tending sky from her tomb of marigolds.

And may my words as patiently as fruit
Lie quiet for the heart's sicklemen, the loosenings of Autumn.

A Cassida for Sadegh Hedayat
(Persian writer, found in a gas-filled room, Paris, 1951)

Like a crested bird from Asia, the East Wind
Has delivered a letter: it says, "A friend is gone."

His exile has choked him in an airless chamber:
Sequana, indifferent goddess, mourns in her palaces.

The crested fire-bird, whose nest is increment, hoots
Of oil, education, bank-notes, fanaticism.

But a nightingale lies strangled in the shade of the poplars,
In a spring of irises and unsheathed swords.

Old men with scrolled texts, climbing to towers at evening,
Watch for the new moon, and proclaim a Unity.

In uplands where the morning hunts down fraternal darkness,
And the martyr tulip leaps to a furnace of holy flames.

O routine moon, at the end of fasting, you watch
Inane and beautiful boys inverting their drained glasses.

Sassanid lions lift up their paws in salute;
The clouds are gross that lean down with carbon monoxide.

At Carthage a queen's beauty crumbled to white cinders,
In a prophecy of skies filled with avenging phoenixes.

Those Uranian birds muster from Seoul to Samarkand:
The statue of Apollo weeps on the Palatine.

Virgil's mirror in Mantua is shattered;
The graal of Jamshid is missing; Isaiah is sawn like lumber.

O Rose, can you care if there is one lover the less –
O Rose of Jericho, in a stony region of goats?

He wandered to strange places, like the banished king he was;
He said: "I am sick of corruption; I shall not come back."

On airs from India there is a voice that announces:
"The city of mud and pearls has broken another poet."

The Last Watch of Empire
for Fred Marnau

The ultimate dream. Arms, eagles, broken banners,
And a blind battle in the naked wood.
Over the brazen birds
Those with black shining feathers that scream and tear;
The angels rending their bright hair
Amid the fog and babel of crying voices,
Where Cyril and Methodius snatch at their split hearts.

Look now, this
Is the last Emperor, whose crown of iron and gold
Drops diamonds like frozen tears, like those smooth stones
The glacier bears from mythological mountains.
Now he has fled into the forest, where
The elk and wild boar their yellowing bones
Abandon to the ghost-led traveller;
With his great hands, heavy with seals, he scratches
For acorns, beech-mast, against hibernation,
Through winters which no rising sun, no moon
Prompting the green unfolded bud, shall loosen,
In his gem-fiery chamber among the roots.
(Sleep Caesar, though the hunter's horn
Be still lamenting over your slate-grey head:
It is not time, not yet).
Till corn and roses rise from his brain, his heart.

The holy Malachi, in a western island, once
Prophesied this: the Roman Peter feeding
His flock amid great tribulations,
Destruction riding over the seven hills.
Now an old man, in a secret mountain cave,
Sits, with wax-white hands to bless, and hair
Light on the wind, and grey as cobwebs;
Where eleven hermits, as spry as wagtails, twitter,
Raising their spare throats to the dawn's cold beams.

Nietzsche's Death-bed

He bristles at the setting sun:
A crevasse is opening in his head. The cells split and explode;
Brightness streams down in music on the mountains,
The hanging birch-woods above Silvaplana.
                    "Wait, my Ariadne,
Wait, on your frozen Naxos. The fuddled god
Is reeling home – Zagreus the holy,
Torn in the manse by his twelve Titan sisters.
And I once more return
To the black magician whom I loved, to the tarantulas,
And all the little men whose problem now
Is to be rid of me – the crucified
On his fanged whirling wheel.
Golden the time comes round with the gold beast,
As to the rotting brain recurs the spirochaet."

Landscape near Geneva, 1950
for Hans-Joachim Haecker

Summer ago
I walked beside that lake, where like presiding elders
Alp and the Jura raised to serene heaven
Their candid heads – lapped in a valley's greenness,
Whose trees were rife with nightingales' synods,
And every tongue of grass

330

A pulpit for the throbbing cicala.
With alien friends I walked, out of a Europe
Broken like bread and scattered on the mountains,
Whose hearts, perturbed and passionate, recalled
The iconographic hand, the gift of tongues,
Silenced and stricken in the room of poverty:
Commemoration of the Christ transfigured,
With Law and Prophecy, upon the hills,
Descending to an epileptic world.

Care in Heaven

How many times they do come (if you will receive it),
So gay, with a light hand, and a brisk pinion
Cutting the blue air, that stands above London, even –
So, in a phrase of song,
In a half-hour's peace, lying like a moment of love
Upon our wounds, affect us;
Telling we are only a footstep from the garden,
From the golden world, from the shoemakers' holiday –
How near we were to finding our lost childhood.

So courteous they are. Then why should we refuse them
If to-morrow they come back in their formal livery,
Their panoply of humiliation, to pummel
With fiery sword-hilts upon the heart's closed doors?
These are dark nuncios; they have the king's commission.

Let it be Michaelmas: the failing of the leaf,
The time of the blue daisy – when the chief of the heavenly birds
Strikes at the glistering snake, who falls
Like a wreath, like a wraith of smoke, among
Those hemlock-umbels, the autumn constellations.

To My Godson, Julian Kollerstrom

Go down, Julian, into the waters;
Into the living waters you go down
Julian, apostate – the emperor,
Crowned and be-laurelled by his clamouring legions,
In the Lutetian mud-town which became
That gay and sensual city, Aphrodite's Paris.

Come up now, Julian. Look, you would never have thought
How easy it was to be born a second time.
Here are the same faces – your father and mother,
Godfathers and godmothers (among them, me).
You come up clean,
A little saint – Saint Julian the Hospitaller:
Saint Oedipus, to whom the pitiful deer
In the dark forest wounded, was accuser.

The landscape, you observe, is much the same.
Here are God's innocuous trees, His special mountains
Just as behind you in the wilderness.

Nothing is changed then? Julian, I thought the same,
Beside the Rhine, the Rhine, Europe's divisive river:
The same mountains and plains, the same pine-forests – but upon
    that side
The Nazi frontier guards, with their fixed bayonets,
And upon this,
The little city of peace, built in her hills,
(Cachemats constructed by imperial Julian)
The small and ill-defended state of Luxembourg.

For the New Cosmology

I saw the lady of galaxies at 12 a.m.,
Leaning over her cradles in a pallium of hydrogen,
The Hyades in her hair, and the Seven Sisters,
Orion crucified to the South, and the polar Bear,
With the nebulae about her like whirling dervishes.
"Oh infinitely I aspire," she said, "I am the ever-virgin

332

And burning bush, created every minute
By the miraculous seed in the vacancy of my loins;
And cumbering my heart,
Singing birds in a rage, an exaltation of nightingales."

Canticle of the Sun
Dancing on Easter Morning

I am the great Sun. This hour begins
My dancing day – pirouetting in a whirl of white light
In my wide orchestral sky, a red ball bouncing
Across the eternal hills;
For now my Lord is restored: with the rising dew
He carries his own up to his glittering kingdom –
Benedicite, benedicite, benedicite omnia opera.

Look, I am one of the morning stars, shouting for joy –
And not the least honoured among those shining brothers,
O my planetary children – now that my dark daughter,
The prodigal Earth, is made an honest woman of;
Out of her gapped womb, her black and grimy tomb,
Breaks forth the Crowned, victory in his pierced hands –
Benedicite, benedicite, benedicite omnia opera.

You too, my lovers – little lark with trembling feathers,
Sing your small heart out in my streaming rays;
And you, grave narrow-browed eagle, straining your eyes
Against my wound – foretell
These fiery dales and flame-anemoned meadows
Shall be a haunt for shy contemplative spirits –
Benedicite, benedicite, benedicite omnia opera.

And now with joy I run my recurring race;
And though again I shall have to hide my face
With a hand of cloud out of the heart of schism,
Yet the time is sure when I once more shall be
A burning giant in his marriage-chamber,
A bright gold cherub, as I came from my Father's halls –
Benedicite, benedicite, benedicite omnia opera.

Dionysius the Areopagite

*(On his return from Egypt, having witnessed the eclipse accompanying Christ's
Crucifixion, he dedicates an altar to the Unknown God)*

Bright god of day, and you, O Athenäis,
Virgin of the city, hard-spear-proffering, gathered
From the clear radiance of the Father's brow – here I salute
My earth of home; the quality of light,
Your shafts, glancing upon grey rock or marble;
Town of the violet-garland, olive and thyme; the landscape
Which only comes alive when crossed by man.
Here dance the feet
Of fairy-goddesses, and here, disturbed at noon,
The sunburnt whistler, wrapped in a goat's hide,
Puts panic on the shepherd in the lonely gully;
Across these hills, under this open sky,
The calm Olympians go. We have defined –
Clear head, and active tongue –
The human stature of a godhead's power.

But there,
Whence now the black-prowed ship has borne me home,
Southward across the sea, southward from Crete,
In a more ancient country, where the Nile
Flows wrinkling from the Mountains of the Moon –
Oh there the gods have unfamiliar faces:
Of scavenging birds, or cats, or grinning tongueless things
That crawled out of the mud, and weeping hawks
Crowded about a king who dies with the parched grain,
Blackened and stiff in his waxed linen grave-clothes.
They are become vast stalking letters, carved
On a mathematical stone tomb – as once in Babylon
A priest with braided beard inscribed
In figures of the stars on a clay pillar
The battles of the abyss, the eagle-taloned
And bull-horned giants who tore and stamped,
And a singing fish-tail, crying of elemental waters
Unloosed for the world's drowning; in Asia, where
A talking flame roared from a dry thorn-bush
And a people's grumbling god, in a little box
Thatched with blue badger-skins,
Waits, to subdue the earth.

Bright charioteer,
Guider of horses and the harmonious lyre
Whose intellectual chords construct,
For us, a ladder of the mind –
(As Plato, once, your child of fable, told) –
To climb through these blue heavens, beyond
The stars, that Delphic quire, the kosmokrators
Turning the world's wheels, above the darkness
Of this stone womb, the body's cave
Haunted by shadows, till we at last are lost
In the still One, the light beyond the image:

         But they have known you
Human no more, soar in the hard sky,
A great red globe, fiery and angry, the twisted serpent
Black on your brow, while your two silver wings
Spanned with their tips the sterile far horizons;
A kestrel, self-brought-forth, you hovered
Above the gulf of darkness beyond time;
A polished metal beetle, trundling the world,
A little ball of dirt, in the illimitable desert;
A bird come wandering from millennium
To die at Heliopolis in flames.

         And then
I saw you suddenly sicken, blacked out in terror –
You ran back, Sun, dropping your reins, as once
Above Thyestes' retching board – a meal of flesh,
Of living flesh – over the vines and wheatfields; something
     obscene,
As if a god died horribly, alone,
There, in that darkness, on a naked hilltop.
Yes, you were mastered, Sun, and all your fires
Livid with fear.... I have my seat
Here, in that tribunal where once by night,
Hands sticky with his own sin, the fugitive
Came trailed by dogs of nightmare, still onward driven,
Even from your sanctuaries, bright one.... What unknown god
Your shuddering eclipse proclaimed, I honour here,
Raising this altar, and with this inscription,
Beside the gates. So, passers-by may read;
Who shall declare?

Pharos

It must be true, one cannot doubt,
What Stesichorus put about;
Helen never came to Troy;
They filched her from her handsome boy,
And here, on Pharos' isle detained,
She all those war-torn years remained;
So Paris, to his shame, conveyed
A succubus to Troy, a shade
Which counterfeited in his arms
The miracle of Helen's charms.
For this the topless towers were burned
And Priam's empire overturned;
For this the Grecian navy sailed,
And Hector, butcher's meat, was trailed –
The draggled hair and the pierced heels –
At the doomed victor's chariot wheels.

Then hold it so. These lines I write
Where strikes the same Egyptian light
That touched the gold of Helen's hair;
I breathe the pristine desert air
That loved to lift her garment's hem.
The midland sea, like a soft gem
Rolls its seductive waters on
Under the pre-dynastic sun,
Where now a different city rises,
With other lotteries, other prizes,
And the good-looking and the glib
Drink coca-cola and zibib.

Like Menelaus have I come,
Tired and a longish step from home,
Here to consult an oracle?
But still the black Hamitic spell
Withholds. That fabulous, lovely witch
I must pursue to the last ditch
By Pharos now denies to me
Her swan-born, white epiphany.

Porphyry and Plotinus gone,
(The alone have fled to the Alone) –

Their tranquil wisdom who shall guess?
But the unappeased distress
Of bitter, thought-crazed, passionate men
Like self-castrated Origen,
The jangling and fanaticism
Of schism and of counter-schism,
With Cyril and his monkish drove
Who hated for sweet Jesus' love –
These come to us across the years
And shadow our own guilt and tears;
We also have Hypatia torn
And reasoned beauty put to scorn.

Rhodian Apollonius,
Nostalgia of Theocritus –
Shall then these lines invoke your grace;
Or that late loiterer of your race,
Cavafy – old, sad, heart untamed,
Who the perfect image framed
To fit this city which he loved:
Antony, when the god removed,
Listening with quiet despair
To music trailing through the air
Which he would not hear again –
The soft-limbed wine-god and his train?

It is the genius of the place
Commends this bitter syrup. Face
The image Homer gave once more:
How Menelaus, cast ashore
Storm-buffeted from the northern sea,
Came stalking here the slippery,
Corrupt, shape-shifting Proteus;
And when he caught him, held him thus –
In a King of Sparta's grip.
For we must never let him slip –
Though he range through his repertoire,
His watery nature change to fire,
Fish, serpent, beast or screaming bird –
Till he consent to give the Word.

Alexandria, 1955

Theogony

If it was not Hesiod, it could have been his colleague –
Nine decorous gentlewomen met him in a dale;
The bees, the tawny-bodied, were rummaging in the blossoms,
And he for garlic-bulbs, to relish his porrage.
Nine miraculous Muses tweaked him there on the mouth:
"Let theogony be your theme, construct upon that thought."
"Ladies," then said that long-shanked bard, "Out of last year's
     comb
Men press ungrateful honey; the ultimate sweetness cloys.
For Ilion's walls lie flat now; Homer's harpstring is slackened,
And civilization a dream among these hard-ribbed hills.
The hypocausts of Crete run cold for lack of plumbing.
This is no season for dithyramb; the rich year departs."
Erato then, and her eight incorruptible sisters,
Smiled to mark his diffidence; "A bard is a die-hard,
And the Muse, a nine-lived mouser, has got her claws in your
     spine –"
(In a mizzle of mist departing, they tricked their violet coronets)
"– Poet, you'll never know what mustard-and-cress you've planted.
Pallas has dreamed up Athens: sing the birth of the gods."

Bird-Song in New England

Jargon of cat-bird, purple finch, or song-sparrow –
Your notes now breathe a life
To stiff Victorian woodcuts, known in boyhood,
From yellowing books of Natural History, *Tableaux
Of Animated Nature*. The chimney-swift
Goes splitter-splutter into the twilight, different
From my shrill subfusc devil-screamer, whirling
Up through Lord Nuffield's smoke-smeared Oxford sky
To doze till dawn, the footless one, his cradle
The lullabying currents of warm air.

The myths retire,
Shyly, to their museums; or here they dwindle
Into a summer haze of Tanglewood tales
Twice-told to children by a nervous student.

For if the emigrant Muse
Forsook Cephissus, Arno, or her Thames,
By Charles's banks to plant her candid footprints,
It was occasional; conceded, Indian ghosts,
Reproachful, haunt these parklands and this outcrop.

And at a bird's cry, should one say:
"Some hapless nymph of chaste Diana's train,
Pursued by hirsute Pan, in her extremity
Besought the prudish goddess – "Aid me, do,
Sweet Phoebe, Phoebe!" – whereat the Delian
Alert in her Olympian mansions heard,
Descended (in machine) and – Ovid mark! –
Transmogrified the virgin to a bird"?

Those syllables relate
Only a whistling, melancholy call.

State of Massachusetts
July 1955

Canso

When spring airs fondle
And the nightingale
In the olivaster
   Harbours and sings,
And the moon's candle
Numinous and pale
Hangs high to foster
   Increase of things –

My heart discourses
Contrariwise:
How beauty is fallible
   In all her pride;
The season passes;
Embrowns the rose;
Nothing perdurable,
   Things faint and fade.

Thus our mortality
Fortune derides;
For love's mutations
   We learn to weep;
And no sodality
But it corrodes
Through time's collusions,
   Darkness, and sleep.

So we, being homeless
When spring rides high,
Should make obeisance
   In her cool vault
To the grave goddess
Of the moonless sky,
That her beneficence
   Go not by default.

It is convenient
We take this guise
To hold her revered;
   That in all terms,
She may be lenient,
And we, likewise,
Not unprepared
   When winter comes

Les Saintes-Maries-de-la-Mer
April 1953

Wild Snowdrops

The Spring returns, Cleobolus;
   Dissolves the snow. And even here –
Among the uncharming Yorkshire hills –
   A certain sweetness in the air;

Crocus and daffodil break out;
   And I observed, a week ago,
By Fountains Abbey, grass white-patched
   With snowdrops, not with lingering snow!

340

Cistercian flowers – no, naked nymphs,
    Cruel and ambiguous as spring,
Ride forth; and migrant love returns
    On purple, gold and garish wing.

In my back-yard the ousel's throat
    Salutes, at half-past six, the sun;
The Spring returns, still dangerous as
    For Horace and Anacreon.

Saint Luke's Summer

Saint Luke's Summer, the Silver Age of the year –
Chryselephantine autumn, white cloud and gold leaf
Recalling an ivory shoulder, the light in your hair –
Let the still rains drip to my heart, and rinse it of grief!

But is there any dabbing could expunge that stain?
Too well and too constant the Shadow has conned his brief
To indict this specious season a common thief,
Filching the warmth from the year, but leaving my pain.

The lackeys of Summer paid off, wood-wren and swallow
In a mythical and inaccessible Africa
Are hoarded and harboured now, where I may not follow.

That you, too, are absent proclaims each vapid evening;
Therefore I make my petition to great Verticordia,
And may love likewise come back with the seasons' returning.

Song

And how did I presume to love
    You, whom the winds and weathers favour;
Who with the moors their secrets share,
    And have the blond-haired sun for lover?
Shoulder and throat that I kiss now
    The all-possessing air may savour.

How in my arms' restricted pale
    Could you find pasture? – who have known
The roads of Europe beckon you,
    And challenged the arrogant hills of Spain;
To you confided like a bride
    Her twilit secrets Carcassonne.

Hearts are at infinite remove
    Though breast on breast lie all this night;
Though thigh and lip and finger play
    The soul is lost to sense and sight:
Between these dark polarities
    Love's rainbow arches, and is bright.

Watching Tennis

Light, in light breezes and a favouring sun,
You moved, like a dancer, to the glancing ball,
And the dance and the game seemed one
To me, unmarked spectator by the wall –

Always spectator, nor apt at any sport –
And you free burgess of the summer air;
Embraced within the Iron Maiden, Thought,
I of my body's poverty am aware.

How could I guess that all-consoling night,
Confider and concealer of secrets, should conduct
You to lie easy in my fumbling arms?

Yet, by the chances of the game betrayed,
Your mouth on mine found out its silent need,
And my discordant nerves peace in your limbs.

Out of the Picture

Half an edge from the claws of the law
    And a hand's tick out of time
They lie, two casual wanderers
    Beyond the picture's frame;
From any Eden but this out-cast,
    For its metaphysical heaven
Spirit forgets to grieve; the beast
    Pastures, and is forgiven –
On ribbed and salty hills he finds
    His sparse, but natural food;
Warm winds from nowhere, favouring, lash
    The five tides of the blood.
While mouth on grinning mouth confirms
    The skull inside the head,
A wholly holy and laughter-loving
    Goddess observes the bed.

The Unpredicted

The goddess Fortune be praised (on her toothed wheel
I have been mincemeat these several years)
Last night, for a whole night, the unpredictable
Lay in my arms, in a tender and unquiet rest –
(I perceived the irrelevance of my former tears) –
Lay, and at dawn departed. I rose and walked the streets,
Where a whitsuntide wind blew fresh, and blackbirds
Incontestably sang, and the people were beautiful.

The Lady's Complaint

I speak of that lady I heard last night,
    Maudlin over her gin and water,
In a sloppy bar with a fulvous light
    And an air that was smeared with smoke and laughter:
    How youth decamps and cold age comes after,

343

In fifty years she had found it true –
    She sighed for the damage that time had brought her:
"Oh, after death there's a judgement due.

"What once was as sleek as a seal's pelt,
    My shapeless body has fallen from grace;
My soul and my shoes are worn down to the welt,
    And no cosmetic can mask my face,
    As under talcum and oxide you trace
How the bones stick out, and the ghost peeps through –
    A wanderer, I, in Wraith-bone Place,
And after death there's a judgement due.

"My roundabout horses have cantered away,
    The gilded and garrulous seasons are flown;
What echo is left of the rag-time bray
    Of the tenor sax and the sousaphone?
    But I was frightened to sleep alone
(As now I must do, as now I must do)
    And a chittering bat-voice pipes 'Atone,
For after death there's a judgement due.'

"Green apples I bit when I was green,
    My teeth are on edge at the maggoty core;
Life is inclement, obscure, obscene;
    Nothing's amusing – not any more;
    But love's abrasions have left me sore –
To hairy Harry and half-mast Hugh
    I gave the love I was starving for,
And after death there's a judgement due.

"Potentate, swirling in stark cold air
    The corn from the husks – I offer to you
My terror-struck and incredulous prayer,
    For after death there's a judgement due."

Girl with Marionettes
(Leeds City Varieties)

to John Betjeman

They hold their own, not the wire-puller's laws,
As each its wicked, sensual life assumes;
The prancing skeleton gained our applause.

That invocation gave our laughter pause:
These manikins our merriment exhumes –
They hold their own, not the wire-puller's laws.

The grave-faced girl, thus, cautiously withdraws
Them from their box, like mummies from old tombs –
The prancing skeleton gained our applause.

The erotic nautch-doll, draped in tinselled gauze,
Twitches her stiff limbs to Ketélby's neumes;
They hold their own, not the wire-puller's laws.

And vanishing at last, as with no cause –
Magnesium flash, and puff of bluish fumes –
The prancing skeleton gained our applause.

To abolish chaos, and restore guffaws,
Three teddy-bears in hand, she now presumes;
They hold their own, not the wire-puller's laws –
The prancing skeleton gained our applause.

Brief Letter to a Friend

Dear friend, since you do not admire
My verse (but true Parnassian fire
Upon occasion's to be found
Mid tinsel wreaths that lap it round –
Or so you give me to suppose)
Therefore in measures close to prose
Familiarly to you I write
On this all-soulless autumn night,
From the disgusting town of Leeds

Which spleen in my condition breeds.
But, looking round the world, in fact
What is there spleen to counteract?
The weather's foul, the news is bad,
The whole creation running mad;
And, totting up the total score,
We half expect a Third World War,
Or advent, at the very least,
Of the ten-horned, abysmal Beast.

But what is to become of that
Ill-clothed and under-nourished brat,
Our little orphan Annie – she
Who once was English poetry?
Time was, her place was near the fire,
Since born in Cædmon's Saxon byre;
A Latin tutor taught her grammar,
Correcting her Teutonic stammer;
And a French tailor made her neat,
And shod her trim syllabic feet,
And tricked her out with glittering rhymes;
But she has fallen on evil times,
And you and I have seen her go
Combing the gutters of Soho.
So academic critics rule:
"Send her to an Approved School:
She needs *our* care and *our* protection."
Poor soul, she'll there get scant affection!
While one in Dublin, kindly-cruel
Feeds her with thin and neutral gruel;
And one in Berkshire will not fail
To prove that Reading has a gaol;
By the whole gang she's soundly rated
By one she's robbed, by one she's bated,
And last, at Downing, suffocated.

But now I mourn a closer grief,
Since cosh-boy Death, the general thief
Our glib-tongued Dylan has struck down,
Half exiled, in a distant town.
I hear Ceridwen, goddess, still,
On some remote and Cambrian hill,

Lamenting for her druid, sigh;
A mountain torrent now is dry.

Long past the stroke of twelve I've penned
This note to you, dear candid friend,
And something of my bile expressed,
(A time for rage, a time for rest!)
Enough – you shall peruse at leisure
This halting, hardly-Swiftian measure.

10 November 1953

A Ballad of Pope Joan

Joan she was an English girl
   Born at West Hartlepool;
Scotus Erigena taught her Greek
   When she sneaked into school.

"From All to Nothing creation goes"
   He said "– *O entium ens!*"
The scholarship-boys rose up like a man,
   Transfixed him with their pens.

Joan she sat with the curate at play:
   "Will ye gang, Lizzie Lindsay," sang he
"Will ye gang to the hieland heights of Religion,
   Your petticoats up to your knee?"

"Oh I will follow my own true love
   In any weather or wind;
I will fly to the forests of Arden and Eden
   And my name is Rosalind."

Fever, famine and fury of Northmen
   On the map of Europe crossed;
The people died like flies, only quicker,
   And the curate, somehow, got lost.

Joanna came to the city of Rome,
  Being discreet and highbrow,
And the shattered statue of Venus Genetrix
  Cocked an ironical eyebrow.

Oh who shall jangle St. Peter's keys,
  And mount the Pontifical throne?
This girlish-faced young monk, demure,
  And relatively unknown.

Solemn procession through the streets:
  "Bless us, and pray for us,
Joannes servus servorum Dei
    Pontifex maximus!"

Joan gazed up at the blank, blue heavens,
  And her heart was a puddle of fear;
"Alas, I have that in my womb..." she muttered,
  For she knew her hour was near.

The seven Archangels before God's throne
  In their adamantine mail
Trembled: "Oh Pillars, support your Church,
  Lest the gates of Hell prevail!"

Then the three Pillars of Peter's dome
  Gasped in their stony lungs,
And over all the astonished city
  Clattered their marble tongues.

And the first Pillar was craggy Cephas;
  He said: "At my nets I haul
For haddock and mackerel, herring and dory,
  But here's queerer fish than all.

"My net is a tough and close-meshed net,
  And if any breaks through and goes,
I curse and swear in my Billingsgate...
  But then the red cock crows."

And the second Pillar was James the Just,
　　And he said: "The accusing Law
Clutches at my Davidic heart
　　With a cold and constricting claw!"

And the third Pillar was John, the thunderbird:
　　"I have seen the Whore and her Snake
Rampaging over the Seven Hills
　　To the incandescent lake.

"But my Love, the terrible brazen-footed
　　Alphabet looks on me:
O adorable, ridiculous children
　　Love one another," said he.

Then Mary leaned from among the Angels,
　　Observing Joan and her fear:
"There are times", she said, "when a girl needs Mother,
　　My dear, but ah my dear."

Then Joan fell down in the public street,
　　With the harsh cobbles for bed:
And the taxis stood and hooted like furies,
　　Till the crossing-lamps turned blood-red.

And "Oh, oh, oh," cried Joan and "oh,
　　Assist me, gentlemen, please!"
Then the baby ripped itself from her womb,
　　And addressed them in words like these:

"I am Long Will of Cumberland,
　　And Will of Malvern Hill,
And Will of the Tyger and the Lamb,
　　And Arden and Avon's Will.

"I voyaged to the Southern polar Seas,
　　And Samson's blindness was mine,
And I twice rode pilgrim to Canterbury
　　To Thomas the Martyr's shrine.

"Immortality flies round my head,
And urns and nightingales;
True Thomas I am of the Eildon Tree,
And Taliesin of Wales."

They buried Joan by the street-crossing,
With the baby at her feet,
And continually circumambulate
To avoid that scandalous street.

Epitaph for Thaïs

Traveller, under this stone lies all that remains – of our sister,
Arete, servant of Christ; alkaline sands of Natroun
Hold here a wonder, those limbs which once lent their contours
to Thaïs
(God has forgiven her sins – scarlet, now whiter than snow).
Ask not how many young men their fortunes let slip, and careers,
Chancing one night on her couch (and it was worth it, they
said);
Neo-Platonic sages failed to show up at their lectures –
Dream of the touch of her lips, metaphysics go hang!
Praising one of her nipples, there was a poet composed an
Epic in twenty-two books (no one peruses it now).
Alexandria's side-streets are always full of such rumours
(Keep to the lives of the Saints, these are the gossip of Heaven).
All is altered now; she who was bound to the shameless
Demon the heathen revere, Aphrodite the Rose,
Now is made free of the golden-causewayed city of Zion
(Love that accomplishes all, glory be given to Thee).
Athanäel our brother with his rough rhetoric tamed this
Lamb that so widely had strayed, coaxing it back to the fold.

Athanäel has left us; dying, they say in despair – he
Could find no quiet nor rest, such are the snares of the Fiend –
So distracted his prayers the rose-tinctured body of Thaïs,
Satan into his den clawed that apostatized soul.

Did you suppose, O you who pass by, this hetaira
  Yielded herself to a god, not exacting her price?
What more costly a gem could Heaven itself afford than,
  Dear-bought and bright, a soul predestined, to her fee?

Carol for Advent

Let love come under your roof:
  Oh house him, vagrant;
Happy the eaves where he builds a space –
  That light-winged migrant.
Italian airs shall echo and hang
  Under each rafter;
He'll touch into silver foil
  Your peeling plaster,
Set geraniums round your door,
  On hearth lay tinder;
So spread your nets to detain him here –
  Don't let him wander.

Love has no manners, and pays no rent,
  Full of evasions,
Is rude to your influential friends,
  And sneaks the rations;
Sulkily packs his bag and is gone
  At your reproof,
Leaving the plaster peeling still,
  A leaking roof.
Likely, he'll not be back any more
  For tea, nor dinner –
Love is, by nature, impossible –
  Learn your dishonour:

Love, Love is a king discrowned;
  In their dumb motion
All the republican stars lament
  His abdication.
Once he taught them solfeggios,
  Danced in their choirs,

Till intellectual pride untuned
    The shining spheres.
If he'd be glad of a share of your board,
    Or a place by the fire,
Draw back the bolts, and give up to Love
    Your easiest chair.

The Dark Planet

There is a dark planet striking against us. Invisible,
Its venomed arrows whisk through the purple air.
It is the masked dancer, shifting among
The beneficent choir, deflecting
All dulcet influence of Aphrodite the gay,
Ingenious Mercury with his legerdemain,
And Artemis on her silver-sandalled way.

It is because the dark planet decrees,
That the rose discards to the dust her flush-fire mantle.
It is the dark planet's malice that has choked
The song of the bird in its throat, and grinds desire
Down to the bitter ashes, the gritty cinders of time,
Where, with the brazen monument, crumbles the rhyme.

Where the dark planet strikes, nothing is innocent;
My boyhood impulses it caught in a net of fear.
My friends it suborns from me. Now you, my dear,
The dark planet has hit in the thick of the night.
It has turned you away from us all, and away from the light,
And the times we in common possessed, that went by like dreams –
With the unquiet speed of all dreams – must likewise fade,
As memory fades, your image become a shade.

In the web of things we perceive, there is nothing the dark planet
    spares;
For not to our condition is granted ever
Perfection of beauty, intellect, power. They fade like those cold
Prismatic garlands, the abstract blossoms of snow,
In the beams of that black sun, whose visage we may not know.
For it is an envious star. Not one, in their hierarchies,

But must bend to its importunate, to its absolute demands.
Though we turn, in our rage, and upbraid, through our tears, its
    assaults,
It will yield no retrograde motion, no slackening of its bands.

The dark planet swings through its ebony kingdom above.
Listen, do you not hear the whoosh-whoosh of its wings?
No, it will not cease fire, till every image is emptied
Of all significance, saving only its own.
Ah my dear, has your parting this hypothesis taught me?
Implacable, that sky-wanderer. Its name is Love.

Quatrains

    The Dog Star now, negating all desires,
    Hurls through the atmosphere destructive fires;
      In mute indifference heart and pen must lie,
    Though Fame still tarries, and though Love expires.

    For we have seen the rage of Time consume
    Those temples which the Muses' lamps illume;
      If their resplendent torches gutter down,
    To smoulder on shall burnt-out stubs presume?

    Some verses still unpublished I avow...
    A sausage-roll, a pint of beer – but Thou?
      The Thou whose image prompts my midnight tears
    Is ash at Mortlake Crematorium now.

    The leaves made languid under August skies
    In Bloomsbury Square reproach my life; and cries
      The voice Verlaine within his prison heard,
    And *"Qu'as-tu fait de ta jeunesse?"* it sighs.

    Sweet-scented, possibly, the manuscript
    Of half my span is closed, and better skipped;
      We slumber in Hope's lap an hour or two
    An unquiet sleep – and wake to find we're gypped.

There was a time when the enchanting bird
Of poetry was in my orchards heard –
    The green boughs whitened with ideas in bloom,
And easy on my lips lighted the word.

Fate's discords have unharmonized those tunes,
And blank abstractions blotted out the runes;
    Each finds his loneliness: FitzGerald knew
Like impotence among the Suffolk dunes.

Time with unpitying and iron feet
Bears down upon us all; we learn to greet,
    Without despair, the inevitable void,
Whether in Nishapur or Russell Street.

Little Russell Street, Bloomsbury
August 1953

Poem Preparatory to my Thirty-fifth Birthday
"I passed by his garden and marked with one eye..."

Tonight the sun enters Cancer – wooing the crustacean
Sidelong, evasive creature that is my patron:
House of the white-faced, introvert, musing Moon,
Goddess and genetrix. I come now, this tells me, soon
In *mezzo dell' cammin* – at fifteen and a score –
To midway this mortal heart, and at my life's core.
But, as for the dark wood, I have been habitual denizen
Of that often re-visited, and so dangerous plantation,
Whose trees, perennial-bloomed with the knowledge of good
        and evil,
Authentically are sprung from the apple-seed of the Devil.
And those three carnivorous beasts distractingly cavort
About my errant steps, here, as in any resort:
The Lion of wrath and pride, with flesh-fumed mouth capacious
To bolt me down to his oven, is (no more than usual) rapacious;
And slinky-sided, mean, with satisfied grin, the Wolf
Exhorts me, as always she does, to be true to my love of myself.
These are malicious vermin; before them, I have to fear

354

The familiar fawning of the pock-marked Panther.
The sickly-breathed Panther, that damasked and diapered beast,
In the sluggard's garden, my soul, with the Owl was sharing a
    feast.
For the Owl, pedantic, hoots through the desolate glades of my
    head,
As the Panther purrs in the no less desolate groves of my bed.
Therefore, these smoke-signs I direct to you, George Barker,
Who of our local fauna have been both stalked and stalker.
Perceiving them, as you stride in some out-of-earshot brake,
Pause, and condone my petition, since now I seek to invoke
The impersonal Wisdom (if she indeed be friend
To Lucy, lady of light, which I lack) condescend
To request from his sigh-wavered castle uprear at my side
The latin and latent tradition, to chide and confide.

To Tom Watt

Painters are diurnal, poets nocturnal animals:
Whoever heard that you had a Muse?
Following, not Phoebus, but a northward radiance,
You, I presume, inhabit where objects are real,
Existing in a world of light. Two dozen egg-shells
Hang here in a basket because you like them.
I, sleeping with ink and paper beside my bed,
Protract my days in a semi-stupor of idleness,
Awaking only in the yellow-lit bar
(Where others relax) – to absorb the human gestures
And fragments of conversation which around me themselves
    deploy.
Only in the darkness, when a winter moon rides without,
She bends and protends to me; and only then
Is silence a word. Companion, we'll therefore
Modulate, in a different sense, the identical dialect.

To Hugh Gordon Porteus

My friend with the eyes of a benevolent weretiger –
A scholar voyaging on Abana and Pharpar,
A poet loyal to words and his material –
I think of you engaged now in Adam's occupation,
And curing your own tobacco with cider or a rotten pear.
On an autumn night, a poet in China saw once
A vision of a huge house, where all the scholars of the Empire
Sat in the warmth of the fire, with enough rice, with poetry, and
     wine.
But his feet stumbled among the lonely hills:
Hoar-frost hangs on the grass-blades, wild geese pass overhead –
Shall I ask one of the latter to carry this message?

On a Picture of Avicenna Lecturing
to his Pupils
for Peter Avery

Seated above a space of grass, a blue dome hovering behind,
Under a white wall where a small tree sprouts,
The Master opined to his class of bearded boys,
Upon the Soul; how she,
A white dove, flickered once among the supernal spinneys.
Anguish and mystery her descent to these ravines;
Anguish and mystery her straining to depart.
Reason beyond our thinking rules the nest of the spheres:
The prophetic spirit reveals, a Man speaking to men,
As a doler out of laws to the political animal.
After the gorgeous steed's ascent, after the absence,
The cords of memory draw, in the mind's right dispositions.
Particulars of geography are hallowed thus by pilgrimage;
In fasting, gifts to the poor, and numbered genuflections,
Against dispositions of nature, the soul strains to her health.
The discourse ended, he rose; all at a hand's clap,
The waiters brought in wine, musicians and dancers entered.
The unspeaking sun goes down to his golden chambers;
Wakened, the soul knows harmony her own:
In a whirl of wordless pleasure, she turns and returns.

Preface to an Anthology of Recorded Poetry
presented to Professor Bonamy Dobrée on his retirement

Tired with the trappings of imperial pride
Caesars have laid their purple pomps aside;
Relinquished sceptre, diadem, and ball,
With flattery that acclaimed them lords of all,
Exchanging for the cares that plague the great
Long dreamed of solace in a private state.
Great Diocletian thus, the Illyrian lord
Who stained with martyrs' blood his Roman sword,
Resigned the crumbling Empire with a sigh
For some spare plots of kale and broccoli;
And Hapsburg Charles divided Europe's strife
Despaired to heal, and sought to end his life
In cloisters cold, and the religious cell,
To tell his beads, and mark the office bell.
But such, ill-starred and of a dubious fame,
The Muse, auspicious, would forbear to name,
Though you, Augustus of our little realm,
Must now, before due season, quit the helm;
In peace you gave your petty senate laws,
And sought for knowledge, not your own applause;
Captives, indeed, your annual triumphs swelled –
That bless the golden chains wherein they're held;
You have made prisoners of our eager youth,
And the light bonds were Eloquence and Truth.
Vandal and Gothic rage you kept at bay,
And what, within the walls, might faith betray;
Grave Pallas proudly reared her classic head,
And academic Dullness, muttering, fled;
The Graces too, and genial Mirth, appear,
And the poor Muses find asylum here
(Since raggle-taggle gypsies they've become
They range the world, yet call no place their home).
Time, only Time, such charms can never hold,
And Time determines now our age of gold.
Like Prospero, you quit the enchanted isle,
Resume your favoured Milan for a while;
But do not sink your book, nor break your wand,
Nor yet release your Ariel from his bond;
For him, the active Genius of your brain,
Still other tasks, and triumphs new, remain:

357

Afresh to compass all that world of wit
In Charles's reign, or Anna's, who more fit?
Great Dryden, bending from his sphere above,
Assigns the task; his peers the choice approve;
And Congreve's shade, and Wycherley's, and Pope's,
Berkeley's and Swift's on this have fixed their hopes –
That you the expectant world their graces show,
And dress those laurels they had won below.

Since you, alas, must go, and we remain,
This random garland you will not disdain,
Of blooms selected from Pieria's bowers,
For these, though few, are still unfading flowers.
If distance parts us, yet, at close of day,
Our loves, and these, our disembodied voices, stay.

To Two Friends Returning to Canada

for John and Helen Carter

Dear friends, the importunate ocean stream
Recalls you, to revoke the dream
Of Europe, and her citadels:
Truth that inhabits not her wells,
Nor yet her wine-vats, but the heart
By love made peaceable, impart
A wise acceptance – so may you
Proceed upon your way, escorted
By flocks of keen-voiced birds, and courted
By the brisk sons of Aeolus;
The adorable and decorous
Soft-breasted, nude Atlantides
Make smooth the world-dividing seas!
Go home dear friends, and leave behind
Cities that only in the mind
Put on that rare, Platonic grace
Which stings us like a lover's face:
Naples, where the siren's grave
Abuts the blue and lucid wave,
And Virgil's dust lies, dry and dumb;
Imperious and infallible Rome;

And London, haunted more than these,
By dark, Dickensian fantasies.
Find your own earth which, unencumbered
With memories, so long had slumbered,
And mark, with new and chastened eyes,
The sun ascendant in those skies.
Not yours the loss. These lines I pen
Because we may not meet again;
Love, if not wit, informs their pace,
And is not bound by time or place.

The Cave of the Nymphs

Hushed, haunted the cave – a gathering point
For time and eternity. One entrance
For men, subject to death,
One, open to the sky,
For the Undying. In this place,
Where the quiet nymphs weave purple cloth,
And hive the learnèd bees – archetypes,
Images, symbols.

                    But Ulysses,
Ulysses of the many stratagems,
Was unaware of this. He shook himself (grandson
of Autolycus, the wolf-man) suddenly awake
Like a great canine. He rubbed the salt from his eyes,
Dismissing the images of night and journeying:
The snatching horror, the sucking whirlpool,
Canticle of the death-birds,
Possessive and beast-attended
Goddesses, the geometrical gardens.
He knew where he was. The landscape
Was not the deceptive pastoral simplicity
Of the cannibals' island, and not
The hothouse vegetation of Lotos-land,
Nor spruce and silver-birch
Of the Laestrygones' fjord. It was limestone;
It was tamarisks; it was olives
And vine-stocks gnawed by goats.
It was Ithaca at last. And was dangerous.

Therefore, out in the sunlight,
Meeting a shepherd-boy,
He started once more to lie –
It was almost routine with him now –
Improvising a cover-story. But with so much blague,
And such a ready tongue,
He began to enjoy it. And that other,
Knowing it would all come out,
Could not refrain from revealing herself –
The goddess who was on his side –
And chaffed him too. So they stood there,
The man and the Immortal, like a pair of friends
Who understand each other
Too well to talk much.

And as he turned to go
She still smiled after him. But if
The perdurable and inviolate heart
Of immortal Wisdom might grieve, it ached then
For what it could never know:
For not to know death is to know nothing
Of the wonder of deliverance; and to be free
Of the wide aether, and the white peaks of Olympos,
And all the bounds of the world and the backward-flowing Ocean,
Is never to know and love
One patch of earth as home.

                    But Ulysses,
Ulysses who had made a good journey,
Was unaware of this. He had gone to look for
A wife he had not met
For twenty years, and a son
Who must now be a stranger to him.
For he had come home;
Which is the whole point of the story.

Not Being Oedipus

Not being Oedipus he did not question the Sphinx
Nor allow it to question him. He thought it expedient
To make friends and try to influence it.
In this he entirely succeeded,

And continued his journey to Thebes. The abominable thing
Now tame as a kitten (though he was not unaware
That its destructive claws were merely sheathed)
Lolloped along beside him –

To the consternation of the Reception Committee.
It posed a nice problem: he had certainly overcome
But not destroyed the creature – was he or was he not
Entitled to the hand of the Princess

Dowager Jocasta? Not being Oedipus
He saw it as a problem too. For frankly he was not
By natural instinct at all attracted to her.
The question was soon solved –

Solved itself, you might say; for while they argued
The hungry Sphinx, which had not been fed all day,
Sneaked off unobserved, penetrated the royal apartments,
And softly consumed the lady.

So he ascended the important throne of Cadmus,
Beginning a distinguished and uneventful reign.
Celibate, he had nothing to fear from ambitious sons;
Although he was lonely at nights,

With only the Sphinx, curled up upon his eiderdown.
Its body exuded a sort of unearthly warmth
(Though in fact cold-blooded) but its capacity
For affection was strictly limited.

Granted, after his death it was inconsolable,
And froze into its own stone effigy
Upon his tomb. But this was self-love, really –
It felt it had failed in its mission.

While Thebes, by common consent of the people, adopted
His extremely liberal and reasonable constitution,
Which should have enshrined his name – but not being Oedipus,
It vanished from history, as from legend.

Theseus on Naxos

1

Mother seldom spoke of Father:
   She'd a faded photograph –
Tall and rather worried figure
   With a great carved oaken staff

(Am I looking somewhat like him
   Now I've got my worries too?) –
That, and a few withered violets
   Which had once been vivid, blue.

These she kept between the pages
   Of – oh, I forget the name –
Odes and Dithyrambs – or something –
   By some modish Lesbian dame.

Darling mother's taste in verses!
   Still, I'm not the one to judge –
What you'd call a man of action;
   Most poetic stuff is fudge.

"Violets, these, from Cecrops' city
   Where your father reigns", she said,
When I coaxed her to display them
   (To delay the time for bed).

Not a wholly normal childhood,
   Being – well, "the fruit of sin" –
Or, to put it bluntly, bastard
   (*And* my school-chums rubbed it in).

362

Then I got "his" sword and sandals –
  Time the local boy made good –
(Mother said she *wasn't* crying) –
  Ventured through the Dangerous Wood.

How I there eliminated
  Various anti-social types
Frequently has been related –
  Kites and crows enjoy their tripes!

(Take, for instance, that Procrustes
  With his calculating eyes,
Who stretched travellers out, or cut them
  Down, to fit his standard size:

In his way a true idealist –
  Never thought it was enormity –
Man a thing to be transcended
  In that Higher Uniformity.)

Thence to violet-crownéd Athens:
  Touching scene with dear old Dad;
Took me two weeks to discover
  That the place was really bad.

First, a rather passée sorceress
  Had poor father on a string;
I was forced to send her packing,
  Borne aloft on dragon's wing –

Whirled on high in a fiery chariot,
  Queen of the Night in a four-wheeled star,
Dragon-drawn, and trilling curses
  Through empty space where no gods are.

Then the Cretan tribute, stifling
  As it came by year, by year,
Streets of that white-paven city
  With a pale, unspoken fear:

Delicate girls in the blush of beauty,
  Boys in their galloping grace, to the Beast –
Product of hideous and comic lust:
  The obscene guzzle, the bull-thing's feast.

363

Aegean-dandled island of Crete:
  Before I dreamed it, I had come,
Voluntary victim, to liberate
  Athens, I now knew was home –
  Suddenly, inexplicably, home.

Corridored palace of Knossos,
  Throne-room of Minos the king,
The bull-games painted, the double axe,
  And young girls dance in a ring –
  Bell-skirts, bare breasts, in a ring;

Eyes of Minos, thalassocrat,
  Lord of the bull-voiced wave,
Who must make up accounts with God
  At the ninth year's end in a cave –
  Is it birth or death in that cave?

And the staring eyes of a girl –
  Ariadne's, that king's daughter –
Bird-eyes that seemed to burn with delight
  (Was it of love or slaughter?)
  On me, destined to slaughter.

Secretly she came that night
  (She had bribed the guards, as I guessed)
To the close dark hell of a man in fear,
  And I lay upon her breast.
  And I dreamed of my mother's breast.

She gave me a thin-spun cord;
  I held it, and walked in a daze
Threading the echoing corridors
  Of a hollow, haunted maze –
  Of the palace, or of the maze.

Princess, or priestess, or goddess,
  It was the ritual task
She had assigned me; I killed
  A bull – or behind that mask
  The king, in a bull's mask?

I do not know; We fled
  Through darkness where snickered no star,
Over shaggy seas to Naxos:

That's precisely where we are.

3

All the time I think of Athens,
  Athens which will now be free:
People needing laws and justice –
  And that business lies with me.

God knows, what can I do for them?
  But it's not for me to choose;
Father will not live for ever;
  I must step into his shoes.

Ariadne, with your witchcraft,
  Life, and all, I owe to you;
But, as queen of civic Athens –
  Really, it would never do.

Ariadne, mountain priestess,
  Wild-eyed enthusiast
Of swift-footed Britomartis...
  I shall live to weep the past.

Dearest, you were very gentle –
  Delicate and white those hands;
May the strange gods whom you worship
  Guard you on these wind-vexed sands.

Look, how peacefully she's sleeping!
  Dark now; it will soon be day.
Quietly set the sails and leave her –
  Surely it's the kindest way.

Plato and the Waters of the Flood

In one of the remoter parts of Asia Minor, near what was once the southern
boundary of the Phrygians, there is a warm spring flanked by a Hittite monument,
and known to the Turks as Plato's Spring. The reason for the name is that it was
at this spot, according to Arab legend, that Plato succeeded in stopping the Flood
by making the waters run underground.

W.K.C. GUTHRIE, *Orpheus and Greek Religion*

When on Armenian Ararat
   Or Parnassus ridge
Scrunched the overloaded keel,
   Pelican, ostrich,
Toad, rabbit, and pangolin –
   All the beasts of the field –
Scrambled out to possess once more
   Their cleansed and desolate world.
      Plato, by that fountain,
        Spoke to the swirling deep:
      "Retire, you waters of Chaos,
        Flow retrograde, and sleep;
      Above the swift revolving heavens
        Rule the intelligible,
      Chaste and undecaying ideas;
        Brackish waters, fall!"

Plato, in the academic grove,
   Among the nightingales,
Expounded to wide-eyed ephebes
   His geometric rules;
Reared a republic in the mind
   Where only noble lies
Reign; he expelled the poets
   (With courtesy, with praise).

Loaded down with useless garlands,
   Down to that fountain
The exiled poets proceeded:
   "When will you rise again,
Ten-horned, seven-headed seraphim,
   Out of your abyss,
Against the beautiful Republic –
   Nor tamed by Plato's kiss?"

Titus and Berenice

"Turn to me in the darkness,
   Asia with your cool
Gardens beyond the desert,
   Your clear, frog-haunted pool;
I seek your reassurance –
   Forget, as I would forget,
Your holy city cast down, the Temple
   That still I desecrate."
"Buzz!" said the blue-fly in his head.

"In darkness master me,
   Rome with your seven hills,
Roads, rhetorical aqueducts,
   And ravaging eagles;
Worlds are at bitter odds, yet we
   Can find our love at least –
Not expedient to the Senate,
   Abominable to the priest."
"Buzz!" said the blue-fly in his head.

Titus the clement Emperor
   And she of Herod's house
Slobbered and clawed each other
   Like creatures of the stews;
Lay together, then lay apart
   And knew they had not subdued –
She the insect in his brain,
   Nor he her angry God.

Note: According to a Jewish tradition Titus was afflicted with an insect in his brain as a punishment for his destruction of the Temple.

The Peacock and the Snake

"It was your fault! It was your fault!" cried the Peacock.
"And it was yours too," whispered the Snake.

"It was lust! It was lust!" shouted the Peacock.
"Yes, and pride, and vanity," – so the Snake.

"I loved him! I loved him!" shrieked the Peacock.
"And she was sweet, sweet," hissed the Snake.

"I look at my feet and I scream" – the Peacock.
"And I have no feet" – the Snake.

"It was your fault!" "Yours also perhaps?" – thus the Peacock-
    Angel
And the diabolical Snake down in the filthiest pot-hole

Where they exist, reproached each other,
Timeless in their torment. But somewhere

Within the innocent jungle, the peacock (which is a bird)
Displayed beneath the bough a fragment of God's splendour;

And the coiled snake (which is a reptile)
Deployed upon the ground a portion of His subtlety.

In Every Sense of the Word

When my heart was young I wasted my body
In every sense of the word Love

Now my body is older I waste my heart
In every sense of the word Love

My mind and my spirit reproach me both
In every sense of the word Love

There will come a wind and disperse all four
In every sense of the word Love

They will meet again on the Judgement Day
In every sense of the word Love

For Heaven can burn, and Hell can burn
In every sense of the word Love

Judgement Judgement Judgement Judgement
In every sense of the word Love

My heart will grieve, my body will groan
In every sense of the word Love

My mind too late will repent, and my spirit –
In every sense of the word Love

My blue cold spirit will still be free
In every sense of the word Love

In Hell to burn, in Heaven to burn
In every sense of the word Love

Bert and the Seven Deadly Sins

Bert
Never showed that he was hurt,
On his side:
That was Pride.

He continued to term her "his Silver Chalice":
That was Malice.

While reacting like a bull to a red cloth:
That was Wrath.

And regretting what, in his stupidity,
He wasted on her: that was Cupidity.

The situation continued – both
Were guilty of Sloth.

But, in middle age, discovered refuges –
Love's febrifuges –
Drink, drugs, a good dinner, the weed:
That was Greed.

Yet he still loved her, for her bitchery:
That was Lechery.

So they were damned,
And into Hell crammed
(After they died) –
Where she became his bride,

To torment him with other Furies:
Decision of celestial juries?

The Ballad of Don and Dave and Di

Don and Dave and Di –

Dave
Was an artist (no man's slave);
But Don
Always got on;
And Di
Was anybody's apple-pie.

Don loved Dave, and Dave
Loved Don
(I wonder why)
And both loved Di,
But Di
Looked after Di.

Di married Dave
(God save
The mark, she thought he'd save
Her from her inner lie.)

But Don
Got on, got on,
And off with Di.
She saw the point of pie
Not in the sky.

Dave hated Don,
But he forgave
(I wonder why).

370

But Don could crave
No hatred then for Dave:
Don still had Di,
And he caressed her thigh.

Said Dave:
"One of us three must die;
And if it's Don
I'm bound to sigh
Over his early grave;
And if it's Di
I know I'll cry."

Don still had Di.
She was his slave.
Till, by and by,

Don killed Dave
(I wonder why).
It was an unmarked grave.

Don still had Di,
He still got on.
Till Di
Drove him to an early grave.
(God knows why.)

Johnny Appleseed

Johnny Appleseed wherever he went
From just-round-the-corner to the Firmament
Planted apple-trees; and they were bent.

The graft they came from was all right
Till a married couple, against the light,
Forewent their lease at one bite.

Johnny was mixed up in that affair,
Disguised as a grass-snake, though Regent of the Air –
But his own account is, that is not fair:

371

He is not interested in Original Sin;
Which is something we have got under our skin,
And he never supposes he can win.

He thrust a seed deep in maternal Nature's
Heart, and distorted her virginal features:
All creatures are unkind to all other creatures.

He flung a fruit in the face of the Goddess of Art,
Who had some connection with the human heart,
And definitely upset *her* applecart.

Involved also the scientific technique,
Which had been invented by an ancient Greek:
Pride, prejudice, stupidity are not far to seek

Meddled also with the political animal,
Therefore each party programme seems so small
And you hate to vote conservative labour or liberal.

In short, affected the whole Universe:
Which is partly why this is such bad verse –
You can't push a ball-point but under a curse.

I think that for the destruction of Man
He hung a split seed in the sky of Japan,
Which we do not seem to be able to ban.

I am telling this story with the lid off:
I do not know how we can get rid of
Johnny Appleseed. But instead of

Hereby invoking the concept of Grace
(Which can hit you like a slap in the face,
And transform, leaving scarcely a trace,

Or in the mode of a still, small voice
Continually advocate a definite choice –
A situation which is not nice)

I recommend merely we should take heed
Not to cultivate that weed; nor breed
The apple-seed of Johnny Appleseed.

Household Devils

Pipes don't draw, gas-fires pop,
Sinks get choked, chains won't pull,
Milk turns sour in steamy kitchens,
Cigarette-lighters burst into flames –

Possessed by the little household devils
That grimace at me from recalcitrant objects.

Towards human beings I generally exercise
Reasonable forbearance and charity
(Being the way they are):
A sneak has picked my heart from my pocket –
I bring myself to forgive him.

But *they* more frequently and effectively
Trip my heels into mortal sins
Of rage and blasphemy.

Seven in particular sit on the typewriter
Transforming it into a fiendish device
For mangling communication
It gnashes its 42 teeth.

So I approach it with the understandable
Reluctance of the male spider
Approaching the female spider
To be chewed up in the act of love.

Articles don't get written,
Poems don't get copied;
The grime of sloth settles on my life.

They remind me also if I only traded
(Like practically everyone else)
My soul and my talent for a little gold
I might after all be graciously living
In easier and sleazier circumstances
Among gadgets and gimmicks which actually work.

Use of Personal Pronouns:
a Lesson in English Grammar

I

I is at the centre of the lyric poem,
And only there not arrogant.

"You begin every sentence with *I*" – the rebuke was well taken:
But how on earth else am I to begin them?

YOU AND THOU

You are a secret *thou*.
Fumbling amongst the devalued currency
Of "dear" and "darling" and "my love"
I do not dare to employ it –

Not even in a poem, not even
If I were a Quaker, any more.

Beginning as an honorific, the unaffectionate *you*,
For English speakers, has put *thou* out of business.
So, in our intimate moments,
We are dumb, in a castle of reserve.

And He alone
From Whom no secrets are hid, to Whom
All hearts be open,
Can be a public *Thou*.

HE, SHE, AND IT

Only in the third person sex raises its
Unattractive – well, "head" is a fair enough euphemism.
The thought of sex in which you and I
Do not participate is (unless we are *voyeurs*)
Either horrifying or ridiculous. He and she
He it and she it.

But, moving outside the human order,
We observe there is no personality
Apart from gender. Animals are *it*,

374

But our own cats, horses, and dogs are *he* or *she*;
The huntsman's Puss is *she*, Reynard is *he*;
And even ships are beloved as *she*,
Cars and bicycles, even.

For the homosexual queening it in the Gimcrack Bar
His colleagues, objects of his scandal, are *she*,
While the inaccessible youth in the tight jeans,
Three buttons undone in his scarlet shirt,
Is, however, an *it*.

ONE

One thinks of *one* as a pronoun employed principally
At Cambridge, modestly to include oneself
And other people in one's own set,
At Cambridge. One appreciates the French usage
Of *on*; one knows one's Henry James;
One does feel (or, of course, alternatively, one does not)
One must, on the whole, concur with Dr Leavis
(or, of course, alternatively, with Mr Rylands).
At Oxford, on the other hand,
One tends to become *we*. At Cambridge
One senses a certain arrogance in the Oxford *we*;
A certain exclusiveness in the Cambridge *one*
Is suspected, at Oxford.

WE

"We", said Queen Victoria, "are not amused."
Subsuming the entire dinner-table into the impersonal
And royal *We*:
No wonder the effect was devastating.
We is also the Editor of *The Times*
While a Greek chorus is a pattern of dancing *I*'s;
The Christian congregation is *I* in the Creed,
Thou in each of the sacraments,
Otherwise solidly *we*. And
"Let Us make man in Our own image."

We is not amused, nor is it interested
In the possiblities of defeat.

They is the hellish enemy of paranoiacs
(And even of Auden and Edward Lear);
They is in a conspiracy, is directing hostile thought-waves, –
Has got everything fixed *their* way. *They* will not let you.

History a deadly and unending struggle
Of class and national *theys*, except when sometimes
An imperial and oecumenical *We* serenely
Frowns at a barbarian and utter *they*.

But for you and for me,
Weeping in our tragic citadel, the horror
Is simply to realize that *they* exist.

Footnote on Epic Diction

Achilles let slip a wingéd word:
Beowulf word-hoard unlocked;
Homer knew, Widsith and Cædmon knew,
Words are not expendable.

For the quick Greek the musical, bee-like creatures
Hiving between the wickerwork of his ribs
In patience confected the honey of his eloquence;
But an errant swarm is no profit.

And the slow Saxon in the dragon's cave of his breast
Concealed the troll-worked and elaborate gold;
Churlish and unthrift not to keep it dark –
It could carry a curse.

But with us the air is pestilent with words,
Loud speakers perambulate the market-place:
The counterfeit penny that cheats and corrupts,
Winged motes that buzz and sting.

Egypt, 1956

Ars Poetica

1

One thing *imprimis* I would have you remember:
Your poetry is no good
Unless it move the heart. And the human heart,
The heart which you must move,
Is corrupt, depraved, and desperately wicked.

Milton denoted poetry
"Simple, sensuous and passionate".
But who has said, my dear,
Human sensuality and human passion
Were ever simple matters?

But poetry is not "emotional truth".
The emotions have much less to do with the business
Than is commonly supposed. No more than the intellect.
The intellect shapes, the emotions feed the poem,
Whose roots are in the senses, whose flower is imagination.

Call it then: "A humane science"
(Like all science concerned
With a world that really exists) – but humane:
Beatrice could request, not command Virgil –
She among the blessed, and he in Limbo –
He can take you as far as the Earthly Paradise
But no further than that.

In Limbo also is the Master of them that know:
But he is a Master. Therefore respect critics,
Especially the uncomfortable ones.

But there is no field of any activity
In which the parable of the wheat and the tares
Is more applicable.

The poem does not propound
Your or anyone else's opinions,
However admirable, however fascinating;
With luck it may touch the skirts
Of universal Wisdom.

And much the same goes for the passions:
The oaf in love *may* be a poet
Or bumpkin tongue-tied still;
A poet in love may be no less oafish.
And so in eloquence remember
All things exist in Love.

I mentioned just now luck – our Lady Fortune
("Bright-haired daughter of Chaos" I once called her)
She also is an exalted goddess,
Germane to the Muse. Therefore revere her.

2

A poem is built out of words;
And words are not your property.
They are common counters, involved
In private chaffering, and international transactions;
They have been tossed into the caps of beggars, and plonked
On the reception-desks of brothels.

In your case they are the English language:
Not the Greek flute, nor the Roman trumpet,
Nor the Welsh harp, nor the Spanish guitar,
Nor the French clavecin,
But a sound bourgeois piano
Capable of something of each.

You have got to make language say
What it has not said before;
Otherwise why bother – after a millennium,
(And a bit more) of English poetry – and you a wren
Rising from the eagle's back?
Work against language. It is your enemy.
Engage in a bout with it.
But like a Japanese wrestler
You will overcome by not resisting.

3

The words come to you from the commercial districts:
From the shop-bench, and from working in the fields;
But contrary to much of the practice of the age

There is something to be said for politely requesting them
To wipe the mud off their boots
Before they tread on your carpet
(Supposing you own one).

And if they should emerge from the reading-room
Tactfully suggest they remove the cheese-parings,
Dead flies and biscuit-crumbs from among their whiskers.

I have no personal objection
If you want to put on singing robes:
At a ritual you don't wear work-a-day clothes.
But the surplice and chasuble, or the Geneva gown
Are nothing more than the Sunday best
Of a Byzantine gentleman, or a Renaissance scholar;
And any clergyman, I suppose, would look pretty silly
If he walked down the street in them.

So under existing social conditions
You had better think over this matter of your costume
With a certain perspicacity.

4

A poem is like an iceberg:
Seven-tenths under water
(And what is below the surface –
This may at first have seemed –
To you the most important.)
Like an iceberg – cold, hard,
Jagged and chaste, glittering
With prismatic colours, as it drifts
On unpredictable deep-sea tides. Against it also
The titanic folly of the age
May shatter itself as it goes through its joyless night.

5

"Patience and perseverance
Made a bishop in his reverence."
The proverb ought to have added
"And the charisma of the Holy Ghost."

Mutatis mutandis
(And it is very much *mutandis*)
This likewise is relevant.

So through patience, perseverance, luck and that sort of thing
(I can only wish you luck)
You may arrive at an actual poem –
An interjected remark
At a party which has been going on
For quite a time (and will, we trust, continue);
A party at which you are not
A specially favoured guest
And which you will have to leave before it is over.

Let us hope the others will occasionally recall it.

But to you it will seem a little world.
You will look at your creation and see that it is good.
In this you will be mistaken:
You are not, after all, God.

Poetry Today

The sun is eclipsed; and one by one
The birds stop singing –
Folded their wings:

But I never heard
That the frogs stopped croaking.

May-Fly

Under the willow whose roots are shallow
The dismissed lover laid his head down,
        And down, and down:
May-fly, May-fly, living a day,
It was good while it lasted – even gay?

Under the oak which storm-winds broke
The defeated general laid his head down,
          And down, and down:
May-fly, May-fly, dead in an hour,
What then is glory, what precisely is power?

Under the elm, the treacherous elm,
Whose boughs can break, the ruined businessman,
For his country's sake, laid his head down,
          And down, and down:
May-fly, May-fly, grub in a stream
Eating dirt, for years eating filth – for a dream.

Under the fire of the sweet-briar
The fading beauty laid her head down,
          And down, and down:
Bridal May-flies thick in the haze –
Once and once only! Praise! Praise!

Under crossed boughs the unfrocked priest
Laid his head down – "I have been a beast!" –
          And down, and down:
Finished May-flies falling to death –
God is spirit, spirit is breath.

Under the laurel in continual quarrel
The obscure poet laid his head down,
          And down, and down:
Dead May-flies on the waters strewn,
· And dead words are drifted on.

Lament for the "Old Swan", Notting Hill Gate

The Old Swan has gone. They have widened the road.
A year ago they closed her, and she stood,
The neighbouring houses pulled down, suddenly revealed
In all her touching pretentiousness
Of turret and Gothic pinnacle, like
A stupid and ugly old woman
Unexpectedly struck to dignity by bereavement.

And now she has vanished. The gap elicits
A guarded sentiment. Enough bad poets
Have romanticized beer and pubs,
And those for whom the gimcrack enchantments
Of engraved glass, mahogany, plants in pots,
Were all laid out to please, were fugitives, doubtless,
Nightly self-immersed in a fake splendour.

Yet a Public House perhaps makes manifest also
The hidden City; implies its laws
Of tolerance, hierarchy, exchange.
Friends I remember there, enemies, acquaintances,
Some drabs and drunks, some bores and boors, and many
Indifferent and decent people. They will drink elsewhere.
Anonymous, it harboured
The dreadful, innocent martyrs
Of megalopolis – Christie or Heath.

Now that's finished with. And all the wide
And sober roads of the world walk sensibly onwards
Into the featureless future. But the white swans
That dipped and swam in each great lucid mirror
Remain in the mind only, remain as a lost symbol.

Bryant Park, New York

Adjacent to the Public Library, not far from the public lavatory,
A rectangle, paved; and with trees, and with green –

From an altiloquent and alien beauty
Nostalgically I turn into this enclave

(It recalls London.) I wish they kept it better:
Rain-soggy newspapers; and a few not old

Not young men sit and stare here;
They are slumped behind illegible eyes.

Mine meet instead those of the bust erected
By the Goethe Society of America,

Eyes which equally are turned to stone
(Needed no sculptor to accomplish that),

Pleased to encounter a European acquaintance
(With respect; with, one hopes, humility)

Though personally I have not much loved Goethe –
Tempted to think that he deserves this place?

The Prison of Saint Louis, Mansura

They gave him the judge's house,
The best house in the town – a fine and airy cage
For a royal bird to mew in. The spy-hole
Is pierced in the roof (tactful) where the guards stood,
And the squalid cupboard under the stairs
Was apparently for his chaplain, who, I hope,
Was a monk and a holy man, and had a vocation,
Or at least, was habituated to such quarters.
For courteous they were, and, anyway,
There was money to be had for this, the Christian king.

Only one touch they added –
The door through which he daily had to pass
To take, under surveillance, exercise
Is barely four feet high. So, he must stoop,
Who was taller by a head than any of his knights,
And, for a ransom, would not beggar France.

– (For clear-eyed France, self-violated now,
Playing the harlot under every green tree
On the Algerian hills!) –

                    Blessed Saint Louis,
That our personal freedom shall not
Be based on the ruin of others, and in the hour
Of our humiliation, pray for us.

1957

Zante

Then from the pangs of the Aegean storm we burst,
The crystals of the weather formed once more
Around the sun's gold seeds. And, naked as
That green-haired century of Nereus' daughters,
Promontories and islands in procession
Breasting the sea's clear vintage. So for days
The far-shot arrows of a god beat down
On grey of rock, green-grey of olive-leaves,
Blue-green and dazzle of moving waters; so that the heart
Stands still, and the brain aches, and the eye falters.

The centaur is standing just behind the hill:
The pipes are, but for a moment, hushed.

Aeolian and Ionian names... And now, Zante,
To starboard rising – but not voiceless,
Island of poets and exiles! – You, Foscolo,
And you, Kalvos, whom the east wind of freedom
Swept to that holy city of the Celts
Where I go home; but now recall
The Cyprus gaols, the gallows and the guns – and I
Cannot without shame, cannot without tears
Honour this beauty.

1957

Note: The poets Ugo Foscolo (1778-1827) and Andreas Kalvos (1796-1869) were natives of the Ionian island of Zante. Both became Liberal refugees in England. The phrase "the holy city of the Celts" is applied to London in a poem by Kalvos.

The Parthenon

Where they tamed the wild Libyan
Unmarried war-goddess, goatskin-aproned;
Transmuted the owl-shrieking bugaboo
Into an image of Wisdom –

A dash in a reckless and exorbitant taxi
Will get you there; then climb

384

Above the esurient, lively, and stuffy city,
Feet slipping on loose stones.

Suddenly it stands there; like a familiar quotation
From dusty oleographs, the model
Of every second-rate "classical" building –
Church or museum –

Off-white like a sea-worn shell,
Like a bird's skull,
Under remorseless light;
Denuded the colour and gold

Long since; the centaurs and heroes
Shanghaied to Bloomsbury.
It seems very small:
And She has departed.

So that's all. There is nothing to do
But stand and gape like any other
Romantic tourist; and then go.

But turn your back, and stumble
Down the steep track – then suddenly
The mathematical candour,
Neither over- nor under-statement,

Owl-clawed, hooks to the heart.

The Sphinx

It is not feminine: this crouching cat-beast
Kneading a vacant temple between its claws –
Napoleon and the rest
Can fire their guns in its face. In the vicinity
Of the pyramidical Pyramids, where the lanner
Nested, and boys can easily scale,
For a few piastres, an old cove's tombstone,
It will stay, it will gaze

At the rising, rising sun, until the sun
Forgets to rise, and Time ruins, and it, too,
Crumbles – the implacable image
Of male power that smoothly worships itself.

To Edmund Blunden
on his 60th Birthday

Thyrsis, or Meliboeus, or old Damoetas –
I must address you
By some such green, Virgilian-vowelled name –
You, the last and truly-tempered voice
Of all our lovely, dead, and pastoral England:
The radio brings that voice to me tonight,
Reading your poem, the vocables
With Kentish loam adhering to them still.
You on the Chinese shore, and I
In Alexandrian garboils? No –
For fourteen years are abrogated now;
The evening sun is gilding Abingdon,
And Kirk White's verse, and Bloomfield's, and Clare's
Our topic as we sit here in the bar,
And brown-haired boys are playing in the street.

1957

First Steps in Physiologus:
a Little Bestiary for Beginners

THE PIG

Not improved by domestication. Wallows
In its own filth. Screams
As loud at feeding-time
As when it is killed – throat slit,
Hung up by the heels, the blood
Drip-dripping out of it.

Omnivorous, adaptable – like us;
He has secured a good Second
In Evolution. He is cunning –
You cannot fence him in –
But the ring in his nose is no badge of honour.

The pig has much the same idea
Of sensuality as you have. Scratch his back,
With your hand (if you don't mind),
With a stick (if you are particular),
He will pay you in grunts. He is the hero
Of so many of our sagas
(From Curly Wee to George Orwell); and ought to have been
A wild boar rushing out of the Ardennes,
All tusks and bristles, the crest
Of our thundering Saxon ancestors
And of the last
(And possibly maligned) Plantagenet.

But has no tragedy now – unless a flood
Overtakes him: then he swims
Until he cuts his throat (in a combination
Of fat and despair) with his little, bifid hooves,
Which will never play Bach, or paint a picture.

THE HARE

Would rather run up-hill than down-hill;
Would rather look backwards than forwards;
Escapes by going the long way round,
Or by lying still.

Mad? A wild lover,
And a bouncing prize-fighter;
But, a careful mother,
In tussocks of couch-grass
Abandons her leverets.

Wounded, captured, screams
Horribly, like a child;
Is eaten half-putrid, boiled
In its own dark blood;

And is sacred to the Moon,
A type of innocent sacrifice.

THE TORTOISE

Always to be at home
For the tortoise may be as burdensome
As for the human being,
His continuing exile:

The foxes have hide-outs,
The birds of the air their cradles –
They are free to come and go:
To the tortoise, his dome.

"Stroking, a waste of time,"
(Şaid Sydney Smith) "You might as well think,
Caressing St Paul's, to please
The dean and Chapter."

                    But was wrong,
For he is sensitive,
Even to the roof-tops;
Vegetarian, inoffensive, longaeval,
Condemned, through seven generations
Of men, to trundle
The load of his home-keeping.

THE GECKO

I don't know how many thousand years
Of evolution have not taught the gecko
You can't jump *up* downwards.

Blue-flecked, pink-flecked, semi-transparent,
Sucker-footed, he creeps
Across the ceiling. He sees
With his extraordinary protuberant eyes
A fly, just hovering below him...He
                              jumps
                                    and
Flick!
        He falls to the floor:
Poor little half-dazed lizard!

How did this absurd, this innocent creature
Become a symbol of evil?

The Copts say:
"Saint Shenouda has commanded us to destroy you!"
Whereat the thing is supposed to curl up and die,
Or at least depart, embarrassed.

And everyone, Moslem or Christian, is agreed
It sneaks into houses, it spits
Into the salt-box, tabernacle of life,
Contagious of leprosy;
Like its own whiteness it fades to in the dark.

Shenouda, intransigently holy father,
Striding out of the desert with grit in your beard,
Do you concern yourself, then,
With such trivialities?

It could be so. In your day,
In those of Pachomius, Anthony,
The wastelands pullulated with dragons.
This is a parody, a miniature.

There is so much evil in the world
Anything can be a symbol of it.

THE STARLING

The starling is my darling, although
I don't much approve of its
Habits. Proletarian bird,
Nesting in holes and corners, making a mess,
And sometimes dropping its eggs
Just any old where – on the front lawn, for instance.

It thinks it can sing too. In springtime
They are on every rooftop, or high bough,
Or telegraph pole, blithering away
Discords, with clichés picked up
From the other melodists.

389

But go to Trafalgar Square,
And stand, about sundown, on the steps of St Martin's;
Mark then, in the air,
The starlings, before they roost, at their evolutions –
Scores of starlings, wheeling,
Streaming and twisting, the whole murmuration
Turning like one bird: an image
Realized, of the City.

THE NIGHTJAR

Less bird than voice,
Than the ghost of a voice of a bird,
Of a ghost-bird – moth-owl, fern-owl,
Twilight's great moth-winged, moth-pursuing swallow,
Bark-mottled invisible squatter – Oh why,
Walking now through the garish streets
Of London's noisy midnight, recall this? –
The nightjars each to each, at their churning and spinning,
Over the New Forest heath –
(Years ago now: dwindled the air's gold) –
And soft death-rattle of a pleasing day.

THE CHOUGH
at the London Zoo

So you've got King Arthur's soul inside you, have you?
You certainly look it, gazing
Over your aristocratic, arched, and vintage
Coral bill. Your nostrils
Are covered with soft plumes, and not with bristles
Like the crows with which you are usually classified.
Sundevall, I know, that square-headed Swede,
Put you in the phalanx *Humilinares*,
Or "humble-nostrils," amongst a flock of starlings.
I trust you regret that "*Ay-ow, ay-ow*" you cry
With an accent indistinguishable from
The jackdaws which replace you. You are no longer
Cornish; you are barely Welsh, or Manx.
You are in mourning for something.
For you, like others, palpably must
Become extinct, unless kept in a cage.

AN APOLOGY TO THE FISH

I apologize to the fish (or fishes)
Because there is not much about them
In this series, sequence, collocation or whatever
Of verse, prose, poetry or whatever.

Anyway, I think fish have been fairly well dealt with
By others I would not wish to emulate
And would be embarrassed to have excelled –

Such as Leigh Hunt, Rupert Brooke, &c.
(And I've not forgotten Diaper, Mr Grigson.)

To tell the truth, I'm not very good on fish:
A goggle-eyed, cool, un-talkative, elegant people –
The royal, small-mouthed sturgeon: the mackerel,
Pure as a cirrhus sky,
Feeding on corruption; the carp
That does not flinch when the Japanese eat him alive;
The pike, pickerel, perch, tench, roach, and so on;
The trout, the salmon-trout, and the salmon –
They are so much alike and I forget how to classify them.

Perhaps there are more poetic possibilities
In the invertebrata – the octopus,
Sacred to the Goddess, and subject to nervous breakdowns;

The starfish with five bodies and one head; the sponge,
Which draws in through its pores and respires through its mouth,
And is both a city and an individual;

And the sea-anemone –
The carnivorous flower, the sucking rose of the sea.

THE LOCUST

It is only a grasshopper, after all:
I had a good look at one once
In Alexandria, as it climbed up a wall
In the hot, hot Egyptian autumn – the same great eyes,
The grave and horsey face, and the angular,
Arched and leaping shanks.

Some Russian or other
(I forget the name) has proved it – innocuous grasshoppers

Mutate, in the starved lands
(Incompetently or greedily farmed
Till they are desert). So, locusts are created,
A sign of judgement,
And no green thing withstands.

So here it is, climbing up a wall
In the hot, hot autumn; a straggler from its army,
Bearing in itself the prophecy
Of Abaddon's abominable hordes –
The scorpion-tailed, the woman-tressed, the kingly-crowned
Troop, that will occupy us.

THE ANTS

You could have been human, but you aren't.

THE CICADAS

Cicadas of Greece – persistent
Chirr chirr chirr – unambiguous, almost harsh
(Rock off-white, glaucous leaves,
Sun-beat Aegean splendour).

The voice of poetry, this, in the ear of Socrates;
It takes its dram of dew; it is loved
By the slim-ankled maids of Piera.

The American model is different:
Begins, jaunty on tree-tops,
To whirr like a tiny, delicate dynamo;
But soon stops.

THE BED BUG

The bed bug is like Cain
A wanderer on the face of the earth –
Perpetual immigrant,
Being an intimate lover of Man;
An exiguous Count Dracula.

By nature he is sub-tropical:
He likes warm places – snug
As a bug in a rug.

His name, I fancy, is originally Arabic
(He returned with us from the Crusades)
But "contaminated", as philologists say,
With Anglo-Saxon *bug* – "goblin" or "devil"
(Cf. Slavonic *Bog* = "God").

I have been eaten by bed bugs
In three continents so far:
Those in the Parisian Latin Quarter
Were certainly the worst
(They had had Villon and Verlaine before).

A ruthless spraying of DDT,
Burning sulphur, arsenical smoke-bombs
Will get rid of bed bugs. But the natives
Generally seem to prefer to be bitten
Until they become immune from the irritation.

Or you can simply learn to sleep with the light on:
The bug is afraid of light.
But this is to take a rather Manichaean attitude –
Exchange of blood with any of God's creatures
Is (as of course John Donne knew)
A matter with serious implications.
It has something to do with love.

America has a variety
Known as the "kissing bug"...

Note: This insect is placed by entomologists as a close relative of those described in the preceding poem.

THE TWO FLIES
Or "Windows"

The fly inside says,
   "I see unattainable
Sky – sublime azure! –
   It exists?" The fly outside,
She says, "He does not love me!"

Note: The subject "Windows" for a poem in the *waka* form (31 syllables) was given by his Imperial Majesty the Emperor of Japan for the annual Japanese Poetry festival of 1959.

The History of the Flood

Bang Bang Bang
Said the nails in the Ark.

It's getting rather dark
Said the nails in the Ark.

For the rain is coming down
Said the nails in the Ark.

And you're all like to drown
Said the nails in the Ark.

Dark and black as sin
Said the nails in the Ark.

So won't you all come in
Said the nails in the Ark.

But only two by two
Said the nails in the Ark.

So they came in two by two,
The elephant, the kangaroo,
And the gnu,
And the little tiny shrew.

Then the birds
Flocked in like wingèd words:
Two racket-tailed motmots, two macaws,
Two nuthatches and two
Little bright robins.

And the reptiles: the gila monster, the slow-worm,
The green mamba, the cottonmouth and the alligator –
All squirmed in;
And after a very lengthy walk,
Two giant Galapagos tortoises.

And the insects in their hierarchies:
A queen ant, a king ant, a queen wasp, a king wasp,
A queen bee, a king bee,

And all the beetles, bugs, and mosquitoes,
Cascaded in like glittering, murmurous jewels.

But the fish had their wish;
For the rain came down.
People began to drown:
The wicked, the rich –
They gasped out bubbles of pure gold,
Which exhalations
Rose to the constellations.

So for forty days and forty nights
They were on the waste of waters
In those cramped quarters.
It was very dark, damp and lonely.
There was nothing to see, but only
The rain which continued to drop.
It did not stop.

So Noah sent forth a Raven. The raven said "Kark!
I will not go back to the Ark."
The raven was footloose,
He fed on the bodies of the rich –
Rich with vitamins and goo.
They had become bloated,
And everywhere they floated.
The raven's heart was black,
He did not come back.
It was not a nice thing to do:

Which is why the raven is a token of wrath,
And creaks like a rusty gate
When he crosses your path; and Fate
Will grant you no luck that day:
The raven is fey:
You were meant to have a scare.
Fortunately in England
The raven is rather rare.

Then Noah sent forth a dove
She did not want to rove.
She longed for her love –
The other turtle dove –

(For her no other dove!)
She brought back a twig from an olive-tree.
There is no more beautiful tree
Anywhere on the earth,
Even when it comes to birth
From six weeks under the sea.

She did not want to rove.
She wanted to take her rest,
And to build herself a nest
All in the olive grove.
She wanted to make love.
She thought that was the best.

The dove was not a rover;
So they knew that the rain was over.
Noah and his wife got out
(They had become rather stout)
And Japhet, Ham, and Shem.
(The same could be said of them.)
They looked up at the sky.
The earth was becoming dry.

Then the animals came ashore –
There were more of them than before:
There were two dogs and a litter of puppies;
There were a tom-cat and two tib-cats
And two litters of kittens – cats
Do not obey regulations;
And, as you might expect,
A quantity of rabbits.

God put a rainbow in the sky.
They wondered what it was for.
There had never been a rainbow before.
The rainbow was a sign;
It looked like a neon sign –
Seven colours arched in the skies:
What should it publicize?
They looked up with wondering eyes.

It advertises Mercy
Said the nails in the Ark.

Mercy Mercy Mercy
Said the nails in the Ark.

Our God is merciful
Said the nails in the Ark.

Merciful and gracious
Bang Bang Bang Bang.

Communications

With the philosophers in their beleaguered city
(Besieged by warlock words)
Drinking the last dregs
From the central well, until
There is nothing left to drink
(Excepting of course hemlock):

With the scientists shoving their eyebrows
Into the excrement, studying
Animalculae and atoms
Through the wrong end of a micro-telescope
(Besieged by gibbering, non-factual ghosts):

With the poets, writhing as they chew
Their last scrap of toxic laurel
(Besieged by verbal whores,
And the usual poetry-lovers):

With the politicians dreaming of geometry
(Besieged by faceless men)
And the mathematicians dreaming of justice
(Besieged by infinity) –
Each of them wondering whether their separate games
Are truly worth the candle:

With the theologians lighting that candle,
Before they collapse at the foot of the altar,
Dumb oxen, stupefied by glory
(Besieged by the single and real

Little Devil of Doubt – "*And you won't*
Give me money I'll sweep you all out!"):

With everyone else, stuck
In front of the blind television set,
Or the radio which breaks down
In the middle of an announcement, merely
That the world is about to come to an end
(Besieged by boredom and commonplace death):

– With these what communication, unless
The courteous angel comes and goes
In diplomatic immunity
With authority to reconstitute a fragmented empire,
Delivering code messages
To which the cipher has been lost:
Conjectured to read "Love" –
Itself a meaningless word?

The Magi

The magi I suppose need not have been
Exotic kings or esoteric sages:
This was an eastern country; such as they,
Wandering fortune-tellers, were always tagging around
Deaths, marriages and births
With an eye to the main chance. There was something to be got
Even from a birth in a stable.

They offered token gifts –
A shred of myrrh, a scrap of frankincense,
A scraping or at most a gimcrack trinket
Which they alleged was gold. And Joseph
Of courtesy obliged to pay
Far more than these were worth.

It was Mary who pondered, Mary who magnifies,
And saw in this epiphany,
Emblems of kingship, godhead, and of death.

Song for Saint Valentine's Day

Urbane bishop, Valentine,
  Sexually ensnarling
Tom with Thomasina tit,
  Starling with his darling,
Cob swan with pen swan,
  Dove with truest turtle,
Ducks with drakes, and ruffs with reeves,
  Under Venus' myrtle:

On plastic macs beside tilled fields
  Copulating couples
Do the essentially innocent act –
  Till they bit those apples,
Down in Eden's seminal garden,
  Poor Adam, silly Eve,
Created into a world of matter
  Where scaly worms deceive.

Within your airy diocese
  Feathered reptiles flutter –
Twitter and caw, and bill and coo
  What they cannot utter:
A man and a woman upon a bed
  Gasp and groan and sigh
  "Unto us a child is given,
  But we two must die."

Exalted martyr, Valentine
  Teach me this pervigilium
Why the rape of Helen was worth
  The burning down of Ilium;
Of Love, continually crucified;
  Eternally throned above
Comprehending within itself
  All things. Including love.

Vernal Impromptu

At last a touch of spring –
Returning Favonius;
Adolescent April
With the appropriate flowers.

Go on and on and on
Up in your tower of air
Johann Sebastian skylark:
Improbable though it may seem

Even the winter-encrusted
Heart may find a voice, may climb
Its own invisible towers
Unabashed as you are.

Tiberius on Capri

The old goat sits on the goats' island:
Behind, a fabulous backdrop – garish light
(Subsequently inhabited by tourists).

And Virgil's voice is ashes. Rome's poetry now
Exploration of pain, sensuality:
To a god nothing is forbidden.

Violated bodies of children. A blinded fisherman,
Face rubbed with his own lobster. Inedible slaves
Are flung to edible eels. Hardly stirred

The old man's guttering senses. And dreadful,
The intellect is utterly unappeased.
The wheels of empire grind on, peacefully

Under efficient administration.
This morning conscientiously, he peruses
Reports Greek freedmen hand him:

Priests of Isis have deceived a Roman gentlewoman
With false Annunciations of the god Anubis.
He decrees condign punishment. In Judea

At Procurator's orders another luckless fanatic
Has been put to death:
A commonplace crucifixion –

There is nothing, nothing whatever to engage
His connoisseur's sensibility. It is boring.
Divine Caesar sighs for the lot of man.

Virgin Martyrs

Catherine, describing a perfect circle
    Upon your wheel of fire,
Cecily, improvising three-part inventions
    On the Neronian lyre,

Lucy, squeezing your bright blue eyes out,
    Agatha, with a penknife
Slicing your pretty half-formed titties,
    The might-have-been founts of life,

Ursula, massacred eleven-thousand times
    By the anonymous Huns,
Teasing and stripped Eulalia, with
    A snow-drift about your loins,

Intrepid Margaret, whom even the Dragon
    Found indigestible –
Heavenly Alices of a sadistic
    Wonderland; incorruptible

Lolitas, up in the dock in front of
    A worried Governor,
Declining a minimal pinch of incense
    To poor old Jupiter.

(Who came in a shower of chinking guineas
    To Danäe, in his time,
Outbellowing the bulls of Bashan and Hereford –
    But now was past his prime):

I praise, I celebrate, I invoke your refusal,
    In intricate dances who move,
Garlanded with blood-red lilies, for ever
    And ever and ever, in love.

Another Spring Poem

A daffodil bulb, having consumed
    Its stores of sugar and starch,
Thrusts up green lungs and sexual petals
    Into the winds of March.

Rashly, lots of little blossoms
    Along the boughs break out;
A thrush that has survived the winter
    Repeats its brainless shout

Connecting all this with resurrection
    Of, in some sense, the word
Convention-ridden poets insist;
    Spring has, in fact, recurred.

When Sappho Loved

When Sappho loved a gondolier
    Tongues on Lesbos clacked apace:
Unhappily he had no ear
    For stanzas of Aeolian grace;
        Her lover's leap into the deep
            Fishily-tanged Tyrrhenian tide –
        One sickening drop – soon put a stop
            To lyric passion and to pride.

Lady Mary laughed to view
   Great Mr Pope before her kneeling:
His form seemed ill-designed to woo,
   Much less evoke an answering feeling:
      So Alexander lived to slander
        What else he tenderly had sung,
      And she confessed among the rest
        The Asp of Twickenham's forked tongue.

Dispersed about the Delphic plane
   Grasshopper-witted poets thrum –
You, scurrying ants who haul the grain,
   Envy them not, though you be dumb:
      What's to your mind perhaps you'll find
        At harvest's end among the sheaves
      But those who follow bright Apollo
        Likely embrace cold laurel leaves.

Variation on a Theme by George Darley

It is not beauty I desire
   And not – but not – the virtuous mind:
Marks of potential tragedy –
   These stigmatize the human kind.

And lonely in the darkness, I
   Surmise your pain, your loneliness,
And stretch uneasy arms towards
   That inarticulate distress.

If sons and daughters of the gods
   Stride careless through the market-place
What can we but avert our eyes –
   Acknowledge, not demand, their grace?

Although the smooth olympian brow
   Bids Greece and Ilium beware,
More turbid tides on love's dark sea
   Involve us with the siren's hair.

Each hard-faced doctor who expounds
  Within the rigid schools avers
That God Himself loves His elect
  Yet for no merit that is theirs.

And, fuel to the appalling creed,
  By human analogues we know
We do not love the beautiful
  But, loved, they are imputed so.

The Timeless Nightingale

A nightingale sat perched upon
  The trellis of a Samian vine
Beneath whose shade Anacreon
  Strung his slight lyre, and drank his wine;
Far in the Asian highlands then
  The corpse of great Polycrates
Was scorched by sun and stripped by rain,
  Stretched on the cross-bars of two trees;
But the nightingale's lament
  Was for dismembered Itylus:
White-haired Anacreon vainly schemed –
  How could he move Cleobulus.
    The poet took another glass.

Li Po drank his rice-spirit warm:
  Disgraced at court, he sipped alone –
No-one to talk to or make love –
  Himself, his shadow, and the moon;
Above his head, migrating cranes:
  In the wild gorges monkeys howl:
Red-haired, green-eyed barbarians
  Along the utmost marches prowl;
The nightingale (or what bird else
  Chinese convention had assigned)
Fluted of jewelled gardens where
  Drunken immortals ride the wind.
    The poet took another glass.

Upon a greenish sky at dawn
   The sickle of the moon grew dim:
Hafiz still sat there on the lawn:
   A moon-browed Saki poured for him;
Advanced across the Northern hills
   Timur and his crude Turkish band,
To build their pyramids of skulls,
   And fetch the wine to Samarkand;
But the timeless nightingale
   Enamoured of the eternal rose
Cried "Love's in the dark of the candle-flame,
   And nothing quite what we suppose!"
     The poet took another glass.

The true, the blushful Hippocrene
   Was fairish claret, if you please:
Love a bacillus in his lung,
   John Keats was on those perilous seas;
Into the mills of Yorkshire now
   The Luddite gangs walked stark and grim:
The bourgeois Muse was mousy-haired
   And did not only dance with him;
The nightingale inside his head
   Sang on (at once to him and Ruth)
"You're better off when you are dead –
   Truth's Beauty then, and Beauty truth."
     The poet took another, took another glass.

A Sonata by Scarlatti

This music which you made, Domenico,
To smooth the boredom of a Queen of Spain –
Vivid as darting fireflies, sharp as Naples limes:
Now come the fifes and drums, the hunting-horns,
The bold announcing trumpets, and flambeaux carried
By black-sheathed, silk-eyed pages.
How brave, how gay that bright procession passes
Against the velvet night –
Against the crouching and carnivorous darkness!

Mozart and Salieri

Salieri encountered Mozart;
  Took him friendly by the arm,
And smiled a thin-lipped ambiguous smile.
  This was Italian charm.

Mozart observed the smile of Salieri
  But was not enough observant,
(For the Angel of Death had called already
  In the guise of an upper servant).

"Maestro," said Salieri "Dear Maestro,
  It is happy that we met."
"We'll end this sharp boy's tricks," he thought
  "He'll not get by – not yet!")

"And as for that post of kapellmeister
  We'll do what we can do."
But something black within him whispered:
  "He is greater, is greater than you.

"He is great enough to oust you, one day,
  And take your place at Court."
("Not if Salieri is Salieri,"
  Salieri thought.)

"It is happy that we met," said Salieri
  "I wish I could ask you to dine –
But I have, alas, a pressing engagement.
  You will stay for a glass of wine?"

No one carried Mozart to nobody's grave
  And the skies were glazed and dim
With a spatter of out-of-season rain
  (Or the tears of the Seraphim).

Then two stern angels stood by that grave
  Saying: "Infidel, Freemason,
We are taking your soul where it willed to be judged
  At the throne of Ultimate Reason."

But the Queen of the Night in coloratura
  Horrors trilled at the sun,
For she looked at the soul of Wolfgang Amadeus
  And she knew she had not won.

They lifted that soul where the great musicians
  In contrapuntal fires
Through unlimited heavens of order and energy
  Augment the supernal choirs.

And the spirit of Johann Sebastian, harrowed
  With abstract darts of love,
Escorted the terrible child Mozart
  Through courteous mansions above.

And hundred-fisted Handel erected
  Great baroque arches of song
As the Cherubim and the Seraphim
  Bandied Mozart along.

But Mozart looked back again in compassion
  Below the vault of the stars
To where the body of Beethoven battered
  Its soul on the prison bars.

Successful Salieri lay dying –
  But now his reason was gone –
In a chamber well-fitted with Louis Seize furniture,
  But dying, dying alone.

Then two small devils, like surpliced choirboys,
  Like salamanders in black and red,
Extracted themselves from the fluttering firelight
  And stood beside the bed.

And they sang to him then in two-part harmony,
  With their little, eunuchoid voices:
"You have a pressing engagement, Salieri,
  In the place of no more choices."

So they hauled down his soul and put it away
    In a little cushioned cell
With stereophonic gramophones built into the walls –
    And he knew that this must be Hell.

Salieri sat there under the chandeliers
    (But never the sun or the moon)
With nothing to listen to from eternity to eternity
    But his own little tinkling tune.

To John Gawsworth with a Gift of Croce's Aesthetics

John – I'll say it *sotto voce* –
We're both a little bored by Croce:
He takes up too much space and time
For those whose main concern is rhyme.
But you who have seen Croce plain
This gift, I think, will not disdain.
For then, while Italy awoke
To spurn once more the indecent yoke,
He sat, clothed in a dressing gown
And in a rather vague renown
To prove at least that Latin sanity,
With the centuries-long humanity
And intellectual love of good,
Had still lived on in the dark wood.
You found him courteous, tired and old,
And (be it to your honour told)
In the still doubtful interim
Scrounged beans and bully beef for him.

To Constantine P. Cavafy

If I had arrived sooner, if you had departed later,
We might, Monsieur Cavafy, have met:
Have encountered each other in those undistinguished
Streets – ghost-lanes, which follow
The not obliterated axes
Of a vanished city – still wide enough
To accommodate a Roman chariot.

As it is, I can only look
At the house you occupied (on which
They have put a plaque, of course).
It is more or less like any other
Conurban residence – stone-curlews
Desolately trill from the flat roof.

In your day, they tell me, there was a brothel underneath:
"La bas, le chair," you said *"ici, l'esprit."*

And if we had met then, and were introduced,
Would there, I wonder, have been
Any more chance of communication
For me, than at this moment there is,
With you, who are now dead:
Who walked those streets, conversing
With Byzantine officials, and Hellenistic scholars,
And ordinary street-boys disguised as gods?

But you still walk,
Knowing, as you knew from your youth,
It is always the same city that follows us everywhere
With a sublimity of boredom,
The selfsame city that forever is departing,
The same barren island which does not cheat.

If you had departed later, if I had arrived sooner,
We might, dear poet, have met –
A situation not unfamiliar
In the City, Alexandria, we love.

Poetry as the Tribute Money

Here in the human breast, that microcosm,
Imagination's in the place of God:
The Reason, then, is Caesar. And to each
Is to be rendered.

Remit, poet, remit
Your two-faced coin; and if your worry
Is mainly, where is it to come from?
(The poetry, I mean, and the penny)
Cast your net, Peter, cast:
It will come, in the mouth of a haddock.

The Poet of Bray

Back in the dear old thirties' days
   When politics was passion
A harmless left-wing bard was I
   And so I grew in fashion:
Although I never really *joined*
   The Party of the Masses
I was most awfully chummy with
   The Proletarian classes.
           This is the course I'll always steer
            Until the stars grow dim, sir —
           That howsoever taste may veer
            I'll be in the swim, sir.

But as the tide of war swept on
   I turned Apocalyptic:
With symbol, myth and archetype
   My verse grew crammed and cryptic:
With New Romantic zeal I swore
   That Auden was a fake, sir,
And found the mind of Nicky Moore
   More int'resting than Blake, sir.

White Horsemen down New Roads had run
   But taste required improvement:
I turned to greet the rising sun
   And so I joined the Movement!
Glittering and ambiguous
   In villanelles I sported:
With Dr Leavis I concurred,
   And when he sneezed I snorted.

But seeing that even John Wax might wane
   I left that one-way street, sir;
I modified my style again,
   And now I am a Beat, sir:
So very beat, my soul is beat
   Into a formless jelly:
I set my verses now to jazz
   And read them on the telly.

Perpetual non-conformist I –
   And that's the way I'm staying –
The angriest young man alive
   (Although my hair is greying)
And in my rage I'll not relent –
   No, not one single minute –
Against the base Establishment
   (Until, of course, I'm in it).
         This is the course I'll always steer
           Until the stars grow dim, sir –
         That howsoever taste may veer
         I'll be in the swim, sir.

Song of the Death-Watch Beetle

Here come I, the death-watch beetle
Chewing away at the great cathedral;

Gnawing the mediaeval beams
And the magnificent carved rood screen

Gorging on gospels and epistles
From the illuminated missals;

411

As once I ate the odes of Sappho
And the histories of Manetho,

The lost plays of Euripides
And all the thought of Parmenides.

The Sibyl's leaves which the wind scattered,
And great aunt Delia's love letters.

Turn down the lamp in the cooling room:
There stand I with my little drum.

Death. Watch. You are watching death.
Blow out the lamp with your last breath.

Translations

Maiden Song

(from Alcman)

No longer, young girls with honey-sweet voices ringing,
Have my knees strength to bear me; and I wish, and I wish I could be
An ocean-martlet, that careless-hearted goes flying
Over the bloom of the waves, among the sea-swallows –
That bird of Spring, dark purple in plume like the sea.

From Theognis

I have given you wings, and over the infinite seas
    And the whole earth, they will easily carry you on;
There shall be no meal set, nor feast given, but you
    Will be there, reclining between the lips of the guests,
While still the young and beautiful sing your name,
    Setting your praises in order, to clear flute-notes;
And when you go down to the dreary depths of the earth,
    To Hades' mansion, the place of so much lamenting,
Never, although you are dead, shall you lose your renown,
    But men will think of you as one of a deathless fame;
You'll travel, Cyrnus, about the Hellenic lands
    And islands, across the fishy, unharvested deep,
Not mounted on horseback, but sped by the gracious favour
    And gift of the bright and violet-garlanded Muses
To all who take you in; and sharing their immortality
    You'll live, a song to the future, while Earth and Sun stand firm.
But I, I am nothing to you, either great or little;
    You cheat me with words, as one fobs off a small child.

Sappho's Ode to Aphrodite

God's deathless daughter of the bright-dappled throne,
Foam-cradled, queen, craftswoman, now as I require you,
Let not in my breast the heart be bruised and broken
                    Down with its dangers,

But descend in kindness, as at the catch of my call,
Far-heard, in former days, you at your father's roof-tree
Listening, have left for me those golden lodgings,
                    Yoked the gay and glittering
Curricle for its course: and quickly they conveyed it –
Eagerly, as angels out of the upper air –
The birds, that with whirr of wings down to the dark earth wheeled
                    Through the sky's midmost mansion.
Swiftly and soon they are here; and you with a smile lightening
Most blissful one, your comely and incorruptible countenance,
Asked me what grace I sought, the ground of all my grieving,
                    Why I had haled you hither,
What now would my hot mad heart be having,
"And for whose loveliness must Our lures be laid?
Who, Psappha, has put sadness on you – as if in hatred
                    Frets you with unfriendship?
For though now she flees you, she will follow and be fain,
Though she lets go your gifts, it is she that will be the giver,
And the one that does not love you, however loath or lazy,
                    Shall learn that lesson."
Draw near then, lady, and let my soul be lifted
Out of despair and torment; what I desire you, do,
And shoulder to shoulder, as my shield-companion,
                    Fight out this bitter battle.

Charaxus' Home-Coming

(reconstructed from Sappho)

Cyprian goddess and Mediterranean mermaids
Tender my brother home, unscathed from his voyaging,
And may the true desires of his heart be perfected;
                    Laying aside now

His past indiscretion, let him come once again to us,
The dear delight of all his friends who love him,
Bane to his foemen; nor our poor house be troubled
                    More with this matter.

Make him desire the good report of his sister,
Forgetting the anguish, forgetting the bitter words
Which, at his parting, cruelly he gave me,
                    Wounding the heart's core.

416

This when he does (and let that day come soon now)
Then can he cast all those past ills aside,
Choosing a wife, mid revel of his townsfolk,
                              In honest wedlock,

If he desires one. But as for you, I say,
You black unchancy bitch, you can set your foul snout
Down to the ground – away, and sneak off hunting
                              Some other quarry.

Cyprian Aphrodite, may she find you bitter!
May she never live to boast herself so loud,
A second time to say: "Look what a fine catch
                              Doricha's hooked now."

"A fine sight, some say . . ."
(after Sappho)

A fine sight, some say, is a great army
          Upon the march, or a ship that sails on its way:
But finer the sight of the face that the heart longs for –
          That is what I say.

Moonset
(after Sappho)

Moonset.   Starset.
Midnight.   Time goes.   I lie
Alone.

To the Dioscuri
(from Alcaeus)

Come now, deserting the island home of Pelops,
Brave boys that Zeus begot upon his Leda,
Kindly-disposed ones, show yourselves – O Caster
                              And Polydeuces –

You who go riding swiftly-pacing horses
Over the wide world and its seas, the sailor
Whelmed in the ice-cold terrors of a wave's clutch
                              Ready to ransom:

Lightly you leap to the gallant rowers' ship's-prow,
Climbing with far-seen flash upon the fore-stays,
Bearing to black ships through the midnight's horror
                           Light, with its blessings.

To Artemis
(from Anacreon)

To the deer-quelling Artemis,
God's brown-haired child, and patroness
   Of the wild beasts, I sue:
Now, gazing down the mountain-glen
Where the Lethaeus' water swirls
This city of courageous men
Gladly you mark; these are no churls
   Here, shepherded by you.

To Dionysus
(from Anacreon)

Prince, and playmate of the mighty
Conqueror Eros, with dark-glancing
Blue-eyed nymphs, and Aphrodite
   Tyrian-tinted, dancing;
Wanderer on the high hills' crest –
Appellant now, I seek to move,
May you attend this prayer addressed,
   And generous-hearted prove:
Turn then, O kind Dionysus,
State my case to Cleobulus –
   Make him receive my love.

The Girl from Lesbos
(from Anacreon)

Now golden-haired Eros tosses the purple ball,
Hitting me square – he calls me out to play with
That girl with the harlequin slippers there;
But she's from the Lesbian isle, of stylish houses;
She'll not condescend to smile on my white hairs –
She's all agog after some other girl.

Catullus' Last Message for Lesbia
To Furius and Aurelius

Furius and Aurelius, who are Catullus' friends,
Ready to go with me to the world's ends,
To India, or where the last long wave resounds
                    On beaches of the dawn,

Past Caucasus, or the sensual Saracens,
Among the nomad bowmen, Sacae and Parthians,
Or where, from seven mouths, the Nile stains
                    With Egypt's mud, the sea,

Stepping beyond the lofty Alpine peaks,
To follow in Caesar's monumental tracks,
To see the Rhine, or, lastly, the fierce looks
                    Which the wild Welshmen bear –

Ready, with me, to take up any trail
Over the earth, if such is the sky's will,
Carry this message for me to my girl,
                    These few unpleasing words:

Let her enjoy herself with all her men,
And take three-hundred to her arms, though none
Of them she loves, and each and every one
                    Is hamstrung in the end;

But never more turn back to me her eyes:
My love has wilted, like the flower that grows
On the field's edge, uprooted by the plough's
                    Heedlessly passing coulter.

Three Inscriptions for Statues of Priapus
(attributed to Virgil)

i

In Spring I'm decked with roses, in autumn with apples,
In the summer season with ears of corn:
Winter alone for me is a frightful pest.
I dread the cold – what's more, I shouldn't wonder
If I, being only a wooden god,
End up furnishing firewood
For some uncaring boors.

.ii

Here stand I, a product of folk-art;
Here am I, traveller, a dried up poplar stump,
Guarding this little acre you see here
In front and to the left, with a crofter's homestead
And his small garden-plot – these I protect
From picking and stealing hands.

In spring, a garland of gaily coloured flowers
Is placed on me; beneath the scorching sun
The bearded corn reddening to gold,
A bunch of luscious grapes with green tendrils,
And olives nipped by the early frost.

From these pastures of mine the delicate she-goat
Goes up to town, her udders swollen with milk;
From my sheepcotes the fatted lamb
Sends home again a good handful of brass,
And the tender heifer, while her mother lows,
Pours out her blood before the gods' shrines.

Therefore, traveller, be wary of this god:
Hands up – if you know what's good for you:
There's a gibbet here for you – my tool.
"Gosh," you say, "I could help myself."
But, my gosh, here's the bailiff coming.
His sturdy arm unhitches that tool of mine,
And makes it a cudgel in his strong right hand.

It is I, lads, who look after this place –
This cottage in the marsh, thatched with withies
And rushes by the handful – a dried-up oak-stump
Hacked into shape by a countryman's axe. Year by year
It grows more prosperous. For those who own this shack,
A father and his teenage son, pay their respects
And hold me for their god. The one
Tending me with such assiduous care, that
Weeds and rough brambles are kept away from my shrine;
The other brings me at all times lavish gifts
Out of a small man's handful. In flowering springtime
A gaily coloured garland is placed upon me,
Then, as first-fruits, the delicate spikes
Of the greening corn, with their still-tender beard,
Yellow pansies, and the poppy with its milky juice,
Pale melons, and fragrant smelling apples,
Reddening grape-clusters trained
Under the shade of their own leaves. This weapon of mine –
But keep mum – a bearded billy
And his horny-hoofed nanny-goat stain with their blood.
For all these offerings Priapus now
Will have to do his bit – taking good care of
The master's vineyard and his garden-plot.
Be off with you, boys, and don't you try
Your thieving tricks here! There's a rich neighbour,
And his Priapus is careless. Lift things from him –
The path at your feet itself will take you there.

Horace to Lydia
Odes I, xxv

Of late it's not so often one can hear
Your shutters rattling, nor young wenchers jar
Your slumbers; the accomodating door
                    Hugs close its threshold,

Whose hinges once so easily found occasion:
This serenade grows less and less in fashion:
"Can you, while I am dying out here of passion.
                    Lie sleeping, Lydia?"

You too, a broken-down hag in some dark alley,
Shall weep the insults of your faithless cully,
When, between moons, comes like a drunken bully,
                              The North Wind raging;

While a fierce lust, with unappeasable fires,
Such as in rutting time drives mad the mares,
Sends through your ulcerated guts its flares,
                              And its frustration;

Because young men prefer the fresh green shoot,
The ivy and the myrtle when they're sweet,
And fling the dry leaves that with winter wilt
                              Down the cold river.

After Horace, Odes III, 23

With palms turned upwards to the sky
Beneath a crescent moon, you, Phydile,
Offer, with your country thrift,
Fragrance, this year's garden produce,
And a fat greedy sow.

                    For then your vines
Won't feel sirocco's blast, nor the rust spoil
Your corn, and your hand-reared lambs,
When apples fall in autumn, not turn sickly.

Somewhere below the snowline on the Alban Hills,
Shaded by oaks and holm-oaks, feeds the heifer
Earmarked for Roman ritual butchery,
Sanctified abattoir.

                    No need for you,
A major slaughtering of muttons – you who crown
Your household images with rosemary
And slips of myrtle.

And if pure hands shall tend the altar,
No lavish offerings will serve the more to soften
The small hearthstone gods,
If they should look askance, than barley meal
Given with reverence, than salt –
A spatterdash that fizzles in the flame.

422

The Pervigilium Veneris

Let tomorrow be for lovers, loved they never, loved they long!
Spring is now the world's renewal, youthful Spring, the time of
song.
Love in Spring is single-hearted, birds select their mates again,
While the woods unloose their tresses for the husbanding soft
rain.

Let tomorrow be for lovers, loved they never, loved they long.

Tomorrow she who couples lovers, in the shade of forest leaves,
From the switches of the myrtle her green tabernacles weaves;
Holidaying through the woodlands she shall lead melodious clans;
For Dione from her throne tomorrow publishes her banns.

Let tomorrow be for lovers, loved they never, loved they long.

Tomorrow celebrates the nuptials of the prime ethereal god,
Who upon the sea-spume's droplets by his own sky-fallen blood,
Mid the azure mob of mermen, fish-tailed horses of the main,
Gat Dione, wave-like rising through the husbanding soft rain.

Let tomorrow be for lovers, loved they never, loved they long.

She it is who with the flower-buds gives the year a tinge of red,
Swelling all their rounding nipples, by the West Wind's breathings
fed,
Till they show in knotted clusters; scattering the clear bright dews
Which the night-wind has left lying, freshening moisture to suffuse.

Let tomorrow be for lovers, loved they never, loved they long.

With their weight ready for falling now start forth those tears
quivering,
Till each droplet like a globe down to the earth goes headlong
shivering;
Moisture which the stars rained down through the midnight's
quietude
Early loosens from its bodice virgin nipples of the bud.

Let tomorrow be for lovers, loved they never, loved they long.

How the reddening of the flower-buds publishes their virgin
    shame,
While the roses' glowing clusters start forth in a hectic flame.
For she bids them bare their breasts and cast their mantling cloaks
    aside;
For the naked virgin rose turns an early morning bride.

Let tomorrow be for lovers, loved they never, loved they long.

By Love's kiss created, tinctured with the Cyprian's very blood,
Coloured by the fire of sunlight, is the rose that was a bud;
She, who blushes, hidden in her cloak of woven flame,
Shall reveal herself tomorrow, loose her girdle without shame.

Let tomorrow be for lovers, loved they never, loved they long.

Now the goddess bids her nymphs go into the myrtle-grove;
Sends her son as playmate with them: and, should you suppose
    that Love
Might not wholly be off duty, nor his arrows put away –
Go, nymphs, go! – he lays them down, for Love is now on holiday.

Let tomorrow be for lovers, loved they never, loved they long.

Naked he is told to go, with no weapons in his hand,
Lest, with fire, or bow and arrows, any harm he might have
    planned;
Yet, O nymphs, you must beware of Cupidon with all his charms:
For the Love-god, going naked, bears full panoply of arms.

Let tomorrow be for lovers, loved they never, loved they long.

Of young virgins chaste as you are Venus sends an embassy,
Delian Artemis, to beg one favour of your clemency:
Let the grove be undefiled by slaughtered wild-beasts in their
    blood;
Let fresh flowers alone be decking the green shadows of the wood.

Let tomorrow be for lovers, loved they never, loved they long.

She would like to ask you if you can relax your prudery;
And to join us she'd invite you, if that suited modesty.
For three nights of festival you'll see about your forest ways
Lovers in a rout go wandering, who in chorus sing their lays.

Let tomorrow be for lovers, loved they never, loved they long.

Mid the myrtle tabernacles, and the wreaths of blossoms too,
Vine King and Corn Mother are, and the god whom poets know.
We must spin the whole night out with singing songs, and keep
   our wake:
You must wane, O Delian; Dione queens it in the brake.

Let tomorrow be for lovers, loved they never, loved they long.

She bids deck her high tribunal with all the flowers of Hybla's
   ground,
Seated there in jurisdiction, with her colleague Graces round.
Hybla, pour forth all your blossoms, the new season's legacy;
Hybla, don your flowery cape, like Enna's field in Sicily.

Let tomorrow be for lovers, loved they never, loved they long.

Here are girl-nymphs from the fields, here are maidens from the
   mountains,
Those who live in the woods and spinneys, those whose dwellings
   are the fountains.
Now the wing'd god's mother orders that they shall attend her son;
Warns them they are not to trust him, God of Love, the naked one.

Let tomorrow be for lovers, loved they never, loved they long.

As male power of generation, through Spring clouds this vernal
   tide,
Rain, as husband impregnates the kind womb of his fruitful bride;
Fecund by the sea and sky, fused in substance of the earth,
All things by her mighty body are nourished and are brought to
   birth.

Let tomorrow be for lovers, loved they never, loved they long.

She, the great Creatress, rules the blood, makes the mind to take
   its course,
By her all-pervading spirit, and her hidden secret force.
She it was bade Troy's survivors colonise in Latian land,
Gave the captured Sabine girls as brides to Romulus's band.

Let tomorrow be for lovers, loved they never, loved they long.

425

She it is who opens up a pathway for the vital seeds,
Which through ocean, heaven, and earth, uninterruptedly she
    leads;
Sends the fire of generation coursing briskly through the veins;
By her laws the world discovers all the roads that birth maintains.

Let tomorrow be for lovers, loved they never, loved they long.

Lavinia she chose, a bride for Aeneas, her own son;
From the cloister gave the War God Silvia, the Vestal nun –
Thence the ancient lineage of the Roman clans derives,
Which in founder Romulus, and in Caesar, now survives.

Let tomorrow be for lovers, loved they never, loved they long.

Countryside feels sexual power; fields grow fertile with its joy –
Country-born, the story runs, was Love, the Dionaean boy.
When the plough-land brought him forth, the goddess took him
    to her breast,
Nurturing him among the blossoms that softly kissed him and
    caressed.

Let tomorrow be for lovers, loved they never, loved they long.

See, the young bulls rub their flanks among the broom-plants all
    around,
Each with his own proper mate in natural conjunction bound;
Likewise how the bleating flocks are coupled underneath the
    shade,
And how the goddess bids break silence all the birds in every
    glade.

Let tomorrow be for lovers, loved they never, loved they long.

Hear the swans with clangorous voices noisy all about the mere;
Tereus' girl, the nightingale, answers in the poplar there,
And you would suppose that only through love's power she
    learned to sing,
Mourning not her sister's sorrow, ravished by the barbarous king.

Let tomorrow be for lovers, loved they never, loved they long.

She is singing, I am silent. Oh, when shall my Spring awake?
When shall I be like the swallow, and the chains of silence break?
Keeping mute I miss the Muse, Apollo's gifts elsewhere disposed:
Silence thus destroyed Amyclae, through the ban itself imposed.

Let tomorrow be for lovers, loved they never, loved they long.

Gray's Ode to Richard West

Mother of roses, for whose sake breathes fresh
The soft wind of the west, and Venus comes,
    Your comrade, – hailed by song of birds
      And the nymphs' dancing quire, –

Tell how my friend – this day not idle – now
Consumes his time – in love beneath the shade,
    Leaving to wake his golden lute,
      Or in the Muses' cavern,

Full of sweet madness he withholds himself –
With never a thought for me, who wander now
    Through the cool woods of Tusculum
      Or climb the Alban Hills.

Delight of Faunus and his goat-foot train –
Pine-trees, be witness, and fierce Anio,
    Wherever through steep gullies hurled
      Your swift flood shakes their sides,

His name high Tibur and the lovely woods
Of Aesulum have heard, and, pleased to hear,
    The rocks have echoed back the same
      To Latian Naiades:

Those nymphs have seen me on their watery banks
Where oftentimes descends Venusia's bird,
    Sweet-singing, there in delicate dew
      To bathe his snowy plumes;

And then, a wonder! – woods and hallowed springs
Take up the song; the ancient laurels, and rocks –
   Taught by the Spirit of Music – hold
      The softening melody.

Yet need you wonder not, though all unskilled
I string these halting numbers to my lyre,
   For pleasant Spring and these sweet scenes
      Prompt my unstudied lay;

Believe me, friend, in Phoebus' shadowy grove
Fancies are clinging under every leaf;
   I know not whether winds or clear
      Waters speak livelier here.

Marcabruns

Marcabruns, poor Bruna's son, –
He was begotten under a moon
Taught him no sooner love's begun
      Than it is over:
And so he loved not anyone
Nor none would have him for a lover.

Marcabruns
a poem of the Second Crusade

By a fountain, in an orchard-close,
To the gravel verge where the green grass grows,
And a planted tree its shadow throws,
   All in a setting of white flowers
And spring-time with its usual tune,
I found companionless, alone,
   The one who will not give me ease.

A lady, by her body graceful,
And a baron's daughter of a castle;
The birds' jargon pleasing well,
   The season new, and the green hours,

428

I thought that she might turn and listen,
Attentive to my conversation,
   And quickly alter her affairs.

By the fountain her eyes were weeping,
And in her heart was deep sighing,
"Jesus," she said, "the world's king,
   It is through you that my care grows;
Through your wrongs I am undone,
For the best of all I had is gone –
   God's will be done! – in your service.

"Through you my friend is gone away,
Who was noble and rich, strong and lovely;
Great distress remains with me,
   Continual mourning and desires.
Ah, bad cess be to Louis the king,
Who made the summons and the preaching,
   Through which this pain to my heart goes."

And as I heard her so grieving,
I stepped to her side by the clear spring,
"Sweet," I said, "too much weeping
   Will spoil your colour and your face;
Don't give over to such despair –
Who makes the greenwoods bud once more,
   He surely soon can give you ease."

"Sir," said she, "I am most sure
God will have mercy on me – there
In another world, for evermore,
   With many poor sinners else;
But still I know the king has taken
What my joy grew from; that I am forsaken.
   My friend being far, he little cares."

Ruggieri d'Amici:
Canzone   Of Distance

It is my heart that must remain
From hour to hour in heavy musing,
Through you, my sweet, because you try
It night and day with cruel pain,
By your delaying and refusing;
For with its longings it will die:
You murder me with anxiety.
When I call back into my mind
The love you gave, when you were kind,
All the goodness and solacing,
Then great is my heart's suffering.

Sweet lady, full of worthiness,
To find you at such long distance,
Great heaviness it is to me;
Since you, with so much amorousness,
Proffered me joy with confidence,
When I was in your company.
I cannot say how it may be
That any comfort might belong
To me; but I should do great wrong
In breaking of my faith to you
For anything that you might do.

This heaviness for you, lady,
Comes back into my heart, whenever
I think how sad it was to part,
Seeing all that joy which we
Created when we were together;
The thought of this is in my heart.
Love wills I shall bear a joyful part
When I come back to you once more:
God! I wish that day were here,
When I shall feel all your sweetness,
It falls to my heart that happiness.

Go forth, my song, full of delight,
By all the good which Love commands,
And seek the kingdom of Sicily;
Greet her who is so fortunate,

And tell her, following my demands,
By all the pains that fall to me,
That contented I would not be
To win great wealth, unless her mind
To love me willingly inclined;
For Love has me so sore beset
I can incur no other debt.

From Dante's Inferno
CANTO VI

Then as consciousness came back to my mind which had been
   clouded
  With pity for those cousins, those kinsfolk in their pain,
  Which had astounded me quite and stunned me into stupor,
I saw fresh torments there, and fresh tormented therewith,
  Around me are ranked there wheresoever I range
  My gaze, or my eyes go, or where they turn back again.
I am in the third round's den – deep there is the downpour,
  The timeless, cheerless rain, accurs'd and chillily falling,
  Which knows no change or renewal in nature or quality.
Heavy falling of hailstones, and foul water, and hell's sleet
  Dank through the dark air continually drenching;
  A filthy stench is from the ground and grievous, that takes that
   falling.
Misformed Cerberus here that both fierce is and fell,
  With his three gullets hideous, houndlike bays howling
  Over the people submerged, immersed there in the mud.
Blood crimson his eyes are ablaze, black and greasy his muzzle
  Both wide is his belly and big, and his hands with claws barbed.
  He rends the spirits and wrenches them and rips them into
   quarters.
And the downpour makes them howl dolefully like dogs,
  With one side seeking still to shelter the other
  Thus writhing and turning, those wretches reprobate.
When Cerberus sighted us, and the great slimy maggot saw us,
  He gaped wide his gullets and showed his ghastly fangs
  And from stem to stern no limb of him was still.
My guide then spread out the full span of his grasp,
  Took clods of the clay, whole fistfuls clasping,
  And thrusting he threw them into those ravening throats.

431

And just as a great dog that growls and barks in his greed,
  Soon as his food he grips, silent he grows,
  Since his instinct and aggression are only to that end,
In such manner those foul mouths and filthy muzzles
  Of the rabid devil Cerberus who rants so and roars,
  That those damned souls who hear it are desirous to be deaf.
We passed then over those shades pressed down by the pouring
    rain,
  And fetched the soles of our feet on the false show of their
    seeming,
  The baselessness of their being, which assumes the shape of a
    body.
The lot of them lay there on the ground lubberly,
  Saving a single one who raised himself and sat up
  When he saw and perceived us passing on that pathway.
"O you who are here led through the halls of hell"
  So he cried out to me "Recall me if you can;
  You, man who were made before I was unmade."
And I to him in answer "The anguish in which you are
  Maybe from my memory and from my mind withholds you
  So that it seems to me that I never saw you.
But tell me and teach me too who you are, here in such torment
  Down in this dreadful place, such punishment deserving:
  Greater there may be and grimmer, yet none so disgusting."
And he to me said then "Your own city, surcharged
  With bitter envy brimful, so that the bag overflows,
  In her I led my lifetime in the light of the clear day.
You, native townsfolk, knew me – Ciacco the name was,
  Gluttony was the fault, the foul sin I fell in,
  Wherefore, as now you see, I am soaked in the rain's sluice;
And I, a soul here in sorrow, am not alone in this sadness;
  Like pain and like penalty here is paid us who suffer
  For sins of the same kind." He said no word further.
"Ciacco," I made answer "Your misery moves me,
  Weighs heavily on my mind, and would make me to weep,
  But tell me if you can what is cast, and shall come
For the townsfolk of this town, divided and torn asunder,
  Tell me if any be righteous there, and what the root and reason
  Why to such division and discord it is doomed."
Then he to me: "At length, from long contention and lasting
  They shall come to bloodshed and wounds and war; and the
    backwoods party
  Shall drive out the other faction with force and with much offence.

This it behoves shall happen, and have place within the time
  Of the circling of three suns, then the other side shall prevail
  Through the succour of one who now sets his sails to every wind.
For a long time they shall lord it with scornful front uplifted,
  Breaking the others down with heavy burdens to bear,
  Although overwhelmed they weep, shamefast and woebegone.
Two righteous there are to be rated, but their reason goes there
    unheeded;
  Arrogance and eager envy with avid avarice also
  Are flaming sparks that fire all hearts there as their fuel."
Completed thus his complaint, plangent and fit for tears,
  Made I answer to him then "More, for my mind's enlightenment,
  Furnish me further, and favour me with speech;
Tell me where is Farinata now, and Tegghiaio that were so noble,
  Jacopo Rusticucci, Arrigo, Mosca, and the rest
  Whose minds were bent on the better course and the public
    benefit?
Where are they now I would know, so to have knowledge of them;
  For great longing consumes me to learn of their last end,
  If Heaven sweetens them now, or Hell, envenomed, holds them."
And he: "They are blasted among souls more black and more
    blameworthy;
  Weighted with different sins, down they have gone to the depths:
  If you descend so much more you may meet with them there.
But when your way you shall wend back to the sweet world
  Remember me, I pray, to the minds of men again;
  No more shall I speak nor may, no more will answer."
Then his straight eyes he squinted and turned them aslant from me,
  A little still looked at me, and then at length his head slumped,
  Then dropped with the others, blinded and blinking in the
    blizzard.
Then said my guide "No more will he move or wake in the mire,
  Till that clear sound, and clangour of the Archangels clarion,
  The advent of their Adversary who then His power advances.
Then each one shall seek once more sadly his sepulchre,
  Refledge himself in his own flesh and his own proper form,
  And that day hear his doom through eternity redounding."
Thus through the foul mixture and muddle we made onwards
  Through the shadows and the sheets of rain, with slow pace
    shifting,
  At leisure touching a little there on the life to come.
"Master," I said then, "These torments, will they in time
  Increase more searingly, when is said the great sentence,

Dwindle then or diminish, or burn as they do now?"
He said "Lean on your logic, have you not learned from this,
  It poses that if anything more of perfection possesses,
  The more its potential for pleasure, and for pain likewise?
And though they are incapable, this canaille in their cursedness,
  Forever of possessing the pitch of true perfection,
  Needs must after the Judgement they be nearer it than now."
Thus on that street going, our steps we stayed not,
  Touching on many topics which I forbear of telling,
  Until we reached that slope where it slants down and descends,
Where Plutus we came on plain, the great foe with his plunder.

CANTO VII

"Papè Satan, Papè Satan, Alèppe!"
  Thus the cacodaemon Plutus with his clucking and cackling;
  And that courteous sage, who all things kenned and considered,
Said then to hearten me "Be you not harmed or hurt
  By any fear that you have; for this fiend's power that is fell
  Cannot withhold or hinder you descending here this rock."
He turned and faced those features, that inflated blubber,
  And said he then "Silence, accursed and savage wolf!
  Within yourself consume your insane slavering.
There is cause for our descent down here into the depths:
  From Heaven is the behest, there on high where Michael
  Wreaked vengeance on the proud and the rebellious rape."
And as when bellying sails blown up by the wind's blast
  Fall matted and tangled when the mast breaks and the mizzen,
  So foundered to the earth that fell beast and fierce.
So held we our way herewith into the fourth hollow,
  Thus comprehending more of the miserable marge
  Where all the bad of the universe is bagged and bottled up.
Ah, justice of God! who can gather together
  Such new pains and enormities as now I saw there?
  Wherefore must our sins so wear and so waste us?
As is the way of the waves above Charybdis' whirlpool,
  Each billow compelled against an oncoming billow,
  Such is the case with these people; in a counter-figure they clash.
Here many I saw, more than elsewhere there might be,
  On the one side and the other side, with a sound of great howling,
  Heaving vast weights, heavily and hard, with their chests.
They moved them together amain and at the moment they clashed

Each one of them turned round, retrograde rolling,
  Crying, "Why do you hold and hoard?" and "Why hastily
    squander?"
And thus returned and retraced by the sad circling track,
  Passing on each hand back to the opposing point,
  Bawling and shouting again their shameful burthen.
Then each one of that rout when he had ranged and reached it
  Swung in his circle's arc back to a second joust.
  Then I, with my heart pierced and pounded with compunction,
"Master," I said, "What means this? Show me and make known
  Of what manner are this clan, and if for the clericy claimed
  All those listed on our left, at large with the tonsure?"
And he to me then said: "All these so squintingly saw,
  Their reason so set awry, in their original lifetime,
  That they could make no spending of their substance with
    moderation.
This they bay and bark out boldly and with clarity
  When they pace to the two opposing points of this circle here,
  Where contrary they are separated by complementary sins.
These were all classed as clerics and clergy, without thatch
  Of hair upon their heads, high Popes and cardinals,
  In whom avarice worked its worst and its wickedest."
"Master," I said "Must there not among this crew here be some
  Whose faces I recall and recognize as known,
  Who by suchlike sins were sullied as these are here?"
Then said he to me "In suchwise vainly do you surmise:
  Their life without discernment, which made them so drab and
    so dirty,
  Now makes them too dull and too dim for any kind of distinction.
For eternity they'll tender this twofold butting;
  With closed fists griping, out of the ground of their graves
  These shall arise re-shapen, and those close shaved and
    shorn.
Badly holding, badly giving, the beauty of the world
  Was snatched away from them, and set them to this scuffling –
  With no adornment of diction I delineate what it is.
Here, my son, can you see the swift-passing farce
  Of wealth and worldly goods, whose wielding is given to
    Fortune,
  For which humanity so boldly buffet and bait one another.
Now may not all the gold that is beneath the moon – and more –
  That ever was in the world, buy for these weary souls
  A single moment's solace or a second's pause."

"Master," I said to him "Make known more to my mind;
  Of this Fortune tell me, on which your tongue now touched,
  What is she, that has in her grasp the goods of the world and
     its guerdon?"
And he to me: "O beings that are blind and foolish both,
  In want of knowledge so wide, witlessly beset!
  Be ready now to receive my ruling concerning her.
That One, Whose wisdom transcends all the world,
  Established the starry Heavens and guides to keep them stable,
  So that each part its shining shows forth and shares to each.
Allotting equally the light of the luminaries.
  In like manner He gave for the glory and glitter of the world
  A minister at large, and a manager ordained to their maintenance.
At the time's point to transfer and permutate empty possessions
  From nation unto nation, and from old stock unto new,
  Beyond the wit of man or his wisdom's mastery:
Hence one stock has sovereignty and another is subdued;
  Sequent upon her sentence and on her secret judgement,
  Which is withheld from us, and hidden like a snake among the
     herbage.
Beyond your knowing it is to balance this in belief:
  She foreordains and foresees and follows out her judgements,
  Governing her realm for good, as in theirs the other gods.
There is no rest nor respite in the run of her permutations;
  Swift moving, by necessity, needs she must be, and speedy
  Frequently come they to her favours as they fall.
This is she who without cause is cursed and calumniated
  Pre-eminently by those who ought to praise and approve her,
  Requiting her with blame, and, wrongfully, with reproaches.
But she is blessed and blissful and hears not their blasphemies:
  Full of joy, among the rest of creatures that first were framed,
  She rolls her sphere around, in beatitude rejoicing.
Downwards now let us descend to deeper miseries;
  Each star already is setting which was before ascendant
  When I took my way at first – long tarrying is forbidden."
To the other side of the circle we crossed then to the shore
  Where a spring breaks forth that boils and bubbles
  Downwards through a ditch from its own force derived.
Darker were the waters than if drenched with purple dye;
  And we, taking our way beside those sombre waves,
  Along that stream, made entry by a strange path straightway,
Where is made the marsh and the morass of Styx,
  From that dismal stream, coming down in its descent

By those grey fells to the grim shore at their foot.
And I, halting awhile with wonder to watch it,
  Saw a muddy folk there, filthy in that marsh.
  They were all stripped and stark and angry was their stare.
They hit and hacked each other and not with their hands only,
  But with their heads they buffeted, with their breasts and with
    their heels,
  And with their teeth together tore one another piecemeal.
My good master said then: "My son, you may perceive now
  These are the souls of such as anger did subdue;
  And let you believe and learn, likewise, for a certainty,
Are others submerged beneath who sigh there in the slough,
  Breaking the water with bubbles above them on the surface;
  As your own eye attests and teaches you where it turns.
They say, fixed in the mud: 'Mopers were we and mirthless,
  And sour in the soft air which the sunlight gladdens,
  And the sluggardly smoke let smoulder in our hearts;
Sullenly now we lie in the black sludge and slime.'
  This is the hymn they gurgle gloomily in their gullets.
  Even to articulate outwardly they are not able."
Thus by that fen with its foulness a wide arc we fetched
  Between the dry bankside and the middle there of the bog,
  Fixing our eyes on those folk who gulped at its filth;
Till by that turn we attained to the foot there of a tower.

CANTO VIII

Continuing, I let you know that long before we had come
  And forthwith fetched ourselves to the foot of the high tower,
  Our eyes were there turned up and attracted to its top
By the sight of two small flames which thereupon were set,
  And from afar another flame in answer flickered back,
  So far indeed it seemed, scarcely in the eye's scope.
And I, turning to the sea and source of all intelligence
  Said: "What did it say, and what answer was sent back
  By that other fire over the flood, and who are they that framed it?"
And he to me said then: "Over the soiled waves and squalid,
  You can discern on its way what we now watch and wait for,
  Unless the mist from the marsh makes it invisible."
Never did bowstring impel the bolt so to break forth,
  Shooting with such speed through the air swiftly,
  As I discerned then a skiff, a light and small one,
Towards us at that moment making through the marish waters,

437

It glided on and was governed and guided by a single pilot,
   Who cried: "Now are you come, accursed spirit and fell?"
"Phlegyas, O Phlegyas, you flatter yourself in shouting"
   Said Virgil my lord, "In vain, this time, for the venture,
   You may only have us in hold till we're hoisted over this
      cesspool".
Like one then who listens to a lying and great fraud,
   A deceit which has been done to him, that direfully he resents,
   Such Phlegyas grew, gathering up his grudge.
My guide bent his way down to the bottom of the boat,
   And cast me also to come in after him in that case,
   Nor seemed it laden nor loaded till I was let into it.
Soon as we both were on board, my guide and I, in that boat,
   That primeval prow, cutting the waves, proceeded,
   Dividing them more deeply than with others it had done.
While thus on our course we came through the dead canal,
   One full of mud reared up, rousing himself from the mire,
   And cried: "Who are you who come before your hour has called
      you?"
Making answer to him then I cried: "If I come, I do not remain;
   But you, who are you now, seeming subhuman in your squalor?"
   And he making answer: "You see I am one who mourns in his
      misery."
And I to him: "With weeping and with wailing in your woe,
   Remain you here in mourning, spirit under malediction!
   For I see who you are and discern you, even through your
      sordidness."
Then he held forth both his hands, stretching them out to our
      hull,
   Whereat my guide, on his guard, gave to thrust him away,
   Saying: "Keep off there, you, with the other curs of your kind!"
And then embracing my neck, he bore me to his breast,
   Kissing my countenance, and cried: "Discriminating soul!
   Blessed may she be boasted that bore thee in her womb.
This one, in your world, was arrogant, overweening;
   Nothing of good had he got for gilding of his memory,
   Thus falls it that his shade is foul and furious.
How many up there were counted who called themselves great
      kings,
   Who lie here now loutishly, loathsome as pigs in the muck,
   Leaving behind them reproach ringing horribly in a rumour."
And I said then: "Master, much is it to my mind
   That I might see him ducked, soused here in the soup,

438

Before we fare from hence forwards across this lake."
And he to me: "So shall he, before the shape of the shore
   Swims into your sight you shall be satisfied;
   Justly may it be enjoined you should enjoy such a wish."
Soon after this, as I tell you, such a tearing of him I saw
   Made of him in the mud, there by that people of the mire
   That God I still glorify for it, and praise Him in gratitude.
The whole crew holloed out: "Have at Filippo Argenti!"
   That Florentine spirit outrageous, that rash was and unruly,
   Turned on himself and tore him, even with his own teeth.
There then we left him; let me of him no more relate.
   But a dolorous and a doleful sound dinned upon my ears
   Whereat my eyes together intently I turned forwards.
Then my sage master said: "Now it is, my son
   Draws near the city of Dis, that is so denominated,
   With its solemn citizens and its great assembly."
"Master," I said, "Already its minarets I see there, and its mosques
   Distinctly I discern there within that dale,
   Incandescent in their crimson as if they had come from fire."
And he to me forthwith: "The flame of eternal fires
   Which rages and roars within, lights them up red to you,
   As now you behold them here in this depth of Hell."
We arrived now in the deep ditches that are dug,
   The moat that was made there about that mournful city;
   The ramparts that were around it of iron seemed to be raised.
Nor before we had sailed a long circuit about it
   Did we pitch upon the place where the pilot with a loud voice
   Cried then "Get out here, this is the gate you go in!"
A gathering of more than a thousand, above the gateway thronging,
   Of spirits I saw there that had rained down from the sky,
   Who in their wrath roared out, "Who is this that comes ranging,
Daring to pass undead here through the kingdom of death?"
   Then my sage master made a signal to them,
   Implying it was his will to parley with them in private.
They held back a little their huge disdain and hatred,
   Saying, "Let you come in alone, but let that other one go,
   Who has come so daringly down here in this kingdom.
Solitary let him return by his same mad route;
   Let him try, if he can make it, to retrace, but you remain here,
   Who escorted and conducted him through such dark country."
Reader, you can realize how ruefully I was discouraged
   At the vicious clamour of those accursed voices:
   Surely I could not believe that I should ever get back.

"O my beloved leader, who more than seven times have lent me
   Succour, and secured me in safety, and drawn me forth
   From deep perils and dangers desperate before me,
Do not desert me" I said, "Leaving me thus undone;
   If we cannot press on further and to proceed is not permitted
   Let us together return, and quickly retrace our steps."
And then that lord who had led me thither
   Said "Do not be perturbed, for our passage and pathway
   Cannot be got from us, by such grace it has been granted.
But wait for me here awhile and comfort your weary spirit;
   Let it be made whole and nourished, with good hope to help
      you:
   I will not desert you down here in the depths of the underworld."
My leader thus went away and left me there alone,
   The fair gentle father; full of my doubts I remained,
   In a turmoil of tension, between yes and no contending.
Meanwhile I could not make out what offer he made them;
   But he had not loitered long, lingering among them,
   When they came crowding in, competing with one another.
Then these fiends, our foes, shut the gate fast
   In the face of my master, who perforce remained outside.
   He took his way back towards me, with slow pace returning.
With his eyes bent down and his brows abashed,
   Their confidence shorn away, and sighing he said:
   "Who has denied me entry into these dolorous domes?"
And to me he said: "Do not you be daunted nor yet dismayed,
   Although angry I am now: the assay I will achieve,
   Whatever they do or devise within there for defence.
This truculence of theirs is known, and in nothing is it new:
   On a prior time they proved it at a less secret portal,
   Which now stands unfastened, and still it is found so.
You have seen the deadly writing of wrath that is wrought above it;
   And now already, this side of it, descending down the steep,
   Winging unescorted his way through the wide circles,
Comes one by whom this country shall be cast open to us."

Note

These versions of three cantos from Dante's Inferno were originally commissioned
by the BBC for a translation of Dante's poem done by various hands and broadcast
on the Third Programme. The poets who contributed to this were free to choose
their own methods of translating Dante, and used a variety of metres, ranging
from the Terzarima of the original to free verse. I myself had some difficulty in

determining what metre should be used. I did not want to use the Terzarima, which is a very constricting metre in English, and I felt that to do so would be to challenge comparison with earlier translators, notably Laurence Binyon and Dorothy L. Sayers. Other metres, blank verse for instance, seemed to me to have post-Dantesque connotations in relation to English verse. Then it suddenly came to me that Dante was after all a medieval poet, and that his nearest analogue in English literature was perhaps to be found not in Milton (though Milton certainly knew his Dante, and drew upon him on several occasions), but William Langland. I therefore used a version of the old English alliterative metre. The effect may strike the reader as grotesque, but I think I did at least succeed in bringing out certain features of Dante which have been lost in other English translations. I mean a Gothic quality in him, and a kind of earthiness – both of these are especially marked in the Inferno.

Canzone: To the Lady Pietra
(from Dante)

O Love, thou knowest well how that this lady
Heeds not thy potency in any season
Though of all other fair it be the lady;
And when she did perceive she was my lady
And shining from my face beheld thy light,
Of cruelty she made herself the lady:
To bear the heart, not of a gentle lady,
But of that breast which proves to love most cold;
So through the season of heat and through the cold
She shows to me the semblance of a lady
Made altogether of some beauteous stone
By hand of one who could best carve in stone.

And I, more steadfast-firm than any stone,
Obeying thee for beauty of a lady,
Bear hid in me the mark made by that stone
With which thou smote me as it were a stone
Which thou hadst learned to hate through a long season,
Even striking to my heart, where I am stone;
And never was discovered precious stone,
By splendor of the sun or by his light,
Which did possess such virtue and such light
That it might be my aid against that stone,
So that it should not bring me with its cold
To such a pass that I were dead with cold.

My lord, thou knowest that by freezing cold
Water is turned into a crystal stone
In northern regions, where is the great cold;
The very air to element of cold
Is still converted, water being the lady
Of all those lands by reason of the cold:
And so it is that at her aspect cold
The frost comes in my blood at every season;
And thought of her, which shortens my life's season,
Is all converted into substance cold,
Which issues from my eye, the body's light,
Whither first entered the unpitying light.

In her collected is all beauty's light,
Likewise of cruelty runs all the cold
Into her heart, where never came thy light;
For to my eyes so lovely is her light,
Looking on her, I see her in a stone,
And wheresoever else I turn for light;
For me, out of her eyes comes the sweet light
That makes me heedless of each other lady;
Would that she were more piteous a lady
To me, who seek in darkness and in light,
Serving her only, for due place and season,
Not otherwise would wish to live long season.

Therefore, O power, older than time or season,
Older than motion or the sensible light,
Take pity on me who have such evil season,
And enter now her heart – it is due season:
So shall, by thee, pass forth from her the cold
Which lets me not, as others, have my season;
Should I be overcome by thy strong season,
In such estate, here this most noble stone
Would see me laid within a narrow stone,
Never to rise till end of time and season:
Then shall I see if ever was fair lady
In all the world like to this bitter lady.

My song, I carry in my mind a lady
Such that although to me she be of stone,
I am so brave that all men else seem cold,

And dare to fashion even for this cold,
The novelty which through your form shows light –
That which was never thought in any season.

Zefiro Torna
(from Petrarch)

Zephyr returns and brings us in fair weather,
Sweet retinue of leaves and flowers as well,
With Spring in white and scarlet blent together,
And chattering Progne and sad Philomel;

The meadows smile; once more the skies are clear,
And Jove made glad to look upon his child;
Now full of love are waters, earth and air,
And with desire all creatures reconciled.

And yet too well I feel the season nighs
When she, who bore away to Heaven the key
Of my heart's deep, draws thence the bitterest sighs;

And song of birds, and sight of flowering meads,
And lovely ladies gentle by their deeds
Seem all uncouth, and strange and wild to me.

Angelo Poliziano: Dance Song

I found myself, young girls, while it was May,
In a green garden, at the break of day.

Lilies and violets blossomed all around
On the green turf, and flowers new-sprung and fair –
Yellow, and blue, and red, and white – were found;
Then I reached out my hand to pluck them there,
To decorate with them my own brown hair,
And with a wreath confine its disarray.
   I found myself, young girls, while it was May,
In a green garden, at the break of day.

I pondered to myself, "Of all these roses,
How can I tell among them which are fairest,
Which of them lately now its bud discloses,
Which are still fresh, and which to fading nearest?"
Then Love said, "Gather those which seem in rarest
And fullest blossom on the thorny spray –"
  I found myself, young girls, while it was May,
  In a green garden, at the break of day.

"When first the rose's petals are outspread,
Most lovely and most welcome it appears;
Then weave it in a garland for your head,
In time, before its beauty disappears:
Even so, young girls, while its pride still it wears,
Gather the rose that makes your garden gay."
  I found myself, young girls, while it was May,
  In a green garden, at the break of day.

The Infinite

This lonely hill was always dear to me,
And this hedgerow, that hides so large a part
Of the far sky-line from my view. Sitting and gazing,
I fashion in my mind what lies beyond –
Unearthly silences, and endless space,
And very deepest quiet; then for a while
The heart is not afraid. And when I hear
The wind come blustering among the trees
I set that voice against this infinite silence:
And then I call to mind Eternity,
The ages that are dead, and the living present
And all the noise of it. And thus it is
In that immensity my thought is drowned:
And sweet to me the foundering in that sea.

1819

The Evening after the Holy Day

The night is soft and clear, and no wind blows;
The quiet moon stands over roofs and orchards
Revealing from afar each peaceful hill.
Beloved, now every alleyway is silent;
At intervals along the balconies
The night-long lantern gleams; you are asleep,
And gently slumber now gathers about
Your quiet chamber, and no single care
Gnaws at your heart; you do not know at all,
Nor think that you have opened in my breast
A very grievous wound. You are asleep:
And I have come abroad now to salute
This sky whose aspect seems to be so gentle,
And ancient Nature powerful over all,
Who has fashioned me for trouble. "I deny
All hope to you," she has said, "yea, even hope;
Your eyes shall not be bright for any cause,
Except with weeping." This was a festal day:
And you are resting after its delights;
And maybe in your dreams you still remember
How many eyes took pleasure in your beauty,
How many, too, pleased you: I find no place –
Not that I hoped it now – among your thoughts.
Meantime I ask how many years of life
Remain to me, and therefore here I cast
Myself upon the ground, and cry, and rage.
Oh terrible days, even of our green youth!
Alas, I hear not far along the road
The lonely singing of a workman, coming
Back to his poor home so late at night,
After the sports; and fiercely my heart aches
Thinking how all this world passes away
And leaves no trace. For look, the festival
Is over now, an ordinary day
Succeeds tomorrow; all things our race has known
Time likewise bears away. Where now is the voice
Of the ancient peoples, the clamour of our ancestors
Who were renowned, and that great Empire of Rome,
The arms, and the clash they made by land and sea?
All is silence and peace; the world is still;
There are no tidings now remain of them.

Once in my boyhood, when so eagerly
We would look forward to the holiday,
Finding it over, I lay upon my bed,
Wakeful and very unhappy; late at night
A singing heard along the alleyways,
Little by little dying into the distance,
Even as this does now, gripped at my heart.

1819

To the Moon

O gracious Moon, I call to mind again
It was a year ago I climbed this hill
To gaze upon you in my agony;
And you were hanging then above that wood,
Filling it all with light, as you do now.
But dim and tremulous your face appeared,
Seen through the tears that rose beneath my eyelids,
My life being full of travail; as it is still –
It does not change, O my sweet Moon. And yet
Remembrance helps, and reckoning up
The cycles of my sorrow. How sweet the thought
That brings to mind things past, when we are young –
When long's the road for hope, for memory brief –
Though they were sad, and though our pain endures.

1819

A Fragment

ALCETAS

Hear me, Melissus; I will tell you a dream
I had last night, which comes to mind again,
Now that I see the moon. I stood at the window
Which looks out on the field, and turned my eyes

446

Up to the sky; and then, all of a sudden,
The moon was loosened; and it seemed to me
That coming nearer and nearer as it fell down,
The bigger it appeared, until it tumbled
In the middle of the field, with a crash, and was
As big as a bucket is; and it spewed forth
A cloud of sparks, which spluttered, just as loud
As when you put a live coal under water
Till it goes out. For it was in that way
The moon, I'm telling you, in the middle of the field,
Went out, and little by little it all turned black.
And round about the grass went up in smoke.
And then, looking up at the sky, I saw was left
A kind of glimmer, or mark, or rather a socket,
From which it had been torn, and at that sight
I froze with terror; and don't feel easy yet.

MELISSUS

And well you might, indeed; for sure enough,
The moon *might* tumble down into your field.

ALCETAS

Who knows? For don't we often see in summer
Stars falling?

MELISSUS

    But then, there are so many stars:
And little harm if one or other of them
Do fall – there's thousands left. But there is only
This one moon in the sky, and nobody
Has ever seen it fall, except in dreams....

1819

The Younger Brutus

What time uprooted in the Thracian dust
Lay, an immense ruin
Italy's virtue, from whence the Fates prepared
For green Hesperia's vales and Tiber's banks
Tramp of barbarian horse, and from stark forests,
Oppressed by the frozen Bear,
To the destruction of Rome's famous walls,
Called forth the Gothic swords;
Worn out and dripping with his kindred's blood
Brutus, in blackest night seated alone,
Resolute now on his own death, accused
Avernus and the inexorable Powers, and thus with savage accents,
Vainly made tremulous the drowsy air.

"Stupid Virtue, the hollow clouds, the fields
Haunted by unquiet ghosts –
These are your schools, and at your back comes round
Bitter remorse. To you, marmoreal Powers,
(If Powers there be in hold of Phlegethon
Or here beneath the clouds), a laughing-stock
And scorn is our sad race
From whom you beg temples and with fraudulent laws,
Insult mortality.
Is Heaven's hatred then so much provoked
By earthly piety? Do you, Jove, sit
Impiety's protector? And when exults
The cloudburst through the air, and when
Hurtles the rapid thunder,
Whelm on the good and just your sacred fires?

Unconquerable Fate and iron
Necessity bear down
Upon the sickly slaves of Death; no intermission
Availing for his outrage, the common man
Consoles himself that ills are necessary.
Is the irreparable less harsh? Is grief unfelt
By him who's stripped of hope?
War to the death, eternal, the brave soldier
Wages with you, base Fate,
Not schooled to yield; and with the tyrannous grip
Of your right hand, victorious on him laid,

Shrugs it off unsubdued, with a last gesture
When in his own proud flank
The bitter steel makes entry,
And grimly smiles toward the blackening shades.

Displeasing to the gods is he, who violent, storms
The underworld: such valour
Is not for their feeble, eternal breasts.
The Heavens perhaps devised our sufferings,
Our bitter lot and our tormented passions,
As a mere spectacle to please their sight.
Calamities nor crimes,
But free, unsullied ages in the woods,
Nature ordained for us,
Our queen and goddess once. Now when on earth
Impious custom wrecks her hallowed reign,
Our meagre life kept back by other laws,
When one of manly soul
Rejects the ill-omened days,
Will Nature blame his dart as not her own?

They know no guilt, nor their own suffering,
The fortunate wild herds;
Calmly, their latter age leads on apace
Without foreknowledge. But if distress should urge them
To dash their heads on the rough trunks, or to consign
From mountain rocks their bodies headlong down
Into the wind, no arcane law
Nor dark conceit stands to contend against
Their wretched longings. You, among so many
Stocks Heaven vivifies, for you alone,
Sons of Prometheus, life is a torment;
And Jove to you alone
Forbids, O wretched men,
If tardy Fate delays, the shores of death.

And you, pale moon, rising out of the sea
Our blood incarnadines,
Survey the unquiet night, and these sad plains,
Ill-fated for the might of Italy.
The victor tramples on his kinsmen's hearts;
The hills are loud, from topmost summits ruins
Rome's antique glory down;

And do you watch so calmly, you who saw
The Latin nation's birth, the joyful years
And all its memorable laurels won?
And you, silent above the Alps shall shed
Your still unaltering beams, when mid the wrongs
Of Italy's servile name
That solitary seat
Is deafened by the tramp of barbarous feet.

Among the naked rocks, on the green bough,
The beast and wild bird
In customary oblivion of sleep
Know not the deep ruin nor the changed
State of the world; and when the labouring peasant's
Rooftop is touched by crimson of the dawn,
With morning canticles
The one will wake the valleys, and the other
From the high cliffs
Startle the weaker droves of lesser animals.
Condition vain, vain race of man, we are
The abject part of things! Neither the bloodstained soil
Nor the rebellowing caves
Has our disaster troubled,
Nor does human anguish dim the stars.

Neither to you, Olympus, nor the deaf
Lords of Cocytus, nor to unworthy Earth,
Nor, dying, to the night, do I appeal;
Nor you, the last beam gleaming through black death,
Conscious posterity. Shall the vile crowd's
Sobs placate my arrogant tomb, their words
And offerings deck it out? From bad to worse
The times rush on; not well it is we assign
To our corrupt descendants
The honour of outstanding minds, their woes'
Ultimate vindication. Let the dark bird,
Whose pinions are about me, greedily tear;
Let the beast prey, and the rain cloud
Draw up the unnoted spoils,
The wind receive my name and memory."

December, 1821

450

To Spring
or, Concerning the Ancient Myths

Even though the sun repair
The ruin of the sky, the western breeze
Quicken the sickly air, from whence is fled,
Scattered, the heavy shadow of the clouds,
And though the birds confide
Their undefended bodies to the winds,
The light of day, piercing among the coverts
And loosening the hoar-frost, breed new hope,
Fresh amorous desire among the beasts;
Yet may a thought revisit the tired mind
Of Man, by grief entombed,
Of that fair former age, which all too soon
The obscure splendour of truth
And time's disasters utterly consumed?
For him, must Phoebus' beams be dark, and quenched
For all eternity?
And fragrant Spring, shall you not touch once more
And breathe upon this frozen heart; which age
Embitters in the flowering time of life?

And are you living yet,
O sacred Nature? May our human ears,
So long unused, catch that maternal voice?
The brooks were once a home for the white nymphs,
Their shelter and their glass
The liquid springs; and the high mountain ridges
To secret dancing of immortal feet
Trembled, and the deep forests (now
The lonely haunt of winds). The shepherd boy
Who sought at noontide the uncertain shade
And led his thirsty lambs
Down to the flowery river's brink, might hear
Sounding along those banks
The rustic Pan's shrill song or, struck with wonder,
Gaze on the rippling waters, for unrevealed
The quiver-bearing goddess
Went down to the warm flood, to cleanse away,
After the bloodstained hunt, immodest dust
From off her snowy flank and virgin arms.

The very grass and flowers
And every thicket lived, in former days!
The gentle airs, the clouds, and Titan's lamp
Were mindful of the race of Man, and then,
O Cyprian star of Venus,
The traveller going through the lonely night
Followed your naked beauty with fixed eyes
Over the hills and shores, and made of you
Companion on his way, and fancied, too,
You cared for mortal men. Others, who fled
The tainted intercourse
Of towns, their shame and tumult, deep in woods
Clasping the rough-boled trees,
Believed that in their bloodless veins there surged
The vital flame, while the leaves breathed, and trembled,
Hid in that sad embrace,
Daphne, or mournful Phyllis, or unconsoled,
Some child of Clymene weeping for him
Who plunged the bright sun in Eridanus.

Nor, you harsh cliffs, on you
Could beat unheeded then the sorrowing voice
Of our distress, while lonely Echo haunted
Your fearful hiding places: not the wind's
Empty illusion then –
A nymph's unhappy ghost had dwelling there,
Whom grievous love and fate too harsh had parted
From her soft limbs. And she from the bare shelves,
The caves and desolate places, would proclaim
The not unnoted grief, to the hollow sky
Hurling the broken words
Of our complaint. And legend told of you,
Musical bird, well-versed
In human deeds, amid the leafy coverts
Singing now Spring is born again, you mourned
To the dark silent air,
In stillness of the fields, your ancient wrongs,
And all the dreadful tale of your revenge
In that wan day when wrath and piety met.

But we can claim no kindred
Now with your race; nor human grief informs
Your varied notes; darkling the valley hides you,

Free from all guilt – the less belov'd for that.
Alas, alas, for empty ˙
Stand the Olympian halls, and the blind thunder,
Wandering among the hills and the black clouds,
Indifferently dissolves with a cold horror
Guilty or guiltless breast; strange is become
The soil that bore us, and knowing not her offspring
Is nurse to the sad soul.
But, O fair Nature, heed our griefs, and this
Destiny undeserved,
And touch my spirit once more with the ancient fire;
This, if indeed you be a living power,
Or if there be in heaven,
On earth beneath the sun, or the sea's bosom,
One Being, conscious there of our distress,
Spectator of our pain, though pitiless.

January, 1822

Sappho's Last Song

O tranquil night, and you, O modest beams
Of the setting moon, and you, whose light has pierced
Among the voiceless woods above this rock,
Day's messenger – sights that were dear to me,
Delightful to my eyes in former times,
Still ignorant of Fate and the cruel Fury;
These mild scenes please my despair no more.
But even now for such as I there lives
An unaccustomed joy, when the dusty winds
Turn from the south, and sweep the trembling plain
And liquid fields of ether, and the car,
Jove's heavy chariot, is overhead,
Thundering, and cleaving through the darkening sky;
Fitting it were to plunge among the clouds,
Up on the clifftops and high mountain vales,
Those terror-driven flocks' tremendous flight,
Or in the deep flood's tumult, as it breaks
Upon the treacherous shore –
Anger of waves, triumphant as they roar!

How beautiful your mantle is, O sky:
And you are fair, O dewy earth. Alas,
The hostile Powers to wretched Sappho gave
No part at all in all this infinite beauty!
In vain, O Nature, vanquished at your throne,
I turn my eyes and suppliant heart towards
This haunting loveliness – of no account,
Rejected lover, and unwelcome guest.
Never again the sunny riverbanks
Shall smile for me, nor the ethereal gate
Of earliest dawn; no more shall greet my ears
The carolling of many-coloured birds;
Nor shall I hear the murmur of the beech trees;
And nevermore under the leaning willows,
Where the bright stream lays its pure bosom bare,
The gentle waters turn themselves aside,
Disdain my unlovely feet,
And hurrying press to where the banks lie sweet.

But how have I offended, and what crime
Did I commit before my birth, that Heaven
Should be so grim, and Fortune's face averted?
In childhood did I sin – the time of life
Which knows not of misdoing – that the harsh thread
Winds from the spindle of implacable Fate,
My youth cut short and withered? Upon your lips
Breathed then imprudent words; for things ordained
Work by their own dark counsel. All is dark,
Except our pain. We are neglected children,
And only born to weep; the cause remains
Upon the laps of the Celestial Ones.
Oh cares and hopes, even of our greenest years!
To form alone, to pleasing outward form,
The Father grants always to bear the rule
With men; through worthier powers, through song,
Or the lyre's skilfulness,
No virtue shines in an unlovely dress.

We die; this worthless veil scattered in earth,
The naked spirit fleeing to Dis, amends
The harsh fault of the blind disposing Power.
And you, for whom vain love and lasting faith
Have held me, and the empty fury of

Unsatisfied desire – live happy, if indeed
Such in this world be any mortal's lot.
But Jupiter, for me, out of the urn
Whence flows the pleasant wine of happiness,
Dealt with no generous hand, since perished all
The dear illusions and the dreams of youth.
For the most full of joy of all our days
Are first to fly away, and then creep in
Disease, old age, the shade of frigid death.
Behold, for all the palms I might have won,
And sweet deceiving hopes, Tartarus waits;
And the aspiring mind must Proserpine
Possess forever more,
The sable night, and quiet Stygian shore.

May, 1822

To Sylvia

Sylvia, do you remember yet
The season of your mortal lifetime here,
When beauty shone indeed
In the elusive laughter of your eyes,
And full of joy and wonder you approached
The threshold of your years?

The quiet chambers rang,
And all the ways around,
With your continual song;
When you were sitting at your woman's work,
Intent, happy enough
With what bright future occupied your mind:
It was the fragrant Maytime; even so
You used to pass the day.

I, at my easy task,
Sometimes laying aside the well-thumbed page,
Which had consumed away
My better parts and my first youthful age,
Upon the balcony of my father's house,

455

Pricked up my ears at music of your voice,
And at your hand which sped
About your labours as you wove your web.
I gazed on the clear skies,
Gardens, and golden ways,
And there the far-off sea, and here the mountains.
No mortal tongue can say
What were my feelings then.

What dreams, what pleasing thoughts,
What stirrings of the heart, my Sylvia!
How fair the life of man
And destiny appeared!
When I remember now how much I hoped for,
A passion falls upon me,
Bitter, disconsolate;
I turn again to mourn my evil fate.
O Nature, Nature, why,
Why do you not give now
The things you promised then, why so deceive
Your children, mortal men?

Before the winter's cold withered the grass,
Assailed and conquered by a hid disease
You died, poor gentle child; and never saw
The flowering of your years;
Nor was your heart to melt,
Hearing soft flattery of your dark hair,
Or when they praised your shy enamoured glances;
Nor girl-companions on a holiday
Had talked with you of love.

And even so with me,
All my fond dreams lie dead; for youth itself
The Destinies withheld
From my first years. Alas,
How you are fled, are fled,
Dearest companion of my earliest age,
My Hope, for whom these tears are shed!
Is this that world? And those
Delights, and love, labours, and happenings,
Of which so often we discoursed together?
Is this the lot then of the race of Man?

For when the truth appeared,
Poor thing, you fell away; and from afar
Showed with your hand the cold image of death
And a bare sepulchre.

April 19-20, 1828

The Solitary Thrush

From the high summit of this ancient tower,
O solitary bird, you still sing on
To the wide countryside, while daylight dies;
And down the valley strays your harmony.
Now all around the spring
Shines in the air and triumphs through the fields,
And hearts grow tender but to gaze on it.
Hark to the bleating flocks, the lowing herds,
The other happy birds that chirp together
Or take their wheeling flights through the free heavens,
Thus welcoming the season of their joy.
But pensive and apart you view it all;
You choose no mates, nor fly,
Care not for pleasure, and avoid their play;
But seem to waste in song
The flower of all your lifetime and the year.

Alas, how like indeed
Your way of life and mine! Pleasure and laughter,
Those sweet companions of our youthful age,
And sharp regret of all our later days,
And you, O Love, so near akin to youth –
I do not care for these, I know not why,
But rather fly from them;
Almost a hermit, strange
Even to my native ground,
I pass the springtide of my life away.
This day, which now already yields to evening,
Our little town keeps as a festival:
Hark to the sound of bells through the clear sky!
And often, too, rattle of distant guns

Reverberating back from farm to farm;
In holiday attire,
The young folk of the place
Have left their homes and spread about the roads
To see and to be seen, the light of heart.
Lonely, I take my way
To this remote part of the countryside,
And leave all sports aside
Until some other time; meanwhile I catch,
Athwart the still, bright air,
The sun's glance, which behind the distant hills,
As ends this clear, calm day,
Sinks down and vanishes, and seems to tell
How youth's blest season, too, dwindles away.

You, lonely little bird, when comes the evening
Of that brief life the stars have measured for you,
Surely will not repine
The use you made of it; for all your longings
Were planted there by Nature.
For me, if I must pass
The hateful gate of age,
When these eyes shall become
Mute for all other hearts, and the whole world
Empty for them, and each succeeding day
More sad and tedious than the last – how then
Shall my desires appear,
And these my early years, and I myself?
Alas, I shall repent, and many times
Look back to them, and not be comforted.

c.1828?

Memories

O you bright stars of the Bear, I did not think
That I should come once more, as was my custom,
To gaze upon you glittering above
My father's garden, or converse with you
From the windows of this house, where as a boy

458

I lived, and saw the end of happiness.
Time was, how many mad imaginings
I fashioned in the thought of your bright aspect,
And your companion stars. For then I used
To pass away the most part of the evening
Quietly sitting on the green turf, watching
The sky, and listening to the frogs' remote
Song, from the open country. The firefly wandered
About the hedgerows and above the flowerbeds,
And the wind sighed among the fragrant alleys
And through the cypress trees there in the wood;
While sounded from the house at intervals
Voices of servants at their ordered tasks.
But what vast thoughts and what sweet visions then
That distant sea called forth, and those blue mountains
Discerned from far away! – which then I thought
To cross some day, inventing for myself
An unknown world, and unknown happiness
To suit my life to come – not knowing my fate,
Nor, willingly, how many times I would
Have changed that bare and sorry life for death.

For my heart never told me my green age
Was doomed to waste here, in this barbarous town
Where I was born, with a cheap boorish people,
Who hold in no repute learning or knowledge
(Often indeed their jest, a thing to laugh at),
A folk who hate and shun me, not from envy –
They do not judge me better than themselves –
But they suppose that in my heart I think so,
Although I never showed it any man.
And so I pass the years, alone, obscure,
Loveless, and lifeless; and I am forced to grow
Bitter myself, with this malignant crowd,
And putting off my pity and my manhood,
I make myself despise the human race,
Even as this herd has taught me; and, meanwhile,
The dear season of youth is passing – dearer
Than laureled fame, or the clear light of day,
Than breath itself – and so it is I lose you,
Having reaped not one delight, and all things wasted,
In this inhuman spot, among afflictions,
O solitary flower of barren life!

The tolling of the hour comes on the wind
From the town belfry. A sound which was my comfort,
As I remember, in those fearful nights
Of boyhood, when I lay in my dark room,
Beset by terrors, longing for the dawn.
There is no object here that meets my sense
Which does not bring some image back again,
Or raise some sweet remembrance – sweet in itself,
But then creeps in, with pain, thought of the present,
And so, an empty longing for the past,
Though it was sad, and these words: "I have been."
That gallery I knew, facing the last
Gleams of the daylight, and those painted walls –
Figures of flocks, the sun rising above
A lonely plain – these in my idle times
Proffered so much delight, when still remained
The strong illusion at my side, which spoke
To me at all hours, in whatever place.
In these old rooms, while the snow gleamed outside,
And the wind whistled round the ample windows,
My voice reechoed, gay and full of pleasure
Then, in that season when the harsh unkind
Mystery of things still seems to us to be
So full of sweetness. Like an untried lover,
The boy, deluded still, gazes on life,
Which is untouched and virgin, fashioning
A beauty from the skies to wonder at.

O dreams, O dreams, O you the dear illusions
Of my young years, always I turn again
To you, in musing; though time goes, and though
Our thoughts and passions change, forget you not.
Phantoms – I know it now – are glory and honour;
All good and all delight are mere desire;
The waste and misery of life bear at the last
No single fruit. And though my years are empty,
And this, my life's condition, desert and dark,
Fortune has taken little – too well I see it.
But oh, as often as I think of you,
My early hopes, the dear imaginings
I once possessed, then look, and see how vile
And sorry my life is, and death alone,
Of all I ever hoped for, now remaining,

I feel my heart turn cold, and then I know
Nothing can recompense me for my fate.
When death, invoked so often, stands before me,
And I have reached the end of my misfortunes,
When earth seems a strange valley, and when the future
Eludes my gaze, I know for sure that I
Shall still remember you, my dreams; that image
Shall make me grieve once more, with bitterness
That I have lived in vain, and with distress
Mingle the sweetness of my dying day.

Even in that first youthful tumult of
Delight, anguish, desire, I called on death
Time upon time, and seated for long hours
Beside the fountain, thought of ending there
Beneath those waters all my hope and pain;
Then, brought in peril of life by blind disease,
Mourned for the fair season of youth, the flower
Of my impoverished days untimely fallen;
And often, late at night, seated upon
My bed, the only witness of my sorrow,
Playing the poet by the uncertain lamp,
Lamented with long stillness of the night
The passing of my spirit, and to myself
Chanted a death song for my failing life.

Who can remember you without a sigh,
Our opening time of youth? – Oh indescribable
And lovely days! – When first on the rapt mortal
Young girls begin to smile, and all things vie
To give him pleasure; Envy holds her peace,
Unwaked as yet, or kindly; and the world
(Unprecedented wonder) seems to hold forth
A hand to help him, and forgives his errors,
Makes holiday to greet the newcomer
Who enters thus on life, and bowing down,
Acclaims and owns him lord of all existence.
Fugitive days! – For like a flash of lightning
They are gone away. Is that man ignorant
Then, of misfortune, if this fairest season
Has fled from him, and the best years of life
In youth, ah youth, are all wasted away?

461

But O Nerina, does not this place speak
Of you, and can it be that you indeed
Are faded from my thoughts? Where are you gone?
For memories, O sweetness of my life,
Are all I find of you. This countryside
Where you were born knows you no more. That window
Where once you used to talk with me is empty,
Reflecting the sad glitter of the stars.
Where are you? For the echo of your voice
Is heard no more – whose distant accents once
Falling upon my ears, made me turn pale.
That was another time. Your days are over,
My sweet beloved. You have passed. To others
Is given now to go about the land
And find a dwelling in these fragrant hills.
But swiftly you passed by, and all your life
Was like a dream. For you went dancing forth,
And joy shone on your brow, and in your eyes
The sure imaginings and light of youth,
And then Fate struck you down, and you lay still.
Alas, Nerina! for the old love yet
Reigns in my heart. And if at any time
I take my way on days of festival
Or go to watch the dancing, to myself
I say: "Nerina, now you deck yourself
No more, nor go to dance or festival."
When May returns, and lovers greet their girls
With carolling and gifts of flowering branches,
I say: "Nerina, never more for you
Returns the spring; and love returns no more."
Every fine day and every blossoming bank
I look upon, feeling my heart rejoice,
I say: "Nerina now feels joy no more,
Nor looks upon the fields or on the sky."
For you have passed away, my everlasting
Sorrow – have passed, and made companion
Of all my fair imaginings and all
My tenderest feelings, in the sad and dear
Moods of the heart, a bitter memory.

August 26 – September 12, 1829

462

The Calm after the Storm

The storm has passed away;
I hear the birds rejoice, the barn-door hen,
Gone back into the lane,
Reiterate her call. Look, the clear sky
Breaks through there in the west, above the mountain;
The plains cast off their gloom;
And the bright stream appears down in the valley.
All hearts are glad once more; on every side
Begins the noise and stir
Of labour, as before.
The craftsman, with his work in hand, goes singing,
To view the rain-swept sky
Outside his door; a woman
Comes running out, to be the first to fill
Her pail with fresh rainwater;
The herb-seller again,
Going from lane to lane,
Takes up his daily cry.
Look now, the sun returns and smiles down
On hillsides and on houses. And now the household
Throws open windows, balconies, and rooms;
And mark, upon the high-street, some way off,
Jingle of harness bells, the creaking cart,
As now the traveller renews his journey.

So every heart is glad.
And when, but now, is life
So gracious and so sweet?
When else with so much liking
Does man resume his labours,
Turn to his wonted work, or start some new one?
And when is he less conscious of his ills?
Pleasure is trouble's child;
And empty joy, the fruit
Of terror overpast, makes even the man
Who learned to loathe his life
Tremble with fear at death;
And thus, in long-drawn torment,
Men, cold, and pale, and silent,
Shudder and sweat, the while they see above,

Against them gathering round,
Lightning, and clouds, and wind.

O bounteous Nature, these
Are then your gifts, and this
The happiness you offer
Us mortal men! The issue out of pain
Is happiness enough;
And pains you scatter with a generous hand,
While sorrow springs even of its own accord;
And pleasure, which by some odd miracle
Is born from trouble, is great gain. O human kind,
Dear to the eternal powers, happy indeed
If granted pause for breath
After each grief; most blest
If even these are cured at last by death.

September 17-20, 1829

Saturday Evening in the Village

The young girl now comes back from the open fields,
About the set of sun,
Bearing her swathe of grass, and in her hand
A bunch of roses and of violets,
As is her custom, for
Tomorrow's holiday,
To make more beautiful her breast and hair.
And the old woman sits
Upon the steps among her neighbours, spinning.
Turning herself to where the day goes down,
And telling tales how she, in better times,
Decked herself out against the holiday,
And graceful still, and fresh,
Would dance the evening through among the rest,
Who were companions of her lovely prime.
Darkens the air, the sky
Takes on a deeper blue, and shadows fall
Cast by the roofs and hills
Beneath the whiteness of the rising moon.

And now the bell proclaims
The holy day's approach,
And at that sound, it seems,
Each heart is cheered once more.
The small boys shouting in troops
About the village square
Go leaping hither and thither
And make a cheerful noise;
Meanwhile the labourer goes whistling home,
Back to his frugal meal,
And thinks about the coming day of rest.

When every other light around is out,
All other sound is mute,
Hark to the hammer knocking, and the saw –
The carpenter is up,
Working by lamplight in his shuttered shop,
And labours on, in haste
To get all finished before morning comes.

This is the best-loved day of all the week,
Most full of hope and joy;
The morrow will bring back
Sadness and tedium, and each within his thought
Returns once more to find his usual labour.

You little playful boy,
Even this your flowering time
Is like a day filled up with grace and joy –
A clear, calm day that comes
As a precursor to life's festival.
Be happy, little boy;
A joyful time is this.
More I'd not tell you; but if your holiday
Seems somewhat tardy yet, let not that grieve you.

September 28, 1829

465

Night Song of
a Nomadic Shepherd in Asia

What are you doing in Heaven? O Moon, tell me,
What, O you silent Moon?
You rise at eve, and go
Gazing upon the deserts, and then set.
Are you not weary yet,
Traversing still that everlasting round?
Are you not tired of it, and still desire
To look upon these valleys?
Much like that life of yours
The shepherd's life appears:
Rising at earliest dawn
He moves his flock across the plains, and sees
The herds, and wells, and grass,
And wearied out, rests in the evening's shade;
He hopes for nothing more.
Tell me, O Moon, what worth
The shepherd's life to him,
And yours to you? Tell me, and whither tending
This my brief pilgrimage,
And your undying course?

A weak, white-haired old man,
Half-naked, with bare feet,
A very heavy burden on his shoulders,
Over the hills and valleys,
Over sharp-pointed rocks, deep sands, and thickets,
Through wind, through storm, under the scorching day
And cold that follows it,
Runs on, eager, runs on,
Traversing pools and torrents,
Falls down, rises again, still hastening onward,
Taking no pause nor rest,
Bloodstained and torn, until at last he finds
The end of his long road,
Which he has reached with so much weariness –
A ghastly, huge abyss:
And there he casts him in, all things forgetting.
Such, O you virgin Moon,
Such is the life of man!

Man is brought forth in labour;
There is the risk of death in being born,
And so he learns to know of pain and torment
Even in that first thing. From the beginning
His mother and his father
Seek to console their offspring for his birth,
And as he lives and grows
Strive to encourage him, endeavouring,
By every deed and word,
To keep him in good heart,
To comfort him for this his human station;
No duty is more kindly
That parents may accomplish for their children;
Yet why bring forth to light,
Why, living, still maintain
The child, if such must be his consolation?
If life is our misfortune
Why must we still endure?
Such, O unblemished Moon,
The mortal life of man;
But you, immortal, care,
As it may be, but little for my words.

For you, eternal, lonely wanderer,
Seeming so full of thought, must understand
What is this life below,
And all our sighings and our sufferings;
And what is death, and the last fading out
Of colour from the cheeks,
The vanishing from earth, till we are lost
To all familiar, loving fellowship.
Surely you understand
The reason of it all, and see the fruit
Of evening and of morning,
And of the endless, silent pace of time.
You know, you surely know, for whom spring smiles,
And for what tender love;
Who profits by the heat, what is procured
By winter with its frosts.
You know and search out many thousand things
Which still are hidden from a simple shepherd.
And when I gaze upon you,
Who mutely stand above the desert plains

Which heaven with its far circle but confines,
Or often, when I see you
Following step by step my flock and me,
Or watch the stars that shine there in the sky,
Musing, I say within me:
"Wherefore those many lights,
That boundless atmosphere,
And infinite calm sky? And what the meaning
Of this vast solitude? And what am I?"
Thus reasoning with myself, and of that splendid
Immeasurable hall
And numberless tribe of stars,
The motions and the workings
Of everything on earth or in the sky,
Circling unendingly,
Returning still from whence their course began,
I can divine no plan
Nor guess the purpose there; but surely, you,
Undying maiden, understand it all.
Yet this I know and feel:
The everlasting round,
And my own feeble being,
May be a source of pleasure and of good
To others, but for me this life is bad.

And you, my flock, who take your ease – Oh happy,
Not knowing, as I believe, your wretchedness!
How do I envy you!
Not only that you seem
Made free of all distress,
All harm and all privation
And each inordinate terror soon forgetting;
But more, because you know no tedium.
For, resting in the shade, upon the grass,
Content you are and quiet,
Without repining pass
In this calm manner the year's greater part.
But when, beneath the shade, and on the grass,
I sit, disgust of life
Cumbers my mind, and a goad drives me on,
And sitting there, still am I far removed
From peace or from repose;
And yet I nothing want,

Nor hitherto found cause for my complaint.
I cannot comprehend
The source of all your joy; yet you are bless'd;
My flock, I joy but little,
And yet not only therefore do I mourn;
This I would ask you, had you power to speak:
"Tell me, why every beast
Lying at his fair ease
Is well contented in his idleness;
But if I lie at rest, spleen seizes on me?"

If I, maybe, had wings
To fly above the clouds,
To number one by one the very stars,
Or wander with the storm from peak to peak,
Should I be happier then, my gentle flock?
Should I be happier, O you pale Moon?
Or are my thoughts astray,
Thus contemplating alien destinies?
Perhaps whatever rank or form we take,
In the child's cradle or beast's couching-place,
The day of birth, for each that's born, is dark.

Between 22 October 1829, and 9 April 1830

To Himself

Now be forever still,
Weary my heart. For the last cheat is dead,
I thought eternal. Dead. For us, I know
Not only the dear hope
Of being deluded gone, but the desire.
Rest still forever. You
Have beaten long enough. And to no purpose
Were all your stirrings; earth not worth your sighs.
Boredom and bitterness
Is life; and the rest, nothing; the world is dirt.
Lie quiet now. Despair
For the last time. Fate granted to our kind

Only to die. And now you may despise
Yourself, nature, the brute
Power which, hidden, ordains the common doom,
And all the immeasurable emptiness of things.

Early 1833

On the Portrait of a Beautiful Lady
carved on her sepulchral monument

Even so you must have been;
Who now are only dust and skeleton
Under the ground, while motionless, above
The bones and dirt, is set this empty image
Of all your ravished beauty –
Sole warden now of grief and memory –
That dumbly gazes on the flying years.
The look which made men tremble, being fixed
Upon them steadfastly (as now it seems);
The curving lip, that was
A vessel flowing over with delight;
The throat girt round about once with desire;
The hand, which felt turn cold,
So often, that which it reached forth to hold;
The breast which visibly
Made men turn pale – all these things once were here;
But now you are no more than dirt and bones,
And now a thing of stone
Must hide the sad, malignant spectacle.

And thus does Fate subdue
The likeness which among us seems to be
The heavens' liveliest image. Everlasting
Mystery of our being. Today, on high,
Spring of unerring feelings and vast thoughts,
Beauty mounts up, and seems
A fitful splendour cast
Upon these sands from an undying nature,
Giving our mortal state
Earnest of more than human destinies,

470

And of the fortunate realms
And golden worlds beyond;
Tomorrow, at a touch,
Is all cast down, abominable, and foul
To look upon, what once
Possessed an angel's brightness,
And that which in our minds
Had moved us on to frame
Such wonderful conceits, dissolved away.

Learnèd consort of sounds,
By virtue of their being,
Creates for truant thought
High visions and desirings infinite;
Mysterious, the spirit of man may thus
Wander delightful seas,
As a keen swimmer goes
Among the ocean waves in his disport;
But let one false note strike
Upon the listening ear –
That moment, Paradise is turned to naught.

If, Human Nature, then,
In all things fallible
You are but dust and shade, whence these high feelings?
In any part if noble,
How is it that your worthiest thoughts and passions
Can be so lightly stirred
And roused and quenched even by such base occasions?

Between autumn 1833, and summer 1835

The Broom

or, the Flower of the Desert

And men loved darkness rather than light –
JOHN iii. 19

Upon the arid shoulder
Of this most terrible mountain,
Vesuvius the destroyer,
Graced by no other tree or flowering plant,
You scatter here your solitary shrubs,
O fragrant-blossoming broom,
Contented with the deserts. So have I seen
Your shoots make beautiful that lonely land
Which girds about the city
Who once had been the mistress of the world,
And to the wayfarer,
Even by her grave and ever-silent aspect,
Gives testimony of an empire lost.
I meet you here once more, O you the lover
Of all sad places and deserted worlds,
The constant comrade of afflicted fortune.
Among these fields, now strewn
With barren cinders only, covered up
By lava turned to stone
That rings beneath the passing traveller's feet;
Where the snake nestles, coiled in the hot sun,
Or to his familiar
And scooped-out burrow the rabbit goes again,
Were farmsteads and tilled glebe,
And yellowing blades of wheat, and here the sound
Of lowing herds of cattle,
Gardens and palaces,
Pleasant retreats for leisure
Of great patricians, and here were famous cities,
Which the huge mountain, from its fiery mouth
Pouring forth streams of flame, has overwhelmed
With those that dwelt in them. Now all around,
One single ruin spreads,
Wherein you take your root, O courteous flower,
As if in pity of the doom of others,
And cast a pleasant fragrance to the skies,
Making the desert glad. Now let him come

And view these slopes, whose wont it is to flatter
Our mortal state; here he may gaze and see
How loving Nature cares
For our poor human race, and learn to value
At a just estimate the strength of man,
Whom the harsh Nurse, even when he fears it least,
With a slight motion can in part destroy,
And may, with one no less
Slight than the last, even now and with no warning
Wholly annihilate.
Graven upon these cliffs
Is that *magnificent*
Progressive destiny of Humankind.

Here gaze, and see your image,
O proud and foolish century,
You who have gone astray
And left the path by reawakening thought
Marked out for you till now, and turning back,
Even of your regress boast,
Proclaiming it advance.
All those fine wits their evil fate has made
You father forth, with flattery receive
Your childish words, although
Deep in their hearts at times
They mock at you. But I
Would not go to the grave bearing such shame,
Though easily I might
Vie with the rest to imitate their ravings
And make my song acceptable to you;
Rather would I reveal the deep contempt
That lies locked in my breast,
And show it openly, while still I may;
Although I know oblivion
Lies heavy on whom displeases his own age.
But I have learned to laugh
At that bad fate we both will share together.
You dream of liberty, the while you forge
New bonds for thought – through which
Alone man rose, in part,
From barbarism, whence only civil life
Has grown, and we may guide the commonwealth
To better things. And thus

The truth displeased you, telling
Of that low station and harsh destiny
Nature has given us. So, like a coward
You turned your back upon the light, which showed
This truth to you, and fleeing it, called base
Those who still followed it; and he
Alone was great of soul who, knave or madman,
Could fool himself or others, and would raise
The state of mortal men above the stars.

A man of poor estate, and weak in body,
Being of a high nobility of soul,
Supposes not, nor claims
That he is rich or handsome,
Nor makes himself a laughing-stock for men
By show of splendid living,
Or valour in his person;
But without shame allows it to appear
In strength and wealth he is a beggar still,
Speaks openly of this, rates his condition
According to the truth.
Nor do I think that creature
Of a high mind, but foolish,
Who, born to perish, and reared up in pain,
Says: "I was made for joy,"
And with his festering pride
Covers whole pages, promising on earth
High destinies and new felicity
Which Heaven knows nothing of, much less this earth,
To a people whom one wave
From a troubled sea, one breath
Of poisoned air, one tremor underground
Might utterly destroy
That scarce the memory remained of them.
But noble of soul is he
Who burns to lift his eyes
Against the common doom,
And with free tongue, not docking any truth,
Admits the weak, low state,
The evil lot assigned to us by fate;
He who in suffering,
Shows himself great and strong
And will not add fraternal wrath and hatred –

The worst of ills – to all
His other miseries
By blaming man for his unhappiness,
But lays the fault on her who is indeed
The guilty one, the Power who is our mother
In that she brought us forth, stepmother in will.
He calls her enemy, and thus, believing –
As is indeed the truth –
The human race was from the first conjoined
And ranked against the foe,
He takes all men as his confederates,
Embraces all men with a general love
Which is sincere; he offers
And looks for prompt and valiant aid from them
Amid the anguish and recurring dangers
Of this their common war. But against man
To take up arms, or seek to lay a snare
To cause his neighbour stumble,
Seems mad to him, as if one in the camp
Hemmed in by enemies, beneath the threat
Of their most keen assault,
Forgot the foe, and stirred up bitter strife
Among the allied ranks,
And scattered flight and tumult with his sword
Through his own warriors.
When thoughts like these again
Shall be revealed, as once, unto the crowd,
That horror, which at first
Bound men in fellowship,
Together linked against an evil Nature,
Shall be in part restored
By knowledge of the truth; honour, right-dealing
In civil intercourse,
Justice and piety shall find a different soil
Than those proud follies, founded upon which
The probity of the mob
Stands firm as all things else rooted in error.

By these deserted banks,
On which the hardened flood
Casts a dark cloak, and still seems moving waves,
Often I sit by night and mark on high
In heaven's purest blue,

The stars burning above this mournful plain,
And where the far-off sea
Becomes their mirror, and the whole world ablaze
With glittering sparks circling the empty sky.
And when I fix my eyes upon those lights,
Which seem to them mere points,
Yet are so vast that all
The earth and sea compared with them are truly
Only a point; to which
Not only man, but this
Globe, wherein man is nothing,
Is utterly unknown; and when I see –
Beyond them infinitely more remote –
Those clustering knots of stars
Which look to us like clouds, where are unknown
Not only man and earth, but all together,
So infinite in number and in mass,
The golden sun among the rest, our stars,
Or seeming even as themselves appear
To us on earth – a point
Of nebulous light; then to my questing thought
What is it you appear,
O son of man? Remembering
Your state below, of which the soil I tread
Bears testimony still, and yet that you
Think lordship and a purpose
Assigned you by the Whole; how many times
You have been pleased to say on this obscure
Grainlet of sand, which bears the name of earth,
The authors of the universal cause
Came down, on your account, often conversing
At pleasure with your race, and how this age,
Which seems in knowledge and in civic arts
The most advanced, heaps insult on the wise,
Renewing once again
These long-derided dreams; what feeling then,
Unhappy children of mortality,
What thought of you at last my heart assails?
I cannot say if pity or scorn prevails.

As a small apple falling from the tree,
Which late in autumn-time
Its ripeness and no other force impels,

Crushes the loved homes of a tribe of ants,
Tunnelled in the soft loam
With infinite toil, their works,
And all their wealth, which, jealously collecting,
That busy race had garnered with long care
And patient forethought through the summer season –
Burying and laying waste,
All in a moment; so, falling from on high,
Hurled through the utmost heaven,
A cloud of cinders, pumice-stone, and rocks,
Darkness and ruin, mingled
With boiling streams of lava,
Or down the mountain side,
Raging across the fields,
All in a molten mass
Of red-hot sand and metals mixed together,
A mighty flood swept down,
And overwhelmed, destroyed, and covered up
Those cities which the sea
Washed on the farther shore,
In a few moments; whence above them now
Browses the goat, new towns
Rise in their stead, whose seat is still upon
The sepulchres of those, while the steep mountain
Seems spurning with its foot their prostrate walls.
Nature has no more care
Or value for man's need
Than for the ant's; and if disaster falls
More rarely on the former
No other cause can be
Than when he breeds, man's less fertility.

Full eighteen hundred years
Have passed away, since vanished, overwhelmed
By the force of fire, these peopled seats of men:
And the poor husbandman
Tending his vines, whom scarce the scorched, dead soil
Upon these plains affords a livelihood,
Lifts yet suspicious glances
Toward the fatal summit,
Which, now become no milder than before,
Still full of terror stands, still threatening
Disaster for himself, his sons, and their

Impoverished fields. And often
The wretch, upon the roof
Of his poor cottage, lying
Sleepless all night beneath the wandering air,
Time upon time starts up, to mark the flow
Of that dread simmering, which still pours out
From the unexhausted womb
Over the sandy ridge, and shines upon
The shores about Capri,
And Mergellina, and the Bay of Naples.
And if he sees it coming near, or deep
In his domestic well he hears the water
Gurgling and boiling, he awakes his children,
In haste awakes his wife, and snatching up
Whatever they can seize, they go, and fleeing,
See, far behind, their home,
Their little field, which was
The sole protection they possessed from famine,
Prey to the burning flood,
Which hissing, overtakes it, then unappeased,
Spreads ever-during over all they had.
Returns to light of day,
Which old oblivion had quenched for her,
Pompeii, a skeleton,
Out of the grave by greed or piety
Dragged forth into the open;
From her deserted forum
Upright among the ranks
Of broken colonnades, the traveller
May gaze long on the forked peak of the mountain,
And on its smoking crest,
Which threatens still the ruins scattered round,
And in the horror of the secret night,
Among the empty theatres,
Temples defaced, and shattered dwelling-houses,
Where now the bat conceals its progeny,
Like an ill-omened torch
Which darkly flickers through deserted halls,
Still runs the glimmer of the deadly lava,
Which far off through the shadows
Glows red, and tinges everything around.
Even so, knowing naught of man, or of the ages
Which he calls ancient, or the long succession

Of various generations,
Nature stays ever fresh, or rather she
Travels so long a course,
That still she seems to stay. While empires fall,
While tongues and peoples pass, nothing she sees;
And man presumes to boast eternity.

And you, O gentle broom,
Who with your fragrant thickets
Make beautiful this spoiled and wasted land,
You, too, must shortly fall beneath the cruel
Force of the subterranean fire, returning
To this, its wonted place,
Which soon shall stretch its greedy fringe above
Your tender shrubs. You then
Will bend your harmless head, not obstinate
Beneath the rod of fate;
Nor yet till then in vain and cowardly fashion
Bow down to the oppressor still to come;
Nor upright in mad pride against the stars;
Amid the desert, where
You find your home and birthplace,
Allotted you by fortune, not your will;
But wiser still, and less
Infirm in this than man, you do not think
Your feeble stock immortal,
Made so by destiny or by yourself.

After April, 1836

The Setting of the Moon

As in the lonely night,
Above the waters and the silvered plains,
Where fluttering breezes move,
And distant shadows feign
A thousand images,
Illusory and fair,
Among the quiet waves,
Hedgerows, and trees, and hills, and villages –
Having reached the sky's confine,

479

Past Apennine, or Alp, or in the Tyrrhene
Sea's unsounded bosom,
The moon descends, and all the world grows dim,
The shadows disappear,
And one same darkness blots out vale and mountain.
While night remains, bereaved,
And singing, with a mournful melody,
The wagoner hails the last gleam of that light
Which now is vanishing
And on his journey still had been his guide;

Thus disappears, even so
From human life must go,
The season of youth. Away
Depart the shadowy forms
And beautiful illusions; less now seem
Those far-off hopes on which
Our suffering mortal nature learned to lean.
Desolate, full of darkness,
Our life remains. And gazing round on it,
Bewildered, vainly would the traveller trace
On the long road which lies before him yet
Reason or bourn; he finds
That he has now become
A stranger here where dwells the human race.

Too sweet, too full of joy,
Had seemed our mortal state
To those above, if our first youthful time,
Whose every good is bred from thousand pains,
Had lasted out the whole course of our life.
Too mild were that decree
Which sentences to death each living thing,
Did not the path to it,
Though half completed yet,
First show itself more harsh than terrible death.
The Eternal Ones devised
The last of all our ills,
Worthy invention of immortal minds –
Old age, where still desire
Survives, with hope extinct,
When pleasure's founts run dry, and every pain
Grows more and more, while good comes not again.

You, banks and little hills,
Though hidden be the light which from the west
Had silvered all the mantle of the night,
Orphaned you shall not long
Remain, for very soon you may discern
Once more the eastern skies
Grow pale with morning, till the dawn arise,
Whom the sun follows after, and comes forth,
Blazing and bright again,
And with his ardent beams,
His shining streams of light,
Floods all your summits and the ethereal plain.
But mortal life, when the fair time of youth
Has vanished, never then grows bright again
With any radiance more, or second dawn.
Widowed until the end; and in the night,
Where through the dark we come,
The gods have set a sign for us, the tomb.

Completed 14 June, 1837

Chorus of the Dead

Alone eternal in the world, to whom
Every created thing
Devolves, in you, O Death,
Our naked being finds rest;
Joyless, indeed, but safe
From the ancient pain of thought; profoundest night
From the bewildered brain
Blots out that grievous load;
The dry ghost feeling never impulse more
To hope or to desire
Is likewise free from all distress and fear,
And with no tedium consumes the slow
And vacant centuries.
We lived: and as a terror of the night
And an oppressive dream
Is troubled recollection in the mind
Of child as yet unweaned,

The memory remains
Of our lifetime; but far removed from fear
Is it in the recalling. What were we? –
That bitter point of time
Which bore the name of life?
A dark and awful thing
Is life to our conceiving, as appears
To thought of them that live
This undiscovered Death. And as from Death
The living start appalled, just so with us
Our naked being recoils
Back, from the flame of life;
Joyless, indeed, but safe;
Because the Fates deny
To mortals happiness, and to the dead.

The Horn
(from Alfred de Vigny)

1

I love the notes of the horn, at evening the woods among,
Though of the doe's last agony it be the triumph song,
Or the farewell of the hunter, which the faint echo receives,
And a cold wind from the North scatters between the leaves.

How many times, alone, at midnight, when all else slept,
I have smiled, listening to it – but more often have I wept!
For it seemed to me that I heard those sounds that once foretold
The slaughter of the mighty paladins of old.

O country the heart adores! O dim blue mountains afar!
Maboré's amphitheatre, Frazona of crag and spar,
The cataracts that fall down from the melting snow,
The becks, the torrents and springs, in the Pyrenees that flow!

Frozen and flowering mountains, where Summer and Winter
    meet,
Whose brows are crowned with ice, but the green turf lies at their
    feet!
It's there I would take my rest, and there I would hear again
The distant notes of the horn, with its sad and tender strain!

And often times the traveller, while the air holds no noise,
Makes the night to resound once more with that brazen voice,
And, at those cadences, are wakening all around
The bleating lambs' soft bells with their harmonious sound.

And listening, then, the doe nor cover seeks, nor flight,
But pauses motionless, upon the crag's steep height,
While all the torrents' roar in one vast fall is blent.
And voices of romance join that long-ago lament.

Spirits of warriors past, do you once more return?
And is it you who speak now in the voice of the horn?
Roncevalles! Roncevalles! Does this dark valley hold
The mighty shade of Roland, that is yet unconsoled?

2

The heroes all lay slain, for none had fled, in their pride,
Alone, still upright he stood, and Oliver at his side;
The ranks of Africa that ringed them round, yet reeled.
"Roland," the Moor cried "thou diest, and thou must yield!

"Amid the torrents now do all thy peers lie low";
But with a tiger's roar, he cried "African, know,
When I shall yield, then shall the Pyrenees' high crown
Into the waves be rolled, dragged with those bodies down."

"So yield," the answer came "or die; be it as thou hast said";
And a mighty rock came rolling down from the mountain's head.
Rebounding, to the very depth of the abyss it drops,
And in the waves it shivers all its pine-tree tops.

"I thank thee for that," cried Roland "Thou hast built me a road
    to boot".
And single-handed he rolled it up to the mountain's foot;
Then, upon that firm rock, giant-like he takes his stand:
That instant ready to flee, pauses the Moorish band.

3

Yet Charlemagne, in tranquil mood, with all his chivalry,
Went down the mountain's side, with peaceful colloquy.
Already they discerned, by gleam of waters known,
On the horizon, Luz and Argele's valley shown.

483

The army cheered. And now the minstrel tuned his lute,
Ready, in song, the willow-trees of Adour to salute;
From cups by strangers wrought the wines of France they quaff,
While with the shepherd-girls the soldiers talk and laugh.

Roland guarded the mountains: there was no cause for fear.
Nonchalantly mounted on his black palfrey there,
Which was new-decked in trappings violet-hued and gay,
Grasping his reliquaries, Turpin began to say:

"Sire, what fiery clouds hanging in heaven we see!
Halt you your army's march; nor let God tempted be.
For by holy Saint Denys, those are the souls of the dead –
In flaming exhalations up through the air they are sped.

"A double lightning flickered – and two new flashes were born."
Then all at once was heard the far-off note of a horn.
Astonished at that sound, the Emperor of France
Started backwards, and checked his steed's eager advance.

"You heard?" he said. "Yea, surely; some herdsman his scattered
    flocks
Summoning homewards it was, high on the mountain rocks,"
The Archbishop answered him, "or the voice, faint and falling,
Of the green dwarf Oberon, he to his elf-queen calling."

The Emperor pressed on; but with a brow of care
More black and overcast than the storm in the dark air.
It was treason he feared; while thus he brooding went
The horn's note sounded and died, and again, that long-drawn
    lament.

"Ah grief, it is my nephew, oh bitter grief, for how
Should Roland call for succour, but he were dying now?
Turn back, my knights, turn back; we must cross the mountains
    again!
Tremble once more at our tread, oh treacherous earth of Spain!"

4

On the highest mountain-ridge they drew their horses' rein,
Their flanks all white with foam. Below was Roncevalles seen:
The valley faintly glows with the day's last dying light –
And on the horizon's rim, the Moorish standard in flight.

"Turpin, canst thou see aught in that deep gulley lying?"
"I see two warriors – one dead, the other dying.
Both together are crushed by a black rock downwards borne:
The stronger in his hands lifts up an ivory horn –
His soul, with his last breath parting, that two-fold summons
     rung."

Ah God! but the horn sounds sadly the depths of the woods
     among!

El Desdichado
(from Gerard de Nerval)

I am the shadowy one, widowed, uncomforted,
The Prince of Aquitaine by the ruined tower,
In whose starred lute, where the last gleam is dead,
Still must the black sun of his madness lower.

Oh, in the grave's night, who didst comfort me,
Give back the flower that solaced my heart's wound,
Posilipo and the Italian sea,
The trellis where the vine and rose are wound.

Am I Desire or Phoebus? Biron or Lusignan?
Where the queen kissed me yet my brow's afire;
In siren-caves I dreamed ... and I have gone,

Twice, as a conqueror, over Acheron,
By turns resounding upon Orpheus' lyre
The fairy's cries, the holy maiden's pain.

Prison Poem
(from Paul Verlaine)

The sky is up above the roofs,
     So blue, so calm;
A tree there, up above the roofs,
     Rocks its green palm.

A patch of sky's discerned – a bell
    How gently rings;
Somewhere in that sky, a bird
    Complaining sings.

Dear God – simple and quiet there
    How life goes on!
That peaceable murmur there
    Comes from the town.

What have you done, you here, who shed
    Unceasing tears?
Say, what have you done, and made
    Of your young years?

From Juan Ramon Jimenez

At the side of my dead body
My work lives on.

        The day
Of my life fulfilled
In nothingness and in all things –
The flower that is closed with the opened flower; –
The day of contentment in departure,
Through contentment in remaining –
In remaining through departure; the day
Of pleasant sleep, knowing it so, for ever,
Sleep ineffable and maternal
Of the empty rind and the dry cocoon,
At the side of the eternal fruit
And the infinite butterfly.

As on the Potter's Wheel
(from Ernesto Cardenal)

Bless the Lord, O my soul
Lord my God you are great
      You are clothed with the energy of atoms
        as with a mantle
From a cloud of whirling cosmic dust
as on the potter's wheel
You began to tease out the whorls of the galaxies
and the gas escapes from your fingers condensing and burning
and you were fashioning the stars
You made a spatterdash of planets like spores or seeds
and scattered comets like flowers
A sea of red waves was the whole planet
iron and red-hot molten rock
         rising and falling like tides
and all the water vapour
its dense clouds darkening the whole earth
and it began raining and raining for centuries and centuries
      long rain for centuries on stony continents
and after aeons appeared the seas
and the mountains began to emerge
        (the earth was in labour)
growing like great beasts
and to be eroded by the water
(remaining there like the débris of those times
          like piled-up rubble)
and the first molecule was made fecund by the power of water
    and light
and the first bacterium divided
and in the Precambrian the first tenuous transparent alga
nourished by solar energy
and the flagellates transparent as little bells of glass
or jelly-like flowers
moved and reproduced
(and from thence proceeded the creation that we know)
And thence the first sponges
and jellyfish as of plastic,
polyps – all mouth and stomach
and the first molluscs
and the first echinoderms: the starfish and sea urchin.
And at the beginning of the Cambrian, sponges

covered the whole sea-bed
making reefs from pole to pole.
And in the middle Cambrian all these died out
And the first corals flourished
filling the deep with crimson skyscrapers
In the waters of the Silurian the first pincers: sea scorpions
and at the end of the Silurian the first fish ravening
like a diminutive shark (already with jaws)
The algae have turned into trees in the Devonian
learning to breathe
casting their spores and beginning to grow in forests
and the first stems and first leaves were born.
The first lowly animals colonized the land:
scorpions and spiders fleeing the competitiveness of the sea.
Fins grow and the first amphibians appear
and fins become feet.
Soft fleshy trees grew in the Palaeozoic swamps.
There were no flowers yet
and insects appear
dinosaurs and birds are born
and the first flowers are visited by the first bees.
In the Mesozoic the first timid mammals appear
small and warm-blooded
        They bring forth their young alive and suckle them with milk
and in the Eocene lemurs climbing on the branches
and the tarsiers with stereoscopic eyes like man's
and at the beginning of the Quaternary you created man
You give the polar bear his coat the colour of the glacier
and the Arctic fox his, the colour of snow
You make the stoat brown in summer and white in winter
and you give the praying mantis its camouflage
You camouflage the butterflies with flower-colours
You shewed the beavers how to build their dams of sticks
                and their lodges on the water
The grasshopper comes into the world knowing how to fly and
        sing and what its food is
and the wasp knowing how to bore into tree trunks
to lay its eggs
and the spider how to weave its web
As soon as they are hatched the storks know where north and
        south are
and with no-one to guide them fly in a northward direction
You gave speed to the cheetah

and suckers to the tree-frog
and a sense of smell to the moth
to find out the odour of the female in the night
              at two miles distance
and luminous organs to crustaceans
and you give telescopic eyes to the fish of the great depths
and batteries to the electric eel
You invented the mechanisms whereby flowers are fertilized
You give seeds wings to fly on the wind
membranes as if they were butterflies.
Others have down to float on the wind
or they drop like puffs
           or propellers
              or parachutes
or float on the water like ships looking for markers
and pollen always knows its precise way:
it does not falter on the mesh of the style
before reaching the ovule

    The eyes of all wait upon you, O Lord
      and you give to each his food in due season
You open your hand
and you fill all things living with your blessings
To the humble copepod you give its diatoms
The sea anemones (fierce and voracious flowers)
beg you for nourishment
           and you feed them
The cellophane ragworm
            begs you for food with its hungry tentacles
You give algae and crabs to the dabchick and its young
and for the dunlin you give soft molluscs.
The sparrows have no barns nor tractors
yet you give them the grains that drop from lorries
on the highroad
      on their way to the barn
And you give the nectar of flowers to the hummingbird
You give tender rice-grains to the bobolink
and fish to the kingfisher and his mate
Everyday the seagull finds his fish;
every night the owl his frogs and mice.
You prepare for the cuckoo his lunch of caterpillars
and woolly-bears
         You give the crow his crickets

insects to the cricket chirping in his burrow
You give small red berries to the toucan
and he has more berries than he can eat
The chipmunk spends the winter asleep;
when he wakes up he has his seeds handy
and you open the first flowers of spring
when the first butterflies come out of their chrysalids
You open flowers in the morning for butterflies
and you close them in the evening when they go to sleep
You open others in the night for moths
that spend the whole day asleep in dark crannies
and begin to fly at nightfall
You wake the bumblebees from their winter sleep
the same day that you open the catkins of the willow

I will sing to the Lord as long as I live
I will write him psalms
      May my song please him
Bless the Lord O my soul
        Alleluia

Longer Poems

Artorius

to the memory of Charles Albert Harwood, 1938-67

Si quando indigenas revocabo in carmina reges,
Arturumque etiam sub terris bella moventem.

JOHN MILTON, *Mansus*

From the hag and hungry goblin
That into rags would rend ye,
   All the spirits that stand
   By the naked man
In the book of moons, defend ye.

Tom of Bedlam's Song

CALLIOPE I

Take down, Calliope, your trumpet from its tack:
Rested has it long, and rusted? Give us a rouse, girl:
Your voice I invoke now, and your eight with violets crowned
Sisters to sing, to a star-dance I dispose them,
Through the zone of the zodiac, where Zeus's son,
And Leto's, Apollo, shall lead with his lyre.
Urania in a dialogue shall discourse delightfully;
Thalia come also, colloquial in a clown's mask;
Polyhymnia with a pompous pæan of encomium
Is commanded to a solemn ceremony of crowning,
And blithe Erato with ballads and with badinage
Promises prothalamion for a bride and her paranymph;
And Terpsichore, she too, with her castanets, shall testify,
With a sexual dance, a saraband of death;
Plain-suited Clio, in prose, though she plod;
And grave Melpomene shall give us a goat-song;
Lastly and lyrically Euterpe shall lament
Over the waves, at winter's and world's end.

But principally you, Calliope, I presume to ask preside
At equinox and at solstice, at the sun's turnings to sing
Of War and of Justice, of Warlockry and a Wounding.
Present then for man's life a paradigm, his passage,
Like the sun, through symbols; his season's progress
From spring's heyday to high summer and harvest,
And lastly to the laggard lagoon of old age
Where his son supplants him and the cycle returns.
Labour continual is his lot; Alcides learned this,
In his twelve month of toils, under a hard taskmaster –
Battling against beasts, and against brigands also,
Monsters whose hollow dens are in the mind of Man:
The heart of the human being is its own Heaven's ruler,
Through baleful constellations its course it must keep.
        Let us learn then something of LUCIUS ARTORIUS
Of cognomen CASTUS; come of the Venetic gens;
From Illyria long since with the legionaries they came
But British land they bought with blood now here established.
The first that was his forebear, in former times directed
The rearing and erecting of the rampart, which Hadrian
Set from the Solway to the Germanic sea
Against the blue-cheeked bandits of Scotland, and the bands
Of the Picts beyond that pale, the peoples
Of moss and of moorland, and of mournful forests.
Afterwards in Armorica this first Artorius also
Campaigned with his legion; but no legend is left.
From that stock he stemmed then, the steadfast man,
Artorius name him or Arthur: some said Uther's son
And some gave him Gorlois, the good Duke for a sire,
And some that his battle-hardy blood he borrowed
From Aurelius Ambrosius, that erstwhile endured
In Britain the brunt of the Saxon boar-crests.
But none for a certainty could say sooth of such things:
Comes he was by commission – and after to be King?
        The first labour is of the Lion – as in the lust of his days,
In the youth of his years, a young man desirous
In the crags of Kurdistan, his courage to establish:
He seeks the den of the lion, in dry places of the desert,
With a blade only, a brief one, and a bundle of twine,
The black and harsh hair of a hirsute goat,
To entangle and tie up the terrible predator;
Ranging among the rocks, at last he reaches
The cavern of the cat-beast, the dark-maned carnivore,

With taunts then he twits him, and rhetorical tirades: –
"Come forth, you feline; you flea-bitten quadruped;
You lousy old lion lounging in your cave!
It is a man you must match – which will be the master?
Come out with your claws, and your canine teeth;
Or are you nervous, perhaps? Naked am I, know you
I bait you with only my blade, and a ball of twine!"
Tempted by these taunts, the tawny and narrow-bellied
Beast from among the boulders breaks forth; he sees
Dazzled in the daylight, the shadow delineated
Of Man the murderer. He springs, ready to maul
With cruel cusps and retractile claws.
But his malice is muffled in the black mohair,
All his swiftness is swaddled in the swathe of wool
He is snarled in that softness and impotently swinges,
Until without haste the hunter hauls out
The sword he grips in his grasp, and suddenly
Deals him the death-stroke with that Damascus blade,
And the blood from the bowels of the beast makes royal,
Crimsoning his handsome body, his hands and the whole of him.
Now is his manhood known, and the women make much of him:
All his village calls him valiant. With one voice they praise him.
He is remembered by rhymers, and in rough ballads;
For in this kind was formerly the custom of kings –
Bearded Lords of Babel, as bas reliefs show
A huge hunting of lions in hieratic stone.

     Now Artorius is urged to the establishment of empire,
Embattled upon Badon mound – in former times it was built
As a secure stronghold, with steep sides of earth
And spiralling paths to the centre, a spearman might hold.

     Man's woe is manifest in the night sky of March,
In the darkness before dawn of that day of battles,
And the lilting of the larks that salute the first light –
Outrageous Ares that is arbiter of anger.

     But the guardian of this house is the grey-eyed goddess,
Pallas of the pure brow, with her plumed helmet,
Brandisher of the spear, over her brazen breastplate,
Yet patroness of peace, and of its pastimes –
The women who weave their web upon the loom,
Stability of the state; she stands by the olive-press,
For the glaucous-leaved olive is the gift that she gave.
Pitted against Poseidon, she competed for the city –
The lordship and the love of the land of Attica.

The Earth-shaker to show his prowess shoved then
His trident on the ground. It grumbled and groaned,
And labouring it lifted to the light a marvel –
A high spirited horse, in its harness complete,
A war-steed for warriors, and worthy their courage.
The gift of the god they acclaimed as glorious.
But serenely she smiled, and the rich soil
Touched with the tip of her spear for a token:
Green shoots shot forth, and then the shrub
Gnarly and knotted; thus the olive was known,
With oil for anointing and all other things,
For the fairness of men, and full also of food,
A wood to be worked – for peace and for wisdom.
Then the seniors of the city as their protectress saluted her
The virgin victorious for a virtuous people.
And Poseidon in a pique plunged among the billows;
But evermore for Athens, Athenäis the ægis-bearer
Is gracious and grateful, a favouring goddess.
Some say, when the great and horrible horde of the Goths
Marched over the mountains, through forest and morass,
Furious with fire and with sword affraying
The hills and the erstwhile holy earth of Hellas,
To Attica when they attained, and the approaches of Athens,
Sitting against that city, suddenly they beheld
Superhuman in size, the shape, it seemed, of a woman
In armour gleaming, glauque-eyed and glittering,
Walking about the walls, and waving her spear.
So they turned in their tracks, subdued with terror
Of that serene vision, and the city was saved.
　　　But now he puts him in the power of another Parthenos –
Bearing on his shoulders the embroidered blazon;
Artorius exhibits the icon which images
The Bride unbrided, the Theotokos in brightness.
In a cartouche depicted, the corner of the courtyard,
Of the holy Temple, the House of the All-High,
The Virgin kneels at the knowledge of Annunciation,
And the angelic officer at the opposite end
Poised on the pavement with pinions streaming –
"Hail, highly favoured, Miriam, seed of Hannah,
Gifted with grace, and enhanced in glory,
Blessed be among women, and the breeding of your womb."
　　　So before the outbreak of the bloody battle
He makes, in a paradox, to the Author of peace, petition;

In the hour of annunciation of an ultramundane order
Prayer for the salvation and preservation of the City,
On the outcast edge of an enervate empire.
     The remnant of Troia was entrenched on the ramparts,
The Brythonic band, badly caparisoned,
With ill assorted and out of date equipment –
Army surplus from Imperial stores;
And a few battle-horses of Byzantine breed;
But also barbarian breastplates and byrnies,
Beautified with beads of black jet
Washed up at Whitby, and from Scottish waters
Pearls of price picked out of mussels,
Cairngorm stones, and studs of cornelian,
And gleaming torques of the twisted gold;
Elaborate enamels with abstract insignia.
The roll-call resounded of Roman pedigree,
And senatorial status in the remembered city –
Eugenius and Gerontius, and Urbanus of Gower,
Urbigena of Strathclyde, and Gaius the steward;
Bedwyr the butler, and Flaccus (a by-blow
Of Artorius), had arrived and augmented the armament,
And gaily and graciously the courteous Gwalchmai,
The Hawk of May, in the midst of the host,
With truest Tristan, whom Mark trusted.
     In formation on the field, on all four sides,
With the mound in the midmost, the mighty army
Of the Saxons is assembled, with Cerdic as their leader –
The renegade who renounced his Roman citizenship;
With Mul his half-brother, whose blood was a mixture.
The ancestors of Aella and Offa led the Angles,
And, cheek by jowl, the Jutes joined with them.
There was heathenish headgear of high boar-crests,
And well-tempered swords welded by Weland,
And the serviceable and deadly dagger of the Saxons.
Kite-hawks and hoody crows hung around expectantly,
With a glad and gruesome gleam in their eyes;
The wolf also was waiting in the nearby wood,
And doubtless the Wælkures, the daughters of Woden,
Accompanied these carrion birds, ready to carry off
The souls of the heroes to their high-built hall,
For an imagined eternity of unending aggression,
Of brawling and barding, and unlimited bottle ale.
     Cerdic addressed the spearmen and the swordsmen;

Exalted on an eminence, he uttered an exhortation:
"We are come up against this Cymric confederation,
This tattered remnant of the Roman rapaciousness;
It began as an asylum for bandits and brigands,
To spread its latrocinium at large over the lands.
But now the moth-eaten eagle moults its metal plumes,
They bandy you, honest farmers of the backwoods and the Baltic,
With the pernicious title of pirates and of predators.
We were no horde but a handful that hewed down this state,
A carcase wholly corrupt, and ready for its collapse;
Worm-eaten and warped by the contradictions within.
Was that small group of the Goths that glided across the Danube,
Suppliants to their ferriers, enough to sap the foundations?
Validly the Vandals were invited in as mercenaries –
And Hengist also and Horsa, at the behest of Vortigern
Were brought here into Britain, and established a bridgehead.
The people, the proletariat, receive us peacefully –
What cities have we sacked, excepting only Silchester?
The cities had been abandoned by the burghers and the bankers,
The peasantry were impoverished, or swept away by pestilence,
Crushed into thraldom by the Code of Theodosius.
Better an army of barbarian occupation than to bleed
From the teeth of the tax-collectors, and the taskmasters' whips.
It is of right we are ready here to possess
The all but empty areas which everywhere await us.
We come not as a jumble of Germanic janissaries,
But as Alemanni, the All-men, who are open to everybody,
As Franks the federation of all who would be free.

          "I was reared, as you realise, in the Roman civility;
I ground my teeth on Cicero, on Sallust and on Cæsar,
The verses of Virgil, and the vanities of Ovid;
Also the odd conventions of the cultus of Christ.
Fair enough, freely I fling it all to the winds –
I save only the discipline, for the Saxon *duguth*,
Of the law and the lore of the legions and the cohorts.

          Far away in the woods, beyond the wind-touched foam
Of the northern sea, with no one now to celebrate,
The shrines of your gods lie shrouded in shadows:
Who thinks now of Thor, who wielded the thunder,
Of the wiseacre Woden, with his vatic wisdom,
Of Frig the good housewife, or of phallic Frey?
In the wide empty welkin there is only Wyrd.
To Wyrd we submit, and the sentence of Wyrd –

And the stoutness of our strength, in our own stark existence.
Wyrd goes as it will; did some witty Greek
My tutor told me of, in the time I have forgotten –
Aristotle or Anaximander, or some another egg-head,
Denote that Destiny by a different title?
Anangke over all things everywhere is absolute,
Brute fact, that fastens us with her brazen nails;
For Necessity we therefore now nerve ourselves in our need:
In the freedom of the knowledge of necessity we fight them."

    The trumpets enunciated their traumatic *tantara-tantara*:
The battle was begun, in all its beastliness –
The hewing and the hacking of limbs and headpieces;
The divine icon defaced, in a devil's scrimmage.
In a tension of dubiety the tides turned about –
Assault upon the mound, and sortie from the mound.
Mars was the ruler, red with blood and with rust,
Manifestly, as men mashed one another below.

    But frankly, Calliope, do you find this commodious
For the lilting of your lyre, so late in the day as this is?
I, at any rate, would avoid this argument,
And turn aside from the sanguine spectacle of battle:
Murder in the mass is no matter fitting
For a maiden lady, like you, to muse upon,
Or so I would presume – though precedents suggest themselves.

    Let us glance aside then, and suppose there a glade
Of hazels on a hillside, within hailing distance,
With lambstail catkins, lucid in the light,
Dangling delightfully, and dallying with the wind.
In this place the poets, by the privilege of their office,
Stood as upon a stage, strategically apart:
Interested, they observed, objectively and with irony.
Beetle-browed Gwion was the bard of the Brythons,
And Daegrafn spoke for the sea-born Saxons.
They held in their hands their long-stringed harps,
Ready to rouse them to a rattling pæan
Of victory, for praising the virtue and the valour
Of the successful side, when the signal should be given,
Or in melting and mournful measures to set forth
An austere elegy, for the ignominy of the unfortunate,
Transforming defeat to a tremulous delight.

    They talked of technicalities, of the terms of their art,
The rules of englyns, and of runic riddles.
They were aware of words, and as if unaware

Of the battle that rolled and rattled beneath them,
Though committed to conquest for their own countrymen.
Their warfare was against words; they wanted only
To muster a meaning from the bloody mellay.
They knew, whatever victory at nightfall should be vaunted,
The eventual issue at the end should be only
In long futurity a late told legend,
A matter for lays, and for lyrical laments.
The mind of the masters, in the midst of that tumult –
Or was this their temptation? – touched upon the timeless,
On the silence that remains behind the sound of all song.
　　　Gwion said these staves, striking upon the strings:
"I have caught three drops from the cauldron of Ceridwen,
That flew up from the froth and foam of her brew.
They gave to my tongue the ungrateful gift
Of the telling of truth, and the terrible wisdom,
The bitter privilege the bard is bound to.
That moment transformed me; I moved out of time,
I become what I sing; and soothly I can say
I was in the height of Heaven with the Lord of Hosts
When Lucifer lapsed to the lowmost of Hell;
I bore a banner in the battle-order
Of Alexander, the offspring of Egyptian Ammon;
I was in Canaan when Absalom contested for the crown
And hung by his hair from the highest of the trees;
I was in the court of Danau, that dark deemstress,
Before the world had heard of your Woden and his wisdom;
Erstwhile I was instructor to Elijah and to Enoch;
I stood upon Calvary when the Christ was crucified;
For three periods was I penned in the prison of Arianrod;
A bystander, I directed, when Babylon was in building;
I was in Asia when the Ark anchored upon Ararat;
I saw the cities of the plain plunged in sulphur;
I was in the donkey's manger when Mary delivered,
Lowly and blessedly, the Lord in Bethlehem;
I gave mastery to Moses as he marched by Jordan;
I mounted to the firmament with Mary Magdalene;
I was at the court of Cunobelinus in the castle of London;
I am teacher and tutor to all intelligences,
To all cosmic powers I am called as a catechist,
And I shall dwell upon the Earth till the day of doom;
We find that the poet is neither fish nor flesh."
　　　Dourly deliberating, Daegrafn said:

"I know nothing of Ceridwen, nor of her cauldron;
I brag of my bellyful of the blood-mixed mead
Which Woden delivered from those dangerous dwarfs
Who had murdered, in their murky cave, the primaeval minstrel.
But I too am a traveller, in space and in time:
It is the wyrd of the poet to wander widely:
In the courts of kings and commanders of men,
The mighty and munificent, for the most part I have been.
With the lord of the Lombards in the land of Italy,
Alboin, and otherwhere among the Ostrogoths;
I have vaunted in song the Vandals and the Vikings;
I have exalted Odoacer and Eormanric also,
In the time before his mind was turned to tyranny,
So savagely against Swanhild, that he commanded his servants
To trample her under the hooves of his high-bred horses:
But the horses held back at the horror of that thing –
For the woman's eyes baffled them, they blazed so brightly,
Till he called for her countenance to be covered with a napkin;
I was with Hrothulf and Hrothgar when they ruled together,
And held sway in Heorot, that hall which was haunted;
I was with Finn Folcwalding who ruled over the Frisians;
I have sung my lays to the Letts and the Lithuanians,
And the Finns, those sorcerers, that scud through their fens;
Among Edomites and Israelites and the utmost Indians;
Among Picts and Scots in the peat bogs beyond Solway;
Among Parthians and Medes, and the magian Persians;
And with the Cæsar of the Greeks in their great city.
I can recite the names of rulers, and their racial history,
Monarchs over men, here in this middle garth;
I hold those most highly that are open-handed,
And ready as ring-givers to reward the poet.
These I will pay with praise, the one thing that is permanent
In this world where all things waver, transitory and weak.
Like the flight of a sparrow that fleetingly flits
Through a lighted hall, where is high feasting and laughter,
Dazzled, out of the darkness, and into the darkness once more,
There to be lost, is man's life, and his lot in this world.
At the end of all things shall be only existing
The fire and the frost, as they were at the first.
Things go as they will go; and the gods themselves
Shall know defeat – but they know also defeat
Is no final refutation, when Ragnarok rages.
Tiw, from the highest of the towers of heaven,

Looking down, languished for the love of a woman –
A sacrifice to that love, his sword was lost him;
Lacking that, he is fated at the last to fall
To the fangs of Fenris, the fiendish wolf.
I say this, and survey the uncertainty of this conflict."
        Gwion replied, rapt as in a reverie:
"Bound, in the womb of Britain, are those two Worms,
Which Merddyn discovered by the craft of his magic –
The red worm, as it rampages, stands for the Brythons,
The white one signifies the Saxons from the sea;
They writhe in their wrath, ruthlessly shaking down
All foundations from their fundaments, however fairly built –
Nor shall they stand, save by the blood of a son
From no mortal father; but I find that all our myths
And the horrors of our history, howsoever it is told,
Are images of their dream, the dialectic of those dragons:
They are Gwyrthyr ap Greidawl and Gwynn ap Nudd
Who every May Day morning, for the maiden Cordelia,
Are brought to battle by the blossoming hawthorn;
They are Prince Ferrex, and Porrex whom he fought,
Brothers of one womb; they are Brennus and Belinus –
Of the waning year and the waxing year
Daimones, and doubtful their destructive conflict:
Not till the tales of Time have all been told out
Shall one have the upper hand over the other.
I say this, and survey the uncertainty of this conflict."
        Such was their discourse, till the day star had passed its zenith,
And evening began over the battlefield of Badon.
The uncertain tide was turned; Cerdic and his Saxons
Fled from the field; fiercely the Brythons
Hoisted to Heaven a raucous Hallelujah,
Vaunting in chorus their Christian victory.
Gwalchmai and his henchmen rode to the grove of hazels,
Saluting Gwion, as he gazed upon them gladly
By the resounding title of radiant-browed Taliesin;
Daegrafn was handed over as a hostage to his household.
        Artorius was acclaimed: "We acknowledge the Ymherawdr.
Restore in these islands the regimen of Rome,
By right, after this rout. As our ram-horned Alexander
We salute you, and as Cæsar; seize then the imperium –
By our Prætorian suffrage we promote you to that power."
        But the Comes stood brooding. He turned to Bedwyr his
            butler:

502

"Am I hurried into hubris, or haltingly do I hesitate?
By what authority am I urged to the assumption of empire?
What precedents do they furnish, who put on the purple,
In these utmost islands, encouraged by ambition? –
Carausius cruising about our coasts with his pirates;
Or the murderous Maximus, who led away his mercenaries,
Depleting and debilitating the defences of Britain,
To the very walls of Rome – his reward for that recklessness
The scaffold, and the stroke of the public swordsman –
His end was vile, and Valentinian had the victory;
Or my great-grandsire, Constantine, who greedily
Aimed at empire, while Alaric attacked
The gates of Rome. He ravished Gaul
And seized on Spain. But Honorius sent
Forces to fight him. So he fell in battle;
And left the island leaderless and legionless.
Rome ruined. And we roughly fend
Now, for ourselves, in this northern outpost.
We have turned the tide, perhaps only for a time;
For a generation, maybe: let justice be enjoined –
Propping up a polity that belongs to the past,
Or a new-made redaction of republican rules,
Or count on customs which are local, the laws
Of the musty and mythical Mulmutius Dunwallo?
For the interim that is assigned, we will evoke an order."
        (Musing, Gwion muttered into his moustache:
"We evoke an order: an interim is assigned –
As a poet, perhaps, in the future predicament
Of the doubtfulness and dullness of a third Dark Age,
Might undertake the unfashionable inditing of an epic,
Though his colleagues and his confrères confined themselves
        merely
To little linguistic and logical constructs,
Or deployed their egos in the Dionysiac delirium
Of surreal illumination, or psychedelic self-indulgence –
He might establish an order, by the example of this experiment,
Driving his through-road across the thickets of thoughtlessness,
And he also if temporarily, might turn the tide –
But they come back, they come back again, those currents of
        meaninglessness;
Language lags, and languishes away –
The Daughter of Chaos reconsolidates her reign,
Universal Darkness, and delivers it to the dunces.")

Bedwyr the butler embraced Artorius:
"That the ravished land, my lord, you have recovered –
Forgive me, if I find it, in my fondness a small thing;
Personally, I care little if the purple clothe you,
Or imperial ornaments, if urged, you shall assume.
But I bless the destiny that has brought your body
Safe out of this slaughter, and your breast unscarred,
That I may have you and hold you, as heretofore I have done,
The lord whom I love, and it is my luck to serve –
At season of feasting to set food before you,
To dispose of your dishes, and dispense your drink;
It is the liquor of my heart that wholly I would hand you."
        Gwalchmai said: "Gloriously and grimly,
The bodies of our brothers lie unburied here on the field.
Let them be coffined and the cross of Christ
Be scratched as a signal on the stones that cover them;
Let Bedwini the bishop set about his business,
To direct them with a dirge through the dreary mosses
Of Acheron or Annwyn – anyway to avoid
The prickles of the furze, and the fires of Purgatory.
For that carrion heap of heathenish corpses –
We relinquish them to the kites, the crows and the ravens;
And let their unsanctified souls sneak away to Hell,
Their ghastly goddess, blue-faced and grim,
Holding her court in her cloudy kingdom."
        Artorius with authority answered that asking:
"Send Bedwini to see to the bodies of the baptised.
But as for those others, annexed to this earthwork
Let them be given burial: they were brave in battle.
Whatever rituals their religion, though wrong,
Prescribes for their passage, be duly paid them."
        Gaius the seneschal stood forth and said:
"If we were not here at Badbury, but in the hills above Bath,
We could go down to Bath, boys, and have a bath,
And remove, among the ruins, the relics of this mellay.
That city was first builded, they say, by King Bladud,
Who set up a temple for Sul, whom he served,
The palladium of that place, a peerless goddess,
The white-stoled Minerva of the mineral waters.
And from a pinnacle of that dome perilously he dared
To essay, like Icarus, the unstable air,
Leaping, with waxen wings, into the welkin;
Down to the bottom he fell, and battered out his brains:

A warning to the wise to beware of hubris.
Without benefit of bath we must retain our bloodstains;
But appetite urges us at any rate to eat.
Precious little of the provender I provided you remains –
Subsistence for a siege, surrounded on that mound.
But do you see what I see? – They might have been sent us:
Grazing upon the ground, on the further side of that grove,
Sheep at pasture, peacefully but with no shepherd.
Let us set to and slaughter them, and slake our hunger."
   No sooner had he said it, than they seized upon the flock,
And briefly went to work on the business of butchery,
Cutting their throats, and carving up the carcasses;
And a fire being ready, they fetched them to roasting.
But while their minds were merry at the prospect of the mutton,
They were all at once astonished by an unexpected apparition –
A fantastic figure, flailing its skinny arms,
With a bristly beard blowing in the wind,
And a patched cassock caught about his paunch.
It was Cadoc, the holy man, who with a huddle of hermits,
Woned in this wilderness, in wattle-built cabins,
With *Aves* and orisons at the hours of office.
His extreme squalor might be a scandal to the squeamish,
But denoted, doubtless, to the faithful devotee
He was set on the sanctified road towards Salem.
His wasted body was unwashed, and his beard
Uncombed and uncomely, his clothes all to tatters;
A loathsome legion of lice were at grass
Under his armpits, and all about
The pubic hairs of his personal parts.
He rushed towards the army, rabid in his rage,
Banging his book, clanging his bell,
Clutching his candle, and cantillating his bans:
"The malison of the martyrs, and of the holy maidens,
Of the apostles and of the evangelists, and of all the angels,
Of the prophets and the patriarchs, and all the citizens of Paradise,
Light upon you, you louts, for lawless brigands,
That have filched my flock, and the sheep of my fellows!
Artorius, son of Utherius, against you I urge this –
You bear of Britain, with your gang of bandits –
For your worrisome warfare, and your worthless victories,
Your senseless forays, and your sallies against the Saxons,
You pillage and plunder, stealing your pecks
Of barley-meal for your bag-pudding making,

The property of the saints, and sacred perquisites –
Chalices and chasubles stripped from the churches,
And the ornaments of the altar, apprehended for your armoury,
The metal melted down to be made into weapons;
And now it is my flock of muttons that you fall upon –
Cadoc calls down his curses upon you!"
    Gruffly, Gaius gave him his answer:
"You lazy layabout of a lubbardly priest,
Christ put a curb on your tongue for its carping!
Ungrateful and grudging – God has given us a victory
Over the horde of the heathen for the honour of His house.
You can say your prayers in peace now, by our leader's protection,
Unscared by those Saxons, for a month of Sundays.
Go back to your church and your chancel, and chant
Psalms and hymns to Heaven on our behalf,
Nor grudge us our dinner, after this day's doings."
    Artorius said to his steward and seneschal:
"Cannily, my Kai, answer him with courtesy –
Though I grant you such as he, and his greasy god-sibs,
Penning their jeremiads, punish my patience.
If we commandeered his cattle, we will pay compensation.
He taxes us with taking the treasures of the churches –
It was necessary; we needed them, or nothing would have remained
Of the calling of Christians here among the Cymry
In this savage onrush of the unbaptised Saxons.
But all shall be set in order, now that advantage is ours –
The chapels shall be restored, and the Church shall be cherished."
    Mollified somewhat, the sour-faced monk,
In more aulic accents, answered Artorius:
"If indeed it is your choice to cherish the Church,
Let a synod be assembled for her inward sanitation.
For the Hydra of heresy hisses through the land;
And Manichæans, and Gnostics, and Modalists, and Montanists,
And Monophysites, and Nestorians, and Millenarians, and
    Marciomites.
And Ebionites, and Antinomians, and Origenists, and Arians,
And every false and foolish, feather-pated opinion
Breathes its infection abroad here in Britain –
But principally the Pelagians, with porridge in their brainpans,
Morgan's mob, spread about their madness,
Cunningly confounding the Catholic doctrine,
Bid us haul ourselves into Heaven by our own bootstraps:
A belief congenial to our blunt-headed Britons,

As I daresay it always will be till the Day of Doom.
Let them be anathematised – outlawed, by the outraged orthodox!
I am moved by his zeal to admire Maximus that he meted out
To the proud Priscillian for his puerile fancies
The flame and the faggots, to pay for his falsity."
    Artorius said: "That sending to the stake
Was a horror unheard of heretofore in Christendom,
And a pernicious precedent for the future to preserve;
But the Roman pontiff, the Pope, was enraged
Against Maximus for that murder, who had no mandate for it.
All things shall be ordered, but by argument and exegesis
Of learned men; and let the Lady of Love,
Exalted Urania, be the arbiter of their acts.
This then be my sentence; and a synod shall be summoned."

URANIA

ILLTUD. BEDWINI.

ILLTUD: I would ask you, reverend father, to furnish me with
some account of that synod of the Church in Britain which
Artorius summoned after he had been granted victory on
the field of Mount Badon. For I was only a child at that
time, and later I bore arms in others of the battles which
Artorius fought. And only subsequently I put on the habit
of religion.

BEDWINI: It was held to repress the hydra of heresy; but that
mythical water-snake, you remember, grew three heads
each time one of its nine necks was severed. After the
victory at Badon, Artorius's forces pressed eastwards, with
the object of recapturing the city of London, advancing
along the valley of the Thames. Now where the Thame
and the Isis are conjoined, to form the Thamesis, there is
an island among the marshes. It is said that a certain royal

507

virgin, who had embraced the Christian faith and who wished to consecrate her virginity to God, being pursued by a neighbouring prince, a pagan, who intended to make her his wife, came to this place. She was riding upon an ox, and the waters barred her progress. So she said to the beast: "Ox, forth!," and obeying her it forded the river and carried her to that place of safety. And from that saying of hers the place took its name.

ILLTUD: It was at this spot then, that the synod was held? But I have heard that because of the extreme hostility of that holy maiden to the prince who so importunately pursued her, that island bodes ill luck to any Briton claiming the royal authority who presumes to set foot on it.

BEDWINI: Artorius was as yet only designated by the title of Comes or count. But afterwards he acceded to the requests of the people and assumed the royal and imperial crown.

ILLTUD: At what season of the year was this synod held?

BEDWINI: In the month of April, when the sun enters the sign of Taurus. The planet Venus is the ruler of that house, as astrologers say. And if we are to believe them, her influences might not be unpropitious for such a gathering: for we are to consider that Plato, in his *Symposium*, says that there are two Venuses. Venus Pandemia is she who presides over that love which springs from the senses. But Venus Urania is divine love, and leads the soul to the contemplation of truth.

ILLTUD: Manilius, in his poem, also makes Venus the guardian of that house. For his system differs somewhat from that of the generality of those who have written upon the subject of astronomy. For most of the latter divide the twelve signs of the Zodiac between the seven planetary rulers. They assign the Sun to Leo, and the Moon to Cancer, and to the remaining five planets two each of the other ten signs. Thus the sign of Virgo, which follows Leo, is given to the planet Mercury; and from thence, in succession, we move outwards to Saturn, who is the ruler of Capricorn. Saturn is also the ruler of the next sign, Aquarius; and from thence, again in succession, we move inwards till

508

we reach Mercury, who is the ruler of Gemini, which pre-
cedes the sign of Cancer. But Manilius apportions the
twelve signs to the twelve Olympian deities: beginning
with Pallas in the sign of Aries. Then follow Venus, Apollo,
Mercury, Jupiter (with Juno), Ceres, Vulcan, Mars, Diana,
Vesta, and Juno (with Jupiter), ending with Neptune in
the sign of Pisces.

BEDWINI: I do not possess your detailed learning on this subject.
Nor do I think these matters should very much concern
Christians. For does not the Apostle teach us that neither
height nor depth, nor principalities nor powers, nor
heavenly rulers, nor any creature is able to separate us
from the Love of God?

ILLTUD: It was you, father, who first introduced this topic. But
indeed, we seem to have strayed from the subject of our
discourse. Let Urania, then, be our muse – to lift our eyes
to the stars of doctrine, the constellations not of a visible
but of an invisible heaven.

BEDWINI: The weather of April is uncertain, nevertheless the
synod was held in the open air. Artorius presided under
an oak tree, exercising that diaconal surveyance which in
a Christian commonwealth is the prerogative, and the only
prerogative, of all lawfully constituted authority. He exercised it, not as having yet received the diaconal stole, but
on behalf of the distant Emperor who sat at Byzantium.

ILLTUD: And the weather, it is to be hoped, remained clement?

BEDWINI: The air was loud with early nightingales. Some indeed
complained that the song of these birds distracted their
meditations, and a motion was put that they should be
exorcised. But this suggestion was not generally favoured,
and those who supported it were indeed suspected of
being tainted with the Manichæan heresy.

ILLTUD: And were, in fact, many of the leaders of the heretical
sects in Britain persuaded to attend?

BEDWINI: Very many. On the one side sat various sorts of Gnostics, twiddling their flowers and tinkling their cow-bells.

It was said that demons in flying saucers descended from the celestial spheres to whisper instructions to them. But I cannot find that this was actually observed to occur. On the other side sat the bull-necked Pelagians, believing in the indomitable human spirit and in the march of progress – and with scourges ready for the backs of anyone who failed to live up to these ideals. And in the centre, between these two opposing parties, the Millenarians. They believed in the imminent return of the Saviour, with a large cargo of barrels of salt beef and bottles of cheap wine, and pension-books for all his followers. And hell-fire for everybody else. They were provided with massive documentation – measurements of the Great Pyramid, apocryphal apocalypses, and sibylline and hermetic palimpsests and pseudepigrapha.

ILLTUD: These are the adulteries of the rebellious head and the disordered heart. I hope you will tell me what arguments were put forward to rebut their unfortunate opinions.

BEDWINI: It was many years ago, and I am now an old man. I cannot say that I remember them exactly. Let it suffice that the great definitions of Nicaea and Chalcedon, of Ephesus and Constantinople, were reaffirmed; definitions which do not state what is to be believed, so much as what is not – saying to the deep, "so far and no further."

ILLTUD: For we are not wiser than our fathers. One might regard it as a satisfactory conclusion, and worthy of universal acceptance.

BEDWINI: Many did not accept, and excluded themselves. And I recall that the hermit Cadoc was expelled for an obscure heresy, which no one, including himself, had hitherto suspected that he entertained.

ILLTUD: I have been told that he was not chastened by this experience. Nor have his manners improved.

BEDWINI: But among the most there was great rejoicing that peace and order had been restored to the Church. And the same evening Artorius invited the holy fathers to a lavish supper. The poet Gwion composed an impromptu encomium

for the occasion, and the Saxon poet Daegrafn also furnished the company with a specimen of the interesting
but less subtle art of his people. The wine circulated freely
with Artorius and his courtiers, and the abstract ideas previously mooted were re-discussed, not always with discretion. One must say with regret that Venus Pandemia
replaced Venus Urania. For the sister of Artorius, the
Queen of Orkney, was present. The love between them
was more than is lawful between brother and sister, and
on the night following the day on which purity of doctrine
was restored to the Church in Britain, was Modred begotten.

ILLTUD: I am grateful for all the information you have given me,
and I would gladly hear more. But the sun now begins to
decline in the western sky.

BEDWINI: Let us then, at this hour, make our orisons to the
Unbrided Bride, the Queen of Heaven. And at this season
it will be fitting that we ask her to intercede for us that we
may be guarded from the sin of immoderate laughter.

ILLTUD: In that prayer I will gladly join you.

THALIA

II

*(Scene: Marshy fenland country. Behind a stagnant pool stands
a rude hut of reeds. Enter* GWION *and* DAEGRAFN, *accoutred as
for hunting.)*

GWION: That great white stag, with the nine tines,
Has led us far away from the rest of the party,
Artorius and Gwalchmai and the others
Hunting in these eastern marches. It eludes us,
As the word continually eludes the idea.
Perhaps the white stag of Artemis

511

Which Heracles pursued through the Arcadian mountains,
Till the goddess, descending, claimed it for her own.
But I fear this is no innocent Arcadia,
For we have come to the frontiers where the East Angles
Possess the land, a hostile territory.

DAEGRAFN: I do not think they have found their way
Among these marshy windings of the Cam;
And if they should, I have certain passwords,
Certain secret and runic symbols,
Which may serve to protect us both.
I received them as part of my instruction as a scop.

GWION: I hope then it is permitted
You teach them me sometime. It would be interesting.
Captured in the battle, you were delivered into my house-
hold,
And now I regard you as my brother and my colleague.

DAEGRAFN: I have of course sworn to preserve them inviolate,
With certain very bloody oaths – to gods
I do not any longer think I believe in.
You know that Bedwini receives me as a catechumen.
I have confessed those secrets to him, having an idea
Perhaps he may find them useful one day,
Going on some mission behind the enemy lines.
We Saxons are a perfidious lot.

GWION: But at present the Saxon advance seems checked.
The voice of the people demands
Artorius assume the imperial dignity
Here in this island. He cannot long hold out.
Sooner or later he will go to Caerleon,
There to be crowned. And I shall be commissioned
To compose his coronation poem.
Well, I suppose a Pindaric ode might serve.

DAEGRAFN: The sunshine of May beats down upon these marshes,
Bright with ladies' smock and kingcups.
The cuckoo calls over the water meadows, and the sedge
warbler
Dryly discourses. The spot is pleasant enough.
Let us give up, then, the pursuit of that stag.

Which seems so hopeless. We are both fagged out,
And could do with some rest and refreshment,
If any sojourn here among the fens.

GWION: Now I think of it, there is an old tradition
That King Bladud, one time
Ruler of this land and father of Lear,
Sought to establish here, in former times,
Long centuries ago, a seat of learning.
Philosophers from Athens settled here,
Academics and Peripatetics,
Epicureans far from their garden,
And the austere school of the painted Porch,
Together with rhetoricians and grammarians,
To instruct our blue-stained Brythons
In Ionian subtleties. Here they erected
A temple to the abstract mathematical muse,
Doubtless it is ruined now. But I have heard
One last descendant of those learned men,
Phyllidulus by name, still hangs on,
Delivering daily lectures on poetry.

DAEGRAFN: He must be, one might think,
A trifle short of students.

GWION: That is indeed the case.
He has no one to instruct except the tadpoles,
That swarm in these green pools, all swollen head
And ineffectual tail, and nothing in between.
Eagerly they absorb the Master's judgments;
But nourished only by the handfuls of stale breadcrumbs
He scatters for them on the water's surface,
They are not able to mature in growth,
Remaining fixed in their watery existence,
Instead of becoming, as benevolent Nature
Doubtless intended, mature amphibians –
High-skipping frogs, or respectable toads
(Each with a jewel hidden in his skull)
Or fiery-bellied newts and salamanders.

DAEGRAFN: Something ought to be done
To remedy this distressing situation.

513

GWION: Indeed it should.
          And, as a matter of fact, Artorius
          Commissioned the courteous Gwalchmai, who com-
              missioned me,
          To clear the conduits of rhetoric in this land.
          That was after the synod he held on the Thames,
          By the Ox's ford. Ideas were clarified,
          The hissing and indefinite hydra suppressed.
          Let language also be clarified,
          Here by the banks of Cam.

DAEGRAFN: Someone is coming.
          Perhaps he can direct our way.

          (Enter IANTO.*)*

GWION: Stop a minute, friend
          Though you seem to be in a hurry. Can you kindly direct us
          To the place where the learned Phyllidulus dwells?

IANTO: That I certainly can. And who better than I? –
          For it's I who look after him. I am, in fact, his gyp.
          I am just now going down to the river bank
          To try and capture a roach or a perch or a pike
          To furnish his dinner. This is the very place.
          He lives in that reed hut, and he is inside now,
          Mugging up the notes for his morning lecture.

GWION: Not a very commodious dwelling
          For a distinguished scholar – I hope
          You look after him well?

IANTO: I do my best, sir.
          And then, there is, of course, Miss Lalage
          To give a touch of feminine refinement.

DAEGRAFN: Miss Lalage? – Then, the learned Phyllidulus
          Is not without the consolation
          Of female companionship.

IANTO: Don't get the wrong idea –
          Miss Lalage is his ward. Some sixteen years ago
          He was walking among the swamps, and meditating

About a disputed interpretation in Alciphron,
When he came across the tender infant, lying
Upon a lily-pad, and suckled
By a female water-vole, whose own young
Had been devoured by a marsh harrier.
He took her home to his reed hut,
And, he and his wife, Basilissa, reared her
As their own daughter, educating her
In grammar, rhetoric and dialectic.
She is, in fact, his most promising pupil.
And he has declared that he will give her hand
To whichever of his tadpoles
Shall first attain froghood. She helps about the place,
Rakes out the cinders, and sits among them
To warm her pretty toes; but then she pines
For that imperial palace, whence, she sometimes thinks,
    she came,
In short, she dreams she dwelt in marble halls.

GWION: We would like to meet the learned Phyllidulus;
    And we would certainly like to see poor Lalage –
    Perhaps something can be done for her.

IANTO: The tadpoles will soon be assembling
    To hear his morning lecture. You might
    Discreetly hide behind this alder stump.
    But I must go now.

    (*Exit* IANTO, *full pelt*)

GWION: Let us certainly do as this fellow suggests.

    (GWION *and* DAEGRAFN *conceal themselves. The* CHORUS *of
    tadpoles surfaces in the pool.*)

CHORUS: Mighty Master of the schools,
    Visit these green-mantled pools;
    There's no problem but you'll fix it
    With a resounding *ipse dixit*;
    We, the tadpoles of this damp
    Miasmal and malarial swamp
    Await you, son of Aristotle –
    But each is but an axolotl;

Pituitary deficiency
Hampers our efficiency,
And not the strictest criticism
Can save us from infantilism.
Yet still we trust your scrutiny
In upper air shall make us free,
And from the waters liberate us,
Till we assume batrachian status.
Then, risen from this puddly deep
Through the meadows we shall leap,
Singing to the echoing backs
Our loud "Brekekekek-Koax!"

(Enter PHYLLIDULUS *from the reed hut,* LALAGE *following him.)*

PHYLLIDULUS: Ah, one sees we are all assembled on time.
Lalage, my dear, will you kindly fill up the class register,
And then take your accustomed seat at my feet.
Now I will begin my lecture.

Tadpoles and polywogs, I propose this morning to continue the course I began last May. This is, I think, about the three hundred and sixtieth lecture in the introductory series of my prolegomena to poetry. One would much prefer to expatiate upon one's contemporaries. But, living as we do at the beginning of the Second Dark Age, we can detect little in the landscape which is likely to serve to provide much nourishment for our minds. One is aware that there are grammarians in Massilia, but one is not sure whether one has come across their productions. Here in this island, one notes with a certain hopefulness that the victories of Artorius have initiated a degree of stability – it may be only temporary – in the social situation from which, one might venture, with some optimism, to envisage eventually the burgeoning, if not the flourishing, of a literature which might go beyond, in some measure, the crudities of primordial epic lays or the mere technical virtuosities of Celtic panegyric and bardic exercises, but one cannot, with whatever a degree of sanguineness, even of charitable openness when one casts one's eye on what is currently being produced, discover much to substantiate such expectations. One is aware that a certain brother has made claims for, has even purported to find an interest in, not only the productions of Gwion, who occupies, one gathers, the position of a pensioned poet in the court, but even in those of his friend, the Saxon poet (if that is how one must describe him) Daegrafn. Such of their verses as have come one's way do not, one fears, prompt one to any measure of concurrence.

One is compelled, in short, to go back to the Romans. My remarks this morning will therefore be designed towards a brief revaluation of those Latin poets, which established academic criticism continues to accord, however mistakenly, one may suspect, a certain degree of reverence. One cannot find, for example, that the attempt of Lucretius to unite with poetry the aridities of atomic physics engendered in him any degree of unification of sensibility. There was also, of course, Catullus. One can only peruse with a certain feeling of distaste the lyrics prompted by that unfortunate young man's affair with the notorious Clodia. *'Odi et Amo'*, he says, – and what kind of logical sense, one asks, does that make? One must conclude, with great regret, that that in which some not unperceptive minds have been prepared to detect an expression of passion can only furnish to the reader habituated to a more stringent critical approach to what he reads, little more than the outpourings of a self-indulgent and essentially puerile (one must, it is to be feared, too often add, and prurient) emotionalism. It was said that Augustus found Rome brick and left it marble – and something analogous occurred to poetry in the same generation. One may happen to prefer brick. Marmoreal is a term that has been applied to the *Odes* of Horace. If this style be marble, it is a veneer which does not serve to conceal the writer's essential commonplaces of mind – a commonplaceness which infuses likewise the whole corpus of his epistles: the superficial observations of a man about town, even if he chooses to make them from a convenient country retirement. One has on several previous occasions, one hopes with sufficient cogency, demonstrated the case against the style of Virgil. One presumes, therefore, that it is unnecessary, at this juncture, to go over yet again the *Aeneid*, with its uncolloquial rhetoric and its empty melodising. As for the *Eclogues*, they present us with an unreal world, without even in any effectual degree attempting to imitate the simplicity of rusticity or, for that matter, the rusticity of simplicity. Of the poetry of Ovid, little, one may hope, need now be said. Apart from its diffuseness, and the banality which some would appear to have mistaken for wit, it presents, one can only say, the loose (in every sense of that word) expression of a peculiarly unpleasant mind. This consideration leads me now to Propertius and Tibullus...

(GWION *and* DAEGRAFN *come forward.*)

GWION: Stop! Stop! One cannot bear any more of this.

DAEGRAFN: By what right, sir, do you thus sit adjudicating the
      poets?
      By our English custom, they should be judged by their peers.

PHYLLIDULUS: And who, may I ask, are you gentlemen?
      Having so discourteously interrupted my lecture,
      What account can you give of yourselves?

GWION: Tutor and instructor to all intelligences,
      I was loquacious before the beginning of speech;
      I am of a nature which is not certainly known,
      None can tell if I am fish or flesh.
      I was bound in the cauldron of the hag Ceridwen,
      And now I am come to the remnant of Troia.
      I rode to Canterbury in the sweet showers of April,
      And was fined for beating a Franciscan in Fish Street;
      I was with Samson in the mill of Gaza,
      And in blindness I gazed on the throne of the Distributor;
      I paid the reckoning in the inn of Deptford,
      And was with Tamberlaine when Bajazeth was taken;
      I marked the curfew in the churchyard of Stoke Poges;
      I saw the ladder between Heaven and Charing Cross;
      I howled like a dog in the cloisters of Chichester;
      I was in the firmament at the fall of Hyperion;
      I was subject to an assault in the narrowness of Rose Alley,
      And was with the evil counsellor of Absalom;
      I distributed a pamphlet on the Necessity of Atheism,
      And was with Prometheus in the rocks of Caucasus.

DAEGRAFN: I was instructed by an angel in the cow-byre of Whitby:
      I was distributor of stamps for the County of Westmorland,
      And encountered the leech-gatherer by the solitary pool;

I administered an emetic to the pornographer in the tavern,
And saw the Anarch let fall the curtain;
I heard the chorus of Pities when the Dynasts contended;
I constructed the pleasuredome of Kubla Khan;
I dreamed a dream on the hills of Malvern;
I scrawled the Song of David on the walls of Bedlam;
I perpetrated forgery, I choked upon arsenic;
I held horses outside the Theatre –
And made a threne for the phœnix and the turtle;
I marked the dead stroke of St Mary Woolnoth;
When the bell tolled, it tolled for me.

GWION: I danced around perambulators on Putney Common;
I was in Golgonooza when Albion was awakened;
I was under milkwood on the hill of Llaregyb;
I was with Rustum when Sohrab was slain;
I saw the vanity of testimony in a book and a ring;
I was captive in the Castle of Indolence;
I served the altar in the temple of Bemerton;
I was the queen of the island of Gondal;
I composed the epitaph for a hare never hunted;
I hung on cliffs of fall, in the mind's mountains.

DAEGRAFN: I spoke as a parrot against the pride of the cardinal;
I indited an ode for the Palace of Crystal;
I was in Amalfi when the Duchess was strangled;
I declined a cup of water on the field of Zutphen;
I was present when the congress of philosophers
Detected in astonishment an elephant in the moon;
I suffered the fever at Missolonghi,
And was with Juan in the court of Catherine;
I was in Ireland when the house was burnt,
And by the waters of Thames running softly to my song;
I was alone in the asylum of Northampton...

PHYLLIDULUS: Just now you asked me, somewhat peremptorily,
If I would stop. I think I have the right
To ask the same of you. What is all this?
It can hardly be said to convey
Information in answer to my question.
And if it is supposed to be poetry,
One can only venture the opinion that it is...

DAEGRAFN: Pray, sir, do not re-commence your lecture.
We boasted our credentials here as poets.

PHYLLIDULUS: If poets are to be judged by their peers, who is to
establish
Which are indeed the true poets? One can only answer
A trained, objective, critical mind.

GWION: Such, one presumes, as yours?

PHYLLIDULUS: Well, if not, what else would you propose?
Will you substantiate your claims by miracle?

GWION: Look well at this.

(They draw small phials from the folds of their garments.)

DAEGRAFN: And this.
It contains one drop of the blood-mixed mead,
That Woden stole from the dwarfs who guarded it.

GWION: And this, one drop from the cauldron of Ceridwen –
The nightmare hag at the world centre –
Kindled by the breath of nine maidens.

DAEGRAFN: The contents of these phials
We will pour into your pool,
And then you will see what you will see.

*(They do so. The pool froths and bubbles. Then the waters turn
clear, and a large golden waterlily rises in the centre and opens
to the sun. The tadpoles become frogs and other amphibians, and
leap onto the dry land.)*

CHORUS: Transformed into a higher kind,
At last we leave our tails behind;
Each is now a toad or frog
Hopping gaily round the bog,
Eft or newt or salamander,
In the upper air we wander;
Conforming to a different norm,
And almost, now, of human form;
By water meadow, stream and ford

520

We will sing unto the Lord –
Sing unto the Lord, by heck! –
Koax-brekekekekek!
Is not that a witticism?
A fig for your old criticism!

PHYLLIDULUS: What is all this? Student unrest among the tadpoles?

GWION: No. Dr Phyllidulus, they have simply
    All of a sudden grown up. And remember
    You are committed to give your ward, Lalage here,
    In marriage to whichever of them
    Should first become a frog.

LALAGE: Oh dear,
    But they have all become frogs,
    At one and the same identical moment;
    I can't possibly marry all of them.

PHYLLIDULUS: Then you will have to choose
    Whichever of them you think most beautiful.

DAEGRAFN: Perhaps she may not think any of them very beautiful.
    But maybe they have beautiful voices.

GWION: Then let her choose by that. Come, little frogs,
    Now sing a serenade to Lalage.

CHORUS: Lalage, oh Lalage,
    Our love is like an allergy;
    Your delicious curves and dimples
    Raise upon our skin goose pimples.
    Though we are amphibious
    Do not tell a fib to us;

    Deign, o deign to take in hand
    One of us batrachians.
    You shall have a lover fond
    At the bottom of the pond;
    A bridal bower, it's understood,
    Finely dight in the rich mud,
    Where the mud nymphs dance and play
    To celebrate your wedding day.

PHYLLIDULUS: Bless my soul, this is intolerable!
          All the principles of criticism
          One has been teaching them for years
          Seem completely to be forgotten!

GWION: Well, dear frogs, if your master means by that
          It is not particularly good poetry
          I am forced to agree with him. But it is a beginning.

PHYLLIDULUS: Now, Lalage, my dear
          Which of them will you choose?

LALAGE: They are good creatures in their way, and I suppose
          They even have a certain beauty. But I must confess
          I personally find them very unattractive.
          I don't really want to marry any of them.
          And I don't want to live at the bottom of a pond,
          With only the water scorpions and the whirligig beetles
          To provide me entertainment. I sometimes fancy
          I was meant for better things. Oh sirs,
          Is there nothing you can do for me
          To rescue me from this predicament?

GWION: In cases like this, the only solution
          Is to petition a god or so
          To descend to earth in a machine
          And set things to rights.

DAEGRAFN: Which gods shall we invoke then?

GWION: Whom, but our special patrons, the masters
          Of Eloquence and Poetry: the bright-haired
          Hyperborean Apollo, whom in our Celtic tongue
          We call Maponos, and Mercury –
          Master of the roads and of communication –
          Who is the same with your Germanic Woden,
          The broad-hatted and vatic wanderer.
          Shall we call on them both together, antiphonally?

DAEGRAFN: You have more learning in these things than I.
          I am quite content you should speak for the two of us.

GWION: Bright Apollo, master
  Of the golden lyre, ruler
  Of the Delphian plain, where you quelled
  The mud-engendered snake, and where
  Your sacred prophetess, inspired
  By the toxic laurel, seated upon her tripod,
  Over the cleft of the earth, speaks oracles;

    And you, Hermes, herald, and guide
  Of wayfarers, and of the bloodless
  Wavering shades of the dead
  On their last journey – you we invoke
  Brothers, and friends on Olympus:
  Descend, and attend the supplication
  Which here we offer, prayer on behalf of one
  Distressed in the dark dilemmas of this world!

    You, Hermes, when you had been born
  In the Cylenian cave, ventured out
  Into the air, and left
  Your mother, the white-armed Maia, sleeping:

    At the mouth of the cave you found
  A slow-paced tortoise – Chelone,
  The unpunctual nymph, who was late
  For the wedding feast of Zeus and Hera, transformed,
  As punishment into that shape.

    With a sharp stone you scooped
  The creature from its portable house, and from the entrails
  You made vibrating chords; and these you strung
  Across the empty shell. The lyre was invented.

    And then you spoke; "Chelone,
  From now onwards you will be an honoured guest
  At wedding feasts and festivals – the sweet-toned lyre,
  Dear to the hearts of men!"

    Then you went on your way, until you found
  The white oxen of Apollo, feeding
  Within a flowery meadow; and these you stole,
  Dragging them by their tails back to the cave –
  Patron of thieves – and made a hearty breakfast.

When Apollo, the Lycian archer,
Descending from Olympus, found that his property
Had vanished thus, he was distinctly enraged.

No crime can be concealed from those pure eyes,
Nor go unavenged! The celestial inspector
Examined the clues, put two and two together
And traced his stolen cattle to the cave.

And there he found a marvel, the precocious child
Sitting among the sucked-dry marrow bones,
And contentedly strumming on his new-made toy.

Furious, he haled the delinquent to Olympus,
To appear before the high court of the gods,
And made his accusation. Zeus frowned;
But when the marvellous boy played on his lyre
They were all enchanted, and their hearts softened with
    pleasure.

He offered the wonderful invention to his brother,
As compensation for the theft. Apollo accepted it,
And ever afterwards the lyre
Has been the peculiar delight of the bright god;
With it he leads the Muses in their dances.

Apollo and Hermes are firm friends now on Olympus;
For what is the good of the abstraction of pure Mind
Without Communication? What good is Communication,
Without the grace of Beauty? These we invoke.

(APOLLO *and* MERCURY *descend from heaven in a machine.*)

MERCURY: We are here at your prayer. And kindly tell us
    Of what particular assistance we can be.

GWION: Here is, we have every reason to think, a virgin
    In dire distress. Unless you do something about it
    She is fated to marry a clammy cold-blooded frog.
    Can you not rescue her, as once the Dioscuri
    Delivered their little sister Helen
    From the cold embrace of the ageing Theseus?

APOLLO: Let me observe this virgin. Ah yes,
My all-seeing eye, which discerns the inner nature
Of things in heaven and earth, informs me who she is.
Lalage, child – for so you are called
By mortal men – know that among the gods
You are named Chrysophone: the youngest of the bright
Choir of Muses, that sing eternally
About the throne of Zeus.

MERCURY: Allow me to explain. Mnemosyne,
The Great Memory of the World, is the Mother of the Muses,
Nine sweet-voiced sisters whose immortal names
Are honoured far and wide by gods and men.
But Mnemosyne had a tenth daughter, the child
Of her old age; and I regret to say,
In her old age, Mnemosyne
Grew somewhat absent minded. Walking one day
By the clear river of heaven, the streaming Galaxy,
She put the child down, intending
To take a brief siesta. But while she nodded
The infant slipped into the starry stream,
And was carried along to the limits of the sky,
To where she fell, like a glittering meteor, down to earth;
But none exactly knew upon what spot
Of earth the child landed. Ever since,
The gods have been looking everywhere for you.
Zeus has offered a reward of ten golden apples
To anyone who can find you. We shall claim that now.

APOLLO: Lalage, you must ascend to heaven with us;
So say farewell to the frogs, and say farewell
To the marshy banks of Cam, and the learned Phyllidulus
Who has so kindly looked after you all these years.

LALAGE: So it's goodbye then. And I am half sorry to go;
And if Olympian regulations permit,
I shall come again to visit this western island,
And be its special Muse. And, by the lucid streams of Avon,
Cam and Isis, Thames and Usk and Duddon,
And silver Trent, I'll seek out my elect
And favoured friends – young poets, dreaming
In chequered rides of sunlit woods,
On moon-touched mountains, or in fœtid dens,

Urban or suburban; and I will teach them
The secrets of my new home,
Apollo's music, and swift Hermes' eloquence.

DAEGRAFN: Well, frogs, it seems you must be disappointed.
Lalage shall be bride to none of you. But put a good face on it.
Sing her a final chorus as she ascends –
A song in praise of this island she has chosen!

(*The* GODS, *with* LALAGE, *begin to ascend in their machine.*)

GWION: I will give you the tune, frogs.
Henry Purcell will compose it,
One day, for an opera on King Arthur.

CHORUS: Fairest Isle, all isles excelling,
Vironing the bogs and fens,
Here the Muse shall fix her dwelling,
And forsake Parnassian glens.

Phœbus, from his fav'rite nation
Shall remove (as he thinks fit)
All that curbs poetic passion,
Dullness, too, that stifles wit.

Every critic, as in duty,
To the poets shall be kind:
Those shall be the priests of beauty
These the prophets of the Mind.

DAEGRAFN: You begin to improve, little frogs, so be it.

PHYLLIDULUS: One has, if grudgingly, to concede that. But I
Have been made the protagonist of a shoddy farce –
An improper blend of the Old and the New Comedy.
I shall abandon these ungrateful tadpoles, and these soggy
fens,
And become a shepherd on the northern hills,
Instructing the woolly sheep with a hemlock pipe.

GWION: It would be better, Phyllidulus, if you would consent
To take up residence at the court of Artorius.
Our half-barbarous, half-Roman nobles

Could benefit from contact with a mind
Of critical discrimination.

PHYLLIDULUS: Well, perhaps,
One might bring oneself to consider that.
But Lalage is gone!

GWION: Where none of us can follow her.
But the way up is the way down – so Heraclitus says:
He who would seek the Muse, he who would seek
To marry himself to any kind of sovereignty,
Must make the descent down to the earth's centre,
To face his utmost fears, and his most secret anxieties.

DAEGRAFN: Come, my friend, it is time to continue the chase
Of the White Stag, of the unattainable.

CALLIOPE II

Come back, Calliope, at call; we have been straying
With some of your sisters down sylvan byways.
But now it is the solstice, and the sun in splendour,
Caught in the claws of the watery Crab,
At the topmost of his career turns at the tropic,
And at Midsummer moves to a retrograde motion.
This is the mansion of the Moon, and a time for mysteries:
This sign also signalled the beginning of my sojourn
Upon the earth, and by that augury I am oblique,
Cradled by the Crab, crustaceous and devious,
And moved by the subjective moods of Selene –
The more fitted, by that potency, for this project which I pass to;
To describe a descent to the depths of creation,
And Artorius even underneath the earth
Moving his wars; warily I make for it.
        It is the Vigil of the Baptist; now bonfires are built

To feed and furnish the sun with fire
At his height, and with heat for the ripening harvest.
But my scene is placed on the plain of Sarum,
In the huge circle of the hanging stones;
At the centre of a city of the dead, surrounded
By a vast necropolis of nameless notabilities,
The cairns and barrows of the kings of Britain,
Unmarked and unhonoured from utmost ages.
At midnight, the moon mysteriously casts down,
And lucidly, her cold and colourless light,
On two figures which I find there; and the first I recognise –
It is Artorius, indeed, in armour for his initiation,
As the moonlight glimmers and glances on his greaves.
But the other is of aspect more antique and more awe-ful,
Uncouth and unkempt, and crowned with oak leaves:
The son who had no human, as they say, for a sire,
But an incubus of the air, that urged its embraces
On an enclosed vestal, vowed to virginity,
A Christian nun, clandestinely in the night.
It seems that the devils in their den had devised this,
That the actual Antichrist might issue upon earth,
Being brought to birth; but baptism forestalled it,
And frustrated the filthy politics of the fiends.
It is Merddyn, last master of the magian traditions
Which the Druids deliberated and divulged to their pupils,
Closely guarded in collegiate confraternities,
Among the stone circles and the solitary groves.
        With authority he addressed the armoured Artorius:
"By the popular acclaim of the crowd now, the crown
Will be placed upon your brow; to that power you are bidden –
Useless to avoid it; accept the anointing,
And the blessing that Bedwini the bishop shall confer on you.
But first you must be sent to find what you shall find,
To the centre of the earth, to shred off all your shells,
And know your own nakedness, and your utmost nothingness.
By stages descend through the deepest strata,
Through marl and minerals, to the heart of matter,
Formed at the first by the primæval fires,
Till finally you come to Ceridwen and her cauldron,
Where she sits at the centre; and seek her gift,
Your Luck – and may it last you as long as you live.
        "Hold your heart high, for this is no hunting
Of the Erymanthian Boar, nor his bristly brother

The tusker Trwyth, I tell you. You go after
The subterranean Sow who consumes her farrow.
Do you accept this, Uther's son?" And Artorius made answer:
"If so your wisdom directs. But where is the way,
The gate through which I shall go to this grim descent?"
Merddyn replied, the magian master:
"The entrance to the Underworld is everywhere and anywhere;
But we seek it here in the centre of this Circle.
And I put into your hand a passport to purvey you thither."
          Then he drew from the folds of his dress a flower,
Golden and bright; no botanist gathers it:
The flower of the fern, that is found only
In a timeless moment, at a Midsummer midnight.
He gave it to Artorius, who gazed upon it awestruck.
And he said: "Touch with this that stone which you see
In the heart of the Henge; it was the high altar,
In times long since, of this temple of the Sun."
Artorius obeyed the offspring of the incubus,
Touching the great block with that tremulous blossom;
And with a rending at its roots the rugged slab
Slowly reared up, sucking at the soil.
And underneath was uncovered an enormous abyss,
Darkness going down to the depths of the earth,
Like an unplumbed well; in wonder he peered in,
Nor shrank back in horror of the shadows that showed there.
"I am ready to descend," he said, "But dearly would I desire
You should go with me as my guide into that dim gulf –
As the Cumæan Sybil, for his comfort companioned
Our ancestor Aeneas exploring Avernus,
Or as the sire, Africanus, Scipio in his *Somnium*."
          "Or as Virgil himself," said Merddyn, "In a vision as yet
                    unvouched.
But I cannot undertake to guide you; it is not time for me to go
Down into that womb, though one day I will –
When the Sow, by her name of Nimue, shall ensnare me,
And I am penned in her dungeon till the day of Doom;
You will call then in vain for my comfort and my counsel.
But I will send for a Guide, assigned for your going."
          Then Merddyn forthwith put two fingers in his mouth,
With a shrill, sharp whistle, just as a shepherd
Summons his dog to his side to do him service.
Then silently, silhouetted in the silver of the moonlight,
A shadowy shape showed itself to their gaze,

529

Stepping from behind the standing stones.
The form was human, but its forehead and face
The pointed muzzle of a dog, a prick-eared pariah,
Such as haunts in cemeteries, on solitary hillsides.
Cringingly, the creature crouched before Merddyn,
Who playfully patted it, with the palm of his hand,
And, turning to Artorius: "Accept this towser –
Hermes, Psychopomp of the highroad to Hades,
Acknowledged anciently in Egypt as Anubis.
You will find this fellow a faithful conductor;
For he serves the Sphinx, the Strangler below."
      Artorius with Anubis, entering into that emptiness,
Down into the gulf descending with his guide.
Through grinding gravel, and gritty sand,
They climbed down, clutching at clinging root stocks.
Then the citizens of the subsoil all about surrounded them,
With the faces of infants and feeble accents –
The annulose Earthworm, the Ant and the Earwig,
The mucous Slug, the Snail and the Centipede,
The Cockroach, the Dor-beetle, and the Devil's Coach-horse,
The Burying Beetle, the Wood-louse and the Blaps,
The maggot of the Blow-fly, the Millipede, and the Mole-cricket
With Truffles and Toadstools, and tiny Bacteria;
Eagerly and avidly, encircling Anubis,
Crying: "Daddy, you have brought us a delicious dinner,
He is fresh and fleshy, and full of blood;
We will munch him with our mandibles, and mumble him with
    our labia!"
      "Patience, my children, my pretty poppets!"
Anubis answered that assembly, "Enough!
I bring no dead man, darlings, to dine with you.
We make no stay here, but into the sterile stone
We must force our way firmly and so wend further."
Then they struck into the substance of the solid minerals,
As divers through the waters divide the waves;
They cleft the Cretaceous and Carboniferous strata,
The Permian, the Liassic, and the lithographic limestone,
To the depths of the dusty Devonian, and the Ordovician.
No life was left there, but long-dead relics –
The fossils of a fearsome pre-Adamite fauna
Silently slumbered in sempiternal oblivion.
But they awoke in wonderment at the unwonted intrusion;
In a macabre saraband the monsters surrounded them:

530

The dunderheaded Diplodocus, with all the tribe of Dinosaurs,
The Stegosaurus, and the spindly Struthiomimus,
The horned Triceratops, and the terrible Tyrannosaurus,
The Ichthyosaurus, the Iguanodon, the Ichthyornis, and the
    Archæopteryx,
The monstrous Mastodon, and the Megatherium,
The Sabre-toothed Tiger, and the savage Smilodon,
And, pathetically half-human, at their head, the Pithecanthropus.
Hollowly they hailed the traveller from the Holocene:
"Stay with us, in our wonderful and static world,
While silently and steadily the geological centuries,
Unmarked, march on, over your magnificent bones,
Till the palaeontologists exhume you, and put you on exhibition
In a glass case in a museum for the masses to gawp at!"
        But Anubis, the good barker, bayed at those animals,
Sharply snapping at their shanks and their shin-bones:
"Traipse off, you riff-raff, you rejects of Time!"
And to Artorius he exclaimed: "In these ante-chambers of Annwyn
It is not convenient to linger. Cast off your carapace.
To the first circle I send you and what you shall find there."
        Darkness came down, and consciousness departed;
In an unknown environment Artorius awoke –
In a stable stinking of the stale of horses –
Age-long accumulations of excremental effluvia,
Fæcal matter, muck and merds.
In that fœtid mansion he found himself mastered
To shovel away the shit, and to try to shift it.
But the more he laboured, the loathsome mess
Piled up in heaps, horrible and putrescent,
Till stupefied by the stench, he faltered and swooned away.
But dimly he heard the dog-headed divinity –
"I send you further, to the second circle."
        Artorius stood in a summer arbour,
Golden with sunlight, and the gladsome song
Of garden warblers, linnets, goldfinches and larks;
In a corner of that garden, in courtship of a girl,
A stripling stood, strumming upon a lute.
But the sense of his song, and the words he was singing,
Eluded Artorius; eagerly he advanced,
Hoping he might hear that haunting stave.
But suddenly, from the bushes, a swarm of birds
Flew out, fluttering, with ferocious cries,
Attacking him, and clutching with their clammy talons,

Beating him with their wings, and their beaks for weapons.
That ugly onslaught exhausted Artorius;
He faltered and fell, but the barker followed up:
"Think yourself summoned to the third circle!"
　　　　When Artorius again awoke, was extended
To his vision a vast and vaulted hall,
Consecrate to justice; and to judgment he was come.
In the hushed and solemn silence he saw
A pair of scales, with pans of silver,
Set up upon a stage, and standing beside it
A being, that balanced the ponderous cross-beam;
Human the hands and the body which it boasted,
From the shoulders it showed the shape of a bird –
The neck a whimbrel's or a whaup's, and the neb;
The figure of a crescent flashed on the forehead.
In long garments of linen, gravely
Ministers moved, and mounted to that balancer,
Holding in their hands the hearts of men,
Watchfully to be poised and weighed in those pans.
In awe and astonishment Artorius anxiously,
And in wonder, watched that weighing; till, at length,
A minister, as it seemed, in silence marched
To where he was standing, stark as a stone,
Who held in his hand the haft of a knife
With a fine blade, and formed of the flint;
And suddenly struck, swiftly, at his breast,
And cut out the heart, complete from his carcass –
Yet he did not die, but heartless still, descried
How it fluttered like a bird, in its frantic beating,
As that other held it in his hands aloft,
And bore it to the bird-headed god with the balances;
Finally to be weighed against a frail feather,
A white one, from the wide wing of Truth.
　　　　Then numbly he knew the necessity – on those scales
His living heart must lightly be lifted,
And the feather be forced by its weight to fall,
Or judgment in justice be enjoined. Then he saw,
Crouched by those balances, a beast, like a crocodile,
And half hippopotamus, with hideous jaws,
Ready to devour when his doom was recorded.
In a horror of darkness he heard it divulged –
The sound, not the sense; then suddenly, behind him,
The voice, vouchsafed, of the vigilant Anubis:

"From this sentence you are sent to the fourth circle!"
     On a wide plain, whipped by the wind,
He found himself running, and full and round
The Hunter's Moon hung in the heavens;
Not running alone, but around him a rout
Of men and women, moaning and wailing.
Fair had been their faces, and their flesh, but now
Passion had pined them, and pinched and distorted.
And some, in that vision, that he viewed he seemed
To know and to number, but most were unknown:
With streaming tresses, Sappho and Semiramis,
Catullus and Clodia, Cynthia, and Corinna,
Tibullus with his Delia, Delilah, and Dido,
The incestuous Myrrha, Messalina, and Medea,
Diarmuid and Graine, Deirdre, and Gwendolen,
White-breasted Bronwen, and the blossom-faced Blodeuwedd
With Llew her lord, and many more of the lost.
Through thickets and through thorns precipitously they thrust,
In their terror and their torment, at the sound of the tally-ho
They heard behind them, and the red-eared hounds
Which Gwynn, son of Nudd, through those northern glades
Set upon their scent; through hail and through sleet,
Frantically and frenziedly they fled into the darkness.
Till the barking of another Dog through that dimness bayed:
"To the fifth circle go down, and find a further defeat!"
     Artorius, in armour, in an open arena
Stood, and perceived, opposing him, positioned
An immense array, an army of eunuchs
And bearded hermaphrodites – battalions of half-men;
At the head of this host, imperial and hieratic
A female figure, in formal vestments
Bedizened with diamonds, with dark eyes glaring.
Fiercely, their fiery darts they discharged,
Filling the heavens with flakes of flame,
Against Artorius; then that august Empress
(Who had once been a harlot for the whoremasters of the Hippo-
     drome)
Shifted her crouching shape to a Cat's,
The monstrous Malkin, ferociously miauling,
Pelug, a deadly and Dianic pussy.
Craftily she crouched, then pounced with claws
Extended and eager on Artorius in that arena,
Breaking his spine – he lay senseless, but somewhere

A prim and pedantic and prosy voice,
In a lengthy discourse growing louder and louder,
For futurity defined his defeat and his failure.
Then the bark of Anubis broke in on that bore;
"To the sixth circle go down, the most searing."
          A winter wood – windless, but snow
Hung on the branches and the hollow boles,
Glittering and gleaming coldly through the glade.
From a bush of holly a hideous boar
Rushed upon the man, robbing him of his manhood,
Tearing at his testicles with its scything tusks.
From a thicket of ivy then issued another –
A female form, with hairy flanks,
Shameless and nude, with the nipples of a nanny-goat.
She embraced that brute, unbridled and amorous.
Impotent, and in pain, he witnessed the postures
Of that salacious satyress and her swinish paramour.
          Then Artorius, in anguish, to Anubis: "Is this the end?
Have I reached the butt and the bottom of these rounds?"
          Anubis answered: "Artorius, awaits you
The seventh circle. That also you must suffer."
          In mizzling rain and in rolling mist,
He lay, at his length on a lonesome plain.
A field of battle, and feebly through the fog
The moans and the death-rattles of dying men.
A fearful, fervid, and feverish thirst
Tormented his tongue. In that terrible agony
He craved for a cup, and cried for water.
          Then it seemed, among those butchered that Bedwyr, his
                    butler,
The man that most of all men had loved him,
Came and approached him, carrying a cup,
But leering lewdly, with a loose-lipped mouth.
The cup of water that he wanted he clasped,
And lifted it to his lips, but loathingly he shrank back,
Struck by the stale stench of the blood
That cruelly tainted it, and tinged it with crimson.
          At that bafflement, Bedwyr, with a brash enunciation:
"Sup it up, Cæsar – a suitable potation:
On the blood of the people plenteously you have battened."
In the horror of that humiliation he heard, yet once more,
The growls of Anubis, the gruff guide-dog:
"To the eighth circle I send you, and the uttermost."

He found himself submerged in a subterranean sea;
Cephalopods and hydroids, sea-anemones and holothurians
Groped with their ghastly and grisly feelers;
Tentatively he was touched by their coiling tentacles,
Mumbled by their horny and horrible mouths.
Dreadfully, as an oyster is drunk, he was devoured;
His body melted, his marrow and his bones.
The glutinous hag-fish glided into his guts,
Insidiously eating him inwardly.
      "Artorius, awake!" – the accents of Anubis –
"From this darkness descend, from this total diminishment!
Cast your last shell in the cave of Ceridwen."
      In a long gallery, lit by the glimmer
Of crystals of quartz and carbuncles, Artorius
Stood astounded, stark as he was born,
Still clutching in his fist the flower of the fern.
Distantly through the dimness he discerned a light,
At the other end in an enormous archway –
The bright flicker of flames (by the breath
Of nine maidens mysteriously ignited);
A copper cauldron was set on those coals –
Through the steam continually streaming from it was distinguished,
Fitfully, what seemed a female figure:
Ceridwen, the mother and mistress of that kingdom.
Awe-ful, and unspeakably ugly her appearance:
Full-face her visage, but two vipers formed
With their heads in profile, a horrific portrait;
Around her neck a necklace noisesomely displayed
A chain of skulls, suitable for a charnel,
With severed hands, horribly suspended;
Her own hands were claws, hooked and cruel;
No garment, but at her waist a gruesome girdle
Of hanging snakes that harshly sibilated –
Livelily those reptiles writhed and lashed.
At the aspect of that august one, Anubis advanced,
Fawning like a favourite dog at her feet.
      Artorius gazed at that great goddess –
It seemed for centuries – in silence; then a voice
Hoarsely was heard from that ghastly head:
"Artorius, Uther's son, adventured into Annwyn,
I have chosen you, child, if the choice be yours.
By numerous names I am known among men,
In many lands, and in multifarious languages;

In these islands I am argent and astral Arianrod,
Creiddylad, and Modron, and the crow-faced Morigan,
Rhiannon, and Danau the dark deemstress,
And many more; but those who most
Firmly and fearlessly have looked on my face
Know that my name is *Rerum Natura*.
As Ceridwen I am guardian of this great cauldron,
This grail, the gift which I grant you for your luck.
Will you take, Artorius, in trust this talisman?"
        Artorius answered the arbitress of Annwyn:
"Princely one, I will take it – but what price must I pay?"
Croakingly then came the voice of Ceridwen:
"Look into the steam. Look well, and see."
Visionary shadows shifted in the vapour:
He beheld once more the mound of Badon –
One with his own face stood there with his followers;
It seemed that Cerdic still led the Saxons;
But as both their bands were joined in the battle
The issue was altered, to another outcome:
The Brythons fled, and the fierce barbarians
Drove them from the field, in disarray and defeat.
Then the voice of Ceridwen vibrated through the cavern:
"Look further yet; learn of futurity."
        He saw into the steam; you, too, know what he saw –
The horrors of history, huddling through the years,
Endlessly extended through oncoming ages:
The White Worm he saw driving the Red Worm
Westward to its den in the desolate wilderness;
The shapes of the ships that dragon-like shifted,
Avenging, over the eastern ocean,
From the larch and fir-clad fjords of Lochlin –
The raven of the Vikings raucously victorious;
Then the king of the Saxons slain at Senlac;
The Norman bastard, and his noble brigands,
Oppressing with tolls the poor and the peasantry;
The Red King carried on the collier's cart;
The blood of Becket, the bishop in Canterbury;
Hideously he heard the hollow screams
Of Berkeley and Pontefract, of pitiful butchery;
He saw the people pinched by famine and by pestilence,
And Jack Straw's falchion in the flesh of the Flemings;
The raging of the Roses, the white one and the red one,
In the wasteful wilderness, and the wanted crown

Hanging on a bush, the hawthorn of Bosworth,
The monstrous Tudor mightily towering –
In schism, the shrines shattered and dishallowed;
The headless bodies of the Bullen and the Howard,
The smoke and the torments of Tyburn and Smithfield;
A pedantic Solomon slobbering over Steenie,
And the neck of his son outstretched on the scaffold;
Cumberland in the carnage of the moor of Culloden,
And the sluggish succession – a saturnian age
Of lead and gold – of the loutish Guelphs,
The Germanic Georges, heavily jowled;
New Troy become Sidon and Tyrus and the sons
And daughters of Albion enslaved in the darkness
Of the satanic mills, for the mansions of Mammon.
  And through the whole of those showings, the howls and
    the shrieks
Of war, like a wind, wuthered and blustered;
Till in the mud of Flanders and the Marne, the flower
Of the manhood of Britain was bogged down in murder;
And the fury of flames fell upon London,
Scorching and searing the Augustan city.
  Like a ship, offshore, with shattered masts,
Battered and betrayed, the island of Britain,
Through the thickening dust of a third Dark Age,
Drifted into dimness in a tedious decline,
With two rival crews of contending rats.
  Came through the cavern the voice of Ceridwen,
Asking: "Do you accept, Artorius?" And he "I accept."
"Then take me, and give me in token of that gift,
One kiss on my lips, of your love and of your courage;
You may find me less unlovely and less foul than you fear."
He heard the goddess, and aghast he hesitated;
Then stepped forward steadfastly on the stones of the cave,
And embraced her in his arms in all her ugliness,
And kissed that cruel and uncomely mouth.
  An intense flash of flame enfolded them:
He found himself in a green and flowering garden;
Around him were lilies and royal roses;
The swish of fountains, and the sweet fluting
Of song-birds saluted him, and ravished his senses;
He embraced in his arms, amazed and enchanted,
A graceful girl, in the gladness of her youth,
Garlanded, in a loose gown of silk.

"My name," she said, "Now know as Sovereignty.
I will serve you, my prince, sweetly for a season;
And lightly give you this Luck for my gift."
        Laughingly she held out to him, in her left hand,
A crystal cup, clearer than moonlight,
And in her right, a bright and burnished blade,
A sword of steel, strongly tempered.
"Keep this well," she said, "and call it Caliburn;
While your luck holds fast, it will not fail you in fight."
        Intenser and more brilliant the brightness blazed,
Seeming to consume with its sweetness the senses,
Till consciousness departed in that dazzling clarity.
        When Artorius awoke, he was aware
Of the stark outlines of the circle of stones.
The altar stone was lying where for long ages it had lain.
The moon was setting over the mounds of Sarum.
His armour was heavy on him, but in his hands he held
That cup of crystal, and the great sword Caliburn,
And a brown and bloomless frond of bracken.
Merddyn awaited him, the master of his wanderings
Through the caverns below to the court of Ceridwen –
But those visions in the darkness vanished now like dreams,
Sinking, seminal, to the depths of his soul.
        "Look now," said Merddyn, "At length the light
Of dawn is silvering the skirts of the sky.
The sun will be hoisted, soon over the Heel Stone,
To signal the moment of the Midsummer Solstice.
Come, you must go to your crowning at Cærleon;
The blessing of Bedwini the bishop, and the anointing,
The diaconal stole designate to you for service
Of the imperium in this island. August be the omens.
Look well to your Luck, and keep it while it lasts you,
And the sword likewise: see, in these, symbols
Of the active and passive principles of power."

POLYHYMNIA

Tangling in the Lion's mane,
The Sun, cast up from the Underworld,
Swelters the Cæsarian month; where now
Kronion, gatherer of the clouds,
Directs his rumbling car across
The arid vault of the air, the unsickled fields. And I,

Tutor to all intelligences,
Frame for the diaconal
Anointing, a strophic pæan; for, Samson, you set
Your torch-tailed foxes, aflame
Among the Philistine corn
Bring sweetness out of the lion's strength, as you assume

The radial and imperial diadem:
Victor, son of Scorcher, diaconal
Son of the griddle, remember
What treasure it is you husband.

Victor of the May Day hawthorn,
Remember your course is set towards the Scorpion's
Claws, and the resurgence of your adversary.
The storm-god, with his hammer, drives above,
Breaking the heads of the dragons of the deep,
Releasing the waters of the firmament; and so must you

Sluice out the stables of your land
And turn the straw to sweeten in
The universal justice of the sun's great eye.
The bride, the sister of the corn,
Journeys now across the Gallic
And ripening fields. Bridegroom, prepare to greet her then, as Zeus,

When regal and virginal Hera stood alone
Upon the glacial summit of Ida – he raised
A sudden and seasonal storm,
With mist, and battering hail.

539

Then Zeus assumed the form of a grey
     Cuckoo, with a catch in its throat; bedraggled,
And shivering in the unmerciful rain he flew to her:
     The scornful and inaccessible queen
     In pity took the seductive traitor
Into her breast, to warm him. The clouds dispersed, and all the
     luxurious

     Flowers of the summer cast away their
     Vivid corollas to deck their couch.
Now spread for the people the banquet of your opulence:
     Your cup-bearer stands before you, ready
     To pour the new wine and the mead.
Scour and sluice the cup. Honour ascended Astræa.

     In July prepare to fly, beyond the solstice
     Where the Scorcher is trapped in the bag, and baited
     Like a honey-badger; the sun-king
     Shorn of his locks, and blinded.

ERATO

Hermes, master of the roads, is the tutelar of all those who cross frontiers. His is the standing stone of the cairn to which each traveller adds his pebble so that a landmark may remain. By that stone, in the silent trade, are left goods for others to come and take, and leave what they think a fair equivalent; therefore he is Mercury of the mercatores. Patron of thieves also, for they likewise make silent excursion into alien territory; and immediately he had been born he went as a cattle-reever to carry off the oxen of his brother, Apollo. The herald, in his diplomatic immunity, goes under his protection, with his eloquence and his ribbon-bound staff. And he is also the guide of souls on their last journey to the house of Hades.

Alliance between peoples is sealed by exchange of gifts,

and exchange of women as brides. After Artorius had received the imperial crown of Britain in the City of the Legions, those who counselled him held it fitting that he should take a wife, so that he might beget an heir. It was determined that he should marry Guanhumara, the daughter of Leodegrance, the king of Massilia in Gaul. They said to Artorius, "Let the courteous Gwalchmai, your sister's son, be sent to seal the treaty, and to conduct the lady to this island." But Artorius said, "I cannot spare Gwalchmai from my wars." Then Modred, Gwalchmai's younger brother, said "Sir, let me go." He was so charming that it is told of him that no one could refuse any request that he made, and Artorius regarded him with special affection. Artorius said, "By all means let Modred go on this errand. We hear that Guanhumara is an accomplished lady, and Modred has some skill in music and poetry and will be able to entertain her on her tedious journey." Eugenius said, "That seems an excellent notion. But Modred is young, and only amateur in these matters. I move that the learned Phyllidulus should accompany him. Then the grammarians of Massilia will recognise that we are not without solid scholarship even in remote Britain." This plan was generally agreed on, and, with a suitable escort of fighting men, Modred and Phyllidulus were despatched to Gaul.

Leodegrance, with his men-at-arms, rode out with his daughter, and the waiting women who were to accompany her to Britain, from his city of Massilia. That city had been founded in ancient times as a colony of Greeks from Ephesus; their patroness was the many-breasted Great Mother of Asia. The appointed meeting-place was at the mouth of the River Rhône, where stands the shrine of the Three Marys of the Sea, *Matres Galliæ*. For they had been put on the sea in a rudderless and sailless boat, and they drifted to that spot. And with them was their black servant, the Egyptian Sara: the dark moon, honoured by outcasts and vagabonds, tinkers and itinerant smiths, fortune-tellers, horse-thieves and musicians. To pay his respects to her, Modred descended to the unconsecrated crypt which had been a Mithræum. He said, "Inspire me, Muse," but what other prayers he uttered is not reported. Phyllidulus did not go with him. He remained in the clear air, for he worshipped Apollo Maponos, bright god of day.

When Modred had received Guanhumara, on behalf of Artorius, from her father King Leodegrance, they set out on their northward journey along the valley of the Rhône. Curious birds, pelicans, flamingoes and purple coots, looked at them from

541

between the reeds as they passed. Under the burning southern sun they crossed the desert of the Camargue, and came at length to the fertile lands of central Gaul. They saw olives and vines, and corn ripe for the harvest, the gift of kindly Ceres. On a certain day they rested at noon in the shade of a grove of poplars. The cicadas sang in the heat, and the crested lark from the top of a broken stone wall. Then Guanhumara said to Modred, "Have you any skill in music?" And he replied, "I have such a skill, and I will sing if it please you. Music lightens a journey, and we hope it may sound along our last journey on the roads of the dead. You are about to cross the frontier from the unmarried to the married state, and music will serve for that passage also. I will sing you a song in praise of the married state, a song of a scholar and the birds; and I will sing it also for the learned Phyllidulus." Then he took his lute and began to sing: –

He sat within a vernal grove
    Where birds were practising their scales,
His problems, poverty and love,
    Exhaling to the conscious gales;
The conscious gales did not reply,
    Of course, but the officious birds,
In loud and various harmony,
    Answered his words, answered his words.

"If I pursue the abstract Muse,
    A difficult and thankless task,
Will all her gifts the world refuse
    (Though little it may be I ask)
Until at length I'm bent and balding?
    What then shall my dry senses please?"
Replied the monotonous Yellow Yalding:
    "A little bit of bread and no cheese!"

"Perhaps, like most, I'll find instead
    That flesh and blood will do as well
To bless my board, and grace my bed –
    But how to win her, who can tell?"
It was the jolly speckled Thrush
    That heard his weak despondent sigh,
And hollowed from an ivy-bush:
    "Cheer up, cheer up, cheerily, never say die!"

"The hard and learned terms I own
    Are not the ones with which to greet her;
My tongue must catch a different tone
    If I encountered such a creature."
The bachelor Chaffinch on the spray
    (His was a joyful note to hear)
Taught him the words that he must say:
    "Sweet sweet sweet sweet sweet come kiss me dear!"

"Kind birds, you tell me how to choose,
    Partly direct the way to woo;
I know what language I must use,
    But language spent, what's then to do?"
The little greenish Willow Wren,
    With tones that none could have denied
And silver liquid chimes came in:
    "Ah, lay her down, adown, adown, adown." it sighed.

"My feathered friends, I'll take your cue,
    When time and place, and chance appoint –
And all that after may ensue;
    But how am I to reach that point?"
The plump dactylisonant quail
    Taught him how he should come to it;
Among the grass roots told the tale
    Of *"Bit by bit, bit by bit."*

"But love is jealousy and pain;
    With doubtful anguish I am vexed.
Can so much risk be worth the gain –
    Perhaps the Cuckoo answers next?"
A Ring Dove, sensible and fat,
    On beech-mast corn, and acorns fed,
Lifted its head, and told him flat:
    "You fool you, you fool you, you!" it said.

"Inhuman birds, who are involved
    Only in the instinctive minute,
When shall my question be resolved –
    You seem to find no problem in it?"
A Raven, on the topmost oak,
    Watching, keen-eyed, for things to die,
Opened its sable bill, and spoke:
    "In hora mortis" was its cry.

Guanhumara thanked him for his song. "I found that charming," she said, "But the learned Phyllidulus will be able to express a more considered judgment on the merits of your poem."

"Since you ask my opinion," said Phyllidulus, "I fear one must say that it is an emotionally dishonest and self-indulgent piece. What is it supposed to say? On one level of interpretation the birds appear to put forward a plan of action of doubtful moral validity. Or, if, on the other hand, we are to consider the birds as unfallen creatures, not subject to a morality incumbent upon Man, then their advice can be of no possible service to the scholar. I will say nothing of the too easy slackness of the rhythm, nor of the provincial affectation of calling a yellowhammer a yellow yalding for the sake of a rhyme which has, anyway, a certain touch of, may one venture to call it, vulgarity about it, except that such want of discipline is the correlative of the intellectual slackness which appears to pervade the entire conception. You make the raven talk Latin: the macaronic depends for its effect on a kind of scholarly in-group humour, which is not only pedantic but presents social implications which one must deprecate; and in any case, the phrase given to the raven does not, to my ear at least, seem, in any effectual way to reproduce the cry of that bird – which I presume to be the rather pointless intention of the author in the closing line of each of his stanzas."

"Come," said Modred mildly, "You are not now lecturing to your tadpoles. But I will endeavour something on rather more intellectual lines, which may stand up better under your scrutiny." So, laying his lute aside, and looking ardently upon the princess Guanhumara, he spoke the following quatrains:

> When Jove, and his two brothers, in their rage,
>   Their sire, old Saturn, from Olympus hurled,
>   Astræa, weeping, left the stricken world,
> And from our earth faded the Golden Age;
>
> She stands among the constellations:
>   So do not ask for Justice here below –
>   Justice is gone, and Earth's proud rulers now
> Chastise us with their whips and scorpions.
>
> Justice is gone. But Mercy has her seat,
>   Ladies, within those other stars your eyes:
>   It may be granted for a lover's sighs,
> To him, and her that grants it, proving sweet.

544

"One cannot say" said Phyllidulus, "That one is aware of anything approaching serious intellectual activity in these lines. The first two stanzas are nothing more than a piece of stale mythologising, and the diction throughout is flat and conventional – 'their sire, old Saturn,' 'Astræa, weeping' and so forth. What is the distinction between 'the stricken world' and 'our earth?' If there is none, this is a tautology; and 'from Olympus hurled' is an ugly and awkward inversion. The connection of the final stanza with the rest appears to me to be spurious, as well as morally suspect. Granted the idea that perfect justice is something not to be discerned in any contemporary social situation, the facile romantic solution suggested by the concluding lines is no solution at all. Mature sensibility would recognise that it does not absolve us from the necessity of seeking to establish and of maintaining some sort of social order, however imperfect. To this end the relaxed emotions to which the poem's conclusion points us would, one is obliged to say, in no way conduce. Frankly, one is disturbed."

"Well," said Guanhumara, "It must be very nice to be so clever. I liked Modred's poem, but you seem to have got far more meaning out of it than I was able to do. But the sun is now declined from his midday height, and I think we had better proceed on our journey."

They went on their way, the two young people slyly laughing together at that bumbling marsh-bird, the old butterbump of the fens as he was. They went on along the valleys of the Rhône and the Loire until they reached the port of Burdigala, where they took ship for Britain. And Modred delivered to Artorius his kore, his corn-dolly, his færie queene.

*   *   *

The nuptials of Artorius were celebrated with great pomp at Carlisle. He held his court there that year, for there were rumours that the Picts were mustering beyond the wall of Hadrian. And after Gwion had sung his epithalamium, the planet Venus was shining brightly in the soft sky of a summer evening.

A kite, a long-tongued magpie, and a hoody crow, Stymphalian birds, perched by the midden behind the castle. And this was the song they sang:

THE KITE: Chicken bones, and beef bones,
        And bones of the mountain deer –
      Fragments of a royal feast
        Make us royal cheer.
      Fat of mutton, fat of pork,
        And yellow goose's fat –
      Shall we dine richer, sisters,
        Daintier than that?

THE MAGPIE: Better than that, sisters – listen
        To tattling Margot Pie,
      Who can perch on window sills,
        Who can peep and spy.
      A worthy king – but not so young –
        Has taken a youthful wife:
      May such a match breed jealousy?
        Jealousy breeds strife.

THE HOODY CROW: Hark to my prophetic voice,
        The chooser of the slain:
      I see a bloody field of war,
        In January rain.
      Marrow-fat, and marrow-bones
        Such pickings are delight;
      But a fairer prize is the fine blue eyes
        Of young men fallen in fight.

This was their song. None heard it, but an old blind beggar, who had crawled to the midden to feed on the scraps from the feast. He had no name but Poverty, lying at the door of Justice.

CALLIOPE III

At the autumnal equinox, in even opposition,
The bright and heavenly Balances hold
The softness of summer and the savagery of winter;
As on a field of fighting, the fierce tides

Doubtfully turn, in indecisive tumult.
Yet the doom of Summer is sealed, though the sun
Suffuses the landscape serenely with light.
There is an edge of death in the dank air,
And the fading leaves, as listlessly they fall.
The swallow and the swift, and the sylvan warblers
Have moved off on migration; no more is heard
The note of the nightingale, nor the nightjar's churning,
The calling of the cuckoo, nor the dry-voiced corncrake;
Richly the apples ripen in the orchards;
The harvest is garnered and hauled into granges;
Geese are set in the stubble to glean,
With relish, the residue of the reaped grain,
Fattening their flesh for the feast of Michaelmas.
  Such was the season when Merddyn suddenly
Came to the king, Artorius, in his court.
The wizard addressed these words to the Ymheradwr:
"Confide no more in my counsel and my comfort;
The time is near; for Nimue the nightmare
Summons me to her secret and subterranean kingdom.
I must abide there in darkness till the Day of Doom;
The sweet sunlight will see me no more
On the upper earth, nor the air embrace me.
  "Listen to my words, the last of my wisdom:
In the sign of the Ram, in the raging slaughter
Of the field of Badon, the four-sided fortress,
You prosecuted war for the promotion of peace,
Establishing externally the order of empire;
In the sign of the Bull, the bishops in synod
Determined by dogma the *limes* of doctrine;
In the sign of the Twins, song and sentence,
The lines of communication, by your laureates were cleared;
The conduits of rhetoric were cleansed of rubble:
The frogs of the fens found their vocabulary;
In the sign of the Crab, I sent you to Ceridwen,
From the maddening moonlight to the Mother's cauldron,
To face your futurity, and encounter your fears
And your utmost anxieties – an inner order
Was created in that descent to the darkness of her cavern;
In the sign of the Lion, the loud suffrage
And the plea of the people prompted you to your crowning;
In the sign of the Virgin, this was validated by the solemnity
Of wedlock to a bride – the wine and bread

547

And the common cup, signify the completeness,
The consummation of life: to the crowned couple
The guests do homage, in gladness of that grace:
May the screaming birds of scandal be sent
To their Stymphalian marsh, nor mar the merriment.
      "Now is the time for this knowledge to be translated
Into forms of government, to guide those who follow;
That stability of the state may stand the firmer,
And a code of law be left to the land.
Summon then to council your senators and your commons,
To deliberate and determine, in form of debate,
Wisely and lucidly – of weight and learning,
Knowledgeable for this matter: I shall not be of the number."
      Artorius, with awe, answered his utterance:
"Legislation lodges in the letter that killeth;
For the hardness of the heart it is held a necessity;
But, as who trusts in the sword by the sword shall be slain,
Who leans on the law shall be judged by the Law.
I call to my memory that merciless king,
Feasting in Babylon; but fingers of flame
Scrawled on the stonework the sentence of his doom:
'You are weighed in the balance, and wanting, Belshazzar!'
In that night he was slain, and the sovereignty was to Cyrus."
      Merddyn, the master, answered his misgivings:
"Justice is fixed on no firmer a foundation
Than a fallible construct, for the conservation of freedom;
Apart from her arbitration, in error and anguish,
We wander in the wildness of the primæval wood,
Treacherous and trackless; and terrifying beasts,
Monsters whose dens are in the mind of man,
Perilously couch there – Passion and Pride.
Remember Minos, who mightily and marvellously
Reigned at Knossos, in the realm of Crete:
With the sails of his galleons he swayed the seas
And the isles of the Aegean, and even Athens
Was a feudatory fief, in fear of that potentate;
He laid on them his rule, and the laws he received
From the divine Distributor, in the cavern of Dicte.
In the halls of the dead he is held now as doomster,
With righteous Rhadamanthus, rigid and incorruptible,
And Aeacus also, acting as assessors.
Yet lust and covetousness came upon that king:
The bull he had promised as a present for Poseidon,

To be slaughtered in sacrifice, he slyly withheld,
Captivated by its beauty, he kept it in his byre.
But his queen, likewise, was caught up by love
Of that horned brute, by a hideous and heinous
Stratagem she sought to solace her desire;
Begotten of her body, was brought forth the Minotaur,
The loathsome man-eater, that was lodged in the labyrinth,
Where Theseus subsequently sought it out and slew it.
But the ravished ruminant, in rabid must,
Went raging and rampaging round about the island,
Destroying the cities in seismic disturbance,
Till Heracles butchered the horrible beast:
You have learned the lot of Minos the lawgiver –
How animality injured that island emperor.
         "But supposing the story has a different significance? –
Maybe by the labyrinth is meant the law,
With all its tortuosities, its illogical turns,
Containing the monster of cruelty and malice.
The cunning Dædalus was the craftsman who designed it:
The favoured fosterling of Hephæstus the farrier
(The only honest Olympian, who alone
Toiled, though lame, at a trade for his living).
Put in that dungeon for his part in devising
That prurient subterfuge for salacious Pasiphäe,
He escaped, issuing into the upper air
Flying on wide-spread wings of feathers;
Reasonably, he ranged through the middle regions
Of atmosphere, but Icarus, exalted and enjoying
The new sensation, soared to the sphere
Of the blazing sun, but those burning beams
Mollified the wax of his wings, and they melted –
Downward he crashed in disaster to death.
Alas for Icarus, alas for all
Young men who fly too fast and too far,
Too superbly soaring, so near the sun!
I leave you to negotiate the labyrinth of law,
And ponder this fable. So, farewell my friend."
"By your departure," said Artorius, "I also am diminished."
         It came thus about, that were called together for conference
Rulers and ruled, from the regions of Britain –
A motley congeries: from Celtic clans,
Hereditary holders of hillside raths,
With men of their tribes, a mixture of tongues,

And some who claimed senatorial status,
And relics, by tradition, of Roman rank;
A few traders, who forwarded their traffic
In sea ports undestroyed, or cities undeserted.
        Lud's town, London now lay for a season,
With the region adjacent, in the rule of Artorius.
The congress was convened on the hill (Cornhill
Subsequently to be denominated under Saxon dominion),
In the Church of Michael, which memory maintained
Lucius, that lord, who first in this land
Embraced and established by his authority, the Evangel
Of the Prince of Peace, had founded for his people.
        On the westward wall was displayed for worship
An image of the Assize at the end of the ages:
The Judge Tremendous, with tokens of terror
And majesty of mercy, was enthroned in the midmost
On the clouds in glory – were gathered the goats
And the sheep for deeming, sharply divided,
At the sides of His seat; and before Him was set
A pair of balances with brazen pans,
Where Michael, the bird-winged minister and messenger,
Poised for scrutiny the small souls;
Lower down on the left, loathsome Hell,
Cavernous jowled, with crocodile jaws,
Grim and gluttonous, gaped for the reprobate.
        Artorius addressed the assembled auditors:
"Friends and colleagues, we are come here to consider
A matter of moment – the making of Law,
And the framing of a polity to preserve our freedom:
Stability of the state, and the stablishment of justice.
        "Essentially law is love in action:
It is Venus that grants this – that gracious goddess,
Sprung from the foam of the Cyprian seas;
She who couples the beasts in covert and brake,
The birds of the air, and bride with bridegroom,
Sets her seal on the social bond
Of human solidarity, as habitants of cities.
Aphrodite, like Athene, is exhibited in armour,
Not necessarily like a naked hetaira,
No shameless profligate, but protectress of the *polis*,
And memorialised as the mighty mother of Rome.
Not the hot and hurtful Ares is her husband

(Though sometimes she goes whoring with that handsome
     sargeant) –
The gods in council consulted on her case;
In their wit they assigned her as wife to the Artificer,
The muscular Vulcan, the master of metallurgy,
Lame, and labouring on Lemnos – smeared
With the sweat of his forge, and the smoke of his fires.
On the anvil of Hephæstus it behoves us to hammer out
The forms of the framework we design, not forgetting
The wisdom of Aphrodite that overlooks the work.
     "Let each of you set forth his sentence on this subject,
Urging, from experience, what we ought to aver,
What form of polity it is fitting we proclaim;
But first in this concourse I call on the father,
Bedwini the bishop, to bring forth his words."
     At the behest of Artorius, Bedwini arose:
"Am I supposed, as a Christian, to speak on this subject? –
When the theologians have thrashed out the whole business of
     their theories
Of Law and Grace, what is left but Love?
What sanction for judicature, when we are enjoined not to
     judge?
What place for forfeits and penalties, when forgiveness,
To seventy times seven, is still the command?
When the Saviour constrained the casters of stones,
Dismissing the adultress detected in the act,
What remained, my lords, of the rulings of Law?
But we are come to be pilgrims, pitifully, where the creatures
Groan and travail for a grand transformation –
That existential order we ask in our anguish,
Crying, *de profundis*, for the Kingdom to come:
Freedom without knowledge, finally, of Necessity.
But Sovereignty behoves, and sanctions must stand,
Or monsters of murder would stalk at midday,
Cruelty without a curb, carousing on blood.
     "At your coronation, O King, your sovereignty was
          confirmed,
And signalised by the donation of the deacon's stole:
In that manner you are summoned to a ministry of service –
Husbanding the goods of the household of God,
Particularly for the protection of the widows and the poor.
It is earthly imitation of the angelic orders.
     "Unknown modes of majestic existence

Augustly encompass us; in exalted adoration,
The Dominations and Principalities, in the Divine Presence,
And the ineffable Powers, persisting in that activity;
The excess of brightness those beings absorb,
Flows outward to the flights which they oversee –
The swift winged Cherubim, and the sweet voiced Seraphim,
With the terrific Thrones, transmit and transmute,
In sacerdotal guise, the sacramental glory
To the orders of Virtues, Archangels and Angels,
Who are given surveyance over states and cities,
And a ministry as messengers to men in particularity.
Thus comes the source of the service you are called to.
    "Allow me to illustrate my argument with an exemplum,
A tale which warns us to watch against the temptation
Of Pride, which not seldom princes are subject to:
It seems there was a Cæsar – some say Jovinian;
Confident in his authority, he overheard the choristers
One evening as they celebrated the office in the sanctuary –
The song that Mary sang, the Magnificat.
He asked for interpretation, and an acolyte answered
With the meaning of these verses: 'The mighty and magnificent.
The powerful in their pride, from their seats Thou hast put down,
The humble and the meek Thou hast hoisted to the heights.'
Lightly and recklessly the ruler laughed;
Secure in his royalty, and the stability of his state,
He reckoned himself free from the revolutions of Fortune;
Softly in his chamber he slept like a child.
When the daylight dawned, he found things were different:
Opening his eyelids, he was aware – it was odd –
No grooms nor lackeys graced his levée;
For he lay in straw, in a stinking stable,
In the precincts of his palace, a pitiful buffoon.
He called out, but no one came at his clamour;
He rushed through the corridors, claiming he was the ruler;
No one recognised him, though he raged and ranted –
They mocked him for a madman, as mazed in the head.
He hurried, though hindered, to his presence hall,
Breaking through the guards, and gazed bewildered –
For regally enthroned, in the robes of royalty,
Was a figure whose face and features were his own.
In angered authority, as usurper and imposter
He denounced that phantom – as a fake and a deceiver,
A counterfeit ruler. Calm came the reply:

'This pathetic person is a deluded paranoiac;
It is to be hoped, however, he is fairly harmless:
Carry him to the kitchens, and look after him kindly
With suitable sedatives; when he has calmed down somewhat
We will cast him as our clown, to brighten up this court –
His ragged royalty will be light relief' "
       "For the six months that succeeded this strange turnabout
The Cæsar continued in his calling as a clown
(It is said, with a certain degree of success)
While that unknown other exercised his authority.
Never was the realm more righteously regulated –
Justice and mercy were manifest to the multitude;
The poor were succoured, and peace prevailed,
As not heretofore in the history of humanity.
But finally it faded, that fabulous season.
At its ending, he awoke, with the accustomed accoutrements,
Of his courtly bedchamber, but, beside his bed,
That mysterious figure, with his own face and features,
Was standing still, and spoke these words:
'You are restored now, O Cæsar, to your rule and your royalty,
And I depart, who deprived you of those dignities.
Look on me and learn that a Messenger of Light,
From the courts of Heaven, to curb your hubris,
Was sent to you to govern and to guide your state.
Learn you your lesson, with humility and love
Enjoy and exercise the authority assigned you.'
Then the visitant vanished, on vast wings
Climbing skyward; and the Cæsar continued
To manage his realm as that Messenger recommended,
Though frequently failing, through human frailty;
And did so, they say, till the day of his death."
       Gwion, the bard to Bedwini the bishop
Replied: "The myth Your Reverence relates
Is a tale that has been told, at different times,
In various versions, in verse or in prose:
We have heard of Pwyll, that princely hero –
Hunting with his hounds, he followed a hart,
Which led him at last to the lordly ruler
Arawn of Annwyn, the archon of the Underworld;
By agreement they exchanged each other's empery –
The Dark One for a season, swayed in Dyfed,
The patrimony of Pwyll, while Pwyll was throned
In the realm of the shades in their ruler's shape.

It proceeds, I presume, from a pagan custom
Of far-off times: the tragic fate
Of the king, to be slain for a sacrifice at seed time –
Mystically and magically his blood to be mixed
With the sacred soil, for the setting of the crops;
But as time succeeded they tempered this savagery:
A slave or a criminal was surrogate for the king;
He was housed in his palace and possessed his prerogatives
For the sacrificial season, and thereafter he was slain;
The king, reborn, reassumed his royalty.
     "Pardon this pedantry. But permit me a gloss
To tack on your fable in the form that you told it;
I question if the realm of that ruler was really
So impeccably ordered by the angelic oversight
As you seem to suggest. Could discarnate spirit
Be capable of coping with human confusion?
Maybe not only the monarch was educated,
But the angel also, by that extraordinary episode.
Perhaps peering over the heavenly palisades,
He surveyed our lot with a certain superciliousness.
For this fault, for his correction, he was fated – not to fall –
But to suffer for a season terrestrial sojourn,
Returning with a new and more real knowledge."
     Bedwini smiled benevolently, but suspected
A touch of heterodoxy in the tone of such talk.
But the poet continued to put his case:
"We organise not abstractly for angels and archangels
But for men, who are muddled and mixed by nature.
We are setting up laws for no City of the Sun,
Utopia, or Oceania, or New Atlantis;
To be ground by the politics of Platonic Guardians,
Dedicated to the diffusion of the Noble Deceit,
But propelling the grudgingly garlanded poets,
For falsely fabling, from the frontiers of their State.
I want no such systems. The words I work with
Come to me with the marks of common currency;
Language is to be moulded, not mathematical logic,
To constitute the perfect consort of a poem.
The wise in such matters will work so with men,
Kneading their fallibility to the fruition of freedom,
Which is also an art to be acquired by application."
     Gerontius said, with senatorial gravity:
"The fallibility of subjects, swayed by faction,

Asks for authority to be asserted and exercised.
The Roman Republic was torn by such rivalries
That the sickening state seemed sinking into chaos;
But after Actium, Octavius assumed
The title of *Princeps*, and the public peace
Of that Apollonian avatar overshadowed the Empire;
Overweening Antony, honoured with the attributes
Of dizzy Dionysus, in misery and disaster
Fell on his sword, and that silken seductress,
Cleopatra, in her vanity who claimed to be Venus,
Was blasted by the serpent sucking at her breasts.
　　　"Primitive freedom was in the primæval forest,
Where, nasty and brutish, beset by nightmares,
And the struggle for survival, men lived as savages;
To liberate them from the fear of force and lawlessness
They surrendered their freedom to the first sovereign.
To authority, thus instituted, absolute obedience
Is due, and is demanded – who here can doubt this?"
　　　Urbigena, in alliance, urged this argument:
"That absolute obedience is owing to authority
I will not dispute, but differ in the definition.
The sovereignty of a prince, I say, is patriarchal;
He is the father of his nation, which has the nature of a family,
By ties of blood we are bound as brothers,
To a common father conceding our faith.
This authority was exercised archetypally by Adam,
And devolves, under Christ, on the kings of Christendom."
　　　Gaius the seneschal, with a growing and surly
Impatience, had attended the antecedent argument.
He sprang to his feet: "As your friend and foster-sib,
And your comrade in battle, my king, I conjure you
To take no heed of this high-flown talk.
As your steward and seneschal, my task is to supply
Food to your fighting men, to fill their bellies.
The needs of the people I know – they are paramount;
The suffrage of the people is the source of power.
The monarch rules as magistrate of a republic:
His power being perverted, by process of law
They are dispensed from their duty. A tyrant may be deposed.
A civil contract conveys you your sovereignty."
　　　Further to this, Flaccus, the fair-haired bastard
Of Artorius, advised: "The exercise and advantage
Of the forms of liberty and law are fallacies,

555

If concentration of property be permitted to the powerful.
Augustine avers accumulation of affluence
As *magnum latrocinium*. It mocks at legality.
The property of the people, possessed in common
By natural right, the ruler is to regulate.
The logic of love in this is ineluctable –
For who, having knowledge of the needs of his neighbour,
Would fail to send him, to furnish him sustenance,
Such of his superfluity as most readily he could spare?
Not otherwise the commonwealth should curb our covetousness –
For gross greed is a cankerous growth
That the sword of justice surgeonly must excise."
   The direction the debate was taking disturbed
The mind of Gwalchmai. With the modest grace
Of an aristocrat, he arose, and expressed his opinion:
"Tyranny and Democracy are the twin dragons
That struggle in their den of darkness. They spawn
The rampant and clawed cockatrice, Revolution,
The Orc that issues out of the abyss;
Sorest of evils that afflict the state,
Savagely it consumes continuity and stability,
Which men by nature have as much need of
As of equity, and the enjoyment of an ordered existence,
The bloodstained and murderous blade in the market-place
Reared, to power the most ruthless promoted.
   "What freedom is possible, if we fall in the power
Of either the anger and the ambition and the arrogance
Of the perverse soul of a single potentate,
Or the mobile many, in its merciless cruelty?
Let the Prince rule as prime amongst his peers –
An independent assembly, an elite of excellence,
Rich, yet responsible, recognising a trust
Inherent in wealth, for the welfare of others."
   Flaccus, the bastard, flashed out in his bravery:
"O Hawk of May, if your humane manners,
And your gift of courtesy, more commonly were granted,
What you propose might be pertinent and profitable!
But property is the consummate corrupter of courtesy:
The ugliest of all the orders we envisage
Is a soulless republic of rich senators,
Casting its wedding ring to the cold waves
Of the cruel sea, its suitable spouse.
Its hard-faced hierarchs repress the humanities,

Love of letters, for vocational learning,
And the flamboyant pictures which furbish its palaces."
    "The republic of rich men" Gwalchmai rejoined
"Appals you? I postulate a more heinous polity,
Raised on the pushing of party power
To a total tyranny – the ten-horned Antichrist:
John the Divine dreamed his dictatorship
In a penal camp, the cavern of Patmos."
    Said Artorius, anxious to assuage their argument:
"We are lost in the labyrinth of law; on all sides
We gaze on pitfalls protending perdition,
And gaping monsters, mouthing in the gloom.
Aristotle opined, indeed, from the anatomy
Of the constitutions he collated (a conscientious biologist)
Greek and barbarian, that the best government
Was a mixed polity – partly monarchical,
Partly popular, and in part oligarchical:
With its checks and balances, it might chance to bear up:
Liberty, like Truth, lies in a tension.
But no temporal forms finally translate
The idea or order, which evermore we are urged to.
Politicians are necessary, like policemen and prostitutes;
We will build our polity with bricks of brothels,
And hammer out an order on the anvil of Hephæstus.
While injustice exists, action is imperative."
    Modred had been silent. He spoke now: "It seems
You underrate, my uncle, the advantages of your authority.
I make no connoisseur's claims in this matter;
But listening to these deliberations, this debate on law,
I am earnestly impressed by the august assembly –
Diversity of views – but, doubtless, virtue
Springs from such roots, and is ready to ripen,
Building an order for the island of Britain.
For Britain solely? Sits in Byzantium
The distant Cæsar, serene and dim.
Justinian will be subject, in his season, to senility.
The proud Theodora, the prop of his throne,
Will go to her rest, if rest can reward
So restless a spirit. Is his writ subscribed
Westward in Gaul, now wasted and worried
By the hordes of the Franks – or, further, in Hesperia?
Will Belisarius, rugged in battle, restore,
Indeed, the order of the Empire in Italy,

Grinding to powder the power of the Goths
In the name of Rome? Even now, in their rage,
The fierce Lombards fall on that land,
In armed array, over Alp and Apennine;
Barbarism is born anew in the homeland of Brutus.
      "Supposing you extended, Artorius, the sovereignty
Founded here in Britain, to a broader field?
There are precedents, I fancy, for framing such a project
With justice. The undervalued apostate, Julian –
His lordship was acclaimed by the legions in Lutetia;
Sent by their suffrages to Rome, he successfully
Provided a polity, till the Parthian javelin
Pierced his liver, and laid him prostrate,
His virtue vanquished – 'Vicisti Galilæe!'
But a king who is a Christian need fear no such contingency."
      The king made no comment on this piece of counsel –
Modred's suggestion of a civilising mission;
Was it seen in his face that a seed had fallen?
He adjourned the assembly to another occasion.
In formal procession they passed from the fane.
      But Flaccus delayed by the door, dallying
In talk for a time with the trusted Modred:
The two brothers, both of them begotten
Erstwhile by Artorius, each of them uncanonically,
Of different dams. Delicate Modred
Was the likely lad of the Lady of Orkney,
Artorius's sister; at the sacred session,
The synod of the bishops, she seemed to him bonny.
But Flaccus was begotten on a flaxen bondwoman,
A peasant's daughter, dowered but with poverty.
      "We have heard" said Flaccus "here much hammering
Of words and wisdom, but I wonder to what purpose.
Theoretic propositions these princelings put forward,
But the poor and the simple, in this assembly of the powerful
It seemed to me were lacking, not summoned to these seats.
Differently indeed might those have determined
Of the forms of justice, if their judgment were forthcoming.
And others also were excluded from this assembly –
Guanhumara the Queen, with her gladsome garland
Of waiting-women – their suffrages were wanting.
I learned from my mother, no lady, alas!
The ways of this world go at the will of men –
Of men of property. When the meek and the poor

Are the heirs of the earth, at the end of the ages,
When in the fulness of the Faith there is nor bond nor free,
Nor male nor female, as formerly foretold
By Paul the Apostle, perhaps we shall apprehend
Far different devices framed for our fellowship.
Hasten the happiness of that hoped for day!
I leave you, cousin, to consider this counsel."

     So Modred remained, in religious meditation.
He asked no intercession from the angelic orders,
Nor the pure Virgin. To Venus Pandemia
He proffered his prayers: "Goddess and pastmistress,
Weaver of stratagems, I want your support.
I know more law in the lust of my loins;
I observe more order in the inclination of an arm,
In the glance of sunlight on the golden softness
Of a halo of hair, in the smoothness of a hip,
Than in all the abstractions of these old man's arguments.
The suggestion I set forth – the seed that I planted –
Was the single thing that slipped into my thought;
So bored with those boors booming out their platitudes –
It appeared I was supposed to say something serious.
The deviation will provide a diversion for Dad –
Invading the Empire in the interests of order –
Or a passage to power? And this mouse will play.

     "The queen, I fancy, conceives a kindness for me –
My aunt and my stepmother. I am no stoic nor stickler,
Nor high-minded Hippolytus, whom the wild horses
Tore and savaged by the tumbling sea,
As they panicked at the bull that plunged from the billows.
Shamefast and fearful, he shunned Phædra –
The febrile passion of that foreign princess,
The daughter of Minos. Modred is different.

     "Shoulder to shoulder, as my shield-companion,
Fight out, O Cyprian, this fight of my senses!"

     Thus Modred mused, in the fane of Michael,
While softly the sunlight faded from the sky;
Antares uprose in the arch of the evening,
The heart of the Scorpion at the heel of the Hunter,
Who sank, defeated, in the southern sea.

TERPSICHORE

THE TRAVELLER:

> *Requiem æternum dona eis, Domine,*
> *Et lux perpetua luceat in eos.*
> I am Professor of History in the ancient University of Fen-
> bridge, though not yet a Fellow of All Souls'. I am a
> specialist on the Roman and post-Roman period in Britain,
> poring over the documents of a time often too sparsely
> documented. But why that Latin tag should now be run-
> ning through my head, I do not know. On vacations and
> at weekends I am something of an amateur archaeologist,
> and folk-lorist too. I have visited most of the Neolithic
> stone monuments of Britain: Avebury, and Stonehenge,
> and others, from the Orkneys and Cumberland to Wales
> and Cornwall. But there is one, set among the Scottish
> hills, which I have not seen – Bury Hill, in Strathmore.
> This seems a good opportunity to go and look at it.
>
> I pass by the green wolds of Lincoln,
> I traverse the moors of Yorkshire, where in summer
> The ring ouzel perched and flirted, and now
> The bilberries are ripening to purple,
> Where the grouse call: "Go back, go back!"
> Among the shoots of the heather.
> I cross the Tees and the Tyne, and I go
> By the brown fells of Northumberland,
> Into Scotland I go over the border, and now
> I am among these wind-swept uplands.
>
> I see before me the great stone circle, impressive in its
> antiquity, in the fading light of an autumn evening. In
> such places as this the presence of a human figure seems
> only to emphasise the solitude. I remark a woman walking
> among the stones, picking blackberries. And that is rather
> strange – tomorrow will be November the first, and by the
> old way of reckoning, from the setting of the sun, it is
> already November. I have heard that country people will
> not eat blackberries in November – the devil spits on them,
> they say, and, indeed, at that time of year they are past

their best, small and mawkish and full of maggots. But perhaps it is really because this black fruit is the food of the Dead, who, during this month, are released for a season and wander about our world.

THE WOMAN: "Your fause luve ca'd you till the dance,
    And tuik you by the hand;
But frae your faut comes the bluidy war
    That rages throch the land.

"Ye ligged the nicht in your leman's airms,
    And ye thocht nae thocht o' me;
But ye thocht that the play o' luve was sweet
    As the flur o' the hawthorn tree.

"Ye may wear the stanes wi' your knees in prayer,
    And wet wi' your tears your bread;
But ye willna bring back the braw, braw men
    That lig in a clay-cold bed".

THE TRAVELLER: What is that song you are singing? I do not seem to have heard it before.

THE WOMAN: It is an auld sang I learned lang syne. I dinna mind the lave. But those are the words of Arthur the king to his Queen Gaynor, the faithless woman.

THE TRAVELLER: Queen Gaynor – that is Guinevere, or Guanhum-ara as the earliest sources call her. Now I remember it, is there not some old story connecting Arthur with these very stones?

THE WOMAN: They do say that it was here that he had her drawn in pieces by the wild horses.
And it was for nae guid thing that she did.

THE TRAVELLER: She was the wild mare he could not tame, like Hercules taming the wild horses of the king of Thrace. Was it for her adultery with Lancelot?

THE WOMAN: I ken nae thing of yon laddie, Lancelot.
It was the fause knight, Sir Modred, the King's son
And his sister's son, that tuik her

By the lang hair o' her heid, and pu'd her
Frae the royal throne, while her man
Was awa at his Roman wars.

THE TRAVELLER: That, I think, is the most primitive form of the
story.

THE WOMAN: But for your wild horses, that
Is a foolish tale. The King Arthur wadna do sic a thing, and
the Queen Gaynor
Turnit a nun and made a guid end, they say.

THE TRAVELLER: You seem very certain of what you tell me.
You are a strange woman. And, now I look again,
Strangely dressed too. Why that red,
On the one side of your dress, and the blue on the other?

THE WOMAN: It is a fashion that befits me well – it shows
Whilk side is brennand i' the flames,
And whilk is peinnit i' the cauld.
Pray for me.

THE TRAVELLER: I am not used to pray, unless
The patient study of the actions of the dead,
The search for the truth of the past, may be a kind of prayer.

THE WOMAN: The stream of time is an illusion, the past
Is not dead; it cannot die,
Though it would seek to. The dead are present to you.
And I, who was Guanhumara, the faithless
Queen of Artorius, tell you this,
And bid you to pray for me.

(she vanishes)

*   *   *

(The WOMAN *returns as the ghost of* QUEEN GUANHUMARA*)*

QUEEN GUANHUMARA: The Scorpion, the scorpion in the loins –
Its burning heart is Antares,
The fixed brother of Mars;
Swords, swords – the clouds

Rain swords down from the sky;
Blood, blood – the earth
Is drinking the red dew.

THE TRAVELLER: The battle of Camlan – that last battle,
Where the son and the father lay dead,
Each slain by the other's hand.

QUEEN GUANHUMARA: The starling and the long-tongued magpie
Are tale-bearers about us;
Even in the closed garden the anemone opens her red
    mouth,
A scandalmonger against me;
The roses are in inquisition
Upon my heresy in love.

Like Ishtar I go down,
Dancing a dance of seven veils,
Through the gates of the Underworld;
At each gate I give up
A piece of finery to the scorpion-guardians;
The watchmen of the City of Dis
Have stripped me of my garments.

The men with the masks of goats
Are come against me, they compass me around;
They draw their daggers from under their hairy pelts;
My love takes off his mask:
I look into his eyes, for the first time,
And see no love of me, but love of power.
Pray for me. I cannot tarry. I hear
The red-eared hounds give tongue;
The Wild Huntsman pursues on the autumn wind.

    Pray for me – that I may receive
Enlightenment, that even on me
The light perpetual shine.

THE TRAVELLER: *In paradisum. Amen.*

563

Ladies and Gentlemen: It was with the very greatest pleasure that I accepted the invitation to address this distinguished Society. It is only right that I should begin by paying my tribute to that great scholar in whose memory this Annual Lecture was founded. Whose name for the moment escapes me. I must ask your indulgence; I am not, as one may say, wholly myself. Since I encountered the White Phantom in the circle of stones. White-footed Jennifer, dancing in her foam. The scorpion in the loins, and the mating dance of the scorpions. But we do not have any scorpions in these islands. Only the harmless book-scorpion, *Chelifer*, which has no sting. It is found under mossy stones, and between the pages of old books; feeding on psocids or book-lice, and, I suppose, on the book-worms themselves, which are, in fact, the larvæ of one of the boring beetles. They may sometimes be observed – the book-scorpions, I mean – clinging to the legs of long-legged flies, as they make use of this mode of transport from one place to another.

All this is very interesting. It is only right that I should begin; it is only right that I should begin by – by offering my apologies for not delivering a written paper. I draw a bow, as it were, at a venture. My notes are probably scattered over the uplands of Scotland, driven by the November wind, that drives the withered leaves, and the poor souls that wander between the worlds, while the planet of the god of storms rules above. I hope that is quite clear. The subject of my discourse, as you know, "The Possible Historical Basis for King Arthur's Conquest of the Roman Empire." Now, anyone who has familiarised himself at all widely with Arthurian source material will know that this, on the face of it improbable, legend occupies a prominent position in it. Malory, you will remember, devotes a whole book to it. He is simply following the northern alliterative *Morte Arthure*, reproducing indeed much of its language (this is even more marked in the Winchester Manuscript than in Caxton's text). But if we go back to Geoffrey of Monmouth, we may say that he is almost primarily concerned with this episode, and knows practically nothing of those elements in the story which have preoccupied the minds of later poets and romancers.

Now it is tempting to see, in Geoffrey, the Vergil, or rather the Livy, of Henry II's Angevin empire. Attempts have been made to identify the list which he gives of Arthur's conquests with the actual domains, in Britain and France, of Henry Plantagenet. Alternatively, the theory has been put forward that Geoffrey sought to popularise this body of Celtic legend among the Norman (and in fact they were, of course, to a large extent Breton as much as Norman) ruling caste, at the time when Henry was attempting to incorporate the Celts of Wales and Ireland into his English kingdom, as well as extending his influence over the still Celtic realm of Scotland. According to this hypothesis, the purpose of the *Historia Regum Britonum* was to unite the Norman and Celtic aristocracies by a common myth, in the traditions of which the subjugated Saxon population of England would have no part. But, though this may indeed have been the reason for the later popularity of Geoffrey's work, it can scarcely have been his original intention. For it now appears that he wrote in the reign of Henry's predecessor, Stephen. A difficult time to work in, by any standards. And men said openly that God and his Hallows slept. Geoffrey, it seems, was of the party of Robert of Gloucester and of Henry's mother, Matilda. The Empress fleeing at night, like a white phantom over the white snow. But Clio is also a muse, in prose though she plod, that hard mistress whom I serve. Living, as I do somewhere near the beginning of the third Dark Age of European civilisation. The first was that which intervened between the collapse of the Minoan-Mycenæan culture and the flowering of Hellas. Ilion falling, and Hector slain, and blind Homer turning even defeat to a tremulous delight. The second from the fall of the Western Empire to the First Crusade. And that also an age of epic and not for history. And whether the third began in nineteen hundred and forty five, or in nineteen hundred and fourteen, or as I am much more inclined to think, in seventeen hundred and eighty nine, I must leave you to decide. But where is our epic?

But Geoffrey's pseudo-history was turned, not only into verse by the Norman Wace, but also into poetry by the

Saxon Layamon. A priest, dreaming on the banks of Severn, by the Welsh Marches, his belly full of the blood-mixed mead. And Arthur is carried off at last to Argante, of all the elves the fairest. And she is Arianrod whose castle is the silver circle of the *Corona Borealis* in the northern sky. Ariadne's bridal crown. "And on the mere the wailing died away." But King Arthur became an English king, and Malory's Camelot is Winchester. But Camelodunum was Cymbeline's capital, founded in honour of the sky god. And Shakespeare makes him reject the demands, for suzerainty for Rome, of Caius Lucius, as Arthur defies Lucius, Consul or Emperor of Rome. I was at the court of Cunobelinus in the castle of London.

This is my point, which I trust by this time is becoming entirely clear. The imperial character of Arthur, which may be considered as Geoffrey's creation, as it continued to develop in the mediæval tradition, may be regarded as an English attempt to produce a counterpart to the French history of Charlemagne. But that is surely an over-simplification. In the Welsh sources, Arthur is never called king, but always *Ymherawdr*, that is, Emperor. And there had indeed been Emperors of Britain, such as Maximus, that Spanish usurper, who made a bid for Rome itself, and burnt the heretic Priscillian, which became an old Spanish custom. He is the Macsen Gwledig of the *Red Book of Hergest*. And there his ignominious defeat at the hands of Valentinian and Gratian is turned into a triumph. And if we may suppose that the Arthurian tradition subsumed that earlier one, so that also subsumed those of Constantine, and Constantius Clorus, as the presence of Helena in the Macsen legend shows.

All writers, at least in recent years, who have attempted to elucidate the historical basis of the Arthurian legend – Chambers, Collingwood, Ashe, to say nothing of Saklatvala – have been unanimous in identifying Arthur as a Romano-British leader of the sixth century A.D. Not a king, but a *comes*, or count. We may put aside the views of those who postulate a purely mythological Arthur. Some have seen in him a bear-totem, and it is true that Nennius tells us that his name signified in the British tongue *ursus horribilis*. Others have identified him with the ploughman god Artaios, attested by Gallic inscriptions. The constellation of the Great Bear, or the Plough, is called in Welsh Arthur's Chariot.

But the name Artorius seems to be good Latin; it occurs in Juvenal. The Artorii were a Venetic gens, and it is in the province of their origin, near Split in Dalmatia, that a fragment of a sarcophagus of a Roman officer called Lucius Artorius Castus has been unearthed. But this Artorius belonged to the second century, and according to the inscription, was in command of the legion which we know to have been stationed on the northern frontier of the province of Britain at the time Hadrian's Wall was erected. He also saw service in Armorica. Is he perhaps the true historical Arthur, whose name was associated with a prominent monument, and who became the focus of heroic legend centuries later? Most of the twelve battles of Arthur recorded by Nennius can fairly plausibly be identified with sites not too distant from Hadrian's Wall. The exception, of course, is Mount Badon. This may have been Badbury Rings, an Iron Age hill fort in Dorset; or possibly the downs above Bath.

I stood with my confrère in the glade of hazels when the battle of Badon was fought. And I rode with him in pursuit of the unattainable stag of Artemis into the marshes of Cam, where we found myself lecturing to you tadpoles, as still I do. I have been instructor to Elijah and Enoch. To Elijah Jones of Cardiff and Enoch Pritchard of Pontypridd – both rather awkward pupils, but very good Calvinistic Methodists. Cheiron Chelifer, preceptor to heroes: to Peleus, the father of Achilles, who seized the silver-footed, shape-shifting cuttle fish goddess (Thetis, Tethys, and teuthys, I take to be the same word); much-travelled Jason, who established his right to kingship by ploughing and sowing, and securing the rain-fleece – and Hera was his friend; and the great Alcides, enduring his twelvemonth of toils, under Hera's anger.

It was said that St Ursula and her eleven thousand virgins were intended as brides for the mercenaries whom Maximus had taken overseas to Armorica, depleting and debilitating the defences of Britain. But she begged her father's leave to go first on a three years' pilgrimage with her companions. S. Baring-Gould sees in her the Nordic goddess Hersel, whom he takes to be the Moon "cluster'd about by all her starry Fays." Onward, Christian soldiers, Amazons of the spirit, votaries of Diana. But they fell to the spears of the marauding Huns.

These nomad archers of the steppes are so entirely dependent on their horses as to be almost permanently united to them, drinking the fermented milk of the mares and the blood from a vein in the neck which they open when required. The mongoloid type is almost beardless, and it is said that it is difficult for a European to distinguish a man from a woman among them at a short distance. It is not completely obvious to me how SS Ursula and Undecimilla, Virgin Martyrs, found their way into this lecture. And the Huns also, for that matter. Tartars out of Tartarus, like the Titans in rebellion against the Emperor of the Universe.

I become what I sing. I bore a banner in the battle order of Artorius. I behold him among the dark forests of Armorica, in rebellion against the Emperor, an act of hubris. And to him comes a travel-stained messenger, with tidings of disaster. It is the courteous Gwalchmai, with the news of the wounding of his honour. The unnatural rebellion of Modred, the nephew against his mother's brother. Of the son against the father, unnaturally and incestuously begotten. And I, Taliesin-Tiresias, churchwarden in Gloucester Road or proof-reader for the Press, and evening lecturer in Stukeley Street, foreknew and foresuffered all, and the waste land and the dolorous blow. And I thank you, ladies and gentlemen, for your attention.

Mr Longbotham, in the chair, thanked Professor C. Chelifer, on behalf of the Society, for a most lucid and stimulating lecture. The motion was seconded by Miss Vita Brevis, who expressed the opinion that all their ideas on the subject would now be very much clearer. Coffee and mince pies were then served.

ᚼ

Not even on Olympos are the Immortals exempt
From the ravages of change, and the revolutions of chance;
The sadness of senility likewise seizes them,
Entailing its empty and impotent wisdom.
Saturn with his sceptre once swayed the universe;
And governed the earth in the Age of Gold –
The first men in scattered families followed
The herds of beasts, hunting the bison,
The mammoth and the reindeer, as they ranged, for meat.
A simple collectivity, a classless society,
Not ploughing the soil, nor in seedtime sowing.
Their craft, from the flint crudely to fashion
The tools for their tasks, and with tinted ochre,
In lightless caverns, to limn and character,
Magically, the beasts, to make them breed,
Or slide into the pit, to be pierced by spears.
The bones of their dead they daubed and bedabbled
Likewise with red, for luck and for life,
And gold – prized for its grace and its gladness,
Mysteriously life-giving, not the miser's loot.
But Jove revolted; in rebellion he wrested
The sceptre from his sire, and sent him into exile
To a western island, in the wide ocean;
There he sleeps through time, with the Titans, his siblings –
Grimly, the huge Hundred-hander guards them.
A new age now was known on the earth:
Agriculture was invented, and astronomy also,
To mark the succession of the circling seasons,
For hoeing and sowing, and the hauling in of harvest.
In the stone circles men hallowed the sun,
And the feminine and magical mysteries of the moon.
Human blood, holy and blessing
The soil, was sacrificed, the priest-king was slaughtered
Yearly, for the plenty he yielded to the plants.
Priests also and traders, in the towns, proliferated,
Subsisting from the labour of their serfs on their land;
Silver was hoarded, and a hieratic script
Enrolled their secrets, and recorded their revenues.

The Age of Bronze awoke now in brutality:
Barbarian warriors blustered out of the wastelands,
And wars were waged with more effective weapons.
The handsome heroes exhibited their hardihood
In wild tumult, by windy Troys,
Fighting in chariots, fiercely cheered on
To plunder and pillage, by Homeric poets.
　　　　The Age of Iron, out of Asia, extended
A worse development of destruction – war
Become less human, more horrible and more hideous;
The wheel is in motion, willy-nilly we march on
To the uses of artillery, and atomic overkill.
Each technical gain entails the giving up
Of a spiritual good, of certainty and security.
This puts paid, we presume, to that specious puerility
Which professes to hail, in history, a progress.
Mutability masters us – no myth of improvement
Is the law of life; laugh it off, if you will –
Anangke is the arbitress, and enjoins us: "Adapt!"
　　　　The Saturnalia was celebrated at the Winter Solstice
In remembrance, by the Romans, of the reign of Saturn:
By ritualised ribaldry, and licensed riot –
The posts are decked, the porticos and the doorways,
With gaiety and greenery, and gifts exchanged;
The slaves sit down and are served by their masters,
Reconstructing a far-off and irrecoverable freedom
Nostalgically lost in the long-ago of legend,
When the world was governed by wiser gods.
But at this season of midwinter mirth, the Saviour,
Christ was born, in the cavern at Bethlehem,
To oust from Olympus the etiolated eidola;
Jove and his fellows fell under the judgment
Of old age also, and entered that emptiness
Where man's lost dreams dwindle in darkness.
The stable, for once, was the centre of the world;
Not the dialectical dragons, but the dumb ox
And the ass in humility, hung their heads
By a manger of straw, where Mary the Mother
Looked at her Love and hushed Him with a lullaby.
From the Solstice of Capricorn the Cross stems up,
The ends of the transom transfixing the equinoxes,
The summit at Cancer – Christ in the circle
Of the stars of fatality, to ensure our freedom,

Slain for our salvation, in the celestial wheel,
From the foundation of the world; He was found worthy.
　　At this feast it is the kindly custom of Christians
To honour in each other the Divine Image
By the giving of gifts; as with incense and gold,
And with myrrh, the Magi from the marches of the world
Were beckoned to Bethlehem by a bright comet.
Feasting and frolic and jollity are found here –
Not the mirth of Saturn's mythical magisterium,
But the felt prescience of a possible freedom
Eschatologically offered at the end of the ages,
Whose shoots are burgeoning, and begin now to show.
　　But the Prince of Darkness delights to pervert this:
The affluent honour Gluttony and Avarice,
In spewing drunkenness and a spending spree,
Guzzling their guts and giving for advantage,
Disdaining the Lazaruses who languish at their doors.
In Gehenna these gourmets will get their reward –
Trussed up and transformed into battery turkeys,
With sprigs of holly stuck in their holes;
In the form of a foolish and florid Santa Claus,
With cottonwool whiskers, as a witty contrivance,
Beelzebub bastes them with their own butter.
　　They kept the feast at the castle of Cadbury;
While solid snow silvered the landscape,
And hungrily the wolves howled to the wind.
Artorius and his army were abroad – in Armorica,
Some said. They slogged through sombre forests;
There were rumours that he reared at the authority of Rome,
As Carausius and Constantine and Maximus had claimed to.
No certainty was divulged; despatches were sparse;
A dreary and disappointing campaign dragged on.
　　The governance of his realm was given to Guanhumara –
The Queen ruling, with a Council of Regency;
The sons of his sister had seemed the most fitting:
The courteous Gwalchmai kept at the court,
Arranging all things in the absence of Artorius;
With his younger brother, black-haired and beloved
Of the popular party – for plainly men saw
In Modred the most charming and mannerly of mortals;
Nor guessed, under the guise of that graciousness, his heart
Inwardly consumed, cankered and calloused.
The ferocious passion of a frustrated poet,

571

Self-regarding romanticism, ravaged his soul.
        Resinous pine torches perfumed the palace,
Casting through the gloom a guttering glare.
The hall was gay and garnished with greenery –
The bright holly, with bloody berries,
Decked it, and the ivy dedicate to Dionysus:
Rubicund and pugnacious, the robin redbreast,
Who murders, they say, each midsummer his sire,
Harbours in the holly, and the ivy holds
The King of the ramage, the cutty wren,
A trilling troglodyte. From the topmost rafter
Was suspended a sprig of the sacral mistletoe,
A Golden Bough, from the great boles
Of ancient oaks and Avalonian apple trees
Darkly with incantations by the Druids castrated –
Mysterious, as the flower of the midsummer fern:
It hung there for lovers lightly to hallow.
        The boards were loaded with baked boars' heads,
Venison, and various seasonable viands;
Barrels were broached, of beer and mead.
The dinner being done, they called for diversions
Of mirth and pastime, for the promoting of merriment.
Bards and buffoons and minstrels were brought in.
Dwarfish jesters, and jugglers disported;
Self-pitying songs of amatory suffering,
By acclaimed artists were executed for the auditors.
        Popular plaudits hailed this performance;
But somewhat sadly smiling, the Queen,
Guanhumara, gravely gave her opinion:
"This jejune jangling jars on our nerves;
Nor charms nor cheers us, but the revolutions of chance
Brings into mind, and the bitter memory
Of Artorius, absent oversea in Armorica:
News of his campaign comes niggard to our knowledge.
This occasion asks entertainment more aulic –
Gwion, our poet, is pensioned for this purpose;
Let him touch the high tones of his harp,
And bring forth some lay or legend – of Bronwen,
White-bosomed sister of Bran the Blessed;
Of her sorrow, the victim of a vicious slander;
Of her heart's breaking for the brave men, the heroes
Laid in the cold clay for her cause,
Two islands destroyed – her tragic destiny."

Gwion answered the Empress: "Alas,
My heart is sick and my senses heavy.
I am haunted by visions of violence and horror,
Of doom and disaster – distinctly imaged,
But the words will not come to their work at my call.
The numbered words are numb and weary;
My play with them seems all a paltry subterfuge.
More potent were Merddyn's prophetic madness.
But Ceridwen now, by her name of Nimue,
In her dark cavern till the Day of Doom,
Secretes him, like Saturn sleeping on the island,
Grimly guarded. With shame, Guanhumara,
I say that I cannot sing for your solace."
Thus Gwion, stupid and silent in his grief.
        Then Modred spoke, with mildness and malice:
"If our pensioned poet grudges to produce,
Radiant-browed Taliesin, his treasured talent,
Perhaps, Gloriana, your princeliness will permit
An unworthy amateur offer an entertainment?
I have devised some mirth, a dance in masquerade.
Some mummers I have summoned for this merry season
Are waiting without in the winter snow.
Shall I fetch them in to furbish our festival?"
        Gladly Guanhumara (for she loved the grace
Of Modred, the manners and the charm of the man)
Granted him permission to produce this garnish.
He went out into the darkness; for some delay they waited
In the fading flicker of the flaming torches,
In silent surmise of the promised spectacle.
        In the castle of Cadbury the Happening commenced:
A grotesque gallimaufry of horned goat-men,
Satyrs and sylvans in a savage rout,
Misshapen forms, monstrously masked,
Trotted into the hall, traipsing among the tables.
The diners in wonderment, dizzy with wine,
Watched this cortège capering and cavorting.
Covered with hair, with clattering hooves,
Their prodigious and priapic codpieces and pricks
They waggled and wobbled, as wildly they lurched
In capriole or carmagnole – a double chorus,
Each team led by a taller leader;
And one, like a black and bearded billy,
Marched in the foremost, framing their music,

573

Squeezing the bellows of a squalling bagpipe,
As brutishly and boorishly they bleated a carol:

"On the first day of Christmas my true love sent to me
The horned man in the holly tree.

"On the second day of Christmas my true love sent to me
Two cut-throat kinsmen, and the horned man in the holly
    tree.

"On the third day of Christmas my true love sent to me
A three-headed dog, and a three-pronged fork,
Two cut-throat kinsmen, and the horned man in the holly
    tree.

"On the fourth day of Christmas my true love sent to me
A four-sided fortress, a three-headed dog, and a three-
    pronged fork,
Two cut-throat kinsmen, and the horned man in the holly
    tree.

"The tune" said Guanhumara, "is a gavotte and Gallic;
It calls to my mind my carefree maidenhood,
The sunshine of Provence, and the pretty salutation
As they finished with a kindly kiss each figure."
"But I wonder at the words, so wild and uncouth;
They do not seem such as are commonly sung
To this burden." Said Gwalchmai, "They bode no good."
But relentlessly the rout roared on its chant:

"On the fifth day of Christmas my true love sent to me
Five bishops belching,
A four-sided fortress, a three-headed dog, and a three-
    pronged fork,
Two cut-throat kinsmen, and the horned man in the holly
    tree.

"On the sixth day of Christmas my true love sent to me
Six frogs a-croaking, five bishops belching,
A four-sided fortress, a three-headed dog, and a three-
    pronged fork,
Two cut-throat kinsmen, and the horned man in the holly
    tree.

"On the seventh day of Christmas my true love sent to me
Seven maddening moons,
Six frogs a-croaking, five bishops belching,
A four-sided fortress, a three-headed dog, and a three-
    pronged fork,
Two cut-throat kinsmen, and the horned man in the holly
    tree.

"On the eighth day of Christmas my true love sent to me
Eight crooked crowns, seven maddening moons,
Six frogs a-croaking, five bishops belching,
A four-sided fortress, a three-headed dog, and a three-
    pronged fork,
Two cut-throat kinsmen, and the horned man in the holly
    tree.

Gradually the goat-men in their grotesque dance,
Had thronged round the dais where the throne was displayed,
On all sides surrounding the Queen where she sat
With Gwalchmai and Gerontius and the rest of her guards.
A menaceful meaning was almost manifest;
Unease awakened; the audience was aware.
Fuddled by fumes of the goatish fœtor,
Suddenly sick, some sought for the exits,
And left for the darkness, looking for the latrines.
But the Queen and her company of courtiers about her
Seemed like rabbits, when red-haired Reynard,
The furtive fox, charms them with his frisking,
Playing his tricks to puzzle them; transfixed,
Foolishly fascinated, they follow his gambols,
In wide-eyed curiosity, and incautious wonder,
Till, swift as thought, he seizes one by the throat.
But the raucous carol roared up to the rafters:

"On the ninth day of Christmas my true love sent to me
Nine screaming birds,
Eight crooked crowns, seven maddening moons,
Six frogs a-croaking, five bishops belching,
A four-sided fortress, a three-headed dog, and a three-
    pronged fork,
Two cut-throat kinsmen, and the horned man in the holly
    tree.

"On the tenth day of Christmas my true love sent to me
Ten stone tables, nine screaming birds,
Eight crooked crowns, seven maddening moons,
Six frogs a-croaking, five bishops belching,
A four-sided fortress, a three-headed dog, and a three-
  pronged fork,
Two cut-throat kinsmen, and the horned man in the holly
  tree.

"On the eleventh day of Christmas my true love sent to me
Eleven ghosts a-gibbering,
Ten stone tables, nine screaming birds,
Eight crooked crowns, seven maddening moons,
Six frogs a-croaking, five bishops belching,
A four-sided fortress, a three-headed dog, and a three-
  pronged fork,
Two cut-throat kinsmen, and the horned man in the holly
  tree.

"On the twelfth day of Christmas my true love sent to me
Twelve slaughtered Cæsars, eleven ghosts a-gibbering,
Ten stone tables, nine screaming birds,
Eight crooked crowns, seven maddening moons,
Six frogs a-croaking, five bishops belching,
A four-sided fortress, a three-headed dog, and a three-
  pronged fork,
Two cut-throat kinsmen, and the horned man in the holly
  tree."

        They had crowded in now, and closely compassed them;
From their hairy disguises they drew the hafts
Of dangerous daggers, and deadly falchions.
There were murmurs of treason. And the traitors unmasked –
The leader of one set of the satyrs was seen:
Cerdic, at the head of his Saxon horde;
And the other, outrageously, outlandish in expression,
The blue stained features of Fergus, the bloody
King of the Picts, with his painted clansmen.
Then the black musician, the monstrous billy,
Slid off his visor, and they saw in view
Modred under the mask, with features moulded
In the cast of Iscariot – and the eyes of Catiline.
        Modred spoke: "Sirs, and madam,

We have you in our hands. Do not be so hardy
To counter or resist. This castle is surrounded.
Outside there are others to augment this ambuscade.
The guards are suborned. My Saxon guests
And my Pictish friends will persist in their purpose;
And there are plenty of your own alienated proletariat,
Young men of Britain, who belong to our band.
I come as the leader of a confederate league
Weary of the protracted and wasteful war
Artorius, your Emperor, engages in Armorica.
The times demand a different discipline,
A clean sweep. I claim the sovereignty;
By seizure of the Queen a sanction is conveyed,
Through a Celtic custom. I claim that person.
The lady will grant she has given me her love,
Solemnised secretly by sacred vows,
Long years since. So, I scorn
Clandestine adultery. I claim my consort."
        In the incredulous horror of the cruelty of heart,
And the malice of the man she had made her lover,
Of his secret frustration like a smothered fire,
A banked up furnace, now breaking into flame,
Thus ruthlessly revealed, the wretched Queen
Reddened, and seemed ready to speak,
But no words sounded. Then, white and silent,
She gazed in her guilt. But the grey haired veteran,
Gerontius, retorted to the rebel and his rabble:
"Appropriately, indeed, you entered as animals,
Disturbing the decency and the dignity of our feast
With brutish slogans and barbarian brags.
You would seize a sovereignty unsanctified by right,
Subverting the law which is the source of liberty –
The authority Artorius established in this island.
The truths we uphold were transmitted by tradition:
The venerable rules of the Roman *res publica*,
Furnished by our fathers aforetime in their wisdom.
Not liberty but license is furthered by your lust,
In course to be turned to a total tyranny –
Ever and inevitably the outcome of anarchy."
        Cerdic, the ruler of the Saxons, replied:
"Old man, the mystifications you mutter,
These archaic arguments, do not even amuse.
I think that I had them thrust down my throat

By my tutor who taught me in the times I have forgotten.
These sordid rags, these remnants of Rome,
Are ripe for burning. A better regimen
I will forge with my sword, and the force of my Saxons."
      Fierce and youthful, Fergus yelled:
"Roman or Saxon, I spit on this rubbish
Of law and logic, a thing to be laughed at!"
His head was elated with the heather ale
Distilled on the heaths of his distant Highlands,
And the psychedelic and spotted scarlet toadstool
Which he gulped at one go down his gullet – it engendered
Leprechauns in his brain, and the lucid brightness
Of terrestrial paradises, the plain of Tir na n-Og.
Understandably uninterested in abstract ideas
He would rather fool you with fables of the fairies.
In his view was the vision of a vasty palace
With battlements of bannocks and ramparts of bacon
For himself and his comrades to keep and to hold.
"Who is high in heart need take no heed
Of law –" he said, "It is for louts and lubbers;
I am bound by honour and my own boast."
      Mordantly, Gwalchmai, glancing at Modred:
"Brother, you command a curious band
Of Saxon pirates and Pictish savages –
Are you come to be reckoned with the cattle-reevers?"
      Modred laughed: "Maybe I match
With the potent Hercules in that high profession:
The cattle of Geryon, the king of Gades,
The triple giant, we are told that he took.
My friends Fergus and Cerdic formulate
Arguments to account for their actions – his honour,
Or the workings of wyrd. I want no pretexts.
A cattle-reever, I claim this cow!"
      Then starkly he strode to the exalted stage
Where, silent, the Queen sat, and seizing her
By the hair of her head, he hauled her down.
By that ruthless act, a relationship that had ripened,
Declined, and dragged on, was destroyed; she became
No longer a person, for power possessed him,
But an object only, to be acquired and used.
      Swiftly the sword of Gwalchmai from its scabbard
Flashed, but it faltered to flesh itself in the body
Of the brother of his blood; but the battle-tried Gerontius,

Ineffectual in his age, offered to intervene.
Cerdic and Fergus as with one stroke felled him;
He toppled like a tall tree to the floor.
        Then a frenzy of fierce fighting broke out;
In the hall of Cadbury was wholesale carnage.
There were few to resist the relentless fury
Of the Saxons and Picts, with swords and poniards.
The able-bodied were with the army of Artorius in Armorica;
And these feasters were fuddled with the fumes of wine,
And unprepared altogether for the unexpected onslaught.
In that murderous confusion Modred carried off
The Queen on his horse's crupper from the hall.
They galloped over the plain; Gwalchmai pursued,
But lost them at length in the lowering darkness.

                    *   *   *

        In the White Tower, which traditions told
Cæsar had erected to seal his sovereignty,
In the town of London in the loamy lagoon,
Was a secluded cell – there was kept solitary,
And closely guarded, Guanhumara the Queen.
The Middle Saxons, a stolid sept,
Possessed the place. She was put into their keeping.
        On a night of January her gaolers nodded,
It seemed, for silently slid on the waters
A barge under the battlements, on the breast of Thames.
The Queen heard a hurried conference
With the guard at the gate, and the chink of gold,
As a pouch or a bag presumably was passed;
The steps on the stone of the stairs, and a key
Grated in the lock. Guanhumara looked,
As the door, opening, disclosed to her eyes
Three figures – the form and features
Of Bedwini the bishop, and Modred's brother,
The courteous Gwalchmai, and concealed in a cowl,
Another, unknown, but whose eyes examined her
Searchingly, and it seemed with disapproving scorn.
        Gwalchmai spoke, swiftly and softly:
"We come to deliver you from this dark captivity.
How we found out the place, through what perils we passed,
Braving the barbarians; how we bribed your guards,
There is no time to tell – we may talk of it hereafter.

Suffice it to say that somehow we got here.
Daegrafn, now dead, to Bedwini delivered
Certain secrets, and runic symbols:
They have come in useful, to convey us in this contingency.
The boat is ready by the bank of the river.
You shall sail to a place of succour and safety.
I go, Guanhumara, overseas to Gaul,
To alert Artorius of this attempt on his imperium.
Rapidly he will return; order will be restored.
Modred, my brother, the miscreant and his mob
Of Picts and Saxons, will pay for their perversity,
And flee, as before on the field of Badon."
      Guanhumara answered: "Gwalchmai, I guess
Order, annihilated once, not so easy
To build anew, being broken; have you the knowledge
To organise an omelette again into eggs?"
(Gallic Guanhumara, the good housewife,
Smiled slightly at the kitchen similitude).
"It seems not likely I shall see my lord,
Artorius again. With anguish I admit
My disordered passion produced this predicament.
I would seek out somewhere some solitary refuge,
A place of religion, where with prayers and penitence,
Austerely I may endeavour to expiate these acts."
      Bedwini replied: "It is ready, as you bid;
Away in the island of Ireland it awaits you.
Bridget petitioned the blessed Patrick
For a piece of ground, a place where to plan
A convent for her nuns, a convenient cloister.
But Patrick was grudging of that parcel of ground:
'How much' he said, 'will serve for your sisters?'
'And sure' she answered, 'for this shrine I ask
No more than my cloak will cover.' Then she cast it
Down on the mould – this Dido, meditating
Her Christian Carthage – and a miracle was consummated,
For it covered the whole of the County Kildare.
Nine virgins, vestals in vigil,
Feed and tend there an unfailing flame,
On a holy hearth, in the heart of the land.
In that sacred place you shall be put for protection.
I cannot go with you, Guanhumara, to convey you:
It is a time of testing and turmoil in Britain –
Everywhere, as always, the innocents will undergo

Furious massacre; I must feed my flock,
And, if the Lord require it, lay down my life."
      "Gladly I will go," said Guanhumara, "But who
Will escort me to Ireland, among uncertainties and evils?"
      Bedwini said: "This stranger, and brother,
Is come to convey you. His name is Cadoc.
Cast out, at the council from communion, for his stubborness,
Churlishness and uncharity, I have chosen him for this –
There is no one else now, to serve us in our need."
      Then Cadoc, harshly: "Have we here the whore,
Whom in holy courtesy I must convoy to Kildare –
Whose deed of darkness has brought us to this destruction?"
      Said Gwalchmai, grimly: "More gracious be your tongue,
And cautious, to a Queen, and with that my kinswoman;
And call to your memory *'quia multum amavit.'*"
      Cadoc replied: "In religion, I am ready
To take on, in holiness and humility, this task.
The poorest of creatures, I crave this for a penance.
I will escort the adulteress, your aunt, to Ireland."

                    *   *   *

      In the shrine of Kildare, shone and coruscated
The perpetual flame as it flickered and flashed.
Guanhumara knelt, in that ground, on her knees.
In a midnight vigil she mourned among the vestals.
Broken with contrition, the Queen of Britain,
In anguished orisons asking intercession,
Held up her heart to the Queen of Heaven.
      Brutally lowered over the land of Britain
Civil war, in the wanness of winter,
And savage death; and still in the darkness
The perpetual flame of prayer persisted.
      In the castle of Cadbury, casks were broached,
Beer bubbled from the broken tuns,
And wine, wasted wantonly by the plunderers.
A party of Picts, with Fergus presiding,
Tunelessly still ground out the garbled goat-song.
Somewhat more sober, the Saxons apart
Marked their merriment with a certain menace.
      Cerdic motioned to Mul his sibling:
"Brother, I would breathe it in your ear – this Briton,
This madman Modred, thinks he is master,

Consumed with pride – a peacock, a capercailzie,
He spreads his tail, and trumpets his taunts,
With tight-closed eyes. Eagerly he will take
The brunt of the battle to brave his father.
If they eat each other, it is our advantage.
For this fellow, Fergus, and our friends the Picts,
Their anarchic energy augments our army,
Disdaining discipline, with a desperate courage;
When the fighting is finished, we can settle them finally,
By massacre, cut them down carousing in their cups.
Trust in Wyrd, and your trenchant weapons:
Anangke relegates this realm to the English."

      The drinking was deep: they honoured Dionysus,
The ivy-crowned deity, in exalted dizziness
And transported frenzy – the father of Tragedy.

MELPOMENE

*(Scene: Near the battlefield of Camlann, outside the tent of
Artorius. It is the late afternoon of a bleak January day. The flap
of the tent lifts, and a tall woman with the head of a crow emerges.
She holds in her hands a crystal cup).*

THE MORIGAN: I am the Queen of Heaven – of the empty spaces
    Between the stars, and consort
    Of silver-handed Nuada, rider of the storm;
    I am arbitress of battles, and chooser of the slain.
    This field is Camlann, the sedgy moor
    In the western marshes: Oh Absalom, Absalom,
    In the vale of Hebron, by Avalon's isle!
    But now it is Modred who challenges Artorius;
    He heads the band of the yelling Picts,
    And the silent Saxons. And I have come
    To take back my Luck, the luck of Artorius,
    This gleaming grail. And do not ask me
    Why, feminine, my mind is changed,

Nor to whom I shall deliver it. I do not choose
Modred – the onion man; he will play any part, but peel off
His masks and skins, he has no centre
To be committed to. And I do not choose
Fergus and his blue tattoo of Picts:
They go to battle and they always fall,
An æsthetically satisfying gesture. And as for Cerdic,
He trusts in wyrd and his own sword;
His seed shall reign at Winchester, and in course of time
Maybe my irony ensures
A better and gentler civilisation out of these cinders
Than the wildness of the Celt, and the relics of Rome:
And England's Darling fights once more
The battles of Artorius by Athelney and Avalon,
Against a further threat from the Germanic sea.
To the uncertain battle now
I flap on my crow's wing.

(Exit)

(Enter the CHORUS *of superannuated non-combatants).*

CHORUS: They contend, they contend, the kinsmen contend –
As on the banks of the sacred Nile,
The red-haired Set, the wild ass, and Horus,
Kestrel of the morning – the hot wind
Out of the desert, the green strip
By the bank of the river, where the lettuce sprouts.
It is past midwinter, but not yet
The sun glints on the candour
Of Abyssinian snows; not yet
The heavenly Water-bearer reverses
His fruitful urn.

Blessing on the wells and springs of Britain –
The red dew falls from the incensed heaven;
There shall be a stirring in the waters, the river comes down,
From the cataracts, from the anemonied woods
Of Lebanon, tinged with the blood
Of the eternally slain and slain eternal
Master of the garden, of the buried, burgeoning wheat.

They contend, they contend – the remnant of Troia,
The reliques of Rome, and the inchoate hordes

Of the unharvested sea, and the sterile moorlands.
Under the razor of the January wind,
We, old men of Britain, children
Of Locrine and Llyr, recalling
The misfortunes of Arthur, await,
From the arbitress of battles, the uncertain event.
But who approaches now, his figure marred
With the shed blood? I discern the features
Of Bedwyr, the king's butler; and it is shame
If, wearied, he shifts from the field.

(*Enter*BEDWYR)

BEDWYR: Weep, men of Britain, lament
For the flower of the land this day scorched up
Shed your tears for Urien of Rheged,
And Urien of Gower, lopped like trees
Under the woodman's axe; lament
For the Hawk of May, for the grace
Of courtesy cut off, for Gwalchmai;
For Owain, his brother, whose fine eyes
The kite and the crow are ready to pluck out;
For Kai, the steward, who was not niggard
To furnish the tables with bread and flesh.
In the morning they rode out, a brilliant company,
Adorned with gold torques and bright enamels,
To make good their words that they boasted aforetime,
In the hall of their king on the eve of battle,
Over the red wine and the yellow mead;
The close of the day sees them fallen, and trodden
In the iron-hard ground of winter. The well-whetted spear
Has failed them, and the keen sword is shattered,
The shield-wall is broken to the foe's onrush.
Let your tears be down dropping for this field of disaster!

LEADER OF THE CHORUS: But what of the emperor? What of
        Artorius?

BEDWYR: Artorius fights on, and seeks out his opponent.

LEADER OF THE CHORUS: And why is Bedwyr absent from the field?

BEDWYR: Only at the behest of my king and my dear love,
        Do I shift from the field. When Artorius saw

How many of his men were fallen in the fight,
He turned to me and spoke: "It is the guilty issue
Of my own blood that has brought this upon us.
In the thick of the battle I must seek out Modred
In single combat, and conclude this matter.
Retire you, my friend and my faithful servitor,
To my tent by the field. And there you will find
That cup of crystal which I call my Luck.
Make it ready for my return. If I come victorious,
We will drink again from it. And if otherwise,
Put it between my hands, for burial with my body."
And for this I am come here, as he commanded.

LEADER OF THE CHORUS: Let him come victorious, and the tide be
   turned!

BEDWYR: But lament, O men, for those who have fallen!

CHORUS: To the shadowy paths of Annwyn, and the wan
   Eddies of Acheron, they are passing now,
   The spirits of men. They went out to find
   If it was real, this life they were leading.
   Fame is their proper meed. Fame should run on
   To ages of futurity, but it rests on the tongues
   Of old men, chirping like crickets
   By a cooling oven. Old men who soon
   Will lie cold and forgotten in the frozen ground.
   We are less real than those whom we celebrate.
   But one comes running, stained with the dust
   Of the labour of this day.

   (*Enter a* MESSENGER)

MESSENGER: I seek for Bedwyr, the cup-bearer of the king.

BEDWYR: I am present. Do you come from Artorius?

MESSENGER: Artorius lives. But now they are carrying
   His body from the field, stricken
   With a deadly wound.

BEDWYR: Who struck the blow? And what of Modred?

585

MESSENGER: Modred, who struck the blow, has perished.

BEDWYR: What brought about this double wounding?

MESSENGER: In the thickest part of the battle, Artorius
    Sought out his son and his sister's son.
    At last they confronted each other, but seemed
    As if transformed, their nature changed
    To that of the twin dragons, the warring worms of the earth.
    Artorius lifted Caliburn his sword,
    Firmly gripping it in both of his hands,
    And made to strike down on the helmet of Modred.
    But out of its scabbard Modred discased
    His subtle rapier – they say that the tip
    Was smeared with a secret and corrosive poison;
    The Black Annis of the Dane Hills,
    The hag who has her cave there, who lurks
    Concealed in the branches of trees to snatch and devour
    Straying children, it was who gave it him
    On a moonless night in summer. It seemed
    In a timeless moment each stood there poised,
    And ready to deal the other his death. Then, as if by chance,
    Down from the sky distraction swooped:
    A crow, one of the many necrophilous coveys,
    That hung and haunted about the field,
    Came cawing and croaking down, its black
    And fœtid wings beating about
    The eyes of the combatant kinsmen. Blindly and confusedly
    Their arms and weapons flailed. Caliburn
    Glanced from the helmet and breastplate, and thrust
    Deep into the belly and bowels of Modred. At that moment
    The rebel's thin and envenomed rapier
    Found a mark in the groin of Artorius. Modred
    Stumbled and swooned to the slippery ground, and, dying,
    Gasped out a final and raucous word:
    "*Vicisti!*" – to his sire was it said?
    It seemed rather to the emptiness of the air.

    Seeing their Ymherawdr stricken, the Brythonic
    Host faltered, appalled. And then,
    From behind the horde of the disorganised Picts,
    Cerdic and his Saxons swung into action,
    Moving as if they mastered a Roman regimen.

They are pressing hard the dispirited remnant,
Who still fight on; but defeat seems certain.

BEDWYR: These disasters that power, who rules
         The turbulent tides of our being, has brought upon us,
         For the destruction of the island. And who can tell
         Out of what depths she sprang at her birth?

CHORUS: Three drops of blood mingled with sperm
         (Kronos of crooked councils reaping
         His father's sex – mandrake and mistletoe)
         Through the bright æther slid,
         Like dragon's teeth.
         The first drop fell on the earth.
         Unsheathed from harsh bark
         Nymphs of the Melian grove, of ash trees, shaking
         Their straight and deadly spears. Possession,
         Berserk fury, bitter frenzy of battle,
         Bane to the sons of men.

         A second drop into the unfathomable,
         Unnamed reaches of Night and Erebos –
         Realms of the dead, regions of the unborn:
         Blood-lipped, serpent-skirted, leaden-cheeked, upreared
         The unmentionable Avengers.

         Into the jewelled, light-enraptured sea
         A third drop spurted. Caressed by favouring winds
         A delicate scallop-shell drifted to Cyprus.
         Naked, virgin she rose, and cleansed
         The brine from pearly flanks and sun-bright hair.
         She also is possession; blood-born and laughter-loving
         Even as those others.

         (ARTORIUS, *wounded, is brought in*).

ARTORIUS: Fetch me, Bedwyr, water to drink. The poison
           Runs through my veins. My brain
           Begins to cloud. I see
           A fire flickering before my eyes,
           Kindled by the breath of nine maidens – the cauldron
           Of Ceridwen, as once I beheld it
           At the centre of the earth? Or is it

587

The perpetual flame that burns in the shrine of Kildare,
Tended by vestals? A solitary, veiled woman
Kneels before it, holding a small candle,
As if for the feast of the Purification.
It is the pale face of Guanhumara I see.
The wild horses, the wild horses –
Tear the white limbs of the false woman!

BEDWYR: Forgive her, Oh king, forgive your wife –
Who now in the sanctuary of Bridget,
Repents, and prays for you in her repentance.

ARTORIUS: Oh you lay all night in your lover's arms
And you took no thought of me;
But you thought that the play of love was sweet
As the flower of the hawthorn tree.

Oh you may wear the stones with your knees...
But you will not bring back...
Poor woman

I should rather ask forgiveness of her! What good did I do
her?
I gave her no child but only a false lover,
That issued from my incestuous loins. And now I am dying
With no one to follow me to prop the falling realm. Llachew
Perished in the Caledonian wood,
Pierced by a Pictish dart.
I must not die, Bedwyr, pour water
Into the crystal cup I call my Luck,
And bring it to me here.

(BEDWYR *goes into the tent*).

ARTORIUS: ...will not bring back the brave young men,
That lie in a clay-cold bed.

(BEDWYR *comes out of the tent again*).

BEDWYR: Your Luck is gone. It stands no more
In its appropriate place. The tent is dark.
The strange light that used to glow from that crystal
No longer illumines it. Has some sneak-thief
Slunk in, under cover of the battle's tumult?

ARTORIUS: She who formerly gave it me in trust
      Has taken back her lending. This was the thief.

BEDWYR: The sword remains. The active power remains.

ARTORIUS: It did not fail me in the fight, but its stroke
      Swerved awry from my will. There is no right potency
      In the active power when the passive power departs. Take
        it –
      Fling it to the oblivion of the stagnant lake of sedges!

BEDWYR: I return it with reverence to her who gave it.

ARTORIUS: Fling it rather with scorn to that fickle
      Lady of the glimmering lake – with scorn and defiance.
      But I am freed now from the grasp of Necessity;
      So bring me, in an earthen cup, some drink.

BEDWYR: By privilege of my office I have already brought it.

    (He proffers a cup to ARTORIUS, *who is about to drink, but
    hesitates).*

ARTORIUS: The water is red. It is tinged with the people's blood.

BEDWYR: Not water, but wine – Falernian,
      The last of it, from the cellars
      Of Constantine, your great-grandsire, or perhaps
      From the store of Aurelius Ambrosius. Drink, Cæsar –
      A suitable potation.

ARTORIUS: I drink it for the love it is offered with. Bedwyr,
      You were silent when we sat in the fane of Michael,
      Debating about the laws.

BEDWYR: Was I supposed to say something serious? –
      The single thing that slipped into my thought
      Was my simple love. And it could find no word.

ARTORIUS: Let that wordless word endure. For the makeshift
      Of law is shattered now. The polity crumbles.
      The radial crown that was placed on me,
      Under the uncertain weather of July,

Devolves, by right, on Custennyn my cousin;
But what can he achieve, leading a band
Of refugees and guerillas in the mountains of Wales?
Anangke assigns this realm to the English.
And the stables are still to be cleansed. But not by me.
Carry me now out of the biting air.

(ARTORIUS *is carried into the tent,* BEDWYR *following*).

CHORUS: In that island of the apple trees,
       Contraries are reconciled; the great
       Beneficent and ancient Snake is coiled
       About the gnarly bole, where from the boughs
       Depend the golden fruit; and lean
       The hazels over the deep pool, and the salmon plunging.
       Quietly they walk in the shade and on green lawns,
       The lovers there, and the friends;
       Those whose hearts had beaten with integrity.
       They listen to the timeless song of the white-breasted
       Birds of Rhiannon, and they forget
       Their bitter anguish, their rage and pride,
       And all they endured for passion, or in war.

       Thither you too Artorius, are passing now –
       To rest in the softened sunset of our dream
       For long, long ages; till the circling, starry wheel
       Summon you once again into the tumult
       To save your falling island.

(Re-enter BEDWYR*)*.

BEDWYR: Artorius is dead – your friend and mine:
       The prop is fallen – the image of an order
       That momentarily flashed, a meteor in the night, is gone.
       Returns the darkness and the accustomed horror.
         As for the dead, it is not possible,
       In the shock of such a loss, for the mind to imagine
       Them wholly gone, a snuffed-out candle flame.
       But if they anywhere exist
       It is in another mode of being, and further
       Than the furthest star that flickers in the utmost galaxy;
       Yet, in this aching wound of our bereavement,
       Nearer than the neck-vein. But I cannot help

But think of him as stumbling through the darkness on a
    strange path.
    And I want to be there
Where he is, if I could help and comfort him
With the touch of a hand. But I must not:
We stand as sentries, and the order
For knock-off is not yet given.
And I have his orders too. I go
To throw the bitter sword into the bitter lake.
By that gesture, I affirm, on his behalf,
My own and his existence – not bound
By myth, the starry returning wheels.

CHORUS: As the darkness gathers, enrol him
        With those whose human stature
        Is heightened, not diminished, by their death.
        Not true, not true what the ancient poet said
        Speaking of the misfortune
        Of birth into this harsh world – for not
        Not to be born, to exist,
        This is the best for man.

EUTERPE

After the last battle, Camlann, three men only
Survived, it is said; and the first
Was Sandde Bryd Angel – so beautiful
The grace of his limbs and the light of his face,
Men would not strike him; they took him for an angel
Ministering in that agony. And the second
Was Morvran the son of Tegid, hideous,
Shagged with hair like a rutting stag.
Men took him for a devil, auxiliary
In that unnatural fight, and would not strike him.
And the third was Glewlwyd Gavælvawr,

The dusky hero of the mighty grasp,
A thick-thewed muscleman, the porter
Of the court of Artorius.
None struck at him, not risking
That terrible grip. So these lived on
In the extremes of their humanity.
After the battle, silence. Silence, not peace,
Over the exhausted land. And then
The pluvial god sent rain,
A steady drizzle, filling the dykes,
Flooding the brown fallows,
In purification, till fishes of the sea
Played in the empty furrows.

They passed to westward, those three men,
Dragging on a rough sled or raft of boughs
The coffined body. They crossed the dark moors
Of Damnonia, and reached at last
The ancient igneous rocks – granite, alabaster
And serpentine – of the horn of the land.
The edge of time, the frayed edge:
Ghosts of the dead and of the unborn
Began to crowd upon them. Beneath their feet
Were subterranean knockings, the spirits
Of Phœnician slaves in the hollow tin-mines.

As they passed by
The holy place at Morwenstow, an old priest
In a fisherman's jersey and heavy sea-boots,
And the green headgear of an Armenian archimandrite,
Looked out and blessed them. At length they came
To a bare treeless headland, with a few dwellings:
The village where the cow ate the bell rope.

A sea-morgan, a mermaid, haunted those coasts,
Lily-white and lustful, insatiate and frigid.
Fishermen, stripped to the waist, mending their nets
In lonely coves, or boys,
With unbroken voices, on the edge of puberty,
Singing in the choir, awakened her desires.
She scrambled up the grating shingle, or slithered
Into the chancel, and seized them in her arms.
She dragged them down to her coral and pearl dight hall;
But as the waters closed over them, she found she held

Only a draggled corpse. Her terrible
Frustrated shrieks thickened men's blood,
Made cattle drop their calves untimely.

With difficulty they hauled down to the beach
The body on its raft of boughs. And stood there,
Gazing out over the endless waters
To the last lurid glow of the sinking sun.
A flock of red-footed choughs wheeled inshore to the cliffs.
Sandde said: "Maybe
His soul flies among that lot."
And Morvran: "But we must shove his body
Into the waves. The tide will take it."
And Glewlwyd: "There is here no priest
To hallow his parting. Modred
With his Saxon and Pictish friends, has hunted and harried
The priests through the land. And there is no poet
To speak the praise of our Ymherawdr:
Gwion fell in the fight in the hall
Under the holly and ivy boughs; and Daegrafn also,
The hostage, knifed by his own kith.
And we have no heart to sing." Then, as they looked,
They saw a figure striding over the sands,
A woman taller than a man, clothed from head to foot
In a coarse dark gown. Her hair was white
As the cotton-grass, and her face dead-white,
Like a bleached bone that lay upon the shore.

It was the virgin Sinora, who dwelt
In a cranny of the cliff, among the scooped-out holes
Of shearwater and puffin. None could remember
A time when she did not dwell there, even the oldest;
Nor knew for a certainty what manner of woman she was.
Some said a Christian votaress, and some
A Druid lady of the standing stones;
And some said Merddyn's sister.
Her food was the bulbs of the wild garlic
That flourished all about, and fish
Which her three seals brought her
Out of the deep waters –
Silkie, Sæhund and Slippa.
And these attended her now,
Clumsily lolloping along behind her.

When the men saw those creatures,
With their great liquid eyes, they crossed themselves.
They thought them human souls who, for some unknown sin,
Did penance in those bodies. They were wrong,
Construing thus those harmless beasts.

They saw that she held in her hands a great crowd,
Or a lyre, formed from the shell of a green sea-turtle,
Strung with dolphin's sinews. She greeted them
In a gruff deep voice: "Men, what do you here,
In your beauty, strength, and hideousness,
Carrying a corpse?" And Glewlwyd: "This body is
Artorius, erstwhile Emperor in this island;
And we consign it to the sea. It is our wyrd."
And she: "You do well:
Not wise the thought, a grave for Arthur."
Then Morvran: "There is no one here
To hallow this parting, or to sing
The praises of the dead. Lady, if you have any skill
In music, sing for us." And she: "I have such skill,
And I will sing."

Then, while they pushed the raft of boughs and the coffin
Into the outgoing tide, she took her crowd,
Preluding among the strings – they awoke
Sea-echoes of deep caves, and the moan of breakers
On grinding shingle. Enchanted by the sound,
Silkie, Sæhund and Slippa
Were still and listened, their eyes wide,
Forgetting their fear of man. The raft drifted
Further and further from the shore,
Over the darkening waves. Then she began to sing,
Her voice booming over the waters:

>"We send you, body of a notable man,
>By the waste paths of the sea,
>The salt, unharvested element,
>
>"To the polity of the fish,
>To the furtiveness of the crab,
>To the tentacle of the squid,
>
>"To the red ruler of the tornado,
>To the green ruler of the undersea,
>To the black ruler of the dead,

"To the three-headed dog,
To the sharp-toothed Scylla –
Cuttle fish, and sea-bitch.

"O Lord, who said to the deep:
'So far, and no further!'
Deliver Thy darling from the tooth of the shark.

"O Christ descending
To the profound, redeem him
From the belly of the fish.

"O Spirit, brooding on tohu-bohu, save
From the embrace of the sea-morgan,
From Tiamat, the formless –

"Dove, bearing your olive leaf
Through the rains of the new year,
Breathe into the nostrils of the drowned.

"Star of the Sea,
In intercession gleam
Over the black waters.

"And our vows follow him,
Like petrels flittering
Over the crests and troughs of the waves.

"To the verdict and oblivion of the sea,
Artorius, we consign
Your actions, your defeat."

She ceased; and Silkie and his two brothers
Shook themselves out of their trance, and saw
The strangers standing by.
Then Sæhund gave a soft and sudden "Bao!"
They slid into the sea, following the raft
Far out from shore. They bobbed and plunged,
Joyfully, in the rolling waves.
The unfallen creatures danced in the salt element:
The source and origin of all life.

Hang up Euterpe, on the coral bough your harp:
Take down, Calliope your trumpet.

The Triumph of the Muse

Tongueless the forest now,
Under the arctic Plough;
Where she with lucid brow
   Walked in fine weather;
Each bird of learned trill –
Woodlark and whippoorwill –
Sits, hunched, with tuneless bill
   And drooping feather.

Here, where the turf was sweet,
Danced, with their unshod feet,
Faun-girls and dryads neat –
   All her relations –
Culling delightful flowers
To decorate their bowers,
Through now quite cancelled hours,
   In these plantations.

Goddess and Muse was she,
Patron of prosody,
Seeming benign to me
   Till she had fled;
She has directed far
Venus, her silver car:
Saturn, a thoughtful star
   Spins overhead.

This unkind season proves
I should forsake these groves,
Scene of our decent loves;
   Northward I turn,
Even in my distress
Knowing that none can guess
Her metamorphoses;
   Or her return.

Now listen, reader, if, as I am able
I here recall a dream I had last night,
In formal guise of allegory or fable –

Poetic *genres*, I grant, which can be trite,
And, at the best of times, are hardly new,
Nor, at the present, fashionable to indite:

The whole thing done in *terza rima* too! –
This metre, with its three-fold rhyme in layers,
I find, the knack once caught, I can construe

Almost as well as Dorothy L. Sayers,
(If not as Dante). So, let's pour a cup
In due libation, with the usual prayers,

To bright Apollo, and take the matter up.
(We poets live a life that is *askesis* –
Our dreams aren't caused by that on which we sup.)

Then patience, reader, while I state my thesis:
Last night it seemed, as on my bed I lay
(Which is quite comfortable, in spite of creases),

That suddenly the room was bright as day
(Which was, I must point out, extremely strange,
Because the light's not working, anyway),

But otherwise, there was no obvious change,
Except a figure who stood by my bed,
Close at my pillow, just in my vision's range –

A grave, black-coated form, with a fine head
And features of a somewhat Jewish cast
In which one marked knowledge to suffering wed.

At this intrusion I was not aghast,
But most surprised, and just a bit annoyed;
At first, too, tongue-tied: then I spoke at last –

"Sir, who are you, and why are you thus employed?"
In measured, hollow tones the answer came:
"I'm the long-suffering spirit of Sigmund Freud,

"By Mercy loosed from purgatorial flame
For the brief season of an earthly night
To expiate the sins donė in my name.

"All my life long, with patience infinite
I strove to plumb the depths of that dank puddle
The human soul, till I had sounded quite

"Its pits of sickness, an infernal muddle
Of pride and lust, and childish cruelty,
Where man's pale phantasies in darkness huddle.

"I fancied not ignoble it might be –
The task myself imposed – to show some gleams
Of Science to those sewers of infamy

"Where never before had glanced her sacred beams;
And bring back something, by which men might decode
The message that is ciphered in their dreams.

"I was reviled; not easy was my road.
I died" (here pain twisted the Viennese face)
"An exile, bearing through strange lands the load

"Which is not for me alone, but my whole race,
To find the God I'd analysed away –
Imagine my professional loss of face –

"Was still in charge. On that tribunal-day
I'd scarce a scrap of grace to call my own,
And who of all the Saints for me would pray,

"Or state my case before the sapphire throne?
Who, but God's holy Prophet, who gave the Law
To Israel, graven upon Sinai's stone?

"O father Moses, then it was I saw,
There in that realm where law gives way to grace,
You learned to make eternal justice thaw.

"The God of Jacob did not hide his face
From me, mean child of these our latter days!
So, prisoned in a purgatorial place,

"In pain I learn the lost technique of praise,
Until my time of expiation's ended.
And thus, with patience, I consume my days;

"But more than this has Justice condescended:
I, who through dreams and dreamers had my skill,
By nights have further leave to me extended.

"Through men's subconscious minds I wander at will
(Rather like that Queen Mab in Shakespeare's play)
And they, by me, of visions have their fill

"Until I vanish at the dawn's first grey.
But not of their unrecognized desire,
Sexual phantasy, a mere shadow-play,

"Now am I hierophant – but what is higher:
Images of Truth – as once in the dark wood
The Florentine from his poetic sire

"Had courteous guidance – which may do them good,
If only they have wit to apprehend,
Rightly interpreted and understood.

"And so it is I come to you, my friend:
I am informed – if they have told me right –
You are a poet of the modern trend.

"There is a journey we must go tonight;
You shall learn something useful for your trade.
Step off this window-ledge – the moon shines bright

"Here over Kensington; don't be afraid."
At this he grasped my hand; before I dare
Make any protest, with that august shade

I was out floating through the wintry air.

Swiftly we cut the air, our speed increasing
(I guess) in geometrical progression,
And bent our course without delay or ceasing.

A midnight peeler (who dared not make concession
To this improbable fact, not worth preserving
When he wrote up his log – he feared the impression

On his superiors) alone observing.
Anyone else who watched us go, like Chaucer's
Eagle (see *House of Fame*) so deftly swerving

Probably put it down to flying saucers.
Now London was laid out before us, from
Paul's to the docks, with ships moored by their hawsers,

From Mile End Road to Wembley Stadium –
London, like a black rose, in innocent sleep,
With her dark strength, imperial as Rome.

All this soon left behind – and now the deep
Tides of the English Channel lay below;
And long white tracks of foam were seen to creep,

Curled by the north winds as they boldly blow;
And here we blundered in a migrant skein
Of Arctic wildfowl, fleeing the northern snow –

Dotterel, wildgeese, woodcock (birds without brain) –
That we were fitting company for them,
Poet and psycho-analyst, is plain.

Southwards we steered, towards Orion's hem,
And Europe's form beneath us lay disclosed,
Giantess, with an Alpine diadem.

Now easterly my practised guide disposed
Our course, where on Hellenic rock and reef
The peaceful Mediterranean Sea reposed,

A siren, chanting of some ancient grief
Mytho-scatological, out of Lemprière,
A first-rate scandal on his every leaf.

I was enchanted by the classic air,
And felt like Andrew Lang reading the *Odyssey*;
Grey olives glimmered in the moonlight there –

The atmosphere was very god-and-goddessy;
One thought of Bliss or Tippett's operatics,
With *corps de ballet* chlamysy and bodicey.

I heard cicadas sing (the Athenian *tettix*)
But not dumb insect-song, for here they chanted
Authentic fragments from the pre-Socratics.

"What is that mountain, with the temple planted
Upon its highest peak," (I asked my guide)
"About whose flanks a river's course is slanted

From the clear fountain springing on its side?"
"That is the Muse's sacred hill, high Helicon,
Where we must go; here ends our aerial ride."

Then stooping down, like an alighting pelican,
He drew me with him. I gave a qualmish shiver;
For swings, or lifts, are never things my belly can

Readily cope with. As regards the liver
And diaphragm, the sensation was the same.
But safe we stood beside that rapid river.

"This is the place to visit which you came."
Went on my guide, "This is the Muse's shrine –
Bright goddess honoured wide by many a name,

"And sometimes three-fold known, sometimes as nine;
Whose children's richest gift perhaps may be,
For an untidy life, one perfect line –

"Which they suppose will last eternally,
Like her own laurel growing ever green,
But the axe is at the root even of that tree.

"These are her sacred groves, as you have seen;
Here, where the winged horse struck the sounding rock,
This springing fountain is clear Hippocrene.

"These are her temple's gates; before you knock,
Read the inscription placed above them here."
"TO NONE WITH LIPS UNBLEST WILL THESE UNLOCK;

"TO NONE, UNLESS THE GODDESS HOLDS HIM DEAR,
AND IN THE CRADLE GAVE HER ACCOLADE.
HENCE, YE PROFANE! NO AMATEURS WANTED HERE.

"NO BOTANIZING IN THE MUSE'S GLADE"
Was written plain in letters all of gold,
(Probably genuine) under a cypress shade.

"Pay due regard to what you have been told";
Then said my guide, "but I must leave you now;
I am not one of this initiate fold:

"In life the laurel did not shade my brow."
Polite, as ever, in his life, to all
His patients, then he vanished with a bow;

While I passed through into the Muse's hall.

CANTO III

But how can my weak verse even begin
To tell of that so much renowned and gracious
Temple of song, which now I stood within?

Tall marble pillars there held up the spacious
High-vaulted roof of the celestial fane;
The Muse's hall's sufficiently capacious

All, even her meanest servants, to contain
Though critics still endeavour to contract it
By laws not known at all in her domain.

But, though so vast, I noticed that in fact it
Was crowded full, for all the walls around
Were those from whom her homage is exacted –

The holy poets, with green laurel crowned,
With myrtle, ivy, and the unfading rose,
From every land and epoch, still renowned.

Of course, I knew at once the names of those
Whose pictures are in Blank's Encyclopaedia
(A work which I assisted to compose –

And since I left its staff I have been needier;
But I would rather carve out for myself
A place in letters, than write their annals – greedier

For fame than guineas, for freedom than for pelf.
Likely enough, I shall end up with neither –
Both Fame and Fortune leave me on the shelf).

But I digress, with not much reason either:
I now intend to tell, if I have luck,
Of the great poets which I could descry there.

For all, from Homer down to Stephen Duck,
Had places there assigned, and due degrees,
Who once had learned the sacred bough to pluck.

I saw great Aeschylus and Sophocles,
Who sway the melting soul with tragic thunders;
Also their colleague, Aristophanes,

Whose target was the still recurrent blunders
Of popular politicians – but today
Whether he'd get away with it one wonders.

Homer himself I saw, with the sea-spray
Of all Odysseus' voyagings on his lips,
Who told the glories of the Trojan fray

(With a rather lengthy catalogue of ships,
Like this of poets). These Greeks all sat together;
And with them Hesiod, still retailing tips

On agriculture, grumbling at the weather
As farmers always do – and all the rest –
I don't suppose it really matters whether

I list their names, though I will do my best:
The Theban Pindar, for his high-sounding Odes
Renowned even in those Islands of the Blest

Which once he sang; and, in their Lesbian modes
Sappho, Alcaeus, chanting to the lyre;
Theognis, Apollonius of Rhodes,

Bion, and Moschus, who mourned his funeral pyre.
Next these a Roman legion met my gaze,
Whose chief was Virgil, the great Mantuan sire;

Catullus, who tuned his sweetest notes to praise
A high-born tart, yet had a blistering tongue,
As Julius Caesar knew for all his bays;

Juvenal, the king vulture, who in dung
Of world dictators sought his cowering prey;
And lastly Claudian, who his harp still strung

To the high Roman measures, when the day
At last blacked out on that imperial town,
And the glow of all her conquests died away.

And next I saw, in a coarse cloak of brown,
The Anglo-Saxon Cædmon, with his beard
Parted in the middle, to whom, as he lay down

Among the straw and cow-turds, there appeared
A heavenly angel, who could teach poetics;
I wish that some who in our days are reared

Went to as pure a source for their aesthetics –
If their verse flows it's not divine afflatus,
But something, I should think, more like emetics.

The Celtic bards, with all the apparatus
Of art's complexities, I noticed then,
Who in their lives enjoyed an honoured status:

Merddyn, Taliesin, Llewarch Hen;
And those who ripened in Provençal sun,
In days when poets ranked with noblemen:

604

Arnaut, Marcabrun, the *trouvères* every one;
And next the Italians – Guido Cavalcanti,
And Guido Guinicelli – I'll have done,

And only name the impressive shade of Dante,
Which towered above them all – turn up Rossetti's
Translations, if you think my list too scanty –

I'll not extend it further; for my bet is
Dear English reader, that you're all agog
About your countrymen. If laurel, or lettuce,

Parsley or henbane, crown the Wop and Frog,
It's all the same to you. Right then, I'll tell:
To think up English names, I need not flog

My brains unduly – for they ring the bell.
I'll just note down a few who caught my eye;
Your wishes suit my purpose very well,

And in the ensuing Canto I'll comply.

CANTO IV

Shakespeare was there, above the rest sublime,
A bit embarrassed by his exalted station;
Milton was there, and looked, just at that time

Rather surprised to find his reputation
Was still intact, in spite of Dr Leavis:
I felt that he deserved congratulation;

And Burns was there, but he could scarce believe his
Luck at not being roasted down below;
Jonson was there, though hardly could he heave his

Great bulk, which at the "Mermaid" made a show,
Into the seat of honour there assigned him;
And Isaac Watts was there, though shocked to know

With what loose company they had aligned him;
And Tennyson was there; and Johnny Keats,
And poor John Clare – you must look sharp to find him.

While the great shade of William Butler Yeats,
Lately arrived, complained it was absurd
There was no foam to copulate in – and in those seats,

He'd hoped to be a golden clockwork bird;
Charles Doughty in the dictionary was poring,
Trying to track down a palaeolithic word;

Coleridge was being vague, and Wordsworth boring,
And Shelley shrill, and Swinburne in a rage,
And Thomson (James) was in a corner, snoring;

Byron's hangover seemed in a vicious stage;
John Donne was rather gloomy in his shroud;
But Samuel Rogers hardly looked his age.

I'll say no more of this be-laurelled crowd;
For as I stood and gazed upon them there,
Suddenly came a sound – brilliant and loud

Bray of the trumpet, piercing through the ear,
To announce to all who stood within this place
The most high Muse herself was drawing near.

Then through the temple, with the wind's swift pace,
In triumph drove her ceremonial car,
Drawn by four stallions of celestial race

Whose manes and tails streamed like a shooting-star;
These had the flame-winged Pegasus for sire,
Who skims on the Caucasian hills afar.

But he is much too skittish and full of fire
To draw a lady's curricle far and wide:
These steeds were tempered by what they might acquire

From blood inherited on the distaff side;
Their dam was Common Sense, or Shanks's Mare,
Who grazes pastures on that mountain's side

Where Pegasus feeds on refined dew and air,
High on the peaks. Yet all their father's mettle
Shone in their eyes, and flanks, and unclipped hair.

They were well-groomed, and in the highest fettle;
They feed on an ambrosial mash, prepared
By Vulcan's self, in an Olympian kettle.

Thus to her devotees the Muse appeared;
And then, alighting from her car of state,
Mounted her throne, by all around revered.

Deep silence reigned. There was not long to wait;
For now once more the herald trumpets blew,
To announce what she would next communicate:

"To you assembled here in order due,
Greeting and peace. On this her festal day
The Muse receives all those who wish to sue

"For favours at her hand, if so they may
Make good their claims to approach this holy place.
You candidates for fame, step up this way.

"Show your credentials, you word-huckstering race!"
Then forward rushed a variegated crew,
In which I noticed many a well-known face –

Well known in modern letters. Not a few
Were my acquaintances, and some, my friends.
No orderly attempt to form a queue

Could be discerned. For each of them extends
His powers in that mad scramble to the throne,
As others do for cash or dividends.

Only a few marched doggedly alone
With not much time to spare for all the others –
An attitude I rather would condone.

And so, to deal with these impatient shovers,
The Muse discreetly issued her decree
To impose some order on that band of brothers,

Which they accepted rather sulkily:
They should be quietly called out one by one,
Since over precedence they'd not agree.

And now you are to hear how this was done.

Auspicious be the opening of this book!
I saw that one now stood before the throne
Of the high Muse; with an ambiguous look,

Thus, he approached – as used to stand alone
Before the ignorant or the hostile stare
Of indiscriminate crowds – and yet was shown

Great gentleness in his face, patience and care.
I knew those features, for they daily look
Upon the fading trees of Russell Square;

And the Muse knew them too – well pleased to praise
One who had done brave service in her ranks
In what he knew were unpropitious days –

And in such words as these, expressed her thanks:
"Soar on, my aged eagle, stretch your wing
Above the deserts, and the shrunken banks

"Of rivers, till they learn once more to sing;
Or furl them only when you take your rest
In the ruined shrine which housed a broken king –

"There, phoenix, build your purgatorial nest!"
Then he, with manners modest and discreet,
Withdrew, and took his place where suited best,

Quietly, in the dust at Dante's feet.
The next, a poetess, upmounted there,
Extended a gloved hand, ready to greet

The Muse, as a great lady greets her peer.
Which greeting the bright goddess did not refuse –
Though feminine, she knows no jealous care.

So, to this Sibyl, spoke the gracious Muse:
"Doctor, you wake the most ancient notes of song;
Acceptable to our ears the themes you choose –

"But please don't let them be drawn out too long.
Remember that the Delphian tripod you
Have mounted, may to others yet belong:

"Kathleen and Anne can sometimes use it too;
Though you, perhaps, we most delight to honour."
Admonished thus, the lady took her pew

With Sappho and Vittoria Colonna.
These staid exchanges done, a more alarming
Suitor to the goddess rushed upon her,

To the Toreador song out of Bizet's *Carmen*;
He tried to noose her like an unroped steer,
By methods learnt in Spanish cattle-farming.

But the immortal Muse, smiling austere,
Met his attentions with untroubled gaze,
Pointing him to his place, not far from where

John Dryden sat, shaded by greenest bays.
And now four well-known names the heralds call,
And to their lips the clanging trumpets raise;

There was no movement in the crowded hall;
All eyes were turned, all necks were craned, but none
Saw any sign of that quartet at all.

Just as a passing cloud darkens the sun,
A faint displeasure tinged the Muse's brow,
And with a gesture then, she summoned one

Thomas Warton, who, it seemed, was now
Her secretary, once her chronicler,
And briefly made inquiry of him, how

It was that none of those bright boys was there.
Warton, with some embarrassment, replied
That each was much too busy to appear.

"Cultural activities on either side
The Atlantic Ocean now engage this school;
And they'll be here, at turning of the tide."

"They may, to find the place already full."
The goddess said, in accents somewhat stern.
"It is not often I relax my rule.

"Frivolities like these can only turn
Their sacred art, our province, to derision;
Who seeks my grace must single-hearted burn.

But next there came to seek her high decision
A biting barker with a coloured coat,
In tatters slashed – yet oddly, with precision.

A chimaera, blent of lion, snake and goat –
Or was it St John's seven-headed Beast? –
Followed his steps, and had him by the throat;

Half Mephistopheles, half spoiled priest
Or spoiled child – a man none could agree on,
Yet, at this levee, he was not the least.

The Muse presented him a loud carillon
Of sounding words, with which the Beast to tame,
And let him find a place by François Villon –

May Flavus note, and count it to his shame!

CANTO VI

There was a pause; and then a fresh disturbance
Upset the decorous ordering of the day,
As a small knot of Helicon's suburbans

In close formation tried to force their way:
Some linked by vows of comradeship cemented
In Cairo, beneath Farouk's paternal sway,

Some by the slogans which they had invented,
Blazoned upon apocalyptic banners.
A uniform appearance they presented,

As any nest of sun-spawned iguanas.
The Muse, who never yet was taken by storm,
Bid them to learn more sense and better manners.

610

And others too, who tried to study form
By the new schoolman's rules, she chased away;
"With me, the neutral tone is not the norm."

Now all this time, I must beg leave to say
That I, being merely a spectator there,
Had not presumed to join the eager fray:

Imagine, then, my embarrassment and fear
When, as the heralds once more blew their cornets,
I heard my own name called, in summons clear.

There was a buzzing, like a nest of hornets,
From those waiting their turn, and a mixed look
Of curiosity, surprise, or scorn – it's

The worst half-minute I've had in all my days;
I really thought there must be some misprision –
For who was I to claim immortal bays?

The temple seemed to swim before my vision,
And round me came a host of hideous shapes,
Who bated me with gestures of derision,

And gibbered like a pack of forest apes.
I knew them for the bastard progeny
Of my own brain – of the Intellect when it rapes

The Imagination – oh, too well known to me:
Slack lines, blurred images, epithets imprecise –
The ectoparasites of poetry,

Which cling about its body like crab-lice,
While deep within, the worm, *accidia*,
Claims inspiration's life-blood as its price.

And all my vanity, like a great macaw,
Screamed in my ears, and beat about my face;
And yet, in spite of all my terror, I saw

The Muse still sitting with her archaic grace,
Her garments bright as a magnesium flare,
And with a smile that hovered on her face.

And all around, as in a theatre,
Faces from beyond the footlights are discerned –
A circle of dim white blobs which do not stir,

I saw the faces of the Dead, all turned
To me, who stood there stammering and alone –
The calm eyes of the mighty Dead, that burned.

Their voices gathering slowly, like the moan
Of an advancing sea, or mountain stream,
Grew to a roar, until its thunderous tone

Scattered the thin-spun threads which formed my dream –
And then I saw once more the room I'd known,
And at the window, the first daylight's gleam.

And yet, before the Vision quite was flown,
I seemed to know the voice of the high Muse
Speaking assurance, and her hand grasping my own;

And if deceived, I have not much to lose.

EPILOGUE – SAPPHIC ODE

Now I who once knew favour from those high-bred
Ladies frequenting daleheads of Parnassus,
Finding my lute slack, and my skiff in doldrums,
                    Seek to re-call them,

Framing a measure which perhaps remembers
Rose-weaving Sappho; linsey-woolsey English
Draped for the folds of chlamys or of chiton;
                    Twanged lyre and flute-call;

Nosegays plucked on the isle of Mytilenë,
Though now the dew's dry on their fresh corollas,
Melilot, crocos, cyclamen with flesh-pink
                    Back-folded petals.

And will they come then, as they came in boyhood
Blandly consoling loneliness and terror,
When, by the Stour, or by the Hampshire Avon's
                    Woods, I invoked them;

Or must my songs to drought be relegated –
Night, with her dark plumes, brood among my laurels,
Art unforeseen then be my only study,
                              Patient in dumbness?

O Muse, descend now, Cinderella goddess –
If not to my lips, yet descend, astounding
(Lambent with terrors, or in clear compassion)
                              These sand-blind English!

Cataract, come down – or as cat-o'-nine-tails –
Striking the waves of Isis, Usk, and Duddon,
Since in their reed-beds, geese are counted swans now,
                              Kestrels, gyrfalcons.

Cloud-signs are ill-set; light departs – permit not
We should allow the things your wings had taught us,
As in a dream's shame, utterly to vanish,
                              Through keeping silence.

Wounded Thammuz

Thammuz...
Whose annual wound, in Lebanon, allured
The Syrian damsels to lament his fate,
In amorous ditties, all a summer's day;
While smooth Adonis from his native rock,
Ran purple to the sea, supposed with blood
Of Thammuz yearly wounded...

MILTON: *Paradise Lost*, Book I

I   AUTUMN RITE

I

Dull Time's unwinking sickle has close-clipped
My laurel-boughs (Once more, and yet once more
Ye myrtles brown) and winter's cat's-tongue breeze
Has rasped away my roses, and has stripped
The quivering covering of my garden trees,
Hurling along the brown neap-tided shore
Autumnal discontent of unquiet seas.

And O you wind, as you come chattering
Between these broken strings, choke not my speech.
Break not this song, O break not this one song,
But bear about the winter-world some smattering
Of spring's shrill bird-bright runes, song-spells, and each
Flower-character inscribed my summer long.

This is that dying season when the Dead
Thicken the air, out of the still-born night
Wandering with yellow leaves, drifting with thin-
Spun webs of spider-silk; now should be said,
In the old way, for them, some litany, some rite.
I have no strength, but yet I will begin.

II

All the year's gold and silver is gone underground
    Into your cold dark caves, you fortunate Dead.
Helen and Cleopatra and all the crowned
    Queens of the ancient world lie low in that bed;
King Caesar has cast aside his sword and his diadem,
And Homer untuned his fiddle, to sleep with them.

It's time, oh it is high time, I should be lying
    Down in those shadowy fields where no wind blows;
In funeral garlands for me they will be tying
    With death-cold ivory fingers the deathless rose.
Up in this autumn world will the naked trees be mourning,
In twisted smoke from dank fires the old year burning.

III

A sieve of shell has sifted
The firstlings of the vine;
Are lifted on the pillar
Bunched leaf and dangling bell –
Pom'granate, tendril-twine,
And golden-throated bell.

The barren sheaves are gilded
And swept towards the fire,
Are builded up for tinder;
Dry shells, autumnal leaves
Are pillowed for the pyre
Whose flames are scarlet leaves.

IV

This is the garden of the Dead –
Carved stone at each cold-pillowed head.
No dancing feet disturb the dew
Beneath the cypress and stiff yew,
Nor can the winds bend, as they pass,
The waxen lilies under glass.
Lichen and northward-thriving moss
In gold and velvet hide the Cross,
And angels by the unfruitful urn

615

Furl their broad marble wings and mourn
This is the place where fragrance fades –
Wasted ambrosia of shades;
Rosemary and remembrance die
On beds where sullied lilies lie.
'How soon the freshest grass is cropped,
And the proud-turbaned tulip lopped,
The cockled ear of corn rejected,
The violet's sweetness neglected.
The crown-imperial droops and weeps,
While in his cave the Gardener sleeps.

V

Up on the high hill-tops and in their hollow caves,
Among rough rocks and raggedly-hewn crags,
Hard by the condor's eyrie and caverns of the cougar,
The centaurs dwell, those savage sagittaries,
With their shoulders unharnessed nor their trampling hooves
    shod –
But their broad brows are brother to the human.
They are leapers and laughers by the limpid cataracts,
Their moot the burnt-out crater, the crag and the crevasse.
With strong voice they shout to the strung shell of the tortoise,
Their corrugated trumpet the tragelaphe's curved horn;
They are harpers in the hollows of the unshadowy hills.
The wine of all their wisdom is the mead of the wild heather;
The light of the white-arched sky is still their lore and lust.
The shelves and the great ridges are their green grazing-places;
They search out the salt-lick and fountains tinged with sulphur,
And they watch the dawn dancing over the dales and the steep
    cliffs
Reddening the stark stones and slopes all stippled with snow.
There is music in the mountains unmuffled by the nipping air
As they run with wild worship against the autumn wind.

VI

Bring fennel, and fresh parsley-garlands, and
The southern-scented vervain; bring carved bowls
        With maple-leaves entwined –
        Jaggéd and burned to gold;

Brim them with sweet new milk and stone-ground flour
Meddled with filmy must of sanguine wine,
      And honey, though the bees
      Now seek their torpid cells;

And bind your brows with ivy growing green
The winter through, and sharp bright apples from
      The rowan; range the white
      And crimson agaric

Around this dolmen-altar, older than
Delphos or Cumae or the Latmian hill
      Or Syrian gardens where
      Wounded Adonis sleeps.

Come you goat-footed dancers, shaggy-sided,
      Out of your panthered shades,
And you harsh-whinnying ones with chestnut-shiny
      Flanks and swishing tails,
Trample our vintage with your heavy hooves
And rouse to uncouth din these old unechoing woods.

For we have sour and sweet glassy-cool clustering
      Grapes for the sore-parched mouth;
Our tangled hair hangs loose to the dappled fluttering
      Tags of a fawn-skin clout.
Disturb the fallen leaves with cone-tipped staff
Where through the woods there winds our mazy dancing path;

Where shoulder-high grows all the fire-fringed bracken,
      Or where the squirrel whisks,
Or green to needled ant-hills' turgid traffic
      The hobbling wood-spite dips;
Away, white-flagged, the startled rabbit goes,
Out of her thorn-thatched bed leaps up the bouncing doe.

And wake we with our clamour Echoes pined
In their dry stony cells, with tambourine,
      Cymbals, and wavering shawms,
      And round-toned kettle-drum.

And you, harp-player, snap those withered bays
That bind your long wire strings, conduct our rout
            To valleys whose steep rocks
            Shall bellow back your song.

Now through the waters of this quiet lake
Trundle the sacred cart, whose axle-tree
            And slow-revolving wheels
            The lucent wave shall purge.

Eastward, O wine-stained charioteer, lead on
To empires swart with shade, whose kings shall doff
            Their diamond crowns to deck
Our maypole hung with bells.

VII

Aurora Borealis fills the sky,
Bohemian birds the woods, both signs of war
Or pestilence. And whirl and whirl and whirl
The eddying leaves – Herodias' daughter
At her eternal dancing. Over the waters
Of this unfathomed lake glides a canoe,
Spattered with war-paint, hung with scalps and skulls,
And mouldering finger-flesh clutches the paddles;
The helm is guided by a bony hand...
These are the vanguard; ground cannot contain them,
But corpses sprout like luminous mushroom-spawn
In dark damp cellars, and the heavens sag
With the dull weight of ghosts; and now you hear
From every wood and garden and cross-road
(Cold cradle of the blasphemous suicide)
The petulant and uncomfortable voices of the Dead.

"Oh Life, Life, Life! Why have you stolen our life? –
The moon's green blood in the mid-rib, and the rich red
Blood that is shed in the sunlight? Why must we
Be creeping back again to this damp dead world, slinking
Down by the howling chimney and snuffling keyhole, scaring
Only the nerve-sick and ignorant, seeking
The carelessly minded child, the unwary sleeper
Who lies with his throat exposed?

"We were the wise and strong – but now only
Psalm-singing in stuffy rooms, the squab-like medium,
The joggling automatic-writer and the juggling crystal,
The dog-eared Tarot with its train of senseless images –
The Emperor, the Female Pope, the Fool, the Hanging Man,
And the Lightning-Struck Tower which is the House of God.

"We are that impatient rider of the sea-shore,
With Beauty across his saddle-bow; his marriage-chamber
Is dark in the earth, and many a fresh young bride
Has he brought thither – ah, but a cold bed
Have those Lenoras and rare Margarets.

"We are the surgeon whose frozen hands were lopped;
The envious brain under an acid sky
Worm-screwed among the clamorous machines.
We are the poet within whose honeyed mouth
The ants have built their citadel. We are the patriot
Without a country; all tormented prisoners;
Lamia the child-devourer; the murdered usurer
Into whose poky cottage the young men broke
One night of curses, and spilt his lovingly garnered
Gold-seeds of power on wine and trumpery women.
We are the shadow out of the broken mirror;
The burglar under the bed or in the cupboard.
We are the rats in the cellar. With our long nails
We'll undermine your palaces; with them
Is timbered Hell's ship she at last shall launch,
Pledged to destroy the world."

VIII

A voice as of the wind, a Voice out of the Whirlwind:
"I am the Wild Huntsman, the wanderer of these mountains,
A whining among the woods, the word of the waving fir-tree;
I have wound the wounds of the sunset round with a winding
    cloud-wrack,
And you, wan things, are my quarry, as withered leaves to the
    wind.
My path is over the mountains, beyond the watchfires
And the blazing beacons of the clangorous marchmen;
By moors and mosses where no shepherd shoves
His sturdily-shod staff; by pinnacles

That turn the eagle dizzy and dislodge
The antelope, sure-footed ballador;
Up where the patient glacier-goddess drags
Her plough of glass; by frozen caves
Where cherubim their dreaming hermits cheer
With fire whose coal is more than diamonds.
O cower you down in your small burial-mounds? –
My thundering hooves shall break your earth-dome in,
Scatter your singing shin-bones, and shall mock
The ridged and rigid smile of the skull.
My ravens, Thought and Memory, shall pluck off
The golden bracelet from the fleshless arm,
The pearls which were your eyes. Oh withered leaf
That restless hang upon a restless tree,
Let the wind take you, and be lifted up
Into his own importunate energy!
And you, wild goats of the mountains, and goat-footed
Men, you horse-hooved dancers of the hills,
More madly urge your measure, frenzied be,
With the world's wine made drunk, and with the music
Of my inordinate pursuit; for I will drive you
To fields fenced round with lightning, and at last
Into my unimaginable folds."

IX

"Southward, O wind, seeking the trellised vine,
Long has the fickle-pinioned swallow flown,
To amethystine clusters; but your breath,
Though nursing next year's seeds, rudely shall pine
Those birds who salt with song your bitter teeth,
Shall snuff the orange crocus-flambeau, blown
Too soon in months of all-tempestuous death."

So sang the poet, softly, by the hearth
Of an old house, with embers raked together,
Warming himself by that uncertain glow,
(He who had served proud kings of the old earth –
But their bright livery was all for show,
And pitiful against the winter weather)
Then rose, and went on through the quiet snow.

I

In a long midwinter valley of dry snow
The sphered and cavernous skulls by two by two
Lying. But in that sleep of death
What dreams may come? What images
Trouble the eyeless socket, haunt
This stony scaffolding? What thoughts revisit
The swept and garnished chambers of the skull?
                              Only the wind,
Incessantly breathing over the chalk-white bones
With a high thin whizzing sound – as among sand-dunes
Siliceous windlestraw all night and day
Is pan-piped by an unempassioned breeze
While overhead a forked and arrowy bird
Plunges for glittering fish in glaring seas.

II

Then cold and hot and moist and dry –
Colourless mote-minuet within those cloistral spaces,
Echoes of stringless harps, and tetrachords
Invented by old gold Time's unstained centaur –
Steadfast, my eyeless friends, behold in sleep
The still blue flame within its cone of ice,
The pyramid among the flaring sands that stands
And looms and glooms under monotonous sun;
But you, Intelligences,
O tenuous-handed ones that twist and twine
A rope of twinkling pearls about the brain
That disembodied squats within its empty chamber,
Whose hands and lips and – ah, bird-poignant feet
Strike out no fire, no sparks along the nerve
But wind in formal dance like the thistledown –
(With down upon your feet, ye nights and days!)
All with high movement of the seeds of things,
You circling ministers of crystal snow-dust
And all prismatic artifice of frost
Shake your frail sistra through our unwaked dream;
Then cold and hot and moist and dry –
Thin tunings of a twilight orchestra,
A rustling of primaeval fifths and octaves,

621

Tightening of strings and titterings through the air –
Not yet the angels move with shifting feet
Over God's polished floor in high pavane
Trailing their lace-like wings on bright mosaics
Inscribed with pentagons are still unread,
What time the trumpet shall be heard,
And rattling bones together fly
And Music shall untune the sky.

III

High up above my head I heard the golden plover's
Unearthly fluting, standing in a sad estuary
Where tufted lugworms bubbled, broken shells
Littered the muddy runnels. Bird, O bird,
O wisp of flesh and feather, web and mesh,
Unstaunched and inarticulate desire! Oh, and whither,
Threading these mists and miserable shores,
Treading these lone sea-beaches, and where tending,
Frail and tenacious one? Oh, without ending
The fumbling of numb waters with the sand,
While restless winter combs these bad sea-reaches.

IV

O can you not suspend
Your swift and singing spheres?
You bird-eyed stars unbind your glittering shoes,
Leave silent and untrod
God's sombre dancing-floor,
And cluster like ripe fruit in our damp woods.
But they shrill on, trembling like bright wine-glasses,
Nor yet the darkness passes.

Can you not soar so high,
You star-aspiring birds,
To build and breed in those moon-laden boughs?
You sharp-browed phoenix-clan
Climb through alternate skies
Of fire and snow to reach those radiant fields.
But Earth has still her fowling-nets to tighten,
Nor can the long night lighten.

And still the stream flowed on
Through the embowering darkness, a glittering
Great ring of glow-worm milk, trembling and swirled
By moonlight-bellied violins, a dance
Of swansdown, whirling with noiseless feet
Over a water-smooth, sedge-mirroring floor.
Below that music wooden puppets jerked,
Snapped their sharp fingers, mouthed with painted face –
And no light glinted on the spider-wires
That strung those jointy sockets, tenuous woof
Spun through and through the shrill Æolian air
Where quivering music shadowed voiceless dreams –
Thoughts of a dead man naked of his flesh
In blank midwinter valleys of the mind.

3 SPRING PASTORAL

I

Over the crumpled jaw-bones of the deep
All the long night, blowing the sharp salt spray
Inland, snapping the unglued chestnut-bud,
Howled the infuriate wind, rousing from sleep
Snow-sliding mountains, sending far astray
The homeward birds bewildered to the steep
Where shocked by the foul blast a lighthouse stood,
Till weary morning watched the grey tides creep.

Spring's cradle rudely rocked and heralded
By clarion storm out of the dank South-West;
The pale fruit-blossom shivered from the tree,
And young leaves mingled with the last year's dead;
Builds the undaunted thrush his mud-lined nest,
Shouting defiance from his bridal-bed
While wet winds raked along the grumbling sea.

II

So gaunt and sallow-visaged Spring came forth
Across polluted Europe; uncouth paths
Stalked he in green and fiery slippers, spread
His Eastern carpets over the rubble-heaps,
Pranked with the naked snowdrop, saffron-flower
Of Colchis, Muslim tulip, mortuary
Daffodil. Men marked with hungry eyes
In those Armenian and Sabaean mats
Embroidered pictures of forgotten lust.
But squint-eyed Spring
Squatted, prepared to haggle. Through the woods –
The old, the savage, devastated woods –
Was heard the mad and mocking cuckoo's cry.

III

Come in the early morning, Shepherds, bring
    Your tufted willow-wands,
Long hazel-catkins, and new-garnished knots
Clipped from the fresh-leaved hawthorn-tree, and all
    The season's flowers.

Now the lush woods weep pools of hyacinth,
    And green primroses fade
Around the roots of venerable trees
And mossy banks where all the winter through
    They skulked unseen.

Bring these, and bring pert-flowering daisies, and
    The small blue violet,
The star-limbed celandine, and sanguine-tongued
Anemones wind-tottering, to this
    Dark woodland bier.

For now is time to lay in ground those limbs,
    Those towzled trampling feet,
And brows, grown hoary-fronted, with high horns,
Red lips that curled to many an ancient tune,
    Bright listening eyes.

Carry him down with songs and pipe-playing,
    Nor let the birds be mute –
But now in all their fresh spring plumage mourn;
They knew him well, and to his pastoral flute
    Made shrill reply.

Who knows, as round about his turf-built tomb
    We wind with mournful tread,
What shadowy feet shall echo as we dance
Our sad funereal measure, what cool hands
    Shall smooth our flowers?

But nevermore, you shepherds, nevermore
    Shall his pipe cheer your hills;
Your folds his watch, the shearing-feast his song
Shall lack, and these green lawns shall know
    His tread no more.

Nymphs and Shepherds, dance no more....

IV

Iron vineyards, stables for the fire-drake,
Forges, and mills, and wombs of molten metal,
Where rattling wheels together fly
As though they would untune the sky,
And men with sweaty faces walking among those fires...
They bring last year's corn, and coal, and diamonds –
Fodder for those great beasts; those which half-human
Champ like centaurs, with their shining steel flanks,
In their splendid pride and insolent lust of creation
Singing.
Some stretch forth, iron-pinioned demiurges,
Over a fiery chaos their measuring rods.
Others with delicate organs, fan-like antennae,
Intricate as hares' eyes, electric ears to catch
The inconceivable music of atomic dancing...
And these with shining hands
Have wrenched all our life's roots eternally awry.
Yet with magnificent plunging, let us set out to make
Tall towers our children, and plant blazing gardens
New-dight with quickfire and the steel-frost beauty
Of all the thick-set orchards of the sky.

625

Though nailed down
Under a leaden coffin-lid, stir ourselves to create,
Driving with a fearless ship through forward complexities,
Nor regretting the frail grace of our begetting.
For there is no turning backwards, and if need be, you must thrust
Your hardening man's face through fire-sleet desolation.
And so shall our maimed hero climb to his wry-faced throne.

V

My Love is over the sea to Spain
 And it's blow, you South Wind, blow!
And he'll bring me a pair of scarlet slippers
 That I to church may go.

My Love has sailed for Mexique Bay,
 And it's come, you ship, to land!
And he will bring me a golden ring
 To deck my lily hand.

My Love is gone into Muscovy,
 And it's oh, that he were sped!
And he'll bring me a pair of silken sheets
 Are sewn for our marriage bed.

Last summer we walked in my garden
 And the flowers they were never so bright.
"But heavy shall be the evening dew
 And your roses be withered tonight!

"Your roses shall wither tonight, my dear,
 But they will all be in flower
When I have sailed back over the water
 And come again to your bower."

My roses are red, they are all full-blown,
 And my garden is gay to see,
The swallow has builded beneath the beam,
 But my Love comes not to me!

And I'd sooner the waters were turned to blood
 And I drowned under that sea
Than I should live to another spring
 And my Love proved false to me!

626

VI

What is this, dark against the setting sun?
A crooked tree, a vine whose iron tendrils
Are twisted to toothed wheels, and snake-sheathed chains,
And for fruit, a Man hanging. This is the Vine-tender
Who clambered to his spring-time throne to curb
And gather grapes are full of blood. Even the wind
That howls so sharply and is twisted sore
Among those metal branches, is the shadow –
The moving shadow of a shifting star-dance
In his heroic halls.

Out of a silver wood
That waves above the mountain's silver-birches,
A bird has come, with strange sweet speaking-voice,
To sing imprisoned in our tarnished roses
Whose leaves are blood, whose thorns are iron nails.

This way turn, you women weeping
In the Temple porch, or by the little brook
That runs blood-red with the red earth of the hillside,
This way turn. And you who scour the mountains
Seeking in cool dark woods the boar-marred beauty,
Look here and see your ship-compelling Lover.

Long-lorn, forlorn tree, worn by Adam's serpent,
You bent and bowed, embraced by the meek Hero,
And the world groaned, where writhed your ancient roots.
But now your new leaves shake as the Spring wind
Disturbs the whispering souls that nest between
Crying of Southern gardens and of spices
Which tall flower-censers lift to clearer skies,
Lilies of fire, song of untaloned birds...
O Wind, break not my song!...

VII

Through skies as sweet as milk, and over grass
Tufted with velvet glumes, and whispering
Of sunlight-promise in the morning's mouth,
By tumbling seas gayer than painted glass,
By warm and naked hills, and over uncouth
Crags where rising birds gossip of spring,
Return, winged breezes dancing from the South!

Soft wind, come you, and blow away the rime
Of winter from the leaves, and fan to flame
Of flowers each slender fruit-tree branch, and rouse
New birds to song, now at the young year's prime.
Fresh wind, prevail, so shall you put to shame
Death; Spring wind, so shall you conquer Time
Whose sickle has close-clipped my laurel-boughs.